THE BALANCE OF POWER

Also by Evan Luard

BRITAIN AND CHINA
NATIONALITY AND WEALTH
*CONFLICT AND PEACE IN THE MODERN
   INTERNATIONAL SYSTEM
THE CONTROL OF THE SEABED
*INTERNATIONAL AGENCIES: The Emerging Framework of
   Interdependence
SOCIALISM WITHOUT THE STATE
TYPES OF INTERNATIONAL SOCIETY
*THE UNITED NATIONS: How it Works and What it Does
*THE MANAGEMENT OF THE WORLD ECONOMY
*ECONOMIC RELATIONS AMONG STATES
*INTERNATIONAL SOCIETY
*A HISTORY OF THE UNITED NATIONS
   Volume 1: The Years of Western Domination, 1945–1955
   Volume 2: The Age of Decolonization, 1955–1965
*THE GLOBALIZATION OF POLITICS
*BASIC TEXTS IN INTERNATIONAL RELATIONS

*Also published by Macmillan

The Balance of Power

The System of International Relations, 1648–1815

Evan Luard

First published by
MACMILLAN PRESS LTD
Houndmills, Basingstoke, Hampshire RG21 6XS
and London
Companies and representatives
throughout the world

ISBN 0–333–55046–3

A catalogue record for this book is available
from the British Library.

This book is printed on paper suitable for recycling and
made from fully managed and sustained forest sources.

Transferred to digital printing 1999

Contents

List of Tables

List of Maps

Preface

It is not the aim of this work to provide a new history of international relations during the period it covers. There already exist a number of excellent diplomatic histories providing accounts, on a chronological basis, of dealings between European states at this time. The aim of the present volume (and of the volumes which are planned to follow it) is to present a more analytical survey of events. While it includes a brief account of the main developments (Chapter 3), most of the book is devoted to examining the ideas, the issues and the institutions which shaped relations among states in this age; and on that basis to consider the character of the system as a whole.

There are a number of questions which may legitimately be raised about such an endeavour. The most obvious is: how far are we justified in presupposing that there existed, whether in this period or those which followed, anything that can be described as a "system" at all? Are we not, in making use of that concept, seeking to impose on the history of the period a logic, a pattern, which may not in fact be justified by the haphazard and untidy reality of relationships at the time?

This is a pertinent question, to which we shall need to return when we draw conclusions from our survey. For the moment it may be sufficient to note that the idea that there existed a "system" of international relations was undoubtedly current at the time;[1] and that, in a more general way, commentators and statesmen of the period spoke of the existence of a "society", "commonwealth", or "federation" of states – even that the countries of Europe represented a single "republic", linked together by bonds of close intercourse and common interest. The fact that such beliefs were held at all might be regarded as evidence that there existed at least the preconditions for a "system" at this time.

Beliefs alone, however, are scarcely enough. If a system existed, it should be demonstrated by actions as well as words: the actions of the states of which it was constituted. But we still need to know how these would demonstrate the existence of a system. In other words, what does the concept of a system imply?

Over the past twenty or thirty years a vast literature has developed on the subject of "international systems". Many of these works have been influenced by "systems theory", originally evolved for the analysis of engineering problems[2] but later applied by other writers to social and political systems.[3] Such writings often sought to analyse relations among states in terms of mechanical systems, employing the terminology appropriate to such systems: inputs, outputs, feedback, negative feedback, parameter values, operational rules, capability variables, homeostatic control and so on.[4] There were understandable attractions in this approach. There are undoubtedly inviting analogies to be drawn between the two kinds of system. But the approach begged the crucial initial question: does there exist an international system, and if so what is its nature? It was an initial assumption that there was an international system resembling a mechanical system; that relations among states are therefore governed by predictable forces – based on relative national power and other factors – in the same way that a piece of machinery may be by electrical and other impulses. It thus implied that human beings in a social setting can be expected to act with the reliability and precision of the parts of a machine. And it correspondingly *underplayed* the effect of intangible factors deriving from the complexities of individual decision-making, social relationships and human psychology: factors which cannot easily be allowed for in such an analysis.

If this therefore is too restrictive and specialised a use of the concept of system, what better one can be found? What is the minimum meaning to be attached to the idea?

First, the concept implies that there must be some *interconnectedness* between the component parts. An entity which is totally disconnected cannot be part of a "system". Thus a state which has no contact whatever with other states cannot be said to belong to a system of states. This means that one of the matters to be considered in relation to the international system (in this and in later volumes) is what form precisely this connectedness takes. Does it require diplomatic relations, or would military contacts be enough? Is mutual knowledge sufficient, or is mutual *understanding* also required? This may determine the further question: which states belong to the system; that is, what are its international boundaries? Is it possible for a state to be (as Turkey might be said to have been during the period we are concerned with) partly within the system and partly without? In other words what degree of belongingness is required for a state to be a member of the system?

Secondly, within a social system there must be not only interconnection but *communication*. Members of a social system are normally influenced not only by the actions of other members but by their words. So, in an international system, the conduct of one state can be influenced by threats, inducements, persuasions or injunctions of one kind or another as well as by an act of war. It is here that the human factor, ignored in the concept of a mechanical system, becomes important. For communication differs from control. Thus in an international system, though one or more members may *seek* to influence another, for example by threats or promises, they cannot be sure that they will succeed in doing so in the way desired. The responses that are made depend not only on power factors, not only on the nature of the communication – threat, promise or invitation – but on the nature of the entity that responds. It will depend, that is, on internal processes, which may vary greatly from one member to another. Knowledge of these internal factors may be essential to an understanding of the system as a whole.

Thirdly, within a social system there exists another factor, also not found in a mechanical system, but which to some extent counters this unpredictability of response. This is a set of *common expectations*. These are the essential motive force that sustains the system, for it is normally these that secure the response needed from the individual members. They are, however, much weaker than the forces at work in a mechanical system, which can normally be absolutely relied on to obtain the response required: a sufficient electrical impulse, dynamic force or gravity pull will have an effect which is automatic. Within a social system, including an international system, the forces at work – the expectations – are much more uncertain in their effect. While they may usually be sufficient to bring about a certain response, they cannot be relied on to do so. Human psychology is sufficiently variable for unexpected responses still to be possible.

Finally in consequence, the concept of system implies some degree of *regularity* in relationships. Where behaviour is entirely unpredictable, arbitrary and wayward, no "system" of relations can be said to exist. This does not mean that in a system the responses that occur must be entirely automatic (if so it would be genuinely akin to a mechanical system). But it does mean that behaviour must be sufficiently consistent and regular that, over the long term, a recognisable pattern results: that it appears "systematic".

The relationships we are here describing, it may well be argued, are those that occur within a "society" rather than within a system. There are indeed good grounds for treating of "international society" rather than of "the international system" (a thesis which the present author has strongly argued in the past).[5] But international society, it can reasonably be maintained, is a broader concept than that of the international system: within a society there exist many actors, including individuals, groups and associations of various kinds, and many types of activity, including social, cultural and economic activities, which range far beyond the political and diplomatic relationships among states. The idea of the international "system" may therefore be useful in analysing the latter, more limited field. It refers, that is, to this particular aspect of international society alone.

But even if this definition is accepted, how do we identify a *particular* system of states? How do we locate it? An international system occupies a place in time. We may speak in a loose way about the "contemporary international system", but when did that system begin? If we are considering, as in the present study, a particular period in the past, how can we decide where to place it? Are we justified in considering the stretch of 167 years covered in this book, as a distinct and recognisable "system"; or should it be split into three, five or more such systems, each covering only a part of that period? Clearly the way international relations were conducted changed in the course of the age. The system which operated between, say, 1780 and 1815 was not identical with that which prevailed in the second half of the seventeenth century. Should it be seen, therefore, as something different altogether: a new "system"?

The dividing of history into distinct periods always involves some arbitrary choice. But there do seem to be good reasons for considering the period under consideration as a distinct whole.[6] The Peace of Westphalia is generally accepted as marking a turning-point in European history. It was not only the settlement which concluded a long and bitter war which had involved most of the states of Europe. It not only brought to an end a century of Spain's dominance in European affairs. More important, it created the framework within which international relations were conducted in the period that followed. It marked the close of a century of conflict on religious questions, which had preoccupied most of the countries of the continent during a hundred years, and ushered in a wholly new age, in which religious concerns played only a minor part. Competition now took place among sovereign states, competing for territory, status and power. Power was now more evenly shared. Eight or ten states of comparable size, together with innumerable lesser ones, established increasingly close relations and arrived at certain conventions about the way relations were to be conducted. There may be room for argument about the terminal date of the period. Some would perhaps hold that this should be placed in 1789, when the French revolution ushered in a new era, an age of nationalism which was to last for over a century. Since, however, in 1815 the first revolutionary upsurge was defeated, and an attempt then made to establish a new and different framework, it can reasonably be maintained that it is premature to date the beginning of the new age in 1789; and it has been thought here more logical to place the conclusion of the system we are concerned with in 1815.

If this is the period to be considered, how should it be analysed? What are the particular features which need to be examined?

First, we shall need to look at the individual members of the system: that is the states themselves. The character of any system, and the relations undertaken within it, will clearly be decisively affected by the nature of the individual units: their internal political structures (determining, for example, what type of leaders and groups determine their policies); their relative size and power; the way in which they determine their foreign policy; and the mechanism through which they conduct their relations with each other. These are the factors which will help to determine whether they are competitive or cooperative; war-like or peace-loving; inward-turned or outward-turned, and so the type of relationships that they undertake: that is, the nature of the system. And these are the factors which will therefore be considered in Chapter 2 of this study.

Secondly, the character of the system will be determined not only by these static features, but by dynamic factors as well: the motives which determine how the units react towards each other. One feature affecting this will be the ideology and beliefs which prevail within the international system: the views which are held about that system and the way in which relations ought to be conducted. International societies clearly differ greatly in the nature of the beliefs that are held on these points. In examining this particular system, therefore, we shall need to consider some of the dominant ideas affecting the way relations among the states were conducted. These included the idea of the balance of power, a highly influential notion in this age (considered in Chapter 1); the idea of sovereignty, the principle which upheld the essential independence of each state and their right to freedom from interference from abroad (considered in Chapter 4); and ideas concerning the way the existing structure of the international system should be protected and the duties which states owed each other (considered in Chapter 12).

But in examining a system we need not only to consider general ideas of this kind, but the *particular* goals which were pursued by states (sometimes influenced by those ideas). It is clear that a system in which the acquisition of territory is a widely held goal will be very different from one in which the promotion of the right of self-determination, or the pursuit of rapid economic growth, are the main objectives of states. Just as, within smaller human societies, the character of the political system will be determined partly by the nature of the goals held by individuals – for political influence or economic power, for maximum equality or maximum wealth, more rapid growth or a well-protected environment, for example – so the character of international systems will be determined by the goals and values upheld by states. Thus in studying this society we shall need to consider some of the objectives which were of special concern to the member-states: for example, the demand for status, concerns about territory, about succession in foreign states, or about the means of winning trading opportunities and colonies abroad (Chapters 5 to 9 below).

Next, an international system is characterised by the institutions which are established within it. Some of these will be partial institutions, arrangements made among certain members of the society only, to attain their common ends. Of this kind are alliances, leagues and coalitions established among two or more states to promote their common purposes against other states (Chapter 9 below). Others are wider institutions, involving all the states of the system, intended to protect their common interests by promoting the security of all or by establishing widely accepted conventions concerning state behaviour (Chapter 11). The nature of the system is also demonstrated by the relationships undertaken within it, in other words its history; and we shall need to consider briefly the changing balance of power among the principal members (Chapter 3). Finally, having completed this survey we shall seek to arrive at some conclusions about the nature of the system as a whole.

It is obviously not possible, in a book of these dimensions, to provide more than a sketch of the essential features of the international relationships of this age. It has been necessary to concentrate on the characteristic features of the system and a great deal of important detail is inevitably omitted. It is the author's hope that the book may none the less be of interest, not only to professional students of international history but to many others who are interested in the way relations among states have evolved over the years. It represents the first part of a wider study of the evolution of the international system: a study undertaken in the hope, perhaps not altogether Utopian, that a better understanding of the way that system has developed over previous centuries, may assist in the establishment of a more stable and civilised relationship among states in our own generation.

Publishers' Note

Evan Luard died on 8 February 1991 before he was able to correct the proofs of this book. The references in the text to later volumes have been left to show the reader how Evan Luard planned to extend the work. Shortly before his death he did in fact complete the second volume, *The Concert of Europe: The System of International Relations, 1815–1914.*

1 The Idea of the Balance

THE ORIGIN OF THE CONCEPT

A dominant preoccupation in the international society with which we are concerned in this book, strongly influencing the beliefs that were held about the way relations among its members should be conducted, was the idea of the "balance of power".

There has probably been no society of states in which that term was so widely used and so deeply revered. It was frequently quoted by writers and commentators as an *explanation* of state actions. It was appealed to by statesmen as a *justification* for their policies. It was explicitly alluded to in treaties of peace. It even affected the development of international law.

The concept did not, of course, suddenly appear, unheralded, at the moment our age begins. It was an elaboration and refinement of ideas which can be traced back to much earlier times.

It has always been recognised that, among states which come regularly into conflict with each other, the power of one state will sometimes be used to balance that of others. Whenever a state forms an alliance with another against a third, a balancing of a kind takes place. When a coalition is built up among several states to resist another which appears to have acquired excessive dominance, their aim is to create a counterbalance. And where a state holds itself equidistant from two rival powers, so that it is in a position to throw its weight on one side or the other to suit its own advantage, a different kind of balancing occurs. Such policies have been pursued throughout history without being labelled as a manifestation of the "balance of power" principle. A true balance of power policy occurs only when a state allies itself with the *weaker* of two possible partners, because it recognises that the other may finally prove the greater menace. It is this which, in the age we are concerned with, was generally understood as a balance of power policy.

The origin of such policies was often traced back to classical times. There was frequent mention of Hiero, the ruler of Syracuse, who was praised by Polybius[1] because he decided that, although the ally of Rome, he should lend support to Carthage when it was threatened by Rome, in order to prevent Rome becoming, by her victory, all-powerful. This example was quoted by a number of writers in our age

1

as a prudent exercise of balance of power policy (among others by Gentili, Hume and Brougham). Other examples were found from antiquity. Hume asserted that "in all the policies of Greece, the anxiety with regard to the balance of power is apparent, and is expressly pointed out to us, even by the ancient historians".[2] The league formed by Sparta against Athens, he claimed, had been created "entirely owing to this principle". When Thebes and Sparta were later in contention, the Athenians, he maintained, always "threw themselves into the lighter scale and endeavoured to preserve the balance". And he cited the confederation later formed by the Greek states against the rising power of Macedonia as a further example of the principle at work.

There were less ancient examples which were widely known and sometimes quoted. Commynes, the fifteenth-century diplomat in the service of Charles the Bold of Burgundy and later of Louis XI of France, had described in his *Memoirs* how throughout Europe the power of various rulers was balanced by that of their rivals within their own areas: England against France, Scotland against England, Portugal against Spain, Aragon against Anjou in Naples, Venice against Florence in North Italy, the Visconti against the Orleans family in Milan, and so on.[3] But such accounts described the way rivalry for power could automatically bring about a balance, rather than a policy deliberately designed to create it. For balance of power *strategies* the history of the states of Italy in the fifteenth century was more relevant. During the fifteenth century it was known that Florence had habitually allied herself with the power or powers opposed to the one which she saw as the greatest threat to herself and to the peace of the peninsula as a whole. At the time when Milan, under the Sforzas, was the main threat, for example, Florence allied herself with Venice to resist her; from 1551, when Venice became the dominant power, she joined instead with Milan in opposition.

This story was known to many in our period from the account given of it by Guicciardini in his famous *History of Italy*. This had first appeared in 1561 (more than twenty years after it was written) and been rapidly translated into most other European languages: a new and improved English translation appeared in 1753–6 at the time when discussion of balance of power ideas in Europe was at its height. Guicciardini described this policy as it had been pursued, towards the end of the fifteenth century, by Lorenzo de Medici:

Realising that it would be most perilous to the Florentine republic and to himself if any of the major powers should extend their area of dominion, he carefully saw to it that the Italian situation should be maintained in a state of balance, not leaning more towards one side than the other. This could not be achieved without preserving the peace and without being vigilantly on the watch against every incident, even the slightest.[4]

The mutual suspicion among the other states served to create a balance and so to maintain peace among them:

> Full of emulation and jealousy among themselves, they did not cease to observe assiduously what the others were doing, each of them reciprocally aborting all the plans whereby any of the others might become more powerful or renowned. This did not result in rendering the peace less stable; on the contrary it aroused greater vigilance in all of them to stamp out any sparks which might be the cause of a new conflagration. . . . Such were the foundations of the tranquility of Italy, disposed and counter-posed in such a way that not only was there no fear of any present change, but neither could anyone easily conceive of any policies or situations or wars that might disrupt such peace.[5]

This example of successful balancing came to be widely quoted. Lorenzo's policies were praised by Gentili, the international lawyer, for example, writing towards the end of the sixteenth century. Himself concerned at the dominant power of Spain at that time, he described Lorenzo as "a wise man, friend of peace and father of peace", who had a "constant care . . . that the balance of power should be maintained among the princes of Italy. This he believed would give peace to Italy, as indeed it did, so long as he lived and preserved that condition of affairs. But both peace and the balance of power ended with him."[6] Giovanni Botero in his book *Reason of State* published in the same year as Gentili's, described the creation of "counterpoises" or defensive alliances as the best way to maintain peace among a number of states in a particular region: and he too quoted the example of Lorenzo de Medici, who "kept Italy at peace for a long time by balancing the powers".[7]

By the beginning of the seventeenth century, therefore, the idea of the "balance of power" was already widely current. By many it was seen primarily, as by these writers, as a means of maintaining peace. Others, however, saw it rather as a way of promoting the interests of their own state. A well-known example was the policy of the Italian popes in the period after the invasion of Italy by the French king,

Charles VIII, in 1494. For forty years these turned to one power after another to back them against whichever external state represented the greater threat at the time. That policy brought not peace but continual war. Thus Alexander VI mobilised Spain, Venice, Milan and the emperor to join in ejecting the French in 1495–6. Julius II won the help of France and Spain against Venice in 1508; then formed the Holy League, including Spain, Venice, the emperor and England, against France in 1511. His successors formed an alliance with the emperor against France in 1515 and 1521–3; and another with France against the emperor in 1526. This policy was generally admired by later writers. Criticism was made only when a pope *failed* to join the weaker ruler against the stronger; as when Paolo Paruta, the Venetian writer, criticised Leo X for joining with Charles V against France in 1521, so helping him to acquire an overwhelming power in Italy.[8] This was contrasted with the policy of his own state, Venice, during the same period, which "had often changed friendship according to the condition of the time and affairs, maintaining the constant aim to keep their forces as equally balanced as they could, so that they should both be weakened by their contention with one another".

Outside Italy such policies were also admired. Henry VIII of England prided himself that he too had held the balance between Charles V and Francis I. At the Field of the Cloth of Gold, he wore a banner inscribed with the device *Cui adhaero praeest* – "the one that I join will prevail". Wolsey, Henry's minister, was generally credited with pursuing a deliberate balance of power policy. In the succession of diplomatic conferences which took place in 1520–1, he set himself up as arbiter between the two rival European sovereigns (although in fact he quickly placed himself in alliance with the emperor). As a result, he was told by an English diplomat, the French feared that he "would make your profit with them and the emperor both", so that they might "continue at war and the one destroy the other": in consequence Henry VIII would become "their arbiter and superior".[9] Though the precise term "balance of power" was apparently not used, either by Wolsey or by others in this context,[10] such a policy was undoubtedly attributed to Henry VIII and his minister in subsequent generations. Thus in the eighteenth century it was held that Henry had "held the balance of power in his hand, and the scale had turned according to his directions",[11] and Wolsey came to be credited with following the "good rule" of "preserving the balance of power in his hands".[12]

Elizabeth was believed by some to have maintained her father's policy. Fenton, translator of Guicciardini's *History*, dedicating the work to Elizabeth in 1579, declared that God "had erected your seate upon a high hill or sanctuarie, and put into your hands the balance of power and justice, to peaze and counterpeaze [appease and counter-poise] at your will the actions and counsels of all the Christian Kingdoms of your time".[13] William Camden, in his *History of Elizabeth* written in 1675, not long after the beginning of our period, when the balance of power had become a widely discussed concept, said that she "sat as an heroical princess and umpire" between the Spaniards and the French and might equally have adopted her father's motto (*Cui adhaero praeest*): "France and Spain are, as it were, the scale in the balance of Europe, and England the tongue or the holder of the balance".[14] Similarly the Abbé de Mably, writing in the eighteenth century, attributed to Elizabeth the statement that "it is a matter of dividing Europe into states almost equal, in order that, their forces being balanced, they will fear to offend one another, and hesitate to plan too great designs".[15]

By the middle of the seventeenth century, when our period begins, therefore, there was already widespread recognition of the benefits a ruler could secure by holding the balance. It was understood that it was often the weaker states of the system which had the greatest incentive to pursue such a policy. It was seen for example, that the rulers of the Alpine kingdom of Savoy, wedged between the emperor in the east and France in the west, derived an obvious advantage from calling in whichever could best help them against the most threatening at the time. Venice, seeking to resist the power of Spain in Italy, sought a variety of balancing partners – including even the protestant Netherlands – to counter her influence: policies which had the effect that the idea of the balance of power was particularly attributed to that state during this period. (Mazarin, writing in 1646, for example, attributed this policy to the Republic).[16] Denmark, like Henry VIII of England, had switched from side to side during the struggle between Charles V and Francis I; and a century later, fought each side in turn during the Thirty Years War. Saxony and Branden-burg during the same war sought, so far as they could, to avoid abetting the dominance which either the emperor or Sweden could acquire in Germany. These smaller states, more than any others, it was perceived, had an interest in preventing the excessive domination of a single powerful state on which they might become dependent.

There were, however, two factors which limited the pursuit of balance of power policies in the years before 1648. It was limited, first, by religious sentiment. Such policies can be operated effectively only if each state within a system is entirely unconstrained by ideological allegiance, so that it can choose partners according to the imperatives of the balance alone. During the period between 1559 and 1648, when international policies were dominated above all by religious passion, that freedom did not exist. In general, Catholic states felt obliged to support Catholic partners, whether strong or weak, while Protestant states supported Protestant allies, whatever the demands of balance. So, in the Thirty Years War, the Catholic states of Europe, in Germany and elsewhere, mainly joined the Hapsburg powers of Austria and Spain, despite their dominance; while Protestant powers, such as Sweden, England and Denmark, supported the Protestant cause for religious reasons, or to promote purely national purposes, rather than in the interests of a continental balance. It is true that there were, even in that ideological age, always exceptions: times when religious inclinations were not regarded as decisive. So Protestant England, under James I, was willing for years to contemplate an alliance with Catholic Spain; and was deterred from this only after the outbreak of the Thirty Years War, when religious and political objections in both countries made it impossible. Venice, as we saw, was willing to ignore religious feeling in entering into an alliance with the United Provinces in 1617–18 so that she could better defend her interests against all-powerful Spain. France, most conspicuously of all, consistently disregarded religious sympathies in seeking allies against her arch-rival Spain: Francis I had been willing to call in the heretic Turks against Charles V in 1527 and again in 1536; Henry IV planned to intervene on the Protestant side in the contest for Cleves-Julich in 1609; and in 1635, above all, Richelieu threw France on the side of the Protestant powers, even in a largely religious war, as a means of overcoming the power of Spain and promoting the national interest of France. But these were exceptions. Generally speaking, religious ties discouraged any single-minded pursuit of balancing policies at that time.

The second factor which inhibited resort to balance of power policies in this earlier period was the dominance of Spain. It was not a situation, such as was to prevail after 1648, in which eight or ten principal states, together with numerous smaller ones, were able to group themselves in various combinations so as to create a balance among them. From 1559 a single power, Spain, dominated the continent; and the real question was only: Were you for Spain or against her? Many different states had their reasons to be against her: France, from ancient dynastic rivalry, Britain, Venice and the Netherlands to maintain or secure their independence, Sweden and the German Protestant rulers, to defend their religion. But in general they fought their battles with her, for much of the period, separately rather than together. There was little doubt that they would nearly always see their interests as opposed to the principal hegemonic power. But, in choosing that course, they did not think in terms of a continental balance. Conversely, Austria, for family as well as religious reasons, was automatically committed to Spain's side. There was thus little scope for choosing partners, for deliberate decisions to throw a country's power into the balance on one side or the other, as was to occur so frequently in the period to follow. While, as in all periods, balances often emerged, local or general, they were rarely created as deliberate instruments of policy to maintain the equilibrium of the continent. There was not yet any sense of Europe as an interrelated community, a single entity within which a balance had always to be maintained.

After 1648 both these factors were to change. Religion ceased to count for much in determining the policy of states, and so ceased to inhibit the pursuit of balance of power policies. Alliances were, as we shall see, continually made across religious barriers, and often specifically for balance of power reasons. Secondly, at the Peace of Westphalia Spanish power had been humbled; and it was further weakened in her settlement with France in 1659. From this point Spain became only one among the states of Europe, and soon an increasingly insignificant factor in European politics. From about 1660 France occupied for fifty years a position almost as powerful as Spain's had been. But from 1713 she too was reduced (precisely as a result of the balance of power policies pursued by her opponents) to a rank similar to that of her main competitors. At the same time, the authority of the emperor in Germany was reduced by the Westphalia Settlement and the principal German states increasingly became sovereign powers like any others. Russia, Sweden, the United Provinces, Prussia, Portugal and Denmark all now joined the ranks of significant European states while Turkey, previously so widely feared, fell into decline. A far greater equality of power was thus established among the members of the system. Conditions were created which were uniquely favourable to the pursuit of balance of power policies.

EVOLUTION OF THE THEORY AFTER 1648

It was, as a result, especially in the age that began after the Peace of Westphalia that the notion of "balance of power" began to secure widespread currency. From this point that particular expression – no longer merely a vague notion of "balance" – began to feature widely in discussions of European politics.*

The more favourable circumstances now existing were reflected in the policies actually pursued by states. A new flexibility in alliances became visible. So, during the war between Sweden and Poland of 1655–60, Brandenburg, allied herself first with the one and then with the other (securing recognition of her sovereignty in Prussia from each in turn in consequence). So, during the twenty-year struggle undertaken in three separate wars between England and United Provinces from 1652 to 1674, France gave her support first to one side and then to the other. Russia committed herself against Poland from 1654–6 and again from 1658–68, but in the interval was with Poland against Sweden. Brandenburg shifted rapidly from alliance with France in 1672 to alliance against her a year or so later. Though these twists and turns represented only an elaboration of traditional alliance policies, they demonstrated a still greater flexibility. The states of the system no longer felt constrained, by traditional, religious or other loyalties, from seeking the short-term alliances which they thought would best promote their interests at the time in question.

But it was above all the growth in the power of France, now replacing Spain as the dominant state of the system, which stimulated such intense discussion of the "balance of power" at this time. It was France which had secured the most striking gains from the Peace of Westphalia. Her ambition for further gains became increasingly evident over the years that followed. This was soon manifested in the war launched by Louis XIV against Spain in 1667 to promote bogus claims on behalf of his wife in the Spanish Netherlands, the so-called War of Devolution. That endeavour prompted a clear manifestation of balance of power policies in action: the establishment in 1668 of

---

* Cf. Herbert Butterfield, in Butterfield and Wight (eds), *Diplomatic Investigations*, p. 139: "It is my experience that if, as a general student of history, one collects references to the balance of power, or studies the ones that the experts have collected, they are comparatively few in the sixteenth century, but after 1600 not only do they become more numerous – their meaning is less clouded by ambiguities. It is after about the middle of the seventeenth century, however, that the references begin to come in an amazing flood. And, so far as I can see, it is only at this point in the story that the doctrine has its remarkable development."

But this gave rise to the first and most obvious objection to the doctrine. It was only too clear (even to contemporary observers) that this principle could provide an almost inexhaustible source of justification for any state which wished to plan a war against another. If, for example, Austria wished (as she did) as soon as the War of Austrian Succession was completed to plan a new war against Frederick the Great to recover the territory she had lost, she could always claim (assuming that she felt the need to find a justification) that this was because of the threat to the European balance of power now represented by Prussia, newly enlarged through its acquisition of Silesia and twice a victor in the recent conflict. Because the doctrine could so easily be used in this way some doubts began to be expressed. It was suggested that the balance of power doctrine was sometimes merely an excuse, a rationalisation that could be put forward by any state which wished to justify the use of force against another power. This was the view put forward in 1758, the same year as Vattel's work appeared (and two years after Austria again embarked on war against Frederick the Great), by the German writer, Johann von Justi, in his work *Die Chimära des Gleichgewichts von Europa* (The Chimera of the Balance of Power of Europe).[31] In this he declared that

> when a state which has grown more powerful . . . is attacked . . . in order to weaken it, such action is motivated least of all by the balance of power. This would be a war which is waged by the several states against a strong state for specific interests, and the rules of the balance of power will only be camouflage under which these interests are hidden. . . . States, like private persons, are guided by nothing but their private interests, real or imaginary, and they are far from being guided by chimerical balance of power. Name one state which has participated in a war contrary to its interests or without a specific interest, only to maintain the balance of power.[32]

General adoption of the so-called balance of power principle would make possible continual intervention by one state into the affairs of another:

> If the equilibrium were ever realised nothing would be more

terrible than the enslavement of every state in regard to its neighbours: it would be necessary to recognise in every state the right to
intervene in the domestic affairs of the others. It would be better
indeed to have a universal monarchy, for to subject several states
at the same time would be much harder than to be dependent on
the one.

Thus the doctrine could be a recipe for war rather than peace. This
was the equally cynical view expressed by Burke two years later.
Whatever its success in preventing domination by the powerful, he
asserted, the pursuit of the balance of power had certainly not
brought peace.

> The balance of power, the pride of modern policy, and originally
> invented to preserve the general peace as well as the freedom of
> Europe, has only preserved its liberty. It has been the origin of
> innumerable and fruitless wars. That political torture by which
> powers are to be enlarged or abridged, according to a standard . . .
> ever has been . . . a cause of infinite contention and bloodshed.

The concern with the continental balance meant that wars were now
vast in extent, yet had only limited results.

> The foreign ambassadors constantly residing in all courts, the
> negotiations incessantly carrying on, spread both confederacies
> and quarrels so wide that, whenever hostilities commence, the
> theatre of war is always of a prodigious extent.

This meant that no state could be successful in war everywhere.

> What they gain in one part is lost in another; and in conclusion
> their affairs become so balanced, that all the powers concerned are
> certain to lose a great deal. In modern treaties of peace . . . none
> can properly be called conquerors or conquered.[33]

This judgement, made at the height of the Seven Years War accurately assessed the final outcome of that war, at least on the continent
of Europe. Though losses in men and *matériel* were huge, especially
for Prussia which made the first move, the final result was nil: the
status quo ante was restored throughout the continent.

This cynical view of the balance of power, seen as a rationalisation for purely self-interested motives – the homage which vice played to virtue – began to be fairly widely shared.[34] It was to be stated many times, especially by radical politicians, in the following century, and beyond: by such writers as Cobden and Bright and Brailsford in England, and by Woodrow Wilson in the United States. Rousseau shared their scepticism but for different reasons. He did not doubt that a balance of a kind existed. But he did not think it was created by the deliberate action of states. Under existing governments (it might be different in an ideal world, where the "general will" prevailed in each state) nations were naturally competitive in their conduct; and, whatever the motives they claimed, they would always vie to boost their own power. From that competition, inevitably, a balance of a sort resulted. But "we are not suppose", he declared, "that the boasted balance of power in Europe has been actually deliberately established; or that anybody has done anything really with a view to supporting it." It was simply that "those who have found that they have not weight enough to destroy it cover their own particular designs with the pretence of maintaining it". The balance thus came about automatically "and needs no other support than itself, without anyone interfering; and even if it were upset for a moment on one side, it would soon be restored on the other". But though competition inevitably produced balance, it did not necessarily bring peace. "Though the present system is unshakeable, it is for that very reason the more tempestuous; and there subsists between the European powers a kind of continual action and reaction, which, without entirely displacing them, keeps them in constant agitation."[35]

This criticism suggested that if the actions of states created a balance it was accidentally rather than deliberately. But in practice their policies often overturned the balance in the interests of the states which undertook it. Thus Vergennes, French Minister of Foreign Affairs, in his *Memoire* of 1774, condemned the first partition of Poland on the grounds that, though it purported to maintain the balance of power,[36] it did so at the expense of a smaller state which was unable to protect its own interests.

During the course of almost two centuries the great powers have concentrated all their designs, and devoted almost all their means towards preventing any of them becoming preponderant. A new combination is now supplanting that system of general equilibrium.

> Three powers have endeavoured to establish a particular one
> which they found on the equality of their susurpations. Thus they
> cause the balance of power to lean strongly in their favour.[37]

In other words, the concept could be used to justify policies which
secured not an even balance but one favourable to particular powers.

Despite these various criticisms, the old-fashioned view of the
balance continued to be held by many. The defence of the traditional
view was put most passionately at the end of the century, when the
balance of the continent seemed to have been fatally disturbed by the
victories of Napoleon. Von Gentz, a Prussian official who later wrote
widely about European affairs and eventually became an adviser to
Metternich, had for a brief time welcomed the French Revolution.
But he became a passionate opponent of Napoleon's domination of
the continent; and in his work *On the States of Europe before and
after the French Revolution*, published in 1802, he attributed the
disastrous state of the continent to the neglect of the balance of
power by some of its principal states. He rejected the claim which
had been put forward by Comte d'Hauterive, propagandist for the
French government,[38] that European politics had degenerated into
anarchy during the previous fifty years and that only the dominant
position which France had now secured had restored order to the
continent. On the contrary, he argued, France's dominance had
destroyed the equilibrium of earlier days.

> The political system cannot but be extremely defective when it
> contains such a disproportion of power as nothing but a general
> league can rectify. . . . All the dictates of sound policy prescribe
> the necessity of a natural or an artificial balance of power, not only
> to prevent the wanton . . . abuse of power by a preponderating
> state, but . . . to preserve the [European] political system from
> shocks that might prove fatal to its existence.[39]

Four years later, in a better-known work, his *Fragments Upon the
Present State of the Political Balance of Europe*, he reaffirmed the
basic principles of the balance of power; once more asserting the idea
of community needs. Echoing Fénelon and Vattel he asserted that
there existed in Europe "an extensive social commonwealth, of
which the characteristic object was the preservation and reciprocal
guarantee of the rights of all its members". For this to be maintained
certain conditions must be fulfilled: namely that "no one of its

members must ever become so powerful as to be able to coerce all the rest put together"; that any member which disrupted the system "must be in a condition to be coerced, not only by the collective threat of the other members, but by any majority of them, if not by one individually"; and that "if ever a European state attempted by an unlawful enterprise to attain to a degree of power . . . which enabled it to defy . . . a union of several of its neighbours . . . such a state should be treated as a common enemy".[40] The maintenance of this system required constant alertness and a willingness to intervene at an early stage to defend a state under attack. The governments of Europe must therefore "watch over, maintain and defend the independence, security and rights of their neighbours, their allies and of every acknowledged and legally constituted power; even those of their rivals and those of their occasional enemies". No state could abdicate from this duty.

> We must hear of no insulary systems . . . no absolute neutrality, no unconditional seclusion from any important transaction. . . . The more industry and vigour is employed in checking the first acts of injustice and violence, the less frequent will be the cases in which it will be necessary to march forth to fight against them in the field; the more steadfastly they hold themselves in a state of preparation, the greater reluctance will be felt to challenge them to combat. In a word, the more perfect, harmonious and stable the federal system of the European states, the greater the sensibility each individual discovers to every violation of common rights, the stronger the ties which binds each member to the collective body, the more rarely wars will occur.[41]

This work, therefore, which became widely known, powerfully justified the need for a European balance, on both the grounds which had been mainly put forward before: to prevent domination by any single power and to maintain the peace of the continent. Brougham in Britain, writing almost simultaneously, came to similar conclusions. In his book *Balance of Power*, written in 1803, he set out to defend the concept from its critics: "both those who attacked it as an unintelligible jargon", invented to "furnish pretexts for every act of national injustice" (as von Justi had done), "and those who held that a balance anyway arose naturally out of the fashions of men" competing with each other and was therefore "useless and superfluous" (as Rousseau had held). In his view, though the system might have been abused from time to time, the main problem was that it had not been consistently implemented. The essence of the system was not particular rules of conduct such as "forming offensive and defensive alliances", "attacking a neighbour in order to weaken his power before he had betrayed his hostile views", or "defending a rival in order to stay . . . the progress of a common enemy". The distinguishing feature of the theory lay in "the perpetual attention to foreign affairs which it inculcates; the constant watchfulness which it prescribes over every movement in all parts of the system . . . the unceasing care which it dictates even of nations most remotely situated and apparently unconnected". Above all, "the general union which is effected of all the European powers in one collective system, obeying certain laws and actuated for the most part by a common principle". This meant that in consequence the right of "mutual inspection" was recognised among civilised states, above all in the appointment of envoys and residents who had that function. Where the "powerful states are, for their own sakes, constantly watching over the safety of the most insignificant" the security of all states was protected so that "a flourishing commonwealth" was not liable to "lose its independence or prosperity by the fate of one battle". It was thus essential for states to "ponder upon the principles which should direct their public conduct . . . and remember that each state forms part of a general system, liable to be affected by every rearrangement which it may experience".[42]

The ideas that were held about the balance of power during this period therefore closely mirrored the changes that occurred in the configuration of European politics. So long as a single state dominated the system, and was feared as a threat to many of the others, the balance was extolled as a means of preventing domination and disturbance to the equilibrium. When, from 1713, that domination was brought to an end and a greater equality in power among European states established, a balance began to appear as a natural feature of international relationships. It no longer made necessary any special policies by particular states, but was increasingly seen as an automatic process which would anyway ensure that some degree of balance was maintained (as when, for example, in the diplomatic revolution of 1756, despite a complete change of alliance partners, a new equilibrium was none the less established). By some, indeed, the concept was denounced as a fig-leaf, used to conceal the self-serving motives of any state desiring to attack another. Only when a single nation – the same one as before – again won domination of the system was the idea restored to respectability again. Once again the balance of power was invoked as the means of re-establishing stability and equilibrium throughout the continent.

DIFFERING CONCEPTIONS OF THE BALANCE

Although, therefore, the idea of the balance of power featured prominently in discussion of international affairs during this period, views on the subject varied widely. Some praised the concept and some denounced it. To some it described a situation; to others a policy; to others again a process, virtually automatic. To some the creation of a balance was an essentially self-interested goal, designed to promote the purposes of a particular state; to others a community objective, required in the interests of the society of states as a whole. To some it was a means of securing peace; to others a policy to prevent the domination of other states, and often therefore requiring war.

One source of difference concerned the time-scale in which policies were conceived. The idea that balance came about as a result of an automatic process (as suggested, for example, by Rousseau in the passage quoted above) implied that states, in forming alliances to prevent the domination of others, would bring about roughly equal alignments, each opposed to the other. The balance was the end-result of actions which they took in their *own* interests: to protect themselves against the threat they perceived from others. Competition alone, under this view, would limit the excessive power of any one state. This, however, is precisely what von Gentz, writing only forty years after Rousseau, contested. There was no such automatic process, he asserted. Because they had sought to pursue their own interests in a *short*-sighted way, such powers as Austria, Prussia and Russia had allowed Napoleon to dominate the whole of Europe and so fatally to disturb the balance of the continent. So, he implied, the self-interested action of states would only result in equilibrium if they looked at their *long-term* interest, in stability and the independence of states, rather than short-term political advantages, which might be secured from opportunistic alliances with the most powerful state.

But differences on the question also derived from differing views as to the *purpose* of the balance. If its purpose was to prevent the domination of a particular state, then it was not illogical to propose war as a means of achieving that aim. But if the purpose was to achieve peace, or at least stability, then that conclusion became less obvious. When legal writers, such as Vattel, justified the use of force to prevent any one state securing domination, they implied that the latter goal had priority over the maintenance of peace. Similarly, when von Gentz denounced the European states which had come to terms with Napoleon for neglecting the needs of the balance of power, he was condemning them for preferring peace (which might have been secured by conceding the domination of Europe to Napoleon) to resistance. But others suggested that the main purpose of a balance of power policy was to maintain the peace. Thus Walpole, speaking in the British House of Commons, declared that it is "by leagues, well concerted and strictly observed, that the weak are defended . . . and empires preserved from those inundations of war that in former times, laid the world in ruins".[43] Frederick the Great defined the balance as "alliance of many princes and states against the over-powerful and ambitious, a balance which is solely designed for maintaining the peace and security of mankind".[44] A French writer, early in the following century declared: "This system [the balance of power] has for its objective the preservation of the public tranquillity, the protection of the weak against the aggression of the strong, the blocking of the ambitious projects of conquerors, and the prevention of discord, which in turn leads to the calamities of war."[45] At root this difference reflected varying views as to the *efficacy* of balance of power policies in deterring aggression. The latter view implied that the creation of alliances alone would effectively dissuade potential aggressors from expansive policies (a thesis which the offensive actions of Louis XIV in 1788, Frederick the Great in 1756 and the French revolutionary government in 1793–5 scarcely supported). Under the former view, of the other hand, deterrence before the event was insufficient: only the aggression itself would stimulate the creation of an alliance, which might then eventually reverse the aggression by military action.

This difference was related to another discrepancy in the way the term was employed. Some believed, as we saw, that the balance was to be aimed at by all states equally, in the interest of the community of states as a whole; while others saw it as something required in the interests of a *particular* state, and so to be achieved by the actions of that one state alone. When Henry VIII prided himself on holding the balance between Charles V and François I, or when Elizabeth was praised for holding the balance of Europe in her hands, this was clearly seen as a benefit enjoyed by one particular state. Savoy, in our own period, was widely seen as seeking a balance between France and Austria in her own interests. Even a powerful state might seek to hold lesser states in balance for that reason: as when it was said by a writer of the period that in Louis XIV's day, France "profited from the national animosity, and from the commercial jealousy, between the English and Dutch to hold the balance between the two maritime powers".[46] Swift, in the *Tale of a Tub*, described how a single power, even if politically weak itself, might yet be able to hold the balance among others as a result of its pivotal position.[47] This view of the balance as the creation of a single state to suit its own purposes is quite different from that of Fénelon or Vattel, seeing the balance as a requirement of the society of states as a whole: seeing Europe as a "kind of community", or as a "political system in which the nations . . . are bound together by their relations and various interests into a single body", or "a sort of Republic whose members unite for the maintenance of order and the preservation of liberty". There is a logical inconsistency between these two conceptions – a device to promote the interests of one power and as a requirement of the whole body of states – which was not always acknowledged.

There were differences too on the question: among *whom* was the balance to be maintained? Was what mattered the *local* balance in particular parts of the world: for example, between Britain and France in North America and India, between Sweden and Russia in the Baltic, between Prussia and Austria in Germany, between Russia and Austria in the Balkans; or was it only the general, the continental balance which counted? In earlier times it would have been absurd to think in terms of a continent-wide balance. So Commynes, as we saw, had discussed only one-to-one balances in particular areas, for example in Italy, Germany or Spain. Even after 1648 there was much discussion of regional balances. Martens, in his *Summary of the Laws of Nations*, wrote of a "system for maintaining a balance of power among the Eastern powers in Europe, among those of the West, or those in the North; among the states of Germany, those of Italy; among the Europeans in America".[48] D'Hauterive, in the work quoted earlier, stated that, besides a general equilibrium for the whole of Europe, there were smaller "*equilibres partiels*" in particular areas: for example Germany, Italy, southern Europe and the North.[49] The Duke de Ripperda, in his *Memoirs*, wrote of the "inferiour balances" existing in different parts of Europe.[50] But increasingly, as time went by, attention was focused on the balance within Europe as a whole, and especially between the seven or eight larger powers of the continent. When it was said of Catherine the

Great, for example, that "she never can see with indifference any essential aggrandisement or essential diminution of any European state take place", it showed that she believed that even distinct events were significant if they affected the balance of the continent as a whole. When von Gentz deplored the destruction of the balance of power by Napoleon, he too was thinking of the continental balance as a whole. Increasingly Europe was seen as an integral interrelated political system, in which any shift in the power balance in any one area would have an effect in other parts as well.

But even if it was the balance within the continent as a whole which was at stake, the question still arose, among which powers must it be maintained? Did every state of Europe, from the largest to the smallest, from the Ottoman empire in the East to the tiniest ministate of Germany, have a part to play within that balance? Or was it only the balance between the major powers which counted? This question was never very carefully addressed. Pitt in 1790–1 wanted to bring Turkey into the European balance and was criticised for this by Burke and Grey (p. 000 below). In some of the writing, such as that of Fénelon and Vattel, concerned with the community of states as a whole, the implication was that every state, at least every state in Christendom, entered into the balance. But increasingly, especially from the beginning of the eighteenth century, it came to be recognised that the larger powers of the continent were those which were significant, and that it was among them in particular that the balance was to be maintained. But a balance among those powers alone would not necessarily prevent domination of others that were smaller and weaker. A classic illustration was provided by the partitions of Poland. These were undertaken specifically to maintain a balance of advantage among the three powers which undertook them but only at the cost of the total elimination of Poland from the map of Europe. A balance between Spain and Austria in Italy was secured only through eliminating most of the smaller states of that peninsula. Outside Europe a balance between France and Britain could be achieved only by dismembering India and the West Indies. Maintaining a balance between Austria and Russia involved successive forays at the expense of Turkey. And so on. It was not therefore a general balance within the continent which, even on the most favourable understanding, could be claimed: only a balance among the dominant powers.

In other words it was an oligarchic system; and one which by the end of the period, with the decline in the power of Sweden, the United Provinces, Spain and Portugal, had been narrowed still further. Eventually the term was increasingly understood to refer to the balance among the major powers alone: Russia, Austria, Prussia, France and Britain.

IMPLICATIONS OF THE CONCEPT FOR THE INTERNATIONAL SYSTEM

If these were the varying ideas held about the balance of power, what were the implications for the way international relations were conducted in this period? The fact that such conceptions were held at all, however much they varied, influenced the image that was held of the international society, and so the actions that were taken within it. Those conceptions both reflected and intensified prevailing views about the way international relations should be conducted.

First, the idea that a balance had to be maintained made *flexibility* in foreign policies, above all in alliance policy, essential. If the balance was to be adjusted to prevent the domination of any one state or group of states, policies needed to be always adaptable. There could be no permanent and indissoluble alliances, since these might need to be abandoned if any one party to them became so strong that its partners needed to join the opposing camp. Versatility, the capacity to form new groupings, to meet new threats and new situations, was the essence of the system. This was seen in the reality of international relations during this period. Nothing is more striking than the continual changes of partners which occurred with such startling rapidity, throughout this period (see Chapter 9 below). Britain and the United Provinces, bitter opponents in three wars between 1652 and 1674, became staunch allies in the wars against Louis XIV which followed. Savoy switched sides twice in the course of seven years between 1696 and 1703. Spain was at war with Austria in 1718–20, was her ally in 1725 and again her enemy after 1729. Austria and France, bitter enemies in the war of 1740–8, fought as allies in 1756–63; Austria and Britain, allies in the first, fought on opposite sides in the second. During the Napoleonic wars, for all their hostility to France, Austria and Prussia continually alternated between war and peace; while the Russian Tsar was willing to join with Napoleon in plans for the control of the continent, in the intervals of fighting bitter and expensive wars against him. The needs of the moment required that friends be made into enemies, and enemies into friends, often at a moment's notice.

Secondly, because of this need for flexibility, alliances could take no account of ideology. England and the United Provinces, the only two significant parliamentary states, both of which had adopted republican constitutions at the beginning of our period, none the less three times made war against each other within twenty years; while the absolute monarchies of France, Prussia, Austria and Russia fought against each other quite as eagerly as they fought the parliamentary states. The foreign policies of Sweden and the Netherlands were only marginally different at times of parliamentary rule to what they were when they were controlled by a single ruler. Religion counted for as little as political viewpoint. Catholic Spain fought Catholic Austria in Italy and the Mediterranean, just as Protestant Sweden fought Protestant Brandenburg in the Baltic. Protestant Britain and Prussia were sometimes allies, sometimes enemies; Catholic France and Catholic Austria likewise. Without such doctrinal indifference the balance of power could not have been maintained.[51] Even the French Revolution, though it undoubtedly created for a time a regime entirely different in ideology from that of other states, and on these grounds aroused the hostility of governments elsewhere, did not fundamentally alter the system. Whatever their opinion of the revolution, most of the other powers of the continent were willing to come to terms with France at one time or another. It was ultimately the needs of the balance of power, not the distrust of a revolutionary political system (anyway largely abandoned by Napoleon), which stimulated Europe at long last to combine to defeat the emperor.

Thirdly, a system based on the balance of power required states to settle for less than total victory. Because alliances were formed to balance the power of others, neither side could usually prevail altogether. In the peace settlements, therefore, deals were done, bargains struck. There was an exchange of assets, territories, colonies, trading rights. The losing states lost while the victors gained; but even after the major wars every state retained the bulk of its territories. Often it was as important to prevent an ally from gaining too much as to defeat the enemy. The needs of the balance of power thus often caused states in alliance to seek separate peaces to promote their own interests, so allowing the defeated states to reduce their losses (p. 000 below). As a result in some cases, as after the Seven Years War, there was, even after years of bitter conflict, a return to the precise status quo before the war began.

Fourthly, the changeability of alliances, and the unpredictability that resulted, meant that there was a constant need for watchfulness: the "sensibility" that each state should show to "any violation of rights" demanded by von Gentz, the "perpetual attention to foreign affairs" advocated by Brougham. One of the reasons for the rapid growth in diplomatic representation during this period (p. 000 below) was the demand of every government to be well-informed about the intentions of other governments, so that they were in a position to conclude new alliances when the necessity arose. It was this, as Vattel recognised in the passage quoted above, which had made necessary the "constant residence of ministers and the perpetual negotiations" which now everywhere took place. The needs of balance forced every state to be continually on its guard; and to be willing if necessary to intervene in conflicts occurring at the other side of the continent. As Brougham put it in a different passage, to maintain the balance every statesman needed to "be instructed in all that passes outside of his kingdom which has relation to him, to his allies, to his enemies", since it was "mutual jealousy, and anxious attention to the affairs of other states, which is the master principle of the modern balance of power system".[52]

Fifthly, another effect of the universal concern for balance was the fact that nearly all the wars of this age – at least those involving the principal powers – became wars between substantial alliances rather than between single powers. This had not been true in earlier times. In the age of dynastic rivalry before 1559 and the age of religious dissension between 1559 and 1648, many of the wars had been between individual rulers: English kings against French kings in France; French against Spanish in Italy; Swedish against Polish, and Danish against Swedish, in the Baltic; Philip II's interventions against France and England (separately). Similarly, during the age of nationalism to come every major conflict, with the exception of the Crimean war, was fought between single states. But from 1648 to 1815 every major war was between large-scale alliances, with anything from two to eight states on either side. Because any war could seriously disturb the balance, even in a different part of the continent, every nation now had a stake in its outcome. In many cases alliances had been formed even before war broke out, so that a widespread participation was inevitable from the outset. In others, alliances were sought in the early stages to boost the chances of success for particular participants. As a result often what were essentially separate disputes – for example between Britain and France in West Europe and overseas, between the United Provinces and France in the Netherlands,

between Spain and Austria in Italy, Austria and Prussia in Germany –
coalesced into single continent wide wars. Even Russia, barely considered a part of the European system when our period begins, from
1720 onwards was increasingly heavily involved in the main conflicts
which took place. While the combinations continually changed,
alliances of a kind were always required. Thus Britain, France,
Prussia and Austria took part in every major war of the period (those
beginning in 1672, 1688, 1702, 1739–40, 1756 and 1792); Russia in all
after 1713 except the War of Austrian Succession. A single continental system had not been established in which all of the principal
competitors took part.

Finally, the concern for balance also affected the type of settlement
reached at the end of each conflict. Sometimes victorious powers
deliberately refrained from extracting gains as large as they might
have done because they did not wish to weaken an opponent unduly
(for example, Britain in 1712–13 and 1763; Prussia in 1742 and 1745;
Russia in 1762). Often they were more concerned to prevent an ally
from acquiring too much than to extort the maximum concessions
from a defeated enemy (the Maritime Powers in 1713–14; most of the
victors in 1814–15). On they would seek to negotiate a separate peace
without regard to the interests of their allies (p. 000 below). As a
result, each settlement not only had to meet the varied requirements
of different allies on the more successful side, each having different
and sometimes conflicting objectives; but also take some account of
the concerns of the losers too. Because many states were involved,
the process of peace-making was complex and protracted (the Westphalia settlement itself had taken six years to arrive at – scarcely
surprising considering its importance and complexity) and in the
major settlements which followed peace negotiations rarely took less
than a year and often much more. In consequence many of the wars
had no clear-cut outcomes (two of the three Anglo-Dutch wars, and
the major international wars ending in 1678, 1697, 1748 and, in
continental Europe, 1763). The overriding concern for balance thus
had a decisive effect on the outcome of the most important conflicts
of the day.

In all these ways the conduct of international relations during this
period was affected by the general concern to maintain the balance.
The winning of excessive power by any individual state, it came to be
accepted, was to be prevented. Unilateral gains were not to be
allowed. In all transactions, above all those involving peace and war,
the interests and concerns of other states had to be taken into
account. Action on the basis of "interest" (that is, self-interest) alone

was widely condemned. A widespread assumption of the age, and the only basis of consensus, was that there existed a *de facto* equilibrium among them greater powers; that this should be maintained; and that all should be ready to act, both in their own interest and to the common advantage, to ensure that it was not too violently disturbed. In practice, as we shall see, these admirable sentiments were not always acted on as wholeheartedly as the doctrine demanded. But it remained the theoretical goal, to be pursued at least within the bounds of prudence; and one that should certainly be demanded of all other states.

BOOKS

Contemporary works

Lord Brougham, *The Balance of Power* (1803) (London, 1857).
Charles Davenant, *Essays upon the Balance of Power* (London, 1701).
Daniel Defoe, *The Balance of Europe* (London, 1711).
Francois de S. de la M. Fénelon, *Two Essays on the Balance of Europe*, English trs. (London, 1720).
F. von Gentz, *Fragments upon the Present State of the Political Balance of Europe*, English trs. (London, 1806).
David Hume, "Of the Balance of Power", in *Essays* (Edinburgh, 1741–2).
J. H. G. von Justi, *Die Chimäre des Gleichgewichts von Europa* (Altona, 1758).
L. M. Kahle, *La Balance de l'Europe* (Paris, 1744).
F. G. Leckie, *A Historical Research into the Nature of the Balance of Power in Europe* (London, 1817).
Duke de Ripperda, "On the Balance of Power", in *Memoirs*, English trs. (London, 1714).
M. Wright (ed.), *Theory and Practice of the Balance of Power, 1486–1914*, Contemporary texts (London, 1975).

Modern works

M. S. Anderson, "Eighteenth-Century Theories of the Balance of Power", in R. Hatton and M. S. Anderson (eds), *Studies in Diplomatic History* (London, 1970).
H. Butterfield and M. Wight, *Diplomatic Investigations* (London, 1966) chs 6 and 7.
C. Dupuis, *Le Principe de l'equilibre et le concert européen depuis le traité de Westphalie* (Paris, 1909).
Arthur Hassall, *The Balance of Power, 1715–89* (New York, 1914).
E. W. Gulick, *Europe's Classical Balance of Power* (Ithaca, N.Y., 1955).
G. Zeller, "Le Principe d'equilibre dans la politique internationale avant 1789", *Revue Historique*, vol. CCXV (1956) pp. 25–37.

2 The States

At first sight it might appear that the establishment of a viable international system at this period would be made impossible by the huge variation in the character of the individual states.

These varied from large empires, such as those ruled over by the Austrian emperor and the Russian tsar, covering vast areas and numbers of territories having little in common, to the tiny mini-states of Germany and Italy; from the highly centralised monarchies of France and England to the amorphous societies of the Cossacks in the Ukraine and the Tartars in the Crimea, with only embryonic political institutions and no clear territorial confines; from the royalist autocracies which existed in much of Europe to the republics of Venice and Genoa, and the parliamentary regimes in England, the United Provinces and (part of the time) Sweden; from the secular, and increasingly secular, states that prevailed in most places, to the ecclesiastical states in the papal lands in Italy, and the bishoprics, some of them large and powerful, in Germany; from compact and tightly-knit units, such as Savoy and Denmark, to the diffuse, disorganised and decentralised systems existing in Poland and the Ottoman empire.

These apparently widespread discrepancies, however, concealed many similarities. Though some states were more highly organised than others, almost everywhere a process of centralisation was occurring. In nearly every country systematic state-building was being undertaken, which itself made the units in time increasingly alike. Whether the ruler was a secular monarch or an ecclesiastical prince, the system of government was generally similar: the archbishops of Cologne and Trier, the pope in his own territories, ruled their lands, formed alliances, and had dealings with each other, in much the same manner as secular rulers. Whether a state was a monarchy or a republic, autocratic or parliamentary, power was always highly concentrated, being held normally by a single powerful figure (if not a king then a doge in Venice or Genoa, or a stadtholder in the United Provinces) advised by a few powerful ministers who they themselves had appointed. Whether a state had clearly defined boundaries (and few did), or only exercised a general dominance in a particular area (like the Crimean Tartars), it still sent diplomatic representatives to negotiate with other states, formed leagues with them or declared war against them, in much the same way as other states of the continent. Even states of alien religion and culture, such as the Barbary states of North Africa and the Ottoman sultanate, accepted diplomatic envoys, signed treaties and granted trading facilities in much the same way as other states. Though it would be wrong to neglect the manifest differences among these highly disparate political organisations, they were not so great as to make impossible the establishment among them of a coherent international system.

Competition itself tended to make the units more homogenous. The desire to keep up with rivals caused all alike to seek to create more powerful and effective political structures. The rulers themselves were often the prime movers in this process. For increasingly they identified their own reputations with those of the states they ruled. In earlier times they had seen themselves as the representatives of a ruling *family* – Hapsburg, Valois, Tudor or Wittelsbach: dynasts engaged in a competition with other dynasts. They now became, above all, the personification of *states*, engaged in a competition with other states. Louis XIV, in declaring himself, in his most famous utterance, to *be* the state, clearly demonstrated not so much the state's subordination to himself (which none doubted), as his own subordination to the purposes of the state. Catherine the Great did the same in declaring to the Russian senate on her accession to the throne that she "belonged to the state" and that "there should in future be no difference between her interests and those of the state".[1] Frederick the Great, in describing himself as the "first servant of the state",[2] the emperor Joseph II, in calling himself the "chief administrator" of his own country, both demonstrated the same commitment. Frederick the Great put the point categorically: "the interest of the state is the only motive which should govern the counsels of princes".[3] Louis echoed the same sentiment: "the true merit of sovereigns is in always aiming at the same end, which is none other than the glory and greatness of their state".[4]

To promote the state's interests abroad effectively, the rulers first had to assert their own power at home. This meant that the great magnates had to be brought to heel. The independence of the church had to be reduced. The "liberties" previously enjoyed by the cities had to be withdrawn or curtailed. Administration had to be centralised. When the period began many of the kingdoms consisted of a jumble of territories, brought together by the hazards of successions or conquest, each still having its own administration, estates, traditions, culture and (sometimes) language, linked only in the most tenuous way by allegiance to a common ruler. Spain remained until the eighteenth century a collection of kingdoms and territories, each with their separate parliament (there were six *cortes* in Castile alone), separate nobilities, separate fiscal systems, separate systems of jurisdiction and different relationships to the crown (three were separate kingdoms). The manifold Austrian lands included ancient kingdoms, such as Bohemia and Hungary (in each of which their rulers were crowned separately), a variety of central European duchies and margravates, some conquered Balkan territory and, after 1714, the southern Netherlands and various Italian territories, lands which had virtually nothing in common with each other except their ruler. Poland and Lithuania, Denmark and Norway, England, Scotland and Ireland (the "three kingdoms"), though each formed part of a single political entity, had remained almost totally separate lands. Now nearly everywhere these divisions were reduced. The component parts were gradually more closely integrated within the body politic of the state to which they belonged. In England the Act of Union of 1707 and the legislation on Ireland of 1800; in Austria the reforms of Maria Theresa and her minister Haugwitz in 1749–52; in Spain the centralising measures of Alberoni and later Charles III; in Russia the administrative changes introduced by Peter the Great in 1708, 1715 and 1719, and the establishment by his successors of the supreme Privy Council (1726), the Cabinet (1731) and the Konferentsiya in the 1750s; the bureaucratic changes introduced in Prussia by the Great Elector and by Frederick II: all of these had the effect of reducing or destroying the autonomy of local regions and creating a more centralised structure. The power of local Estates was removed or reduced; tolls were abolished; tax collection was streamlined and centralised; royal armies were established to replace the *ad hoc* levies and mercenaries of earlier ages; above all, a system of uniform national laws was established, which brought greater unity to hitherto disparate fragments.

To implement these changes and supervise an increasingly complex system of administration, more powerful governmental structures were created. Bureaucracies were expanded. Government became more professional and (sometimes) somewhat less corrupt. Substantial authority was delegated by the rulers to powerful ministers who took responsibility for large areas of policy. Some of these, a Colbert in France because of his abilities, a Heinsius in the United Provinces because of his close links with the ruler, a Kaunitz in Austria because of his forty-odd years of service in positions of influence, could acquire power such as few ministers in earlier years had enjoyed. But nearly always the rulers retained the ultimate authority, and were wary of according too much power for too long to any minister. As Louis XIV warned his successor, kings should "learn not to let their servants become too powerful"; it was better to "divide your confidence among many, so that each one who shares it being naturally opposed to the advancement of his rival, the jealousy of one serves as a brake to the ambition of others".[5] He even deliberately favoured choosing ministers who were not of the highest social rank because "it was above all necessary to establish my own reputation and to make the public realise, by the very rank of those whom I selected, that it was not my intention to share my authority".[6] On these grounds he avoided choosing a chief minister at all and expressed the hope that such an office would "forever be abolished in France". At about the same time (in 1665) the emperor Leopold in Austria declared, on the death of his former chief minister, his determination "to be himself his own prime minister".[7] Similarly in Spain when Haro, the chief minister died in 1661, Philip IV announced that he too would follow the French example in having no prime minister. That term only became widely current in the second and third decade of the eighteenth century when Walpole in Britain and Ostermann in Russia acquired the title. A few years later Frederick the Great expressed the view that France would be better off if governed by a prime minister, since then "at least their policy would be tied to a system instead of going entirely by chance as at present, with the ministers each more jealous of their rivals than France's enemies".[8] It was necessary "to divide my confidence and the execution of my orders without entirely entrusting it to anyone".[9]

But the rulers were advised not only by individual ministers but by their royal councils, which existed almost everywhere. These could not be relied on to rubber-stamp dutifully whatever policies the ruler proposed. Sometimes there were lively debates within them, and a variety of alternative courses of action might be advocated. Even in Louis XIV's France, there were sometimes divisions on policy within the *Conseil d'en haut*: during the War of Spanish Succession, for example, a dovish faction led by the king's grandson, the Duke of Burgundy, urged peace at almost any price, opposed by a more hawkish faction of opposite view, with a moderate party in the middle.[10] In Austria the major policy questions were considered in the *Geheimrad*, where Kaunitz put forward his controversial plan for a reversal of alliances. In England a cabinet system of government began to develop in the early eighteenth century, with the effect that decision-making power was increasingly removed from the hands of the king and his immediate advisers. Similarly in Sweden and the United Provinces during the period of parliamentary power (1719–72 in the former, and 1650–72 and 1702–47 in the latter) the important decision-making was undertaken by groups of ministers and par-liamentarians, rather than by the traditional rulers. But these were the exceptions, not the rule. In most countries throughout the period the monarchs continued to exercise a dominating influence on policy, especially in the foreign relations field.[11]

The power of parliament was still more marginal. In some places the Estates had been abolished altogether (as in France and Prussia). In other places they were used mainly for the authorisation of new taxes and had little effective control of policy, especially in the field of foreign affairs. Louis XIV expressed the view of the majority of the sovereigns in expressing his profound pity for those monarchs who were dependent on the "indiscretions of a popular assembly. . . . The more you grant it the more it demands. . . . Once you defer to them, they claim the right for ever to control your plans according to their fancy"; and he congratulated his son that "you will reign in a state where you will find no authority that is not honoured to derive its origin and its status from you, and no body that dares to depart from expressions of respect, no corporation that does not see its principal greatness in the good of your service and its sole security in its humble subjection".[12] Even in England, the influence of parlia-ment on policy was rarely decisive. Foreign policy, in particular, was mainly in the hands of the monarch. Occasionally the parliament was able to impose a policy on the ruler: as when in 1674 it forced Charles II to make peace with the United Provinces; just as in the United Provinces itself the States General compelled William to make peace with France four years later, earlier than he himself would have wished. But in general the power of parliaments (where they existed at all) was rather to demand and to criticise than to initiate or control policy.

The influence of the people as a whole was still less. In one or two countries a small group of writers and publicists were able, through their pamphlets and other publications, to influence the policies their governments pursued, in foreign as in other affairs. But the great majority had little knowledge of foreign policy, few opinions and no opportunity to make their feelings felt even if they had any. There was probably more opportunity for such influence in England than in most other states. But even there, at the time of the Dutch wars, "public opinion whether spontaneous or in the shape of pressure groups, seems to have had very little effect on those who made the major decisions. It was not just a constitutional fiction that foreign affairs were reserved as exclusively a matter for the government or . . . the royal prerogative. Informed opinion can hardly be said to have existed".[13]

Everywhere, therefore, power was highly concentrated. The policies pursued were devised by a small group of people, dominated by a single ruler. Kings and their ministers alike were preoccupied by the purposes of the states they served. Their main concern was that their own state should prevail in the competition with their rivals in which all were so actively and eagerly engaged.

THE POWER OF THE STATES

Whatever similarity there may have been in the structure of states, there were wide discrepancies in their size and relative power.

When the period began France was, by common consent, the most formidable power of the continent. Her population, around the middle of our period (that is, in the early eighteenth century) was 18–19 million. This was about three times as great as that of her two neighbours and principal rivals, Spain and England, which had only about six million each (if Scotland is included, Britain's was seven and a half million). Sweden had about three million if her territories south of the Baltic were included, but less than two million after she lost most of these in 1721. Portugal and the United Provinces had only about two million each. Prussia's population, scattered among several different territories, was only two and a half million at the beginning of the eighteenth century, but it became five million after the conquest of Silesia in 1740. Austria had nearly ten million, including three million in recently conquered Hungary and Transylvania. Poland-Lithuania, occupying a vast area second only to Russia in size, had about 10–12 million. Russia had about 15 million at the turn of the century, but as a result of her conquests and population growth this more than doubled by 1800.

But population alone was not the deciding factor. A country's power depended on the way its population was organised. A nation such as Poland, in chronic disorder and without any effective central authority, was much weaker than another such as Sweden, with only about a quarter of its population but with an effective administration and a well-trained army. As a measure of effective power the size and efficiencies of armies was a more relative criterion than population. It was symptomatic of this age of state-building that for the first time standing armies, maintained in peacetime as well as in war, and under the direct control of royal governments, were now almost everywhere created in place of the feudal levies and mercenaries previously relied on. Again France had, from about 1660 onwards by far the most imposing establishment. Even in peacetime she regularly kept armed forces of 100,000 and during major wars these were vastly increased: during the Dutch war of 1672–8 she had about 400,000 men under arms and during the War of Spanish Succession this rose to over half a million. In the second half of the next century she still had a peacetime establishment of about 200,000, and during the Napoleonic wars at times had over 600,000 under arms. The only other state with forces of comparable size was Russia. She had an army of about 120,000 when Peter the Great came to the throne. This rose to 330,000 during the Seven Years War and to 800,000 by the end of the Napoleonic wars. Prussia had the most efficient and best-trained army on the continent and its size rose dramatically in the course of our period. It numbered only about 8000 in 1648 and 20,000 in 1675; but it rose to 40,000 in 1713, 80,000 in 1740 and to 190,000 in 1786. Britain's land forces were relatively small – there was a deep distrust in her parliament of a standing army – and her peacetime army was only about 25,000 in the early part of the period. That of the United Provinces at first was about the same, for similar reasons. But both used many mercenaries, mainly Scottish, Irish and German in their foreign wars, as well as "auxiliaries", that is, troops hired from friendly states. Britain's army rose to over 70,000 during the War of Spanish Succession and that of the United Provinces to 130,000, a considerable force for such a small country. Thereafter the balance was reversed: the United Provinces' forces declined to about 40,000 in the middle of the eighteenth century, while those of Britain continued to increase, reaching nearly 200,000 during the Seven Years War. The Austrian emperor too had in the earlier part of the period only limited forces. His own army was only about 30,000 strong in 1678 and he depended heavily on subsidies and auxiliaries to supplement this (in addition to calling on the help of German states if the empire as such was involved). He was able to raise an imperial force of 100,000 including 60,000 from German states, in 1683 at the beginning of his war against the Turks; and after various

TABLE 1:   Approximate size of armies, 1648–1815*

	1648	1710	1760	1790	1814–15
Austria	30–40,000	100,000	200,000	200,000	250,000
France	120,000	250,000	330,000	160,000	600,000
Great Britain	65,000	75,000[†]	200,000	40,000	250,000
Prussia	8,000	40,000	195,000	160,000	270,000
Russia		220,000	330,000	300,000	7–800,000
Spain	150,000	30,000		50,000	
Sweden	70,000	110,000		50,000	
United Provinces	50,000	100,000	40,000		

* These figures include mercenaries and auxiliary forces. Peacetime strengths were often much less than those of wartime (such as those mainly given here). The figures are derived from J. Childs, *Armies and Warfare in Europe, 1648–1789* (Manchester, 1982) p. 42, and Paul Kennedy, *The Rise and Fall of the Great Powers* (London, 1988) pp. 56 and 99, and other sources.
† Great Britain's army was reduced to 16,000 by 1715.

ups and downs, his own forces rose to 200,000 in the Seven Years War and to 300,000 at the end of the century.

But land forces were not the only factor that counted. Peter the Great declared that a nation that had only an army was like a one-armed man: to have the benefit of two arms it required a navy too. He himself built up a powerful navy which, within twenty years of its foundation was a major force, both in the Black Sea (while he had control of Azov) and the Baltic; and in the 1720s he even sent a fleet to the Mediterranean. But Russia still only had 30 or 40 ships of the line at the time of his death; and towards the end of the century the number was still only about 55. Britain's navy at the beginning of the period was smaller than that of the United Provinces, but by the end of the eighteenth century she had easily outstripped the Dutch navy of a little over 60 ships of war. By the end of the War of Spanish Succession she had about 120 ships of the line, and 105 smaller vessels; by 1783 174 ships of the line and 294 smaller vessels; and by the end of the Napoleonic wars she had over 200 ships of the line: more than France, Russia and Spain combined. But France too became increasingly convinced of the importance of naval forces during the course of this age. Colbert was determined to build up a fleet which could match those of England and the United Provinces, and at the beginning of the Nine Years War (1688–97) the French fleet was probably bigger than England's (about 120 against 100). She also made extensive use of privateers to harry English shipping. The French navy was run down as a result of defeat during the wars of the first half of the eighteenth century; but it was rapidly rebuilt after the Seven Years War and by 1780 she again had about 90 ships of the line. Spain was the only other considerable naval power, with about 35 ships of the line in 1740 and around 70 by the end of the century, followed by a rapid decline thereafter.

Whatever their peacetime establishment, armed forces of all kinds needed to be rapidly supplemented in time of war. There were three principal ways of achieving this. First, as in earlier ages, mercenaries could be hired for the purpose: individuals of any nationality willing to fight for whoever would pay for their services. Scots, Irish and Swiss were especially often employed for this purpose. Sometimes an entire regiment was composed of foreigners: in the middle of the eighteenth century the Spanish army had 28 batallions (out of 133) composed of foreigners, while the French army had about 50,000 foreign soldiers altogether at that time.[14] Secondly, contingents from other states – "auxiliaries" – could be hired, usually in return for a subsidy. This method, ensuring the engagement of relatively well-trained and disciplined forces, came to be preferred to the engagement of mercenaries, who were often ill-disciplined and liable to desert – a permanent problem: during the Seven Years War the Austrian Army is said to have lost over 62,000 men through desertion, the French 70,000 and the Prussians 80,000.[15] States with relatively small regular armies, such as Britain and Austria, would frequently pay for contingents obtained from other countries which had larger forces than they required. Conversely, other states would regularly hire out their soldiers to fight for other rulers: Hesse, Mecklenburg, Saxony and other German states, Denmark and the Swiss cantons were often glad to win revenue in this way. Sometimes auxiliaries were found from far afield: Britain and the United Provinces engaged Russian forces to defend the latter in 1747; and Britain seriously considered hiring Russians to fight in North America during the War of American Independence. Thirdly, governments not only supplemented their own forces by using criminals, deserters and even prisoners of war, but increasingly resorted to conscription of various kinds. From the beginning of the period France had a form of conscription for the navy and coastal defence; and she later established a militia which provided a significant part of her land forces (in 1696 there were 63,000 conscripted militia men in the French army).[16] Savoy also introduced a conscripted militia, based on the French system. During the Great Northern War (1700–21) both Sweden and Russia introduced systems by which each district, parish or group of households was required to provide a number of recruits for military service; and twenty years later Prussia introduced a similar system, under which each regiment was given a definite area of the country from which it could draw its own manpower.[17] Even in states where there was no conscription various methods of semi-forcible enlistment – such as the impressment of naval ratings – were frequently employed. But conscription was never nationwide. There were many exceptions, especially for more privileged sections of the population. It was generally believed that recruits should be drawn from the classes of the lowest social value, including criminals: and substantial sections of the population, including the commercial classes, artisans and most peasants were exempted.

But the availability of fighting forces was not enough to sustain a state's power. Equally important as a measure of strength were its financial resources: "the vital sinews of war", as Colbert described them. A substantial proportion of state budgets in this age were devoted to military expenditure. During the Great Northern War, 95 per cent of Russia's budget is said to have been for military purposes. In the middle of the eighteenth century 90 per cent of Prussia's expenditure was on warfare. In 1784 France was spending two-thirds of her income on the army alone, and during the Napoleonic wars the proportion was undoubtedly much higher.[18] Not only were large sums required for maintaining armies of ever-growing size, which had to be armed, clothed, housed and fed, and for building and equipping expensive warships; the auxiliary forces that were so widely used also cost substantial sums, as did more general subsidies to allies. Governments which could mobilise funds effectively thus had a substantial advantage over those which, being unable to do so, had to borrow from elsewhere.[19] Britain and the United Provinces, which had flourishing financial markets, were normally self-sufficient, or even able to lend elsewhere,[20] (though even in these countries financial exhaustion was a major factor causing them to seek peace, for example in 1696–7 and 1747–8). Other governments were less well able to raise the money they needed through taxation, and were often compelled to borrow heavily elsewhere, sometimes at crippling cost: usually turning to the money markets of Amsterdam, and later London, which lent large sums to foreign governments mainly for the purpose of making war.

The power available to each state was also affected by changes in military technology. There were two major changes in military methods during this age. First was an increase in the mobility of armies. During the early part of the period warfare often consisted of long campaigns of manoeuvre, with many sieges, in which large-scale battles were often deliberately avoided. The growth in France's power was based partly on her skill in the art of fortification, developed by Vauban and other engineers, as well as an efficient logistical system, developed by Louvois, for supplying large armies in the field. Armies could generally move only slowly, impeded by long baggage-trains, cumbrous artillery-pieces, poor roads, many camp-followers and the need to remain close to their magazines. During the eighteenth century, however, a new generation of generals – Eugene, Charles XII, Marlborough, Saxe and Frederick the Great – were able to achieve a far more rapid movement. Light infantry and *chasseurs* using less heavy equipment were increasingly employed. Mobile columns were used in place of the extensive, and often stationary, "lines". This development reached its culmination in the breath-takingly rapid thrusts achieved by Napoleon. While Marlborough was believed to have achieved miracles in moving 40,000 men 350 miles in six weeks before the battle of Blenheim, Napoleon moved five times as many men over much the same territory in only two weeks before the battle of Ulm in 1805.[21]

The other important change was the increase in fire-power. The old match-lock musket, fired by a slow-moving match, was replaced in the early part of this period by the flint-lock musket, touched off by the spark of a flint, allowing a more rapid rate of fire. But even in 1700, the well-trained soldier could still only fire about a round a minute. By the middle of the century, with the use of cartridges and iron ramrods, this was increased to three rounds a minute and was considerably faster by the time of the Napoleonic wars. Rapid improvements in artillery, especially those introduced in the French army in the latter part of the eighteenth century, produced guns that were more mobile and, above all, more rapid-firing. Used in much greater concentrations than before, they were able to provide the devastating artillery barrages used by Napoleon against enemy concentrations in some of his major battles.

It would be wrong however to attribute military power mainly to technical factors of this kind. The new technologies were adopted in time by all armies alike. Differences in generalship were probably much more significant in their effect: the military genius of Eugene,

Marlborough and Frederick the Great were of crucial importance in securing victory for their countries in the wars in which they were engaged. Superior organisation, training and discipline could also be crucial, as was demonstrated in Prussia's striking successes. Still more important were differences in political leadership. In an age when wars were long and war-weariness a continual danger, the ability of rulers and statesmen to instil the will to win could have a significant effect on the outcome of wars: the success of the Polish king, John Sobieski, in mobilising the threatened Christian forces in 1683, of Louis XIV in rallying the people of France in 1709, of Maria Theresa in inspiring the loyalty of the Hungarian nobility in 1740–1, of William Pitt in convincing his countrymen, in dire peril in 1757, of the necessity of military success in Germany as well as beyond the seas, or of Napoleon in winning the devotion of his soldiers and the French people, had a far greater effect than differences in armaments, strategies or even numbers in determining the outcome of the wars of this age.

More generally, the ability of a government to mobilise its national forces effectively for war was an essential condition of military success. Military power was now increasingly nationalised, concentrated in the hands of the state. The development of that power was an important element in the process of state-building in which all were engaged. Louis XIV's creation of a war ministry, the appointment of intendants to supervise the financing and organisation of military supplies, the creation by Louvois of an efficient logistical support on the ground, contributed much to France's military successes in the first 50 years of this period. Gradually in the more organised states an extensive military infrastructure, of military barracks, of docks and shipyards, of munitions factories, war academies and training schools was established which, together, could make the difference between victory and defeat.

Since warfare was the principal means by which the competition among states was conducted, the development of the state's military power was one of the principal ambitions of the rulers of the day. The emperor Joseph I typified this attitude in declaring on his deathbed; "I have always considered the military profession as my vocation and the development of the strength, the courage and the prestige of the army as the principal object of my life." A war-like environment encouraged the belief that a successful foreign policy could be conducted only by governments which could back it with effective armed power.

THE MANAGEMENT OF FOREIGN POLICY

The dominance which the rulers exercised over policy was nowhere greater than in the field of foreign affairs. While in many areas of domestic policy there was often some degree of delegation, foreign policy was generally kept under the direct personal control of the monarch. Ambassadors were sent as ruler's personal emissaries. The instructions which guided them came directly from him, or at least were drawn up in close consultation with him. The Secretaries of State who had direct responsibility for foreign affairs would be required to report regularly, sometimes daily or even several times daily, to the ruler on the business they conducted. Louis XIV prided himself on the personal control he maintained on this aspect of policy; claiming to be "informed of everything . . . dealing directly with foreign envoys, receiving and reading despatches, drafting some of the replies personally, and giving the substance of others to my secretary . . . [and] having those whom I placed in important places report directly to me".[22] And he flattered himself that even the ministers themselves "were not merely pleased but somehow surprised to see me, in the most delicate affairs, without adhering precisely to their advice and without affecting to avoid it either, easily take my stand, which was one that always proved to have been the best".[23]

In most other countries the sovereign exercised almost as firm a control. Even in parliamentary states such as England and the United Provinces, foreign affairs remained to a large extent under the control of the rulers. William III personally conducted foreign policy on behalf of both England and the United Provinces, with the minimum consultation with ministers, still less with parliaments.[24] In England, even when other aspects of policy came increasingly under the control of cabinet and parliament, foreign affairs were recognised to fall within the "royal perogative".[25] Even the early Hanoverian kings at first continued to exercise direct control in that area (using it, for example, to protect the interests of their Electorate). Only gradually in the course of the period did the British parliament secure a marginally greater influence: the right, for example, to approve any treaty providing for a loss of territory, as well as subsidy treaties and commercial treaties involving changes in taxation such as excise duties, and the right to call for papers. In the United Provinces, when there was no powerful stadtholder in power, foreign policy was discussed in a special committee of the States-General and, if there was disagreement, in the Estates of the seven provinces.[26] Probably it was in Sweden between 1720 and 1772, when the king's control over foreign policy questions was minimal, that parliamentary control was greatest. But even in those countries the ruler maintained the dominant influence.

It was a widely held belief that this personal control of foreign affairs was desirable. The monarch was able to give a coherence and strength to foreign policy that would be dissipated if too many people were involved. Frederick the Great continually reiterated his belief that a state's international affairs could only be satisfactorily handled if a single person was in sole control:

> Nothing great or useful will be done in a state unless the prince rules personally because a single aim is needed to conceive a plan and unite policy . . . so that all tends towards a single objective. . . . When the prince desires something everybody will confirm; when it is a minister every individual makes his own judgement and does only what he thinks appropriate.[27]

The monarch in his view could be relied on to follow "only the public interest, which is his own, while a minister has a partial viewpoint which corresponds to his private interests".[28] Louis XIV shared this belief that foreign policy could best be conducted by an absolute ruler, undistracted by the private ambitions and personal interest of lesser mortals.[29] Peter the Great manifested the same conviction: he would have liked Sweden to become a republic on the grounds that (because of divided counsels) "republics are less dangerous to their neighbours".[30]

It was thought particularly undesirable that parliaments should interfere in foreign policy questions. Louis XIV expressed his profound pity for Charles II's dependence on parliament in the conduct of affairs, declaring to his son that "this subjection which makes it necessary for a sovereign to take orders from the people is the worst calamity that can befall a man of our rank".[31] His Minister, Colbert, had a similar view, writing in his *Political Testament* that

> assemblies and Estates should not be given too much power and should be given authority only on important occasions, and when it is necessary to secure assent for the ordering of the kingdom. For the rest it is enough that the prince judges with his Council what things are necessary and reasonable.[32]

Similarly, Louis' former ambassador, de Callières, discussing the management of foreign policy, pointed to the deplorable situation in England, "where the authority of parliament frequently obliges the king to make peace or war against his own wish; or again in Poland where the Diets have even more extensive power".[33] In the view of Louis, according power to a popular assembly would create "the continual necessity of defending yourself against their assaults": this would "produce more cares for you than all the other interests of your crown".[34] Still less, of course, should power over such questions be shared with the people as a whole. In Louis' view it would be "perverting the order of things to attribute decisions to the subjects and [only] deference to the sovereign".

But this concentration of authority in the hands of the rulers did not mean that they should simply follow their own whims. In the first place, they ought to follow certain principles of foreign policy. Before the period began the duc de Rohan, in his *Treatise of the Interests of the Princes and States of Christendom* (1638), had discussed the differing interests of the principal states and the principles which ought to guide their policy. Now it came to be a general belief that the policies of each state should be based on its own "maxims": principles which reflected its particular situation. Thus, for example, de Witt, Grand Pensionary in the United Provinces, stated that it was the "first maxim of his own republic to keep French power at a distance";[35] and Pomponne, the French ambassador, replying, stated that if he were a Dutchman he would not seek to change these "ancient maxims by which it had been established".[36] A comparable maxim of English policy was to prevent the Low Countries from falling under foreign, especially French, domination. Charles XII of Sweden declared that "it has always been the maxim here . . . to end matters [i.e. settle accounts] first with Denmark".[37] Louis himself believed that each country had its own "true maxims of state" and that "without knowledge of one's own and everybody else's true maxims no sound policy was possible".[38] The concept was a somewhat nebulous one, which could be used to justify almost any desired policies. But it reflected a sense that each state had its own underlying interests, independent of the views and whims of individual rulers; and it may therefore have served to bring about a greater stability in policy than would otherwise have been seen.

Secondly, in conducting their foreign policies, the rulers were guided not only by general principles of this kind but by the knowledge of foreign countries which they were able to acquire. As Louis

XIV put it, success in foreign affairs "consists . . . in keeping an eye on the whole earth and constantly learning the news of all the provinces and all of the nations, the secrets of all the courts, the dispositions and weaknesses of all the foreign powers and of all their ministers".[39] For this reason "nothing is so necessary for those who work on important affairs than to know what is really happening to their interests. Neither our ministers nor ourselves can deliberate with any assurance unless we have exact knowledge of what goes on around us".[40] Much of this information came from their ambassadors, who were sent abroad in increasing numbers at this time. But there were other, less official sources of knowledge. Most rulers had spies and secret agents in their pay. They could acquire knowledge from travellers, merchants and others with direct acquaintance of foreign lands. Only accurate knowledge of this sort, it was recognised, would enable the rulers to reach sensible decisions on foreign policy.

Thirdly, the rulers had at their disposal increasingly expert advice and guidance. All over Europe senior officials came to be appointed with the specific function of advising rulers on foreign affairs and executing decisions in that field. These were ministers, or "secretaries of state", with special responsibility in this field. In Britain there were two such secretaries of state, one having responsibility for the north of the continent, and the other for the south, until a foreign office was established, under a single secretary of state, in 1782. In Russia, the old "department of embassies", which, despite its name, dealt with internal as well as external affairs, was replaced in 1719 by a College of Foreign Affairs, which supervised the activities of the increasing number of foreign ambassadors appointed by Peter the Great. In the Hapsburg empire, a new permanent committee to control foreign affairs was set up by the emperor Joseph I in 1709; this was reorganised in 1721, and underwent further, more radical reorganisation under Kaunitz in the second half of the century. But by far the largest and most efficient foreign office was that of France, which boasted the most skilled negotiators and controlled the largest number of foreign embassies as well as an increasing number of foreign consulates. It grew rapidly during the reign of Louis XIV and came to be divided into a number of separate departments, manned by a wide range of increasingly specialised officials.[41]

Fourthly, foreign policies were influenced by the deliberations of royal councils. Louis XIV, as we saw, discussed questions of foreign policy within the *Conseil d'en haut*, which included the secretaries of state, including the foreign secretary, various notables, and some members of the royal family. He would ask the views of each member in turn. According to the account of one of those who took part, he would normally go along with the majority view; but in a small minority of cases he would "in order to assert his authority, countermand an order or overrule the advice of a minister".[42] In Austria foreign policy questions were discussed in the privy council (*Geheimrad*); it was there that there were, for example, in 1750–6 prolonged discussions about the desirability of a new war with Prussia for Silesia and the alliances required to prosecute it.[43] In Spain international issues were discussed in the Council of State and the Council of War; but these were advisory bodies, consisting mainly of members of noble families without official experience, and their advice was rarely decisive.[44] In Russia the senate created by Peter the Great could theoretically discuss foreign affairs but in practice its influence was minimal. In Sweden the Council exercised a dominant influence between 1719 and 1772 but in the periods of absolutism (1680–1719 and after 1772) had little influence. In most countries it remained the case, whatever the constitutional position, that the rulers could take as much or as little notice as they liked of the advice of such bodies. And in practice a very large number of actions in the foreign-policy field, including many declarations of war, were taken in total disregard of the views of advisory bodies of that kind.[45]

Thus the foreign policies pursued by a state normally closely reflected the beliefs and attitudes of the ruler. One result was that a change of monarch could have a decisive effect on foreign policy. The succession of Frederick the Great in Prussia in 1740, in place of his more cautious father, brought about the war for Silesia later that year; while, conversely, the antipathy to Britain he conceived as a result of Bute's policy in 1762 dictated Prussia's policy thereafter, so that it was only after his death twenty years later that a new alliance between them could be established. In the same way, so long as Maria Theresa dominated Austrian policy, her hostility to Catherine the Great prevented a close understanding between their two countries; and it was only after her death that the alliance between them was renewed in 1781. The succession of Peter III in Russia in 1762 brought about an immediate reversal of alliances, transforming the course of the Seven Years War and saving Prussia from defeat. The influence of the rulers was also important through their choice of ministers. Thus the accession of George I in Britain in 1714, leading to the recall of a Whig administration, brought about an immediate reversal of Britain's policies, a new concern with German affairs and the longest period of peace with France of the entire period. Conversely, Louis XV's dismissal of Fleury in 1743 led to a new and more bellicose phase of French policy, including a new war with Britain. And so on.

Another effect of the dominance of the rulers was that policies were sometimes influenced by dynastic connections. Close ties between the royal families of France and Spain after 1700, reflected in the three Bourbon family compacts (of 1733, 1743 and 1761) made them close allies and partners for most of the eighteenth century. The fact that the rulers of Naples (after 1738) and Parma (after 1748) were related to the royal families of Spain (and so of France) affected the policies those states pursued. The links between the royal families of England and (later) of Prussia and the House of Orange in the United Provinces affected policies both countries pursued towards that country (for example in the crisis in the latter in 1787). The fact that members of the Holstein-Gottorp family succeeded to the thrones of Sweden and Russia affected the policy those countries pursued towards Denmark with its designs on the Holstein-Gottorp lands. This was another way in which the political structure *within* states, and the continuing dominance exercised by the monarchs, had an effect on the relations that were undertaken *between* states too.

In some cases the sovereigns conducted a foreign policy of their own which was undertaken independently of that pursued by the official organs of the state. Most of the rulers corresponded personally with ambassadors abroad. Sometimes this correspondence was unknown to their foreign ministers. William III, for example, frequently wrote to his diplomats without the knowledge of his English ministers.[46] In that situation it was not always easy to know what was the policy of the king and what the policy of the state. Louis XIV, for example, undertook on some questions a private diplomacy unknown to his ministers.[47] But it was his successor, Louis XV, who institutionalised the system, so that in his time two parallel foreign policies were undertaken simultaneously: the king's policy, *"le secret du roi"*, concerned especially with re-establishing an eastern barrier against Russia, and the official policy undertaken by the foreign minister. Royal free-wheeling of this kind aroused increasing disquiet in some countries. Under the Swedish constitution of 1720, when parliamentary government was established, it was explicitly laid down that the king was not to correspond directly with ambassadors abroad, still less with foreign rulers.

Control over foreign affairs, therefore, as over most other matters, remained in most places firmly under the control of the rulers and their principal advisers. It was their attitudes and ambitions that mainly shaped the policies which were pursued by each state. And it was these attitudes that therefore determined whether or not a viable system of international relationships could be established.

DIPLOMACY

The foreign policy formulated by the rulers and their ministers was carried out by the diplomats stationed abroad.

When the period began the number of diplomats permanently stationed in foreign countries was small. The religious differences that had occurred over the previous century had brought a shrinkage of diplomatic contacts, even from the relatively limited level previously reached.[48] During the period we are concerned with diplomacy began to flourish once more. The number of resident missions abroad maintained by England, for example, rose from only about eight or nine in 1648 to 30 in 1815, of which 25 were in Europe.[49] There were comparable rates of increase for most other states. For some the change was still more dramatic. Russia had no permanent diplomatic missions at all in 1648, and she still had none in 1695 when Peter the Great acquired control of her policy. But by 1721 she had 21 foreign missions (including one in China and one in Central Asia), and this number was only marginally less at the end of the century. For Prussia, another rising power, a similar growth could be seen: from half a dozen foreign posts when the period began to about 20 in 1793. But the most dramatic growth of all was in the diplomatic establishment of France. Already well-represented abroad at the time the period began, she steadily increased the number of her foreign missions until she was represented in every significant European state (and indeed in some which many would have regarded as insignificant), as well as having consulates in many commercial centres.[50]

The diplomats had a number of roles. The first task of the ambassador was partly to represent his sovereign with sufficient splendour and magnificence (see below). But he had also to find out as much as possible about the intentions and capabilities of the state to which he was accredited – and, indeed, if the opportunity occurred of other states represented there. De Callières, who served as one of Louis

XIV's representatives in the negotiations for the Treaty of Ryswick and on subsequent missions, wrote in a famous book on diplomacy that the ambassador needed to keep his master informed about any events in other states that could be damaging to his own and might ultimately disturb the peace of the continent: "actions and reactions between one state and another", he wrote, "oblige the sagacious monarch and his ministers to maintain a continual process of diplomacy . . . for the purpose of recording events as they occur and of reading their true meaning with diligence and exactitude". The welfare of a state could thus depend on "appropriate measures taken in its foreign service to make friends among well-disposed states, and by timely action to resist those who cherish hostile designs".[51] To undertake this task effectively the ambassador "must have an understanding of the material power, the revenues and the whole dominion of each prince or each republic; he must understand the limits of territorial sovereignty, he must inform himself of the manner in which the government was originally established; of the claims which each sovereign makes upon parts he does not possess" and all treaties "concluded between the principal powers of Europe beginning with the Treaty of Westphalia right up to the present".[52] This was quite a tall order. De Callières would have been the first to admit that many of the ambassadors of his own day were far from meeting his exacting requirements.

What were the personal characteristics required to carry out such tasks? This question was widely discussed. According to de Callière it was "desirable for an ambassador to be a man of birth and breeding, especially if he is employed in any of the principal courts of Europe". And he added that "it is by no means a negligible factor that he should have a noble presence and a handsome face, which will enable him to please those with whom he has to converse". Wealth, however, in his view, should not be the main criterion: a wise prince would "serve his own interests much better by choosing an able negotiator of mediocre fortune to one who is well endowed with wealth but possessing poor intelligence".[53] To be able to report effectively a good ambassador needed an "observant mind, a spirit of application which refuses to be distracted by pleasures or frivolous amusements, a sound judgement which takes the measure of things as they are" and "penetration which enables him to discover the thoughts of men . . . a mind so fertile in expedients as easily to smooth away the difficulties which he meets in the course of his duty . . . the presence of mind to find a quick and pregnant reply".[54]

To this imposing list of attributes Frederick the Great added the ability to drink: he believed that to become ambassador in London, in particular, it was necessary to be a "good debauchee who should preferably be able to drink wine better than the English and who, having drunk, would say nothing that should be kept quiet".[55]

It was by no means easy to find appointees with these qualifications.[56] Most ambassadors were untrained and without experience. They were appointed from the aristocracy (England was unusual in having some ambassadors without titles) and without any previous service. They normally secured their posts because of the services they had rendered at home, or through influence or connections. De Callières was scornful of such amateurish negotiators, who often had none of the necessary qualities, deploring the fact that "one may see often men who have never left their own countries, who have never applied themselves to the study of public affairs, being of meagre intelligence, appointed . . . to important embassies in countries of which they know neither the interest, the laws, the customs, the language, nor even the geographical situation".[57] (Very much the kind of criticism made by members of Congress of political appointees to diplomatic posts in recent times.) There were tentative attempts during this period to provide some training for diplomats. Louis XIV established an *Académie politique* for the express purpose of training diplomats. Frederick the Great established a diplomatic academy in 1747, though only a decade later, during the Seven Years War, it ceased to function (it was temporarily revived in 1775). But such establishments in any case only trained diplomatic staff, not the ambassadors themselves who would have scorned the idea that they needed or could be expected to undergo any special education. The amateurishness which characterised the top echelon of diplomats thus continued unchanged.

Nor were they much helped by experienced staff. There were few permanent officials and these mainly served in foreign offices at home. Ambassadors appointed to serve abroad would take with them their own staffs, who usually had little previous experience of foreign representation. Only in a few services, such as that of France, were there permanent officials who would serve as "secretary of embassy" rather than as the personal secretary of the ambassador. In the same way there was normally no permanent embassy building; each ambassador would need to find a suitable house in which to represent his sovereign. To undertake these expenses an ambassador needed to be well-off, often a member of the nobility or higher bourgeoisie seeking advancement in a prestigious foreign post before taking a more lucrative appointment at home.

During this period the ranking of diplomats, previously somewhat arbitrary, came to be more firmly established. The most senior were "ambassadors" and "envoys extraordinary" sent, usually with considerable pomp, to undertake a particular negotiation: to conclude a commercial treaty, to forge an alliance. These were followed by ordinary ambassadors, envoys, residents and agents. In some circumstances there was an additional category of "secretaries", who usually came between residents and agents in rank, paid for by their governments rather than by the ambassador. The rank given to the representative depended on the importance of the individual who was sent, rather than on the importance of the post. Thus the same embassy might be filled at different times by an ambassador, an envoy, a resident or an agent according to the task to be performed or the state of relations. But in general a small country would not normally expect at this time to receive an "ambassador", with all the expense and ceremonial that this entailed; while a major sovereign might be insulted if another ruler sent only an agent. There was also little continuity in representation. Posts were often left unfilled for years on end, because of a breach in relations, some dispute about ceremonial or, most often, because of the difficulties in finding a suitable incumbent.

When an ambassador was first appointed he was usually provided with a formal set of instructions, providing an appreciation of the situation at the court concerned and setting out the tasks he was to fulfill. Considerable care was taken in drafting these instructions. Sometimes they included precise advice about what should be said when the credentials were first presented. Lionne, the French foreign minister, spent weeks personally preparing the instructions for Pomponne, the newly appointed ambassador in the United Provinces in 1669.[58] In theory the instructions were kept strictly confidential but there were exceptions. Thus de Witt, Grand Pensionary in the United Provinces at this time, recognising the special importance of the instructions which had to be given to his own country's ambassador in Paris and hoping to learn more of France's intentions, consulted with the French ambassador in The Hague before drawing up the instructions.[59] In other cases there was consultation with those at home who had special knowledge of the court in question: so Lionne in drawing up his instructions for Pomponne before sending him to The Hague, consulted with Turenne, the marshal of France, who was supposed to have a special knowledge of Dutch affairs because of his military service there. And when Pomponne was later sent as special ambassador in Sweden, he drew up his own instructions because he was himself better informed than others about the situation in that country.[60]

An essential tool of diplomacy in this age was bribery. Present-giving was often seen as part of the civilised conventions of the day. Thus de Callières, noted that "there are various established customs in different countries by which occasion arises for making small presents", and added that "the means by which this little custom is carried out may have an important bearing on high policy. . . . The practised negotiator will soon be aware that at every court there are certain persons . . . who will not refuse a small gratification or secret subsidy which may bring a large result. . . . There are even some ministers who will not refuse it if it is offered with address." This was certainly the experience of many ambassadors of the time. The French ambassador at The Hague counted on being able to bribe a large proportion of the deputies to the Estates General and state assemblies in the United Provinces so as to prevent ratification of the Triple Alliance in 1668 (and was thought so likely to succeed that de Witt refrained from submitting the Treaty for ratification by the provinces).[61] Louis personally instructed his ambassadors to bribe. In his *Memoires* for his son he recounts how he had ordered his ambassador in The Hague "to distribute money to the principal deputies and even to individual cities . . . in order to gain control over their deliberations and over the choice of their magistrates, believing it in my interests to exclude from all the public offices the factions of the Prince of Orange, who I knew to be entirely devoted to the king of England".[62] Frederick the Great similarly prided himself on having "broken Polish Diets by expending a little money at the right moment".[63] Louis mentioned the special value of sweeteners for influential women, describing the presents which he himself made to the queen of Sweden, the queen of Denmark and the Electress of Brandenburg, "having no doubt that these princesses would consider themselves honoured at my efforts to acquire their friendship, and they might for this reason enter more willingly into my interests".[64] And he recounted how in the last case he "subsequently gave a necklace of great value" in order to "engage the Electress even more firmly" on his behalf.[65]

Though there were few governments who were not willing to spend money in this way to gain influence, it was generally accepted that

France was the country which bribed most widely and generously. Louis spent large sums, for example, to persuade other rulers to join in alliance with him (for example, Charles II of England in 1670); to secure the election of a new Archbishop of Cologne (in 1687–8); to win control of the imperial electoral college (Louis himself was a serious candidate during the 1680s); and to secure the election of the French candidate as king of Poland (1696–7). Few other governments had either the resources or the contacts to win foreign policy successes on this scale by that means. But they were rarely constrained by scruples about its morality.[66]

Money paid in "subsidies" to governments was not altogether different from the bribes paid to individuals. In both cases co-operation in policy was expected in return for payment. Once again Louis XIV was probably the most successful in this strategy. Between 1668 and 1688 he spent vast sums for this purpose and was successful in buying, at one time or another, the alliance of England, Sweden, Brandenburg, Cologne, Hanover and other states. In 1669–70, when he was competing with Spain for the alliance of Sweden, he recognised that success would depend on how much each country was willing to pay: Pomponne, Louis' ambassador, told him that he hoped to be able to convince the Swedes of the "solid advantage they had received from the friendship" of the French king, and Louis himself suggested that the Swedish resident in The Hague "was not insensitive to his own interests" and might be interested in a "gratification of a few thousand crowns".[67] The Dukes of Brunswick-Lüneburg, whose alliance was sought by both the Dutch and the French at that time, sold themselves unashamedly to the highest bidder, informing the Dutch simply that if they did not meet their demands for more they would accept the French offer.[68] The Archbishop of Trier offered to join the Triple Alliance in return for a subsidy, and in the 1680s French gratifications were paid to a variety of German rulers, including the Electors of Brandenburg, Mainz and Trier.[69] During the War of Spanish Succession France paid subsidies to Bavaria, Cologne and Sweden and to the rebels in Hungary, amounting to 3.4 million livres and later in the century she paid 46 million livre to Sweden and 75 million to Austria (over a period of 12 years).[70] France was not only willing to pay more than other countries, but demanded less in return, often being content with a commitment to neutrality. The English parliament would only vote the necessary funds in return for the specific promise of an alliance, including military action. But in the eighteenth century, as she grew richer,

England was to become more generous than any other country with subsidies. By the time of the Napoleonic wars she would pay out £11 million to her allies in a single year (1813).

Another major feature of diplomatic life in this age was spying. No statesman of the day denied the importance of information obtained in this way. Frederick the Great prided himself on having in his pay "people who had betrayed ciphers and the secrets of their courts"; and he stressed how important this information was, especially in times of war or if war was expected. He believed that it was valuable for rulers to have in their pay the "servants of foreign ministers so as to know who was frequenting their houses".[71] Foreign despatches were routinely intercepted and read. Thus Pomponne, when French ambassador to The Hague in 1669–70, was able to secure copies of the instructions to the United Provinces ambassador in London as well as of the despatches which he sent in return (at a time when France was competing with the United Provinces for alliance with England).[72] He had in his own pay an agent who was able to obtain for him copies of a draft treaty providing for the entry of the emperor into the anti-French Triple Alliance.[73] The entire correspondence of the British ambassador in Constantinople in 1770–5 was copied by a French agent acting as his servant, and handed to the French ambassador, his principal rival, while the Austrian representative at the same court in the same period was also in French pay, providing full information about confidential affairs.[74] Many states created special organisations (*cabinets noirs*) with the task of intercepting the despatches and mail of foreign diplomats. In Britain the Postmaster General was provided with lists of people, including heads of government, whose correspondence was to be opened and copied; after 1765 these were replaced by general warrants ordering the copying of all diplomatic correspondence.[75] This was the practice of virtually every state of the age. It is scarcely surprising that Napoleon (echoing an earlier aphorism of Sir James Wootton) declared that "ambassadors are, in the full meaning of the term, titled spies".

Diplomacy in this age thus provided better communication among governments than had existed in any earlier age. The use of permanent missions at other courts made them better informed about the intentions and capabilities of other states, and better able to influence their policies. It provided the means through which combinations were formed and alliances countered. It was thus the essential precondition for establishing a system of international relations in which combinations and alliances, intended to safeguard the balance of power, played such an essential part.

BOOKS

Contemporary works

Sidney Bethel, *The Interests of the Princes and States of Europe* (London, 1681).

Baron J. F. de Bielfeld, *Institutions politiques* (The Hague, 1761).

F. de Callières, *On the Manner of Negotiating with Princes* (1716), (English trs. London, 1919).

P. de la Court, *The True Interests and Political Maxims of the Republic of Holland* (1667), (English trs. London, 1702).

A. Lossky (ed.), *The Seventeenth Century*, contemporary documents (New York, 1967).

O. and P. Ranum (eds), *The Century of Louis XIV*, contemporary documents (New York, 1972).

Courtilz de Sandras, *Nouveaux interets des princes de l'Europe* (Cologne, 1685).

G. Symcox (ed.), *War, Diplomacy and Imperialism, 1618–1763*, contemporary documents (London, 1974).

A. W. Wiquefort, *L'Ambassadeur et ses fonctions* (Paris, n.d.).

Modern works

M. S. Anderson, *Europe in the Eighteenth Century* (London, 1961).

M. Beloff, *The Age of Absolutism, 1660–1815* (London, 1954).

G. N. Clark, *The Seventeenth Century* (Oxford, 1929).

W. Doyle, *The Old European Order, 1660–1800* (Oxford, 1978).

F. Hartung, *Enlightened Despotism* (London, 1957).

R. D. Mowat, *The Age of Reason* (New York, 1934).

A. R. Myers, *Parliament and Estates in Europe to 1789* (London, 1975).

R. Palmer, *The Age of the Democratic Revolution* (Princeton, 1964).

H. Rosenberg, *Bureaucracy, Aristocracy and Autocracy: The Prussian Experience, 1660–1815* (Cambridge, Mass., 1958).

J. C. Rule (ed.), *Louis XIV: The Craft of Kingship* (Columbus, Ohio, 1969).

C. H. Tilly (ed.), *The Formation of National States in Western Europe* (New York, 1975).

D. L. Tapie, *L'Europe de Marie Thérèse* (Paris, 1973).

E. N. Williams, *The Ancien Régime in Europe: Government and Society in the Major States, 1648–1789* (London, 1970).

Armed forces

D. G. Chandler, *The Art of Warfare in the Age of Marlborough* (London, 1976).

J. Childs, *Armies and Warfare in Europe, 1648–1789* (Manchester, 1982).

A. Courvoisier, *Armies and Societies in Europe, 1494–1789* (English trs. Bloomington, Ind., 1979).

C. Duffy, *The Army of Frederick the Great* (Newton Abbot, 1974).

——, *The Army of Maria Theresa: The Armed Forces of Imperial Austria, 1740–1780* (London, 1977).

——, *Russia's Military Way to the West: The Origins and Nature of Russia's Military Power* (London, 1981).

P. M. Kennedy, *The Rise and Fall of British Naval Mastery* (London, 1976).

A. T. Mahan, *The Influence of Sea Power upon History* (London, 1890).

G. E. Rothenberg, *The Art of Warfare in the Age of Napoleon* (London, 1977).

A. Vagts, *A History of Militarism* (New York, 1938).

Diplomacy

J. F. Chance, *British Diplomatic Instructions, 1689–1789* (London, 1926).

D. B. Horn, *The British Diplomatic Service, 1689–1789* (Oxford, 1961).

P. S. Lachs, *The Diplomatic Corps under Charles II and James II* (New Brunswick, 1965).

A. Picavet, *La Diplomatie française au temps de Louis XIV* (Paris, 1930).

J. W. Thompson and S. K. Padover, *Secret Diplomacy: Espionage and Cryptography, 1500–1865* (London, 1937).

M. A. Thompson, *The Secretaries of State, 1681–1782* (Oxford, 1932).

3 The Shifting Balance

To the observer of the European scene in 1648 there was little doubt that France had become the strongest power on the continent. In addition to her large population (three times that of her two main rivals, Spain and England), she now enjoyed the additional prestige of spectacular successes at arms. The victory of French troops over the fabled Spanish *tercios* at Rocroi in 1643 demonstrated in dramatic form that Spain's power, which had dominated the continent for a century, was now yielding to that of France. At the Westphalia peacemaking it was she that had gained most conspicuously. She had finally won title to the three bishoprics of Metz, Toul and Verdun that she had occupied since 1552; acquired the important city of Breisach on the right bank of the Rhine; and in Alsace, which French troops had occupied during the war, secured outright title to ten cities, together with ambiguous rights in the province as a whole – rights which would provide a fruitful basis for further claims in the future. She had been explicitly recognised as a guarantor of the settlement in Germany and so secured an acknowledged right to intervene in German affairs. And, soon after, she had underlined this position by helping to create (and to finance) the League of the Rhine, a grouping of German states nominally established to maintain the Westphalia settlement but in practice concerned to resist Hapsburg power in Germany.

Against this her adversary Spain had been manifestly toppled from her dominant place. Her decline did not result only from her military reverses. Since 1640 her strength had also been sapped by a series of revolutions in sensitive areas – Portugal, Catalonia, Naples and Sicily – and she was also suffering from financial exhaustion, experiencing outright bankruptcy in 1627 despite the riches of the Americas. As a result she had been compelled in the Treaty of Munster to acknowledge the independence of the Dutch republic which she had fought for eighty years to subdue. Nor had she, even then, reached a settlement with France, with which she was to continue to fight for a further eleven years. And though she was eventually able to overcome the revolutions in Catalonia, Naples and Sicily (but not that in Portugal) and even recovered some ground in the war against France at a time when the latter was weakened by the aristocratic revolt of the Fronde, she was not able to restore her fortunes significantly. Under the Treaty of the Pyrenees of 1659 she had to cede areas of the Spanish Netherlands, as well as Roussillon and Cerdagne, her last remaining territories north of the Pyrenees. From this point Spain sank, and was seen to sink, to the rank of a second-class European power.

England too had suffered the upheaval of revolution. But this did not much weaken her and affected her foreign relations less than might have been expected. The European country with which her regime seemed to have most in common was the newly-created Dutch republic: the Protestant religion, a non-monarchical system of government and an aversion to the closely-linked Stuart and Orange houses (eliminated in 1648 in England and in 1650 in the United Provinces). But after a brief and unsuccessful attempt by Cromwell to link their fortunes, long-standing conflicts of economic interest proved more powerful than common religious or political sympathies. Differences over sovereignty in the seas, fishing rights, the marine salute, and above all over England's new Navigation Act of 1652 reserving colonial trade to English shipping, soon brought the countries to open war. England had the better of the first encounter in 1652–4; and though she accepted a compromise on fishing rights, she was able to impose her will on the naval salute and sovereignty (of symbolic rather than practical importance) and on the Navigation Acts. Elsewhere she was involved in traditional colonial conflicts, with Portugal in 1650–4 and with Spain in 1655. And in 1657–9 she joined France in a declared war against Spain.

The fortunes of the United Provinces had risen even more dramatically than those of France. Even before she secured her independence in 1648 she had become the leading trading nation of the continent. Overseas her merchants displaced those of Portugal in a number of areas and contested with those of England and Spain elsewhere. On the basis of this trade she had established the strongest economy in Europe. Amsterdam displaced Antwerp as the financial centre of the continent; and her manufacturing and processing industries – engaged for example in textiles, sugar refining, tobacco curing and cutting, tannery, cardboard manufacture and brewing – were the envy of other lands. But this economic strength was itself the cause of conflict. A second war with England in 1665–7 resulted largely from the envy of the English merchants and colonists of Dutch success: in 1664 English settlers in North America had seized the successful

Dutch colony of New Amsterdam, and there was also conflict between the two countries in the Guinea coast. Many in England therefore welcomed the prospect of a new war for trade. This time the Dutch, with minimal assistance from their ally France, had rather the better of the conflict, successfully raiding up the Medway to threaten Chatham. England now had to make some concessions, modifying her law on colonial trade and yielding Surinam, but in return recovering New Amsterdam (New York). Between these two Maritime Powers, therefore, honours were now roughly even.

Sweden was another victor in the Thirty Years War. She too had been significantly strengthened in 1648 and was now recognised as a major power within the system. By her military successes in Germany (as well as yet another victory over Denmark in 1645) she had won control of most of the coast of the Baltic, including Finland, Ingria, Estonia, Livonia and West Pomerania, and held most of the ports on the southern side of the Baltic. In acquiring German territory she had even won representation in the imperial Diet. Paradoxically it was only on her own mainland that she had failed to establish her power successfully: Denmark, though losing some of this territory in 1645, still held Scania and other areas north of the Baltic. When Charles X succeeded Queen Christina, his wayward cousin, on her abdication in 1654, he soon determined to seek further expansion in the Baltic area. He saw his main chance of achieving this in Poland, whose kings had for over fifty years been engaged in a prolonged duel with their Vasa cousins for the Swedish crown.

Poland/Lithuania was to all appearances one of the most considerable states of the continent. Its population of 9–10 million ranked behind only those of France and Russia. It controlled a vast territory, including Lithuania (with which it was joined in a longstanding union), White Russia and the Ukraine. It was however weakened by chronic internal instability and the lack of any strong central power. At this moment there were further causes of weakness. In 1654 she was engulfed by a vast Cossack revolt, which quickly won support from Russia. Taking advantage of this situation, Charles X of Sweden in 1655 declared war on Poland, causing her still further reverses. But Sweden's success, as so often in this age, quickly aroused the fear of other states, anxious that the huge power she already wielded was to be extended further. Denmark, her traditional enemy, and the emperor soon sent assistance to Poland. In 1656 Russia too, for the same reason, changed sides and began attacking Sweden. Brandenburg, which had begun as her ally, also switched sides in 1657, hoping to seize Swedish Pomerania from her. But she quickly defeated Denmark which was obliged to cede all the territory she had controlled to the north of the Baltic. This reverse in turn caused the United Provinces, (which had been allied with her against Denmark in 1643–5) to join the coalition against Sweden to prevent Swedish domination of the Baltic Sea which was so vital to her trade.

In 1660 Charles X died and France mediated to secure a settlement. Sweden kept the territories she had taken from Denmark north of the Baltic, but returned the island of Bornholm. The Polish king was obliged to renounce his claim to the Swedish throne and to recognise Swedish sovereignty in Livonia, though he lost no territory to Sweden. The Elector of Brandenburg secured recognition of his sovereign rights in East Prussia. Finally, in 1661 peace was made between Sweden and Russia. Russia recognised Sweden's rights in her Baltic provinces but won no territory herself. She was however to make substantial gains elsewhere. She now returned to her own war with Poland (with which she had recently been fighting against Sweden), till the two countries made peace in 1667. Under the peace of Andrusovo Russia won a substantial part of the Ukraine, including Kiev and Smolensk. It was Russia therefore that emerged as the most substantial victor from these complex struggles: the beginning of a long but uninterrupted recovery in her power from her time of troubles at the beginning of the century, a rise which was to continue for a century and a half.

The other clear loser – with Spain – in 1648 had been the Hapsburg emperor. Most of his residual power in Germany was taken from him. He was obliged to recognise the right of the German states to act independently in their foreign relations and to make treaties on their own behalf. He had to concede the loss of the bishoprics and part of Alsace, both traditionally part of the empire (though he declared, his determination to recover both). The German states demonstrated their power when the new emperor Leopold, who succeeded in 1658, was obliged to undertake that he would give no help to his Spanish cousin in his war with France. The power of the Austrian rulers henceforth rested primarily on their strength within their own domains. Though these remained extensive, including Bohemia, a part of Hungary and considerable territory in Germany itself, the emperors at this point, with their authority in Germany severely weakened, could not claim the power or status of their predecessors (a weakness demonstrated by the ineffectiveness of their interventions in the war in the north). The armed forces they could normally call on were relatively small and their finances chaotic. Moreover, they now faced serious problems in the east as well.

After a period of quiescence, Ottoman power, under the leadership of the powerful Köprolu vizirs, was now reviving. Since 1644 they had been engaged in a long war with Venice. In 1658–61, however, they had been diverted and launched an attack on their vassal, the prince of Transylvania. Having brought that province fully under their control, they turned on the emperor who had ventured to assist the Transylvanian rebels. The emperor's cause and that of Venice then became that of Christianity as a whole. The pope, Alexander VII, succeeded in arousing the conscience of western rulers, and assistance flowed to the emperor from all over Europe. In 1664 these forces were able to win a conclusive victory over the Turks at St Gotthard. The emperor, however, in his weakness made no attempt to follow this up but reached an immediate truce, leaving the Turks in control of Transylvania, and even agreed to pay them tribute for their own possessions in Hungary. This abject peace (which enabled the Turks to launch a new war on Poland seven years later), soon followed by a serious revolt in the part of Hungary controlled by the emperor, demonstrated to the world the decline that had occurred in his power and reputation in Europe.

The revolution against the emperor in Hungary eventually encouraged a new assault against him by the Turks. Thökoli, the Hungarian rebel leader, called for assistance from the Ottomans, and in 1683 the Turkish sultan, only too glad to respond, launched a massive onslaught against the Hapsburg emperor. Before the latter was able to rally his feeble forces, their troops reached the gates of Vienna. Again the emperor called for assistance from the West, and again the pope (Innocent XI) called for a Christian crusade to rescue the threatened empire. John Sobieski, king of Poland, the duke of Lorraine, and the elector of Bavaria, among others, brought a substantial Christian force to the relief of the city and won a spectacular victory, compelling the Turkish army to retreat. The prestige of Poland, severely dented by her reverses at the hands of Sweden and Russia, was now restored: that of the emperor who had been so nearly overwhelmed was not yet rehabilitated.

By this time, moreover, he faced a new threat arising in the west. The young Louis XIV (who himself had been a serious candidate to become emperor when Leopold was elected in 1658–9) took control of his country's affairs in 1661, and soon embarked on an expansionist

policy. He was particularly concerned to free France from en-
circlement by the two Hapsburg powers controlling north Italy,
Franche-Comté, part of the Rhine and the southern Netherlands. In
1667 he began this assault by putting forward a claim on behalf of his
wife, daughter of the former Spanish king, based on a Brabant
inheritance law (favouring the daughter of a first marriage over any
children of the second) which had never been applied to royal
succession; and sent his forces to the territory to enforce it. This
action aroused the fear of the United Provinces, England and even of
Sweden, formerly closely aligned with France. These together, forming a Triple Alliance, demanded a rapid settlement and in a secret
Article (which nonetheless soon became known to France) agreed to
send their own forces against France if she should refuse. France and
Spain soon came to an agreement, in which Louis was obliged to
abandon his former ambitious claim and to settle for only a handful
of towns near to his border.

This outcome left Louis furious with the Dutch, whom he had
previously seen as his protégés. Jealous also of their economic
success, he determined that his next move would be to make war
against them, humble their pride and win economic gains at their
expense. He planned this war over nearly four years: originally
scheduled to take place in 1671 it had to be postponed to the
following year. Meanwhile Louis built up his own armed forces and
made the necessary diplomatic dispositions. In 1668 he reached
provisional agreement with the emperor for a partition of the Spanish
inheritance (to which both had reasonable claims), should the young
and sickly Spanish king die, agreeing to concede to the emperor the
Spanish throne, the American empire and important Italian territories (the treaty was, however, repudiated by the emperor a few years
later when the two rulers went to war). With the aid of lavish bribes
he secured the alliances of England, Sweden, Cologne and Munster,
all of which either joined in the war or (from the emperor, Bavaria,
Saxony and other German states) the promise of neutrality. He
also intensified economic pressures on the Dutch, raising French
tariffs (already raised in 1664 and 1667) still further in 1671, causing
the United Provinces in retaliation to ban imports from France
altogether in 1672. In the latter year he launched his attack. Crossing
the Spanish Netherlands, French forces marched down the Rhine and
invaded the United Provinces from the east. They advanced rapidly
and only Dutch action in opening the dykes to flood the area south of
the Zuyder Zee halted their progress. At this point – as in 1668 –

French success aroused the apprehension of other states. Spain soon declared war on France. Cologne, Munster and England, France's principal allies, made peace with the Dutch. The emperor (with the authority of the Diet) and Brandenburg, abandoned their pledges of neutrality to come to the assistance of the Dutch; and German forces proceeded to attack in Alsace, hoping to reverse the Westphalia settlement in that area. Nor did France's Swedish allies prove of much help. They were rapidly defeated by Brandenburg's efficient army and found their own southern territories once more occupied by Danish forces. The fortunes of war were therefore reversed.

But there was increasing war-weariness in the United Provinces where the war had begun. At the outset of the fighting, de Witt, who had dominated the country's affairs for twenty years, resigned his office and was shortly afterwards killed by an angry mob. William of Orange, who had then been called to power as Stadtholder, now found himself forced against his will to agree to a settlement; and it was thus the United Provinces itself, the victim of the aggression, which first made peace on relatively favourable terms in 1678. France won no territory from the United Provinces and undertook to relax her tariffs (a major war aim for the Dutch). The main cost of the war fell on Spain: she was compelled to yield Franche-Comté, as well as exchanging some fortresses in the southern Netherlands to create a more logical and defensible frontier. The emperor, too, lost more than he gained: he had to yield Freiburg, well to the east of the Rhine, to France. In Lorraine, because its ruler was understandably unwilling to abandon his capital Nancy to France, the French maintained their occupation. Finally, Louis was able to ensure that in the north as well his ally Sweden came out of the contest without too much loss. Denmark and Brandenburg were compelled to return (apart from a small part of Pomerania acquired by Brandenberg) the Swedish territory which they had occupied. Though France had not therefore won the decisive victory over the United Provinces she had originally planned, she had gained significantly elsewhere. Above all she had dictated the shape of the final settlement, and so proved herself to be, as her ruler desired, the arbiter of Europe.

The French advance continued inexorably in the years that followed. In 1680, to win for himself the rest of Alsace and some neighbouring areas, Louis embarked on the policy of "*réunions*": he secured decisions by compliant magistrates that disputed territories in that area, subject to ancient feudal rights, were legally subject to French authority. In 1681 he occupied the strategically situated free city of Strasbourg (also within the empire). In the same year French troops entered Casale, an important fortress in the Alps which Louis had bought from the Duke of Mantua. And in that year also he embarked on a siege of the fortress of Luxembourg, nominally under Spanish rule. In 1683 Spain went to war to recover this but was quickly defeated; France rapidly invaded Catalonia and captured Luxembourg. The truce of Ratisbon of 1684, which was mediated by the emperor and was in effect a European settlement, signalised the peak of French power. It was agreed that, in return for a twenty-year cease-fire, France should retain Luxembourg, Strasburg and the *réunion* territories which Louis had seized.

Neither the emperor, preoccupied by war in the east, nor any other European power, had come to the assistance of Spain. France's triumph was complete. She paid a price, however: by this time all Europe was aroused against Louis' aggressive policy. Already in 1681 the first League of Augsburg had been established, mainly among German states determined to resist Louis' advance into Germany. At about the same time, for similar reasons, William, the stadtholder of the United Provinces, entered into alliance with Sweden, the emperor, Spain and other states. For the moment the Elector of Brandenburg and other German states, as well as the English Stuart kings, continued to receive French subsidies. In 1685, however, Louis' action in removing the toleration for Protestants in France aroused the hostility of many Protestant countries. The Lutheran Elector of Brandenburg, finally abandoning his alliance with France, again became the ally of the United Provinces. In 1686 the League of Augsburg was renewed among a wider group of states. Most of western Europe had now joined together to resist further French encroachment.

Three times, therefore, in this brief period the balance-of-power mechanism had operated after a fashion. In the north, Swedish success caused a number of powers, including two former allies of Sweden, to join her victim in resisting further French expansion. In the east, Christian powers had rushed to the assistance of the beleaguered emperor to eject Turkish invaders. And in the west in 1668 former allies of France had joined in issuing a warning to her to moderate her claims against Spain; while in the war of 1672 a number of states, again including former allies of France, joined in assisting the country she attacked and at least reduced the scale of her victory; finally, after still further encroachments and her successful war on Luxembourg, a number of states joined in a combination designed to put a halt to further French expansion. Louis' bribes and blandishments were able to slow but not to halt this movement.

In the years since 1648, therefore, there had been a distinct change in the configuration of forces on the continent. Spain, defeated in successive wars (in 1659, 1668 and 1678) had seen her power continue to decline. So too had Poland/Lithuania, subject to defeats at the hands of Russia (1667) and Turkey (1676) and serious civil conflicts (1654–5). Portugal had re-established herself on the map of Europe, but had lost large parts of her colonial power and was no longer a significant power within the continent. The emperor had suffered the humiliation of being twice obliged to call for assistance to rescue him from his traditional enemies in the East. England was weakened by political and religious differences at home and the spineless conduct of the restored Stuart kings. Even Russia, although reviving, was not yet a significant European power. It was France, and France alone, which throughout this period had continued to enhance her position and had finally become, and been seen to become, the superpower of the continent and the main threat to its peace.

THE CONTAINMENT OF FRANCE

The growing solidarity among the other states of Europe was not enough to constrain the ambition of Louis. During the course of 1688 two crises arose which stimulated him to new efforts to extend his power.

The first concerned Cologne, the rich and strategically placed electorate on the Rhine, which had been an important ally of France in the past. In June 1688 the previous archbishop died and Louis was anxious that he should be succeeded by Cardinal von Furstenberg, bishop of Strasbourg, who was closely tied to the French crown, having acted as Louis' diplomatic agent in the past. The post, however, had traditionally gone to a member of the Wittelsbach family and the rival candidature of Joseph Clement, the younger brother of the Elector of Bavaria, was supported by the emperor and most German states. The election by the chapter was indecisive. Pope Innocent XI, previously antagonised by Louis' high-handed actions, awarded the post to Joseph Clement. Louis responded by sending his troops into the electorate (though the city of Cologne itself was occupied by imperial forces). Immediately afterwards, French forces attacked positions in the Palatinate, where Louis claimed to be supporting the rights of his sister-in-law in that disputed electorate, as well as other positions on the Rhine, including the imperial fortress of Philippsburg.

Most of Europe was soon aroused against France. William of Orange, Louis' most implacable opponent, was for the moment otherwise engaged: he had already received an invitation to land in England to save that country from the threat of a Catholic succession. Having landed in November and having been made, with his wife, James II's daughter, ruler of England in February of the following year, he was able to arouse both countries to war against France. The emperor, who had by now won a spectacular victory over the Turks in Belgrade (see below) was now ready to divert his energies to the west. Spain and a number of German states, including Brandenburg, Bavaria, Saxony, Hanover and Hesse, provoked by the devastation of German territory in the Palatinate, also quickly joined the war, as did Savoy in 1690. France was left to fight alone. Even Sweden and Denmark, formerly her allies, sent auxiliaries to fight against her. The Grand Alliance, established during the course of 1689, became committed to reversing the French gains of the previous decade and restoring France to the frontiers of 1648–59 (see above). It also agreed to support the emperor's claims to the Spanish succession, Dutch demands for more favourable trading conditions in France and the Protestant succession in England.

Fighting was widespread. Outside Europe there were conflicts in North America, the Caribbean and, on a small scale, in India, and a wide-ranging war at sea. Sea-power was recognised, especially by England and France, as decisively important. In the early stages France planned a sea-borne invasion of England and prepared a fleet for that purpose. A major victory by Anglo-Dutch vessels in 1692 (reversing the outcome of an earlier battle two years before) ended that possibility, but French privateering continued to cause considerable damage to Anglo-Dutch shipping. The land war was mainly fought out in Flanders, West Germany and Italy. None of the campaigns was decisive. In the Spanish Netherlands, though the French won some successes, the powerful fortifications built by both sides prevented any major territorial gains. On the Rhine German forces were unable to make significant headway against Vauban's skilful structures. In Italy the fortunes of war fluctuated, until Savoy's defection to the French side in 1696, after which the area was neutralised. The only decisive campaign was in Spain where French forces invaded Catalonia and in 1697 captured Barcelona. Against this, however, the war caused serious economic difficulties for France where there was near-famine in 1795–6. Louis, therefore, having had to fight single-handed for most of its course against much of the rest of Europe, finally decided to settle. Under the Treaty of Ryswick of 1697 he agreed to restore all the territory he had acquired since 1678, including Luxembourg and the *réunion* territories, but retained Strasburg, strategically the most important place in contention. On the three succession questions which had been at issue, in England, Cologne, and the Palatinate he had to give way. He undertook to recognise William as king of England (though he made no commitment to expel James II from France); and he agreed not to pursue his demands over the succession in Cologne and the Palatinate. The United Provinces won a new commercial treaty which withdrew the earlier high tariffs against them. Savoy had secured Casale, Pinerolo and Nice under her treaty with France as its price for changing sides. The emperor won little for himself, but was compelled to go along with the terms negotiated between the representatives of William and Louis.

Against this the emperor had a resounding success elsewhere. While the Nine Years War was being fought in the West, an equally fierce contest, with more momentous consequences, was being fought out in the East. After the Turks had been driven from Venice in 1683, they had suffered a series of further defeats. In 1686 the Holy League – the emperor, Poland and Venice – had been joined by Russia, though the latter, beset by internal conflicts, was largely inactive until the war was nearly over. In 1686–7 the Christian forces began to make substantial gains. The emperor's forces conquered the main part of Hungary, since 1527 controlled by the Ottomans, and Transylvania, until a few years earlier ruled by local princes. In 1688 imperial forces advanced into Serbia, occupying Belgrade at the very moment Louis launched his war in the West. In 1690 Venetian forces conquered most of southern Greece. From 1695 Russia began to make substantial progress in the area north of the Black Sea. Finally, in 1697 the Emperor's gifted general, Eugene, won a crushing victory at Zenta and forced the Sultan to make terms. Peace was reached on the basis of *uti possedetis*, that is, the territory held at the time. Turkey, therefore, surrendered vast territories in Hungary and Transylvania to the emperor, while the Morea (the Peleponnese) went to Venice. In a subsequent settlement with Russia she was compelled to yield the port of Azov, so for the first time giving the river-based navy Peter the Great had constructed access to the Black

Sea. In the next twenty years the Turks made some recovery. They regained Azov in a new war against Russia in 1710–13, and in 1716–18 managed to reconquer areas in Greece previously lost to Venice. On the other hand, Austria, intervening to help Venice on the latter occasion, won further gains in northern Serbia, including Belgrade and the Banat of Temesvar. Unsuccessful in the earlier period, Austria had now won two successive victories and reached her furthest territorial extent.

Meanwhile in the west the issue of the Spanish succession had again become imminent. Though the Spanish King, Charles II, had, to some surprise, managed to survive until he was nearly forty, he was known to be ailing and there was concern that the question of the succession should if possible be decided before he died. William III, though neither of the states he ruled had a direct interest in the question, sought to negotiate a new treaty of partition with Louis that might satisfy the two principal claimants, France and Austria.* Louis no longer had any serious hope that he could succeed to the whole Spanish inheritance himself, despite his wife's claims. He was willing, therefore, to negotiate a treaty that would bring to France at least those territories that were of most concern to her. Under the treaty negotiated in 1698 it was agreed that the Spanish throne, the American colonies, the Spanish Netherlands and Sardinia should go to the son of the Elector of Bavaria, who had a claim through his mother; Louis' heir was to have Naples, Sicily and places in north Italy; while the emperor's second son, Charles, was to have Milan. This arrangement would have been most unlikely to satisfy the emperor, but before he could be informed the Bavarian candidate died. A new and simpler partition was then negotiated. This time the Emperor's son (again the younger son) was to have a larger share: Spain itself and the Indies; while the French dauphin would have roughly the same territories as before. But the advantage to France was that Milan would this time be allocated to the duke of Lorraine, who would in return hand over his duchy to the dauphin, all of whose territories would ultimately pass to France.

Even this arrangement was unacceptable to the emperor, who was unwilling to sacrifice his ambitions in Italy, the area of greatest

---

* Both had married the daughters of Spanish kings. While Louis had married the elder daughter, the Emperor also had a claim on the basis of an ancient Hapsburg compact providing that, if the Spanish line died out, the Austrian line should succeed.

interest to him. But the partition treaties were even more unacceptable in Spain. The Spanish court was determined that, whoever ruled in Spain, her territories should remain united. Before Charles II died on 1 November 1700, therefore, he made a will. This provided that the entire Spanish inheritance, undivided, would pass at his death to Louis' younger grandson, the duke of Anjou, who would then renounce any claim to the French throne. If he refused, it should go instead to Charles, the second son of the emperor. In other words, there would be no union of the crowns, either with France or Austria. But whichever prince inherited, the Spanish lands would be kept intact. Louis did not hesitate for long. To accept the will would mean repudiating the partition treaty he had only recently signed and could therefore lead to conflict. But the attraction was obvious: though France herself would get nothing, the entire Spanish inheritance would be closely linked with the French crown, and there would be large strategic and commercial gains. Moreover, if he refused, these benefits would go to Austria and could then be taken only by war. Conflict was therefore possible in either case. He accepted.

Though the emperor might well have fought whatever Louis had decided, it was different with the Maritime Powers. France was not to benefit directly, and if the new Spanish king became genuinely independent their interests would not necessarily be affected. On these grounds both at first recognised Philip V as king of Spain. But it soon became apparent that he was to enjoy no true independence. When Louis sent French forces into the Spanish Netherlands to eject the Dutch garrisons there, when he secured for his own country exclusive trading rights in the Spanish colonies, when French advisers flocked to the Spanish court, it became obvious that Spain was to become a satellite of France. It was only then that the Maritime Powers determined to fight to protect their interests. They entered into a new alliance with the emperor – the second Grand Alliance – committing them to war against France. Philip was – originally – to be allowed to keep Spain and her colonies, provided he again renounced the French throne. The emperor's younger son, Charles, would get the Italian territories and the Spanish Netherlands in return for allowing the Dutch to create a new barrier there. The Maritime Powers would secure the right to acquire Spanish colonies if they wished and commercial rights in Spain itself. The Protestant succession in England was again guaranteed. Only after the accession of Portugal to the alliance in 1703 did it commit itself, as she demanded, to ejecting the Bourbon dynasty from Spain itself.

The conflict was fought out, like the earlier one, mainly in Italy, Germany and the Netherlands. In Italy, Savoy soon rejoined the anti-French camp. An invasion of southern France from Italy to besiege Toulon proved a failure; but an Austrian army evicted Spanish forces from Naples, and in 1706 Eugene's forces won a victory over the French at Turin. In Germany a combined force of English, Dutch and Austrian troops inflicted a major defeat on the French at Blenheim in 1704. In the Netherlands a series of allied victories, especially at Ramillies in 1706 and Oudenarde in 1708, forced the French back to their own frontier. Only in Spain were the allies unsuccessful: for a time they advanced from Barcelona and occupied Madrid, but they were later pushed back towards Catalonia once more. Even so, by 1709 the French position was desperate. Louis agreed to negotiations and would have been willing to withdraw from Spain and surrender most of the major gains of his reign, including Strasburg and Lille. But the allies, overplaying their hand, demanded still more: that he should intervene himself to eject his grandson from Spain within two months. By that demand they lost the opportunity of a crushing victory. Stung by the humiliation, Louis was able to arouse the French people to new efforts. In 1711 a Tory administration coming to power in Britain and wearying of the war decided to seek a separate peace with France. They were followed not long afterwards by the Dutch; and finally, reluctantly by the emperor who, in 1714, without allies, had little choice except to settle too. Each of the principal allied powers won the concessions which were most important to them: Britain won Gibraltar and Minorca, keys to naval power in Mediterranean, Nova Scotia, Newfoundland and Hudson's Bay in North America, as well as recognition of the Protestant succession (this time Louis had to agree to give no further refuge to the Stuart pretenders who moved to Lorraine). The United Provinces secured commercial treaties with France and Spain, and a barrier in the southern Netherlands. Savoy won Sicily and territory on her frontier with France. Even the emperor gained most of what the alliance treaty had promised him; Milan, Naples and Sicily, and the southern Netherlands. Spain was stripped of her possessions in Italy and the Netherlands, but retained her overseas empire and the link with France provided by the Bourbon dynasty. Ironically, though the allies had secured most of what each individually had wanted, they failed to achieve what had come to appear their central war aim (expressed in the slogan "No peace without Spain"): the ending of Spain's dynastic link with France.

The end of the war was succeeded by rapid changes in European politics. In 1715 Louis died. The regent who followed him, fearful for the succession in France and for his own position there (it was still believed possible that Philip might claim the French throne despite the renunciation he had made at Utrecht), entered into an alliance with the new Hanoverian regime in Britain: an alliance that was to last for fifteen years (the only significant period of close relations between the two countries between 1688 and 1815). But the Whig administration in Britain, restored after the Hanoverian succession, was not willing to tie itself to any single power. Britain also renewed her alliance with the emperor and the United Provinces, and the latter became linked to Britain and France in the Triple Alliance of January 1717. On the basis of these understandings with the other principal powers, she played a dominant part in organising a collective response to the next threat to European order which began later that year.

Spain felt she had been made the principal loser in the War of Spanish Succession, even though she was never conquered. She intensely resented the loss of valuable possessions in Italy and the Netherlands. Moreover, the new Spanish queen, the second wife of Philip V, herself Italian, was determined to secure territories for her two recently born sons (who, having an elder step-brother, were not expected to inherit in Spain: see below). The king's scheming minister Alberoni therefore, planned a war of reconquest. In 1717 Spain launched an attack on Sardinia (which she had yielded to Austria in 1714), and in the following year on Sicily (yielded to Savoy at the same time). To meet this threat, Stanhope, one of the British Secretaries of State, put together a "peace plan for the south", designed to resolve the continuing conflicts in southern Europe. Under the Quadruple Alliance of 1718, each of the signatories recognised the succession in the other member-states; reaffirmed the settlement of 1713–14, except that the two islands Spain had attacked were exchanged between Savoy and Austria; and committed themselves to secure the treaty's acceptance by Spain. Accordingly Britain and France used their armed forces to compel Spanish withdrawal from the places she had occupied. As a result in 1720 Spain too accepted the Treaty's provisions. The 1713 territorial settlement in Italy, as revised, was restored. The rulers of Spain and Austria were brought to recognise the succession of the other in the territories they controlled. The conflict in southern Europe seemed to have been successfully resolved.

In the following year another treaty was signed, bringing to an end the equally bitter conflict which had convulsed northern Europe for over twenty years. In 1700, the same year in which, with the death of Charles II, the Spanish issue had erupted, another war broke out in the north of the continent. That war had also been launched against a threat of domination: to loosen the grip that Sweden had extended over much of the area surrounding the Baltic Sea. The Danish king was determined to avenge himself for earlier defeats, and especially to capture the territories of the duke of Holstein-Gottorp, interspersed with his own. Augustus, the recently-elected king of Saxony/Poland, hoped to win control of Livonia. Peter the Great of Russia hoped to regain access to the Baltic, which his country had once enjoyed but had lost to Sweden in its period of weakness nearly a century earlier. In 1700, when Peter had finally secured a settlement of his war against Turkey, the three countries launched their attack.

They were disconcerted by the decisive response of the young Swedish king, Charles XII, who had only succeeded to the Swedish throne three years earlier. Inheriting the warlike qualities of the Vasa family, he quickly defeated Denmark and compelled her, in the peace of Travendal (1700), to recognise the rights of the duke of Holstein/Gottorp in his lands. He then turned to the other end of the Baltic where he inflicted an equally humiliating, though not final, defeat on Russian forces at Narva. Next he moved against Augustus in Poland. Though the campaign there was long and for a time indecisive, complicated by internal Polish conflicts, there too he prevailed eventually, expelling Augustus from that country and replacing him with (for once) a Polish king. Finally, he pursued Augustus to his own electorate where in 1706 he was compelled to sign a treaty finally recognising the loss of the Polish crown. Only then did he turn once more against Russia. But, caught in the Ukraine in the bitter cold with an inadequate force (reinforcements had failed to reach him), he suffered a shattering defeat at Poltava in July 1709. He was compelled to seek sanctuary in Turkey, where he remained for five years, largely isolated from the war.

His discomfiture encouraged his old adversaries, Denmark and Saxony, to rejoin the war. They were joined by others with designs on Sweden's Baltic territory: Prussia, which seized Stettin in 1713, declaring war two years later, and Hanover/Britain which, having acquired Bremen and Verden – Swedish territories previously occupied by Denmark – assisted the anti- Swedish forces in the siege of

Stralsund. By the time Charles finally rejoined his armies in 1714 (having crossed Europe on horseback incognito) it was too late for him, for all his military skill, to restore Sweden's lost fortunes. He was unable to save Stralsund from the assaults of his enemies. And he was faced now by Russian forces, which having moved far to the west, had occupied Mecklenburg and threatened what remained of Swedish Pomerania.

This looming threat from Russia, as so often, aroused concern among her own allies: the emperor and Saxony, worried about the presence of Russian forces on German soil, Britain about the threat to her interests in Hanover, Denmark and the United Provinces about the threat to Baltic trade. The anti-Swedish alliance therefore now began to disintegrate. Charles XII, seeking to take advantage of this, engaged in lengthy negotiations with Russia, in which for a time the two countries contemplated allying themselves against their common enemies. Finally, Charles decided on yet another campaign, designed to wrest Norway from his old enemy, Denmark. During the course of this campaign he was shot and killed. Sweden's will and capacity for war died with him. She soon reached settlements with each of her enemies. Most of the Baltic empire had to be given up: Bremen and Verden to Hanover/Britain; Schleswig to Denmark; Stettin to Prussia; Livonia, Estonia and Ingria to Russia. Sweden's century of glory was at an end.

During this period, therefore, once again the balance-of-power mechanism could be seen at work. Three times, when particular powers appeared to have acquired too great a dominance, other nations came together to halt their progress. The steady expansion of France, almost uninterrupted till 1685, was twice checked, in 1697 and 1713–14, by the combined efforts of the Grand Alliance. Sweden's dominance in the Baltic was finally overcome by neighbouring powers, however crude and unprincipled the methods they used. And when this in turn seemed likely to lead to an almost equal threat from Russia, in Germany as well as the Baltic, a new combination had been formed to keep her too in check.

As a result a significant change took place in the overall balance of power. A number of powers which had been in the first order, or near it, at the beginning of the period sank to the condition of second-class powers. Sweden had now been heavily defeated and stripped of most of her overseas territories. Spain, several times defeated in the period before 1700, and now twice defeated since, despite her powerful new partner, fell into terminal decline. The United Provinces, though undefeated, was increasingly preoccupied with her commercial interests, increasingly incapable of defending her own territory effectively, and increasingly reluctant to becoming involved in war at all (from now on she became so involved, as in 1746, 1780 and 1795–6, only when attacked by another state). Portugal, which made no significant contribution to the War of Spanish Succession, had lost much of her empire and was no longer a significant force, increasingly dependent on the support of allies. Even France had suffered a decline: from being overwhelmingly the most powerful state of the continent, she had now sunk to a level comparable to that of the other major states. Against this, there were three powers which had unquestionably risen in status, power and territory. Britain had demonstrated the strength which a sound financial system and a strong navy could impart, and as a result had been able to win major territorial acquisitions in the Mediterranean and in the colonies. Austria had won spectacular victories against the Turks, so long a threat to Christian Europe, and had won vast territorial gains in consequence, in addition to substantial acquisitions in Italy and the Netherlands. Above all Russia, previously a power of little consequence and scarcely seen even as a member of the European system, had revealed her power in dramatic fashion, establishing herself as a naval as well as a military force to be reckoned with. The configuration of European power had thus taken a new shape.

THE CONTAINMENT OF PRUSSIA AND BRITAIN

The understanding established between Britain and France in 1716 was one of the few stable factors in the decade after 1720. But for a time there was an understanding, equally surprising, between Spain and Austria.

After the two countries finally came to terms in 1720, both had aspirations in which the other could, it was believed, be of assistance. Spain's ambitions still lay in Italy, but now in the north rather than in the island territories she had invaded in 1717–18. In the settlement of 1718–20 the emperor had undertaken that the duchies of Palma and Tuscany, where the existing rulers were without heirs, should pass on their deaths to Don Carlos, elder son of the Spanish king and Elizabeth Farnese. He had reluctantly agreed to allow Swiss troops to garrison the duchy as a pledge that the hand-over would be undertaken as agreed. But he refused the demand of Spain, backed by

France, that these should be replaced by Spanish troops. When, in 1735, in the Treaty of Vienna he entered into a close alliance with Spain it seemed likely that when the time came the hand-over would be completed without a hitch. But he still refused to accept a Spanish garrison, and four years later, after the failure of her renewed assault on Gibraltar, Spain again became disenchanted with Austria. She turned now for support to France, Britain and the United Provinces. These agreed in principle, in the Treaty of Seville (1729), that Spanish troops should be allowed to enter the duchies. But when the duke of Parma finally died in January 1731 the Emperor sent his own troops to occupy the duchy. Only, as a result of British intervention did he later agree, in return for a guarantee of the Pragmatic Sanction, to accept both the introduction of Spanish garrisons and the entry of Don Carlos. In March of the following year Don Carlos entered Parma as duke.

Austria's ambitions were of a different order. One of the emperor's aims was to make Austria a significant power in world trade. Uninhibited by the country's insignificant coastline, he established a merchant fleet in the Mediterranean; created an Eastern Company; and made Trieste and Fiume into free ports. Though never enthusiastic about the acquisition of the Austrian Netherlands he determined that, having acquired it, he should maximise its possible benefits. He therefore established the Ostend Company to trade to the Caribbean and the East, and even contemplated establishing a colonial empire. The new company began to compete successfully with the East India companies of Britain and the United Provinces and was viewed with considerable disquiet by both countries. The Dutch maintained that the trade undertaken from Ostend conflicted with the Treaty of Utrecht, as well as the Westphalia provision for the closure of the river Scheldt. When Austria and Spain entered into alliance in 1725 Spain undertook to allow the new company to trade in any port of her empire except in the Americas and to allow the emperor's traders equal rights with those of the Maritime Powers. The latter still objected strongly and for a time war seemed possible. The Maritime Powers won the support of France with whom they entered into a new alliance. Austria's new ally, Russia on the other hand, was unwilling to provide any support for her. In the preliminaries of Paris (1727) the emperor had to agree to suspend the Ostend Company for seven years and abandoned his commercial agreement with Spain. In 1731 in the Second Treaty of Vienna he undertook to suppress the company altogether. Both Spain and

Austria, therefore, during their intermittent and uneasy alliance, secured only grudging support from the other and suffered major rebuffs.

In 1733 a new European crisis arose as a result of the death of Augustus, the king of Poland. After initial proposals for a Portuguese successor had been abandoned, the principal contenders were the son of the former ruler, Augustus II of Saxony, backed by Russia and Austria, and the father-in-law of the French king, Leszynski, who, at least able to boast a Polish name, was elected king by the Polish parliament. The succession in Poland, however, was never the main issue in the war (except perhaps for Russia). By this time Maria Theresa, increasingly widely recognised as heir to the Austrian throne, was expected to marry Francis Stephen, duke of Lorraine. In French eyes this could prevent French recovery of that province, so long a major aim of successive French rulers. The French king and his advisers were therefore determined not to recognise the Pragmatic Sanction authorising her succession (as almost every other European power had by then done) unless in exchange for the return of Lorraine to France. Spain also had demands on Austria: her queen was now demanding Naples and Sicily for her younger son, and the promise of Mantua (in addition to Parma and Tuscany) for the elder. The death of the Polish king therefore precipitated an anti-Austrian war on these questions. The two Bourbon powers immediately entered into alliance, and won the support of the new duke of Savoy, who had aspirations to Milan, and of some German states. In the east, Russian and Austrian armies invading Poland quickly compelled the parliament there to reverse their earlier choice and to elect Augustus III. In the west, France seized Lorraine as well as Phillipsburg on the Rhine, and helped the duke of Savoy take Naples and Sicily. In order not to provoke the Maritime Powers she made no attack on the Austrian Netherlands, which was declared neutral; nor did the French armies make much effort in Germany. Austria's ally Britain declined to support her (see below), while her other ally Russia took little part in the war in the west. Austria therefore suffered a humiliating defeat. In October 1735 she accepted a provisional settlement ceding Lorraine to France, in return for French recognition of the Pragmatic Sanction and the integrity of the Hapsburg domains. The duke of Lorraine was awarded Tuscany in compensation for the loss of his duchy. Austria had to give a further slice of Lombardy to Savoy, and to hand Naples and Sicily to Don Carlos in return for the less valuable Parma.

A little later Austria suffered a further humiliation. Russia had for some time been planning another war against Turkey. After the end of the Polish war she persuaded Austria, her ally since 1726, to join her in this endeavour. Russia hoped to regain territory around the Black Sea, while Austria saw the chance of a further advance in the Balkans. Hostilities began in 1735 (though Russia did not finally declare war until the following year, nor Austria until 1737). The Turks, engaged in war with Persia at the time, suffered some defeats at first. But when that war ended in 1736 they regrouped their forces and concentrated their attacks on the Austrians. The latter were roundly defeated in Serbia, Bulgaria and Wallachia. By 1739 Belgrade was under siege. In that year Austria accepted France's offer to mediate. The French government undertook this task in a way highly unfavourable to Austria's interests. She was compelled to restore to Turkey much of the territory she had won in 1718, including Belgrade, much of Serbia and western Wallachia. Russia, on the other hand, which had had some military successes, secured Azov and some territory to the east, though she was not permitted to fortify Azov nor to navigate in the Black Sea. The two Eastern powers had thus gained little from their venture, while France, now almost restored to her former greatness, had again played a key role as the arbiter of Europe.

In the same year, 1739, a new war broke out in the west. France's ally Spain in that year became involved in conflict with Britain. When Britain in the Treaty of Utrecht had acquired the right to trade slaves to Spanish America and to send an annual trading voyage, she had hoped to acquire an extensive commerce with the Spanish colonies. Disappointed at the volume of the trade, the merchants adopted various devices to supplement it, exceeding the limits laid down for the annual voyage and engaging in regular smuggling from the Caribbean. Spain not unnaturally sought to curb this illegal trade, but the *costa-gardas* she used for this purpose were high-handed and brutal in the methods they employed, quite frequently stopping and searching innocent ships. During the 1730s these incidents led to increasing friction between the two countries. Though Walpole, the British prime minister, tried desperately to secure a peaceful settlement, the British merchants and their champions in Parliament were much less pacifically inclined. Many openly demanded war and even, if it could be achieved, the conquest of Spanish colonies in South America. Ultimately it was they, and not Walpole, who had their way, and war broke out in 1739. Hostilities began in the Caribbean, and France immediately sent a battle fleet intended to help Spain to recapture Jamaica.

The conflict soon became merged in another and much wider war, arising from a quite different cause. In 1740 the Emperor Charles VI died. Over the previous two decades he had won the support of virtually every state in Europe (except Bavaria) to the succession to his throne of his daughter Maria Theresa. As soon as he died, however, the young Frederick II of Prussia, who had succeeded to the Prussian throne only a few months earlier, immediately invaded and seized Silesia, the most prosperous province among the Hapsburg lands, of special importance to Prussia because of its strategic situation. He offered as he did so to support Maria Theresa's claims to the other Hapsburg territories so long as she agreed to his conquest (for which he offered to pay). But immediately other states – with Bavaria, Saxony, Spain and France in the lead – encouraged by his example, and oblivious of their solemn undertakings to accept the Pragmatic Sanction, proceeded to put forward their own claims, falling like vultures on the remaining Hapsburg lands. By the end of 1741 Franco-Bavarian armies had occupied Bohemia and Upper Austria, while Spanish troops had attacked Austrian territories in Italy. The Bavarian elector had himself crowned king of Bohemia in Prague, and at the beginning of 1742 was elected emperor. Only the British gave half-hearted support to the young Austrian queen. But even they, hoping to deprive their enemy France of support from Prussia, urged her to accept the loss of Silesia and provided little effective military assistance: their king, as ruler of Hanover, came to an agreement with France for the neutralisation of that territory and even gave his vote in favour of the election of the Bavarian elector as emperor.

The young and inexperienced queen, faced with this powerful coalition and inheriting an unsuccessful army and a decayed bureaucracy, had to seek desperate remedies. She turned to the nobles of Hungary and, in return for constitutional concessions, won their military support. Rallying her forces, she succeeded in the course of 1742 in reconquering Bohemia and even in occupying much of Bavaria. The Prussian king, having achieved his own ambitions, made a separate peace with her, as did the elector of Saxony. In June 1743 German mercenary forces, paid for by Britain and led by the British king, won a victory over French forces at Dettingen and expelled them from Germany. In September of that year Maria Theresa, pressed by Britain, came to an arrangement with the duke of Savoy, promising him Piacenza (which he never got) and part of the Milanese (which he did), in return for engaging the Franco-Spanish forces in Italy. The fortunes of war for a time appeared to have been reversed. Soon, however, they turned once more. In 1744 France at last officially declared war on Austria and Britain and, with her Spanish ally, launched a major invasion of Italy. At about the same time Frederick of Prussia re-entered the war against Austria, invaded Bohemia and Saxony (which had rashly re-entered the war now on Austria's side) and in 1745 forced another peace settlement, in which Austria once more surrendered Silesia. In the same year the elector of Bavaria died. His successor made peace with Austria and Maria Theresa's husband was elected emperor. Austria's fortunes thus appeared temporarily to revive. Maria Theresa launched a despairing offensive in Italy and nearly succeeded in evicting the Franco-Spanish armies, but was prevented from attaining one of her main aims by Britain's action in neutralising Naples. In 1745 France successfully invaded the Austrian Netherlands and two years later reached the Dutch border. She then declared war on the United Provinces which, despite desperate measures (including the recall of the House of Orange, as in 1672, and the despatch of auxiliaries from Russia) appeared on the point of defeat.

Overseas too things did not go much better for Austria's ally, Britain. In the Caribbean there was a draw and, although North American forces captured the important fortress of Louisburg, in the same year French troops captured Madras. The growing economic cost of the war caused increasing war-weariness in France and Britain alike. In the negotiations that began at Aix-la-Chapelle, France largely ignored Spanish concerns while Britain took little account of Austria's. The status quo was restored in the southern Netherlands, an area of special concern to Britain, Louisburg was handed back in exchange for Madras, and the succession was recognised in both countries. It was therefore Austria which became the principal loser in the war: in addition to sacrificing Silesia three years earlier, she now had to give up more of the Milanese to Savoy, and to yield another Italian territory, Parma and Piacenza, to Don Felipe, the younger son of the Spanish queen.

Prussia was the principal beneficiary. She had not only won a valuable territory, but had challenged and humbled Austria's power in Germany. But this very success aroused other powers against her. Austria herself was increasingly determined to embark on a new war, perhaps with new allies, to recover what she had lost, and undertook a thorough reform of her finances, administration and armed forces with that in mind. Saxony, defeated and occupied in 1745, wanted revenge. The Russian tsarina was deeply hostile to Frederick and anyway hoped to win territorial gains in East Prussia. Sweden began to see a chance to win back the parts of Pomerania she had lost thirty years earlier. And France, angered at being twice deserted by Prussia in the preceding war, began to consider the possible advantages of alternative allies against her main enemy, Britain.

Among the major powers, therefore, only Britain failed to join the anti-Prussian camp. Though she hoped for peace to develop her overseas trade, she knew that another war with France was only too likely: from 1753 local hostilities had already begun in north America and from 1755 this became an official, though still undeclared war. Britain therefore, for three years from 1753 sought to negotiate a new alliance treaty with Russia (see below.) But the main objectives of the two powers were entirely different. For Russia such an alliance would have been designed above all to make war against Prussia, and so perhaps enable Russia to extend her Baltic possessions towards the west. For Britain (though she too was concerned about Prussia as a possible threat to Hanover), the alliance would have been mainly designed to strengthen her hand in a war against France. When such a war became imminent, therefore, to protect herself from the need to devote major resources to defending Hanover she agreed with the Prussian king an arrangement for the neutralisation of Germany (the Treaty of Westminster). For Russia this destroyed any advantage that might be drawn from an alliance with Britain. The Russian chief minister, who had favoured the British alliance, was thrown from office and was replaced by one who was favourably disposed towards France.

Austria, meanwhile, was moving towards reconciliation with France. This course was especially favoured by Kaunitz, sent as ambassador to Paris in 1750. But here too there was a difference of interest between the two countries. Austria saw France as a potential ally against Prussia, a country still seen in France as an ally; while France wanted Austria to assist her in war against Britain, traditionally Austria's ally. Only in May 1756 therefore, when war with Britain was already imminent, did France agree to join Austria, and then, since she was unwilling to be dragged into an aggressive war for the recovery of Silesia, only in a defensive alliance. But this was enough to place Austria, who already had the support of Russia and Saxony, in a powerful position. War against Prussia was now definitely planned for 1757 and troops began to be mobilised. Frederick, learning from his spies of this plan, had no intention of waiting to be attacked. He demanded of the Austrian queen whether she planned war against him that year or the next. When she refused to answer, he himself precipitated the conflict by invading Saxony and occupying its strategic positions.

In the conflict that followed the fortunes of war fluctuated. At first things went badly for Britain and Prussia. French forces rapidly occupied Minorca. Prussian troops, after some initial successes, suffered defeat at the hands of Austrian and Russian forces, especially in East Prussia. In 1757 Sweden and several German states joined the war against Prussia. In the same year France entered into an offensive alliance with Austria. At first Prussia effectively fought alone on the continent of Europe: the British/Hanoverian force that was intended to defend Hanover and undertake diversionary action surrendered ignominiously in September of 1757. But a few months later the fortunes of war began to change. Frederick won two spectacular victories at Rossbach and Leuthen. Pitt, who became chief minister in Britain in the middle of 1757, recognised that military operations in Europe tying down French troops could be an essential means to securing the victory in the colonies that was his primary concern. In April of the following year he provided a large subsidy for Prussia and despatched a new British "army of observation" to fight in western Germany. Meanwhile British successes overseas also weakened the coalition's cause. British forces won decisive victories in India in 1757 and 1762 and in Canada in 1759, and occupied two of the most valuable French sugar islands. Substantial victories over the French navy were secured. On the continent Prussian troops, though they suffered some reverses at the hands of the Russians, especially at Kunersdorf, won important victories over the Austrians during 1760. When Spain entered the war belatedly in support of France at the end of 1761 it was only to suffer disastrous defeat. Havana and Manila were occupied, and even in Portugal Spanish troops made little headway. In 1761 a new ministry in Britain decided to cut the subsidy to Prussia. Prussia, suffering huge losses in men and material, appeared close to defeat against disorganised but far more numerous forces. But at the beginning of 1762 the death of the Russian empress, Elizabeth, transformed the situation. Peter III, who succeeded her, was fanatically pro-Prussian and immediately called off the war. Austria, which had herself tired of the conflict, then had little choice but to settle too. The settlement reflected the fortunes of war. On the continent, where nobody had won, there was a return to the status quo. In the struggle outside Europe, Britain had been unquestionably the victor. It was she therefore that made the major gains. Although her new government, under Bute, did not seek such punitive terms as Pitt would have favoured, she still made major acquisitions: securing Canada, a dominant position in India, new possessions in the Caribbean and Africa, and retaining her important positions in the Mediterranean. France was correspondingly humiliated, while her ally Spain, which had been most manifestly defeated, was lucky to get away with the loss of only Florida (and even for this she was compensated by France with Louisiana).

There was to be no major war in Europe for the next thirty years. But there were some important political developments which affected the balance among the major powers. In the same year that the Seven Years War ended the king of Poland died. Catherine, the new ruler of Russia, determined to maintain traditional Russian domination of Polish affairs, sought to achieve this by securing the election as king of her former lover, Poniatowski. He proved, however, more independent than she had intended, planning financial and military reforms which would strengthen and modernise the country. In 1768, therefore, she despatched Russian forces to Poland, allegedly to protect the religious freedoms of the non-Catholic minority. Russian forces supervised a meeting of the Diet which, besides guaranteeing the rights of the minorities, passed measures preserving the existing constitution and limiting the size of Polish forces. This blatant intervention provoked a revolution in the south of the country, led by the so called Confederacy of Bar. By 1770 the disorder of the Polish state, and the likelihood that this might give Russia the opportunity to strengthen still further its hold on the country, aroused the anxiety of her neighbours. The Prussian king, who had long had aspirations to acquire Polish Prussia, which divided East Prussia from his other territories sent his brother Henry to the Russian court, where there was discussion about a possible distribution of Polish territory among her three powerful neighbours. In October 1771 Catherine, overruling her foreign minister, accepted this plan. Austria, which had already seized a small area of Polish territory near the Hungarian border in 1769–70, was at first cautious about the proposal: partly because it would benefit Prussia at least as much as Austria (and in her view Austria still deserved "compensation" for the loss of Silesia) and partly because of genuine moral scruples on Maria Theresa's part. The latter was however finally persuaded, and in August 1772 the three countries agreed a treaty under which Austria was to take Galicia, Russia Polish Livonia and Byelorussia, and Prussia Polish Prussia. This plan was imposed on an unwilling Polish Diet in the following year. Between them the three countries seized 30 per cent of Polish territory and 35 per cent of her population.

Russia had meanwhile become involved in war with Turkey. Turkey too had become alarmed at Russian domination of Poland and, when Russian troops, chasing Polish rebels, violated Ottoman territory, she took the opportunity to declare war on Russia. Preoccupied in Poland, Russia took some time to respond. But in 1770–1 she overcame the Turkish forces, occupied the principalities of Moldavia and Wallachia and conquered the Crimea, a strategic area that had for long been under Turkish protection. She demanded, as the price of peace, the cession of substantial territory around the Sea of Azov and a twenty-five year lease of the principalities. Once again the threat of a victory on this scale caused others to unite against the successful power. Austria entered into a treaty with Turkey under which the province of Bukovina was later transferred to Austria, and consulted with Prussia about possible countermeasures. France, equally alarmed, sought to strengthen the resistance to Russia by her old allies, Turkey and Poland. But these measures had little effect. In 1774 under the Treaty of Kutchuk-Karnaji Russia won territory in the Caucasus and the Crimea, the right to fortify Azov, to navigate in the Black Sea and through the Straits, and to protect the adherents of the Orthodox religion in Turkey. Turkey was obliged to accept the independence of the Crimea. In 1779 the Crimea was made a Russian dependency; in 1782 it was brought fully under Russian control; and in the following year annexed. Russian power in the area thus continued to expand. Catherine became increasingly committed to a "Greek project", involving the extension of Russian power into the Balkans. In 1781 she compelled the Turkish Sultan to accept Russian consuls in his European territory. She began to build up a powerful Black Sea fleet. And in 1783 Georgia was brought under Russian protection.

Meanwhile in central Europe Prussia continued to assert her power against Austria. In 1778 the two powers came into conflict over the succession in Bavaria. This proved ultimately to be yet another humiliation for Austria. The Emperor Joseph was anxious to acquire the electorate, in exchange if necessary for the Austrian Netherlands. That aim was entirely understandable and little different from the territorial aspirations of other states, including Prussia herself. But the way he attempted to bring it about was misconceived. If he had recognised from the beginning the need to consult and win the support of other German states he might have had a greater chance of success. He over-estimated the support he was likely to win from Russia and France; and underestimated the opposition he was likely to arouse from Prussia and elsewhere in Germany. Nor did he ever seriously anticipate the implications of a serious military confrontation and plan accordingly. In the event, Prussia opposed his plan by force. He failed to secure the diplomatic backing he required and was eventually obliged to make a humiliating withdrawal, suffering a severe loss of face in consequence.

These east and central European affairs were largely ignored by Britain and were little influenced by France. For a time Europe ceased to be a single closely interrelated international system but was for a time divided into two separate compartments. The states in the west of the continent played little part in the conflicts that had occurred in the eastern half. Conversely, Russia, Prussia and Austria showed equally little interest in the growing confrontation emerging between Britain on the one hand and France and Spain on the other. These mainly concerned areas lying beyond the oceans, of which the east European countries had little knowledge and interest.

From the time of their humiliation in 1763 France and Spain had planned their revenge. For fifteen years after the Seven Years War Britain was diplomatically isolated. Prussia was still deeply resentful at her experience at the end of that war (when Britain had abruptly withdrawn support) while tentative British approaches to Russia and Austria were rebuffed. Meanwhile France steadily rebuilt her navy and other military forces. Spain remained determined to recover Minorca and Gibraltar and knew that this could come about only as a result of a new war against Britain. While their rearmament continued the two countries could not risk a confrontation: for example, over the demilitarisation of Dunkirk which France increasingly resented, and over the Falklands. But it was generally recognised that they might ultimately seek to redress the balance of power overseas.

The opportunity came with the revolution in Britain's American colonies. These were potentially a far greater factor in the balance of power than Canada had been. They contained two million European inhabitants – there were less than a tenth of that number in Canada – and their trade represented a much more significant proportion of

Britain's total trade with the outside world. Far more was at stake, therefore, for both Britain and for France, than had been the case twenty years earlier in Canada. This was recognised in France and from an early stage she had established contacts with the American revolutionaries. From 1776 she began providing substantial assistance in the form of arms and financial support. But she was still doubtful of her capacity to match Britain's naval strength and so cautious about full-scale military intervention. When however in 1776–7 British forces appeared likely to crush the revolution altogether, she accepted the need for a more vigorous approach. In 1778 she signed treaties of friendship, commerce and defensive alliance with the revolutionaries, and became formally committed to the war. In April 1779 Spain (having brought to an end a small colonial war with Portugal in 1776–7) followed, after securing a promise from France that she would help in the recovery of Minorca, Gibraltar and Florida, all former Spanish possessions lost to Britain in the past. The intervention of the two powers substantially worsened Britain's position in the war and possibly altered its outcome. The problems of logistics and communications, anyway considerable in a war conducted 3000 miles from home, were made infinitely worse when it became necessary to confront two powerful navies (which could not be kept bottled up in port as in the last two wars), possible assaults on colonial territories throughout the world, and even (in 1779) an attempted invasion of Britain. Without continental allies, such as she had enjoyed in earlier wars, Britain could no longer seek to "conquer America in Germany". On the contrary, her military effort in America was seriously weakened by the intervention of continental powers and conflicts with neutrals. As a result, in the latter part of 1780 the United Provinces joined her enemies, though this was to prove disastrous for that country. In 1781–2 Spain succeeded in reconquering Minorca, but a long siege of Gibraltar from 1779 to 1782 was unsuccessful. When in 1781 the French navy, now operating freely off the American coast, helped to secure the surrender of British forces at Yorktown, the rebel cause in America was virtually won. Though the British had further successes at sea and in the Caribbean these were not enough to turn the tide, and in 1783 the British finally accepted peace. In the settlement France won Tobago, Senegal and some rights in the Newfoundland fisheries, whilst Spain recovered Florida and Minorca. Britain secured gains from the United Provinces in India and Ceylon and the right to navigate among the Indonesian islands. But the United States won her independence, and as a result Britain lost one of its most important overseas assets.

At first sight the balance-of-power mechanism had worked reasonably well during these decades. Prussia and Britain, both rising powers, were in turn checked by combinations of other states. In fact, however, because the coalitions were even less united than in the past, the balance did not operate effectively. The wars were frequently fought in separate compartments. In the War of Polish Succession French power never even tried to balance that of Russia and Austria in Poland, while in the west Russia never contributed significantly to Austria's struggle against France and Spain. Similarly, in the War of Austrian Succession, Britain never contributed adequately to Austria's struggle in Italy, while Austria played little part in the struggle in the Netherlands, still less in that in the colonies. In the Seven Years War the struggle was still more divided between an eastern campaign, in which Britain played only a marginal role and Prussia was almost overwhelmed, and the colonial struggle, in which most of France's allies played no part and Britain was victorious. Finally, in the War of American Independence, the balance also failed to operate: Britain fought single-handedly against four separate contestants and, winning only against one (the United Provinces), had to make substantial concessions to each of the others. A balance could be maintained only by cohesive alliances, in which the members were genuinely committed to common purposes; and it was this cohesion which during this period was conspicuously lacking.

As a result, further shifts in the balance took place. The states which before had been in decline continued to sink still further. Sweden failed in her attempt to recover territory from Russia in 1741–3 and won nothing from her half-hearted intervention in the Seven Years War. The United Provinces, becoming involved in war against her will both in 1747–8 and in 1780–4, suffered reverses in each case and was now seen as an increasingly insignificant factor in the balance of the continent. Spain failed miserably in 1762–3 and, though she had some successes in the War of American Independence, was still only a shadow of her former greatness. Turkey, after comparative success in the war of 1736–9, suffered a long series of defeats at Russia's hands, a series which was to continue almost without interruption for the next hundred years. Austria, too, had started on a similar, if less obvious, decline: defeated in 1739 and 1748, unvictorious in 1763, she too was to suffer an almost continuous series of defeats, until the final collapse of her empire in 1918. France made a remarkable recovery in the first two decades of this period, and by 1740 had almost regained the position she had enjoyed fifty years earlier: but her relative failure in 1748 and her defeat in 1763 were not significantly redressed by the modest success of 1778–83. There were three powers which rose dramatically in status and power in the first forty years of this period. Prussia won striking successes in 1740–5 and was generally seen to have enhanced her prestige in holding on to her gains in 1756–63; but she had largely exhausted herself in the process, her territories were still divided, and she was obliged to become more modest in her ambitions in the years that followed. Conversely, Britain had some success in 1748 and still more spectacular ones in 1763, acquiring huge territories in the colonies and establishing her mastery of the seas; but she too was chastened as a result of military failure, and the loss of her most important colony, in 1783. The only power to have suffered no serious setbacks was Russia. Though she was inactive in 1740–8, and did not win the gains she hoped for in 1763, her expansion in the east and south continued inexorably in the years that followed. It was towards these three powers, therefore – Prussia, Britain and Russia – that the balance had shifted during this period. But it was Russia which, among the three, grew most unmistakeably in power and prestige.

A FIVE-POWER DIRECTORATE

These changes, however, were relatively marginal. For all her territorial gains, Russia remained backward economically, culturally, and educationally. Though Britain had established undisputed mastery of the seas, her army was by no means formidable and she still found it hard to make her power effective on the mainland of Europe. Prussia was now a much more considerable power than at the beginning of the century, but in terms of resources, economic strength and population she was not yet the equal of her rivals. Conversely France, for all her setbacks and her political and financial weakness, still had the capacity, as she was shortly to show, to win remarkable military successes. Even Austria, after the further reforms introduced by the emperor Joseph, showed considerable powers of resilience, so that in 1815 she could still reasonably, after repeated defeats, present herself as one of the major powers of Europe. Among the five major powers, therefore, there remained a rough equality.

The main shift in power was not among them: it was the increasing gap between any of them and the lesser states of the continent. While the larger powers continued to expand, winning territories from the weaker, such as Sweden and Turkey, or even eliminating them altogether (as Poland was soon to be), the lesser ones were an increasingly insignificant factor in the European equation. And the larger powers, for all their own rivalries, were sometimes willing to act together to promote their own interests at the expense of their weaker neighbours.

One example of this occurred in the United Provinces in the latter half of the 1780s. After the conclusion of her unsuccessful war against Britain in 1784 there was increasing resistance in that country to the role of the stadtholder, William V of Orange. This resistance came not only from the regents, the traditional commercial oligarchy which had often contested Orange power in the past, but also from a new radical party, the Patriots, seeking to establish a more democratic system of government in the country. This party, despite its ideology, secured the support of France which welcomed any opportunity to weaken the influence that both Britain and Prussia exercised in the country through their connections with the Orange family. The Patriots steadily grew in power, winning control of three of the seven provinces by the middle of 1787, but the stadtholder retained power in two, receiving covert support from Britain. During the summer of 1787 William's wife, who was the sister of the Prussian king, was arrested by the Patriot administration and temporarily detained. Both Prussia and Britain became alarmed. The Prussian king, Frederick William, issued an ultimatum to the Patriot leaders, while Britain mobilised against a possible French intervention. But France had no common border with the United Provinces, and was anyway too weak to risk a confrontation. In September Prussia despatched a force of 25,000 men, invaded the republic and restored the stadtholder to power. The combined action of the two outside states had therefore caused the overthrow of Patriot power and re-established the type of government which best suited their own interests. They had at the same time prevented France from acquiring a dominant influence in the United Provinces, for Britain a major motive for action. A year later, in August 1788, this co-operation among the rulers of the three countries was reinforced by a new Triple Alliance between them.

Another example of great-power co-operation occurred during the war of Russia and Austria against Turkey in 1787–92. The war, like that of 1768–74, was imprudently started by Turkey, seeking revenge for her earlier defeat. But Russia quickly determined to use the opportunity to make further territorial gains, and she called on Austria to fulfil her obligations under their alliance of 1781. Since the war clearly resulted from Turkish aggression the emperor Joseph had little choice but to respond, though he delayed his declaration of war for six months. When Austria did join, she hoped to recover Belgrade which she had once was lost to Turkey fifty years earlier, but she was disastrously defeated and soon her own territory was invaded by the Turks. Russia too had little success at first, and in July 1788 her attention was distracted when Sweden (where the king had reimposed absolute government sixteen years earlier) now declared war, hoping to recover territory in Finland and elsewhere. The Swedish king, however, faced considerable opposition to the war at home, and for a time she herself was under attack from Denmark. Moreover, she had little military success. Since Catherine II wished to free her hand for the war with Turkey, peace was made between the two countries in August 1790. Sweden won no territory, but did secure a renunciation by Russia of her right to intervene in Swedish affairs (see below) and a recognition of the 1772 absolutist constitution. By this time both Russian and Austrian armies had begun to win important victories over Turkey. However, when Leopold II succeeded as emperor in 1790 and soon found himself faced with a major revolt in the Austrian Netherlands, he sought a quick settlement and Austria returned almost all her conquests.

Russia remained poised to win a substantial victory and so to gain further concessions from Turkey. At this point, in March 1791 Britain, concerned to limit Russia's gains, issued an ultimatum threatening to attack Russia with a British fleet unless she agreed not to annex the fortress of Otchakov. Pitt's action, however, had no support in Britain (it was even opposed within his own cabinet) and the ultimatum had to be withdrawn. In the settlement of 1792, therefore, Russia won Otchakov and considerable territory in the Black Sea area.

A far more blatant example of co-operation among great powers against the weak was the collusion of Russia, Prussia and Austria in the final destruction of Poland. One of the justifications put forward for the first partition in 1772–3 was the chronic disorder that existed in that country under its traditional constitution. Beginning in 1788 a series of reforms took place there, designed to create a more stable and broadly representative system of government. The Russian protectorate was thrown off, the right of confederation (revolution) and the *librum veto* were abolished, and a system of hereditary constitutional monarchy established. The chaos of the past was ended. But reforms of this kind were by no means to the taste of Poland's powerful neighbours. The threat was now that the country might be governed too well. Russia was determined to crush the new government, making use of the right of intervention she had acquired in her treaties of 1768 and 1775. Prussia for a time, seeking to replace Russian domination of Poland, sought to co-operate with the new government and even entered into a new treaty of alliance in 1790; but three years later, increasingly concerned at the emerging crisis in France, she decided to join forces with Russia. Only Austria still opposed further partition, which she believed could strengthen her chief rivals. In January 1793, purporting to respond to an "invitation" from Polish conservatives, Russian troops invaded Poland and took control of the country. In a new partition, this time with Prussia alone, Russia secured a huge area, including three million people, in western Ukraine and Podolia, while Prussia took Great Poland, including Danzig, Posen and Thorn. A new constitution was imposed, restoring the *librum veto* and abolishing the democratic reforms of the previous few years. In consequence, in March 1794, a revolution broke out, directed against Russian domination of the country. This won some military successes at first but was crushed in December. In the following year the three external countries (after some disagreement among themselves about the share-out) imposed a final partition, now wiping Poland from the map of Europe altogether. Russia secured Lithuania, Courland and other areas in the north-east; Prussia won control of central Poland, including Warsaw; while Austria took Cracow and Little Poland in the south.

By that time a far wider conflict had broken out. The first phase of the French Revolution in 1789–90 had seemed unlikely to threaten the peace of the continent: it was even welcomed in many circles elsewhere. It prevented France from playing an active role in European politics for a time, but other powers had no thoughts of intervening. Political developments in France, however novel, appeared essentially an internal question: in February 1792 Pitt was forecasting fifteen years of peace for Britain and British military expenditure was reduced. But the other major powers became increasingly concerned. In August 1791 the Austrian and Prussian rulers issued a declaration expressing their deep disquiet at the situation of the French king and calling for united action by the great powers to assist him. French emigrés became more active in planning counter-revolution, while German rulers were increasingly concerned at the threat to remaining German rights in Alsace. The increasing hostility of outside opinion coincided with, and perhaps provoked, increasing militancy within France, where more radical factions favoured war as a means of spreading the revolution. Early in the following year an advocate of this course, Dumouriez, became foreign minister. After a series of ultimata had been issued by the Austrian emperor, France declared war in April 1792. In May Prussia joined Austria and during the months that followed many other European countries joined them. Though for a time Britain declared herself neutral, the execution of the French king in January 1793 inflamed British opinion against the revolutionary government, and she would probably have joined the war anyway if the revolutionary government had not itself declared war in the following month.

The coalition which eventually emerged included most of the other significant powers of Europe (see below). Once again the balance of power mechanism appeared to be operating to resist a threat to the system: this time ideological as much as military. In fact, however, the coalition was never united, either in aims or action. Its members were linked only by a series of bilateral treaties, not a single coalition treaty. Each of the major powers had territorial or other aspirations which were frequently in conflict. Russia and Prussia were far more concerned with events in Poland than with those in France, and this in turn distracted Austria, increasingly apprehensive about their intentions there.

In the first military encounter in September 1792, a joint force of Prussian and emigré troops was defeated. The initiative was then taken by the French revolutionary forces. They invaded the Rhineland; occupied much of the Austrian Netherlands (opening the Scheldt river, to the anger of the Dutch and British) in 1794; and conquered the United Provinces, where they were widely welcomed, in 1795, at the same time annexing Belgium to France. They advanced into Spain, inducing that country to make a separate peace in 1795 and to join in an alliance in the following year. Prussia too was persuaded in April 1795 to sign a separate peace, ceding all her territory on the left bank of the Rhine and even agreeing to neutralise north Germany, including Hanover. This enabled the French revolutionary forces to launch themselves against Austria, both in Germany and Italy. Allied armies suffered setbacks almost everywhere. A British expedition in the Low Countries in 1793–5 was defeated and had to be withdrawn. Operations in the Caribbean in 1793–6 were even more disastrous: 80,000 men were killed or made unfit by disease. In Italy French forces, among whom Napoleon became an important commander, won spectacular victories, forcing Sardinia to make peace in 1796 and Austria in the following year. France now effectively dominated the whole of western Europe.

Once again the collusion of the great powers at the expense of weaker ones was evident. At the Peace of Campo Formio Austria agreed to the destruction of Venice, Genoa, Modena and the Papal states (which had not been involved in the war) and so in effect agreed a partition of Italy between herself and France. France established two puppet states in north Italy, and acquired the Ionian Islands in the Adriatic. Early in 1798 French forces intervened in the Papal states where they set up a "Roman republic"; a month later they did the same in Switzerland, where they established the "Helvetic republic"; and a month after that in Holland once more, where they established the "Batavian republic" and imposed a new constitution. At the end of the year they took control of Sardinia and a month later of Naples. By this time Britain was the only European country with which they were still at war. The war to crush the revolution, which had appeared a relatively simple task, had been a total failure.

During this time, though she had played little part in the land fighting in Europe, Britain had already begun to win significant colonial gains (see below). Her navy had re-established control of the seas and effectively blockaded the French coast; and she won a major naval victory over France in 1794 and over her two allies, Spain and Holland, in the following years. But if France was to be defeated, land victories too were required. In 1798, therefore, she set about establishing a second coalition which might be in a position to roll back French power in the continent. But once more this foundered on the divisions and jealousies among the three eastern powers. Prussia, after showing some initial interest, refused to join. Russia, which apart from sending a few naval vessels to the North Sea, had taken no part in the first coalition's war, was also at first reluctant to take part, but was finally spurred to do so by France's seizure of Malta in 1798 (Paul, the new tsar of Russia, had made himself the protector of the Knights of Malta). Finally, in 1799 Austria too agreed to join. Austro-Russian forces largely cleared north Italy of French troops and advanced into Switzerland, while the British expelled the French from Naples. But a new British attempt to invade the Low Countries, in co-operation with Russian forces, was a disaster, and helped to disillusion Russia with the second coalition's efforts. There were equally bitter recriminations between Russia and Austria over policy in Italy and Switzerland; the tsar accused the Austrians of using the war for purposes of Austrian aggrandisement. So once again the coalition disintegrated because of mutual jealousies.

In the summer of 1798 Napoleon invaded Egypt. This caused the Turkish sultan, still nominally the suzerain there, to declare war on France, and brought the unusual spectacle of an alliance between Turkey and Russia. The two countries successfully occupied the Ionian Islands. But the main counter to the invasion came from Britain, which won two important naval victories off the Egyptian coast and left Napoleon's forces stranded there. Napoleon returned to France to lead the army coup against the Directoire in November 1799. Having effectively taken control of France's affairs, he proposed negotiations with Britain and Austria. When both refused he returned to arms and won new and spectacular victories over Austria in Italy. Austria again sued for peace and was obliged to cede further territory in Italy. But once more it was the smaller countries that suffered most. Napoleon now turned against Portugal and Naples which, receiving little help from elsewhere, were conquered in turn, while Britain destroyed Denmark's navy because she had presumed to join the Russian-led Armed Neutrality.

Finally, in 1801 Britain too consented to negotiate and in March of the following year the Peace of Amiens brought a temporary truce. France agreed to withdraw from Naples and the papal states. Britain agreed to hand back Ceylon and Trinidad. Egypt was to be returned to the Ottoman sultan and Malta to the Knights of Malta. During the truce, however, Napoleon continued to strengthen his position, annexing Piedmont and Elba later that year, intervening in Switzerland once more, and bringing Spain and Holland increasingly under his control. He was also believed to be planning a new assault on Egypt.

The peace was generally seen as a respite only. Britain was unlikely to tolerate Napoleon's continued domination of the continent for long. She refused to withdraw from Malta, as she was pledged to do under the peace terms, demanding that France should withdraw from Switzerland and Holland, should cease building up her navy, and allow Britain to trade freely in the continent. In May 1803 the war was resumed.

Napoleon assembled a Franco-Spanish fleet intended to mount an invasion of Britain. But Britain's crushing naval victory at Trafalgar in 1805 demonstrated that France lacked the naval power to mount such a project. There again appeared the possibility of stalemate, with France unable to prevail at sea or Britain on land. When Napoleon made his brother "king" of Italy and annexed Genoa in 1805, Britain tried to mobilise a new coalition, offering massive subsidies to Austria and Russia for the purpose. No sooner was this coalition established in August 1805, however, than Napoleon, with devastating speed, rushed his armies to the east to defeat Austrian forces at Ulm and, a month later, win an even more imposing victory over Austria and Russia at Austerlitz. A year later Prussia, after co-operating with Napoleon for several years (and being permitted to occupy Hanover in return), made a brief and unsuccessful effort to join the war against him, but was crushed within a month. Finally, in June 1807 Napoleon (having incited Turkey to start a new war against Russia in the south in the previous year) defeated a large Russian army at Friedland. In less than two years three of the most powerful states in Europe had been conquered in turn. All then agreed to become the accomplices of France against their former ally Britain. In 1807–8 all declared war on Britain and agreed to apply Napoleon's economic sanctions against her. Austria was obliged to hand over Venice and Dalmatia to Napoleon's Italian satellite and German territory to his allies in south Germany (Bavaria and Württemberg). Prussia became a virtual satellite of France. Russia, in return for acquiring a small piece of Prussian Poland, agreed to join the French alliance, even consenting to compel Sweden, Denmark and Portugal to join the war against Britain. Meanwhile Napoleon annexed Tuscany, Parma, Piacenza and (once more) the papal states, where the pope was imprisoned for five years for daring to excommunicate him; reorganised the German states; abolished the Holy Roman Empire; created the Confederation of the Rhine and the new kingdom of Westphalia in West Germany; and turned western Poland into a new grand duchy of Warsaw, largely under French control. He made his brothers kings of Naples, Holland, Westphalia and Spain, and himself king of Italy; married other members of his family to a variety of German princes; and even, for a time, contemplated establishing a single European state, comparable to the Roman Empire. Europe was virtually under the control of one man. The balance of power was at an end.

For five years from 1807 to 1812 Britain and France engaged in economic warfare against each other. Napoleon tried through his

Berlin decrees of 1806 and subsequent measures – the "continental system" – to close the European market to British goods and so cripple the British economy. Though at certain times – in 1808 and 1811 – these measures caused some problems for British industry, they also caused hardships within Europe itself and there was widespread evasion and smuggling. Britain retaliated, both by blockading the French coast and by taking advantage of new markets overseas, including Spanish America and captured French colonies. She was, however, still without allies and Napoleon even won some further military successes. Another attempted British landing in the Low Countries in 1709 was yet again defeated; and an attempt to defend Switzerland failed. A rash attempt by Austria in the same year to resume the war was again rapidly defeated. The former emperor, besides once more forfeiting territory, was obliged to nourish Napoleon's imperial ambitions by marrying his daughter to the French "emperor". The French ruler had acquired the dynastic appetites of his enemies.

The only hope for Britain, apart from overseas conquests, was the campaign which began in Spain in 1808. French troops had been sent to Spain the previous year to bring Portugal under French control and to compel her too to apply the continental system. Renewed French domination of Spain caused a revolution in that country. Directed at first against the weak Spanish king who had brought such humiliation, it was later turned against the French forces and those of the new king imposed by Napoleon, his brother Joseph. In August 1808 a British army landed in Spain under the command of the future Duke of Wellington. Though its first offensive in Spain was unsuccessful, it successfully defended Portugal when it was attacked in force in 1810–11. Only in 1812 was it able, with the assistance of widespread Spanish guerrilla forces, to inflict a series of defeats on the large French army (at one time 350,000 strong). And during the next year and a half it was able to advance steadily to the French frontier.

By the time it reached it, Napoleon had suffered an even greater defeat in Russia. The subjugation of Prussia and Austria meant that increasingly Russia was the only significant independent power of Europe, which he would need to eliminate if he was to control the continent. In 1808 she had strengthened her position by attacking Sweden and seizing the remaining part of Finland. In the south she had won substantial successes in fighting wars both with Turkey (1806–12) and with Persia (1805–13): successes which could ultimately have threatened Constantinople. She had provided no effective aid to Napoleon during his brief war with Austria in 1809, despite her alliance obligation. And from 1810 she had increasingly declined to apply his continental system against Britain. Above all in Poland, where Russia was determined to reassert her influence, the interests of the two states came into conflict. From the autumn of 1811 Napoleon prepared for war against Russia: in June of the following year he launched his invasion. The French force of 500,000 (of whom less than a third were French), assisted by contingents from Austria and Prussia, far outnumbered the Russian army. After a brief but bloody encounter at Borodino the French army was able to occupy Moscow in September. But the capital was largely deserted and Napoleon was unable to impose peace terms. In the middle of October he had to give the order for withdrawal. In its long retreat, harried by Cossacks, the French force was decimated by cold, disease and desertion. Only 40,000 got back to Poland. 270,000 were killed (rather less than the total French casualties in Spain) and another 200,000 taken prisoner. The two defeats, in Spain and Russia, meant that for the first time Napoleon was forced on to the defensive.

The reversal in his fortunes caused a rapid change of policy among the powers that had been collaborating with him. Austria from 1809, like Prussia from 1795 to 1805 and again after 1806, and Russia herself from 1807 to 1812, had been willing to make common cause with Napoleon when this seemed the best way of promoting their own national interests. When Napoleon himself appeared on the verge of defeat this was no longer a sensible policy. A Prussian general who had acted in support of Napoleon during the invasion of Russia now welcomed Russian forces, and even allowed them to occupy East Prussia. In February 1813 Prussia entered into an alliance with Russia against France. Sweden, too, joined the new coalition (Napoleon had occupied Swedish Pomerania in 1812), driving Sweden (in which Bernadotte, a former Napoleonic general, now controlled policy) into the arms of Russia, as did Spain and Portugal. Finally even Austria which, deeply suspicious of Russian ambitions, had for a time hoped that alliance with Napoleon might provide the opportunity to restore her own power, in August 1813 declared war on France. All the major powers of the continent were therefore now once more ranged against Napoleon. In a new alliance treaty, Russia, Prussia and Austria each pledged themselves to commit 150,000 men to the remaining struggle, while Britain pledged vast subsidies. At the battle of Leipzig in October of that year, in which over half a million men were engaged, Napoleon, outnum-bered, suffered a defeat. And though he continued for the next year by skilful manoeuvring to stave off the end, his capacity to call up ever more, and ever younger, recruits to throw into yet more battles was by this time exhausted. In April 1814, recognising imminent defeat, he abdicated. Under the Treaty of Fontainebleu a few days later he was permitted to keep his imperial title, awarded a revenue of two million francs and granted "sovereignty" in Elba. His return and further defeat at Waterloo in 1815 did not materially affect the settlement to be reached, except so far as his own personal future was concerned: it condemned him to be held henceforth a prisoner of the British in St Helena. France herself was still treated with reasonable leniency: though no longer allowed to acquire the Saar and a part of the Savoy, as previously intended, she was still permitted to retain the frontiers of 1790, in effect her pre-revolutionary border, and lost territory only overseas (almost entirely to Britain).

But the other changes to the map of Europe were spectacular. The final distribution of territories, resulting from a complex series of negotiations, represented a deal among the allies themselves, rather than one between them as a group and France. Each of the three continental powers made substantial gains (despite the fact that all had been defeated at least once and had been at war with Napoleon for less than half the period of the struggle). Russia acquired the areas of Poland not previously under her control (she had already gained Bessarabia from Turkey in 1812). Prussia secured two-fifths of Saxony, Swedish Pomerania, Posen, substantial Rhineland territory and Westphalia. Austria gained Venetia and part of Bavaria, and recovered Lombardy and Galicia. It was the smaller states of Europe, who had little say in the proceedings, who were the principal losers: Saxony was truncated; innumerable smaller German states were diminished or extinguished altogether, Luxemburg was placed under Dutch and German condominium; Venice and Genoa were elimi-nated; Modena and Parma effectively made puppet states of Austria, as Tuscany was before. Others were switched from one master to another: Norway from Denmark to Sweden; Belgium from Austria to Holland; and so on. The treaty explicitly declared that it was designed to create a "lasting balance of power" in Europe. But it was a balance among the great powers themselves that was intended, designed to suit their own interests, not a balance among the states of the continent as a whole.

Since 1785, therefore, Europe had passed through a transformation.

For a brief period France had acquired a domination of the continent such as even Louis XIV had never dreamed of. But this time this did not bring into operation the balance-of-power mechanism which had so often in the past created effective combinations against the main threat to the peace. The other powers combined only fitfully, or not at all, to withstand the threat. For long most were willing to collaborate actively with the dominant state. Only after twenty years did they finally wholeheartedly combine effectively to restore the balance. Then, once they had conquered their enemy, they colluded in a typical settlement of the period, redistributing territories in their own favour with a supreme disregard for ethnic, linguistic, historical or cultural considerations, still less in accordance with the desire of populations. At the end of the day they managed to secure what appeared to them a reasonable balance of advantage among themselves. And at the same time they established a system by which they themselves would from then on supervise the affairs of the continent, to ensure that the settlement they had arrived at and the governments they had installed should not be too seriously disturbed.

Among themselves none was any longer dominant. France, still potentially the most powerful, was temporarily subdued. Britain, the only country that had fought consistently and single-mindedly against her, was overwhelmingly the strongest at sea and in the colonies (as well as financially and industrially), but was still not a formidable land power. Russia remained a lurking danger in the east but was to decline in subsequent years. Austria and Prussia, though still powerful, were too preoccupied by their fears of revolution, abroad as well as at home, to harbour expansionist designs. For the moment all the major powers were territorially satisfied and had few designs against each other. They had, after all, secured for themselves a dominance of the affairs of the continent which made further gains at each other's expense, for the moment at least, unnecessary.

BOOKS

Modern works

G. Bruun, *Europe and the French Imperium, 1799–1814* (New York, 1938).
W. L. Dorn, *Competition for Empire, 1740–1763* (New York, 1940).
S. Favier, *Politique de tous les cabinets* (Paris, 1773).

F. L. Ford, *Europe, 1780–1830* (London, 1970).

L. Gershoy, *From Despotism to Revolution* (New York, 1944).

R. M. Hatton, *Europe in the Age of Louis XIV* (London, 1969).

——, *Louis XIV and Europe* (London, 1976).

—— and M. S. Anderson (eds), *Studies in Diplomatic History* (London, 1970).

—— and J. S. Bromley (eds), *William III and Louis XIV* (Liverpool, 1968).

D. B. Horn, *Great Britain and Europe in the Eighteenth Century* (London, 1967).

O. Hufton, *Europe: Privilege and Protest, 1730–1789* (London, 1980).

J. R. Jones, *Britain and the World, 1649–1815* (Brighton, 1980).

P. Langford, *The Eighteenth Century, 1688–1815* (London, 1976).

D. McKay and H. M. Scott, *The Rise of the Great Powers, 1648–1815* (London, 1983).

The New Cambridge Modern History, vols v–ix (Cambridge, 1961–70).

B. Roberts, *The Quest for Security, 1715–1740* (New York, 1947).

H. H. Rowen, *The Ambassador Prepares for War* (The Hague, 1957).

G. Rude, *Revolutionary Europe, 1783–1815* (London, 1964).

S. T. Ross, *European Diplomatic History, 1789–1815* (New York, 1969).

J. W. Stoye, *Europe Unfolding, 1648–1688* (London, 1969).

A. Sorel, *Europe and the French Revolution* (Paris, 1885–1905).

J. B. Wolf, *The Emergence of the Great Powers, 1685–1715* (New York, 1951).

G. Zeller, *De Louis XIV à 1789* (Paris, 1955).

Contemporary works

Catherine the Great, *Memoirs*, English trs. (London, 1955).

J. B. Colbert (Courtilz de Santras), *Testament politique*, English trs. (London, 1695).

Frederick the Great, *Testament politique*, 1752 (Berlin, 1920).

——, *Testament politique*, 1768 (Berlin, 1920).

Louis XIV, *Memoires for the Instruction of the Dauphin*, ed. Paul Sonnino (New York, 1970).

Empress Maria Theresa, *Politisches Testament* (Munich, 1952).

S. Pufendorf, *Introduction to the History of the Principal States*, 1684, English trs. (London, 1697).

4 Sovereignty

THE IDEA OF SOVEREIGNTY

The attitudes and actions of rulers and statesmen towards international affairs in this age were partly shaped by the new ideas which emerged about authority within the state.

During mediaeval times authority within each state had been divided on a horizontal basis. It was exercised by different authorities at different levels and for different purposes. Even the king did not claim absolute power within his own territories. He conceded, for example, to his immediate vassals, in return for their loyalty and their service in war, a wide range of control, even including rights of jurisdiction, within their own lands. Within the towns municipalities exercised an almost total authority over all local affairs, an authority which the ruler himself often recognised in a royal charter. Royal authority of the rulers was shared also with religious powers which, within their own sphere at least, was supreme. (In large parts of Europe ecclesiastical rulers held secular power as well, ruling substantial territories as absolute governors.) Finally, their power was limited by customary or common law, embodying the traditions of the people: in many cases they were obliged on ascending the throne to commit themselves to respect local traditions, grant customary liberties or to speak only the local language. Thus although Justinian, one of the most widely quoted authorities in mediaeval times, had declared that "what the prince desires has the force of law" – at first sight a clear assertion of his sovereign powers – he also made clear that this came about only because "the people had conceded to him their whole power and authority".[1] At that time then the power of the rulers was always limited: exercised only in certain spheres and for certain purposes, and even then it was conditional.

During the period we are concerned with there was a deliberate effort to replace this horizontal and functional distribution of power by a vertical structure, in which unquestioned authority was wielded from the top. This process had begun long before Royal rulers, such as Louis XI in France, the Tudor sovereigns in England, Ferdinand and Isabella in Spain, had sought to strengthen the authority of the monarch in relation to other centres of power. They had increasingly imposed their will on the great magnates. They had challenged the power of the pope and the church to intervene in secular matters and even on doctrinal questions. They had limited the authority of the municipalities and the guilds to regulate local affairs. They had gradually strengthened their powers in the field of taxation. They had formulated an increasing body of royal legislation to supplement and sometimes replace local customary law. And they had begun a systematic process of centralisation, in which the strings of power were placed increasingly in the hands of their own officials.

It was to support and justify this process that political theorists began to involve the concept of "sovereignty". It was increasingly held that the authority of the rulers was unlimited, and obedience to it unconditional. Machiavelli described the strategies by which a ruler could best promote and protect his own power. He was careful to insist that "it is necessary for a prince to possess the friendship of the people", and that "a wise prince will seek means by which his subjects will always and in every possible condition of things have need of a government, so that they will always be faithful to him".[2] But he also maintained that "it is much safer to be feared than loved"; and that a ruler must not mind "incurring the charge of cruelty for the purpose of keeping his subjects united and faithful".[3] In other words the ruler must not hesitate to exercise effective authority if only in the interests of those he ruled.

The need for unconditional obedience to a supreme authority was stated more categorically by Bodin. Writing at a time of disorder (during the wars of religion) in France, he was concerned to justify the power of the king to maintain order within his realm. Writing specifically "On Sovereignty" he declared that this created "absolute and perpetual power": "The distinguishing mark of the sovereign is that he cannot in any way be subject to the commands of another, for it is he who makes the laws for the subjects. . . . That is why it is laid down . . . that the prince is above the law."[4] For him, therefore, the essence of sovereignty was the power to command.

Hobbes, also writing at a time of civil war, asserted equally firmly the needs of kingly power. Sovereignty, he held, derived originally from the fact that individual citizens had agreed among themselves "to confer all their power and strength upon one man, or upon an assembly of men, that may reduce all their wills . . . under one rule" in the interests of their mutual security. Such a ruler would be "called Sovereign, and said to have sovereign power"; and everyone else would be "his subjects".[5]

The sovereignty which Bodin and Hobbes demanded was required, they held, mainly for domestic purposes: to provide a single undisputed centre of authority within the state, able to resolve the conflicts and disorders so evident in their own day. Both emphasised the right of the sovereign to command unquestioning obedience in every sphere. It was this omnicompetence of the sovereign power which above all distinguished the new belief from that prevailing in the mediaeval polity, with its multiple sources of authority. That is why Hobbes declared that, whether it was "despotical", that is acquired by force, or "paternal", acquired as the result of a social contract between ruler and people, the sovereign should be accepted as the "judge of what is necessary for peace; judge of doctrines; he is sole legislator, and supreme judge of controversies; and of the times and occasions of war and peace".[6] The sovereign was not only a judge who could decide all controversies which might arise concerning the law; but a legislator "prescribing the rules whereby every man may know what goods he may enjoy and what actions he may do, without being molested by any of his fellow-subjects".

Because a great deal of conflict in the century before 1648 concerned religious questions, it was particularly important, both writers believed, that the sovereign should have authority to settle religious differences; to judge, as Hobbes put it "what opinions and doctrines are averse and what conducing to peace". This aspect of sovereignty was explicitly endorsed in the Peace of Westphalia at the opening of our period. This reaffirmed the principle of *cujus regio ejus religio*: that is, that the ruler could determine what religion was to be practised in his own territory. First adopted in the Peace of Augsburg nearly a century earlier, that doctrine had at that time proved unable to resolve religious conflicts as easily as had been hoped. The strength of feeling that existed in Germany on those questions had placed it everywhere under challenge. Religious minorities were not always willing to have their opinions dictated to them by their current rulers, who anyway (as the inhabitants of Germany, like those in England, found) might change their religion from one reign to another. Elsewhere Huguenots in France, Protestants in the Low Countries, Bohemia and Hungary, Catholics in Ireland and Calvinists in Scotland, had fought bitter wars to resist the imposition of royally-imposed faiths. In 1648, however, at the end of the widest and bitterest ideological conflict of the age, the principle was again asserted. This time it was often applied with some toleration. But the general doctrine that the rulers could determine the religion of all their subjects was not contested.[7] However bitterly they might disagree on everything else this was the one principle on which all were at one. It was put into effect in the Act of Uniformity in England in 1679; in Louis' expulsion of the Huguenots from France six years later and his subsequent destruction of the Jansenists; in the continued extirpation of protestant heresy in the Hapsburg territories; in the elimination of Catholics from Sweden and of Protestants from Spain. No more categorical assertion of royal authority – that is, of the principle of "sovereignty" – could have been found. The rulers now claimed the right not only to rule the bodies of their subjects but their consciences as well.

In theory the sovereign power need not lie in the hands of a single ruler. It might, as Hobbes had accepted, lie in an "assembly of men". But in practice, because it was sovereigns – personal rulers – who in most places held power, the idea of sovereignty became associated with such rulers. The duality of meaning – either the rule of sovereigns or absolute authority – was not always distinguished. Sovereignty, in the general understanding, was inevitably held by sovereigns: the sovereign was, equally naturally, "sovereign". For the rulers, therefore, the concept was a valuable ideological tool, since it appeared to justify the strengthening of their own authority which they anyway fought to achieve.

For many it came to symbolise not merely the kingly power but absolute power. They therefore underlined the aspect of sovereignty on which Bodin had laid stress: the right of the ruler to command unconditional obedience. When Charles XI of Sweden issued his Declaration of Sovereignty in 1693, he asserted his rights as "an absolute, all-commanding and governing sovereign king" who was not responsible to anyone on earth for the actions which he took.[8] Frederick William of Prussia declared, "I will stabilise the *souveraineté* like a rock of bronze", and made it clear what he meant when he declared "we are king and master and we do as we please".[9] Sovereignty among the German rulers of the day, a French writer asserted, "consists in the magnificent privilege of killing people with impunity. . . . To kill a man when the prince feels inclined is an act of sovereignty".[10] Even in England, where absolutism was rejected, the jurist Blackstone declared in 1769 that there must exist in every state an absolute authority wielding coercive powers in which the right of sovereignty – the *jura summa imperii* – resided (though that view was rightly derided by Bentham, who pointed out that in federal states, such as Switzerland, or in the German empire, no such single source of authority existed). Everywhere, therefore, in absolutist and non-absolutist states alike, the fundamental principle of "sovereignty" was increasingly accepted. And everywhere the statute law promulgated by princes or parliaments came to displace the customary law once held to protect the inalienable rights of the people as a whole.

The simplest way of justifying this extension of the sovereign's power was, of course, to declare that it was ordained by God. This was the view expressed by Bossuet, the French divine, in his *Politics Drawn from the Very Words of the Scriptures*, written for Louis XIV's son, the dauphin. Royal authority, he declared came from God, "who established the king".[11] The rulers themselves should, because of this, "have regard to their power, for it is not theirs but God's power, to be used righteously and in fear".[12] But it was above all their subjects, who should recognise the king's authority as "absolute", since "without the absolute authority he could neither do good nor suppress evil". Thus, "he who refuses obedience to the prince is not to be referred to another judgement but condemned to death without appeal, as an enemy of the public peace and of human society."[13] Louis himself accepted this view of the duty of his subjects. "He who has given kings to men", he declared, "has wanted them to be respected. . . . His will is that, whoever is born a subject, must obey without qualification."[14] This was in the interests of the subject as much as of the ruler. "The tranquillity of subjects lies only in obedience. . . . There is always greater evil in popular control than in enduring even the bad rule of kings". For this reason "bad as a prince may be, the revolt of his subjects is infinitely criminal".[15]

This traditional doctrine of divine right was now buttressed by the new doctrine of sovereignty, which provided an apparently rational non-metaphysical justification of the rulers' power. Whether or not associated with the idea of divine right, the concept of sovereignty appeared to endorse the *legitimacy* of personal rule: rule by sovereigns. While sovereigns now increasingly identified with the states they ruled (see above), their states – that is their populations, their parliaments, and above all their chief ministers – increasingly identified their states with their rulers. They were more and more seen as personifications of the state, rather than of dynasties or peoples, as in earlier times. Often they were the only factor unifying political entities that were formed out of scattered territories and peoples, having little else in common. They afforded legitimacy to the states so constituted. The sovereigns themselves were, not surprisingly, those who were most convinced of their own legitimacy. They would even accept the legitimacy of their enemies. Thus the French court could,

even at the height of the War of Spanish Succession, go into mourn-
ing on the death of an Austrian princess; and Louis XIV, for all his
hatred of some of his royal rivals, could never condone an act of
regicide. Closely bound by marriage ties, the royal families of the
continent shared a common interest in preserving their royal power.
And while they might challenge the right of a rival to rule a particular
territory, they did not challenge the continuation of royal rule itself.
The principle of sovereignty in this sense served their common
interests.

Essentially that principle embodied the idea of a single source of
authority in every state, replacing the multiple sources which had
existed in mediaeval times. In theory that single source could as well
be a parliament as a royal ruler: this was the doctrine increasingly
propounded in England, the United Provinces and other states.
Sovereignty could even be held, as was asserted at the end of the
period by the American and French revolutionaries, to reside in the
"people" as a whole. But for the moment, "sovereignty" was generally taken to justify the rule of existing sovereigns: the monarchs who
held power within their own states.

Ironically, that was the idea which was reasserted, at the very end
of our period, when the assembled states of Europe finally defeated
the French revolution, which had propounded a different view.
Under the Treaty of Fontainebleau of 1814, Napoleon was not only
allowed by his former enemies to retain the personal title of "emperor". He was given personal "sovereignty" in Elba (just as his wife
Marie-Louise was given similar sovereignty in Parma). By this singu-
lar honour to a defeated tyrant, the victorious powers could hardly
have demonstrated more subtly, nor more emphatically, the defeat of
the principle of the French revolution had purported to represent,
and the victory of the concept that they had defended. The ideals of
the revolution had finally been overcome: the *ancien régime* – the era
of personal sovereignty – had been restored.

EXTERNAL SOVEREIGNTY

But the new doctrine not only asserted the authority of the sovereign
within his state. It also proclaimed that power in relation to other
states.

It was inevitable that an assertion of the sovereign's authority
within the state implied a denial of the right of foreign powers within

its jurisdiction. There no longer existed any willingness to share authority with outside forces. In earlier days such a sharing of authority had been normal. The notion of "Christendom" had operated transnationally: it implied not only common beliefs, but common institutions, recognised throughout the continent. Pope and emperor, canon law and chivalric tradition had all exercised some influence in many lands. Now the authority of the pope was increasingly rejected. He was ignored not only in countries which had adopted the reformed religion but by Catholic rulers equally. In almost every country the power of the state over the church was extended, and the authority enjoyed by the pope restricted. Everywhere church lands were seized, the right of the church to impose taxation was abolished or limited, the immunity of the clergy from taxation and other duties was removed. Louis XIV was, as so often, symptomatic of the attitude of many rulers. For all his frequently expressed religious devotion, he rejected the pope's right to direct the affairs of the church in France, demanded abject apologies from him for trivial incidents (see below) and expelled him from his territories at Avignon. Even in intensely Catholic Spain the publication of papal decrees and other papal documents was prohibited in 1768. The papal enclave in Naples was seized in the same year. The once-powerful Jesuits were expelled from Portugal in 1759, from France in 1762, from Spain in 1767, from Naples and Parma in the same year, from Poland a year or two later; and in 1774 the entire order was dissolved. The Inquisition was placed under the direct control of the Spanish crown in 1768–70, while in Portugal its sentences were made subject to royal assent. In the Hapsburg empire, too, the Inquisition was abolished by the emperor Joseph, together with clerical immunity, Mortmain and the right of sanctuary. Religion was, so far as was possible, nationalised. And the transnational influence that the church had exercised on every state disappeared forever.*

The authority once exercised by the emperors was also drastically curtailed. The authority they had once enjoyed in The Netherlands, Switzerland and northern Italy had disappeared long before this period began. It was now only marginal even in Germany, the heartland of the empire. The Peace of Westphalia explicitly recog-

---

* It was symptomatic of the decline in the pope's influence that his denunciation of the Peace of Westphalia as "null, void, invalid, unjust, iniquitous, inane, reprobate and damnable" was universally ignored, by Catholic as much as by Protestant rulers.

nised the right of the German rulers to form allegiances and to establish diplomatic relations with other states, on the same basis as other rulers. Though in theory they were not to ally themselves against the emperor, even this injunction was widely ignored. Thus the League of the Rhine, formed under French auspices in 1658, was, at least by implication, hostile to the emperor, as was the League of German princes (the *Fürstenburd*) established by Frederick the Great in 1785 to resist Joseph II's ambitions in Bavaria. Though the emperors still regarded themselves as responsible for mobilising the empire when its frontiers were under attack, they were often ignored. And in practice all the larger states of Germany and some of the smaller ones undertook their own foreign relations entirely independently.

Frederick the Great, for example, did not even attempt to consult the emperor when he agreed with Britain on the "neutralisation" of the whole of Germany in 1756. The rulers of smaller states demanded for themselves the trappings of sovereignty, seeing themselves as the rulers of independent states running their own affairs like other states. The imperial institutions were increasingly moribund, and were now far more concerned with disputes between German states or between German rulers and their Estates than with any external questions. To all intents and purposes, though not formally endowed with that status,[16] the German states had now become sovereign powers as much as any others.

Other non-sovereign bodies, which had been prominent actors in the previous international system, now disappeared or declined in significance. The Hanseatic League, the Teutonic Order, the Knights of the Sword, the Knights of Malta, the Cossacks and Tartars, had all exercised authority of a kind in their own areas. But they never claimed to exercise "sovereignty". They had no clear territorial basis. They had generally conducted no diplomatic relations. In the new world of sovereign states there was no room for entities of that kind. Their lands now fell under the authority of the new political entities that did claim such sovereignty.

Other relics of the feudal order declined in significance. At the beginning of our period a number of territories were still held to be "fiefs", owing ultimate allegiance to rulers elsewhere. During the course of this period most of these either became sovereign themselves, or were absorbed in sovereign states. East Prussia, formerly a fief to the Polish crown, was absorbed by Brandenburg in 1667–8. Courland, also a fief of Poland, was finally swallowed up by Russia in 1795. Milan, Tuscany, Parma and Naples, all claimed as imperial fiefs in the early part of the period, were either (as in the first two cases) absorbed by other states, or (as in the latter two), granted independence under foreign rulers. The Crimean Tartars, for long tributaries of the Ottoman empire, were first accorded independence in 1774, and finally annexed by Russia a few years later. The mini-states of Germany, theoretically subject to the emperor, were in many cases absorbed by larger neighbours (see below); and were finally regrouped by Napoleon into larger entities in 1806. And in that same year the empire itself, perhaps the strangest of all the non-sovereign relics of an earlier day, was finally abolished and never seriously revived.

So everywhere a world of sovereign states was brought into existence. All such states were held to enjoy a natural right to independence, to be free of interference – especially dictatorial interference – from other states. In the words of Vattel in the most famous work of international law of the age:

> Nations being free and independent of each other, in the same manner as men are naturally free and independent. . . . The natural society of nations cannot subsist unless the natural rights of each be duly respected. . . . No other nations can compel them to act in such or such particular manner: for any attempt at such compulsion would be an infringement on the liberty of nations.[17]

It was this independence which came to be seen as the essential mark of sovereignty.

Sovereign states not only had the right to be free of interference from other states; they were also, it now came to be held, naturally equal (another idea which had never been subscribed to in earlier ages). By the very fact of being sovereign, states acquired the same rights of sovereignty and so, regardless of size and power, an essential equality. Just as individual men were by nature equals, Vattel declared, so

> nations composed of men . . . are naturally equal, and inherit from nature the same obligations and rights. Power or weakness does not in this respect produce any difference. A dwarf is as much a man as a giant; a small republic is no less a sovereign state than the most powerful kingdom.[18]

In other words, every state, however small and however weak, equally enjoyed (at least in theory) the right of sovereignty, and the independence that implied. Such states were held to have the right to enter into diplomatic relations and to make agreements by which they would subsequently be bound. *Pacta sunt servunda* – treaties are to be observed – was one of the most generally accepted rules of this world of sovereignty.

But such states also, in the final resort, had the right to make war to protect their interests. As Hobbes had observed, "covenants without the sword are vain". Vattel now asserted a wider right to make war: not merely to protect a nation but to preserve the society of states. Because "all men and all states have a perfect right to those things that are necessary for their preservation", they also have the right "to resort to forcible means for the purpose of repressing any one particular nation who openly violates the laws of the society which nature has established between them, or who directly attack the welfare and safety of that society".[19] However, as Vattel himself accepted, since each nation "maintains that she has justice on her side in every dispute that happens to arise", this could lead to constant warfare. On these grounds he proposed an important new distinction between what he called the "voluntary law of nations", based on conscience alone, and "conventional" and "customary" law, based on explicit agreements reached between states or on the custom of nations which had been generally accepted (and even this latter was not "obligatory except on those nations who had adopted it").[20]

Such ideas represented a radical change from traditional beliefs about the sources of international law: a change reflecting above all the emergence of the new idea of sovereignty. In earlier times the provisions of international law had been held to be based on "natural" law: principles of justice recognised everywhere in Christendom (there was no obligation to apply that law, most believed, to those who were not Christians). Natural law had been, therefore, among those transnational elements, independent of the will of individual states and rulers, which had provided the basis of inter-state relations. In a world of sovereign states those ideas were now increasingly discarded. It was increasingly asserted, as by Vattel in the passage quoted above, that states were fully bound only by undertakings, explicit or tacit, to which they gave their positive consent. Even lawyers such as Pufendorf, who retained a belief in "natural law," now hedged it with restrictions deriving from the purposes of sovereign states. In his *Law of Nations*, published in 1688, he expressed the view that a sovereign was bound by a duty only so far as it did not conflict with the interests of his state, because his bond with his own subjects took precedence over all other engagements.[21]

Vattel, too, accepted natural law as the basis of "the voluntary law of nations", based on conscience: but held that it was not part of the "necessary law of nations", by which states were (except in the case of customs which were "unjust and unlawful") absolutely bound. The voluntary law, the conventional law and the customary law, all proceeded from the will of nations: the voluntary from their presumed consent, the conventional from an expressed consent, and the customary from tacit consent. Together they represented "the positive law of nations" which therefore all depended, in one sense or another, on the positive consent of the states concerned.[22] Later writers were still more insistent on the need for the explicit consent of states. Johan Jacob Moser, in the late eighteenth century, sought to base international law on the observed behaviour of states, rather than on the abstract principles of an assumed "law of nature", which, he believed (with some reason), meant many things to many people. The "science" of the law of nations should be concerned, therefore, only with treaties and customs which had been generally accepted by states.[23] That view was followed by the better-known von Martens. He too saw international law as a "science" (among his first works was an *Essay on the Existence of a Positive European Law of Nations and on the Advantage of this Science*). And in the very title of his best known work – *Précis of Modern European International Law, Founded on the Treaties and on Custom* – he affirmed his belief that international law was based on treaties and accepted customs alone; while much of his later writing was devoted to assembling the treaties and other documents of the day which, in his view, provided the sole foundation of that law.

The emergence of "sovereign" states, each claiming sole jurisdiction in the areas under their own control, affected the way states undertook their relations in many ways. It was now made more necessary, for example, to determine the limits of the jurisdiction which each claimed. At the beginning of the period there was considerable doubt about this. Spain had claimed that it ruled all the oceans on either side of South America: England that the seas around her could be closed to others (*mare clausum*);[24] France that she had the right, even on the open seas, to compel ships of any other state to dip their flags to hers (see below). There now began to be an attempt to regulate such questions: in other words, to determine the limits of the "sovereignty" any state could claim. It came to be accepted (though not universally) that the limits of national jurisdiction in the seas was defined by the distance reached by a cannon-ball shot from the shore: usually measured as three miles (sometimes four). Within that limit each state demanded the right of absolute control – "sovereignty" – including the right to prevent foreign fishing and arrest foreign criminals. There were attempts to define the actions which could be taken against the shipping of other states in time of war, though here too there remained widespread disagreement. Diplomatic protocol, including the status of ambassadors and the immunities to be accorded to them, came to be more accurately defined.

In other words, the nature of a sovereign state, and the rights which each such state could expect to enjoy, began to be more clearly established. The heart of that doctrine was the right of each state to independence. And the state which demanded such independence for itself was expected – at least according to the doctrine – to accord a similar independence to all others.

REASONS OF STATE

In theory, if every state in demanding sovereignty for itself was equally willing to concede sovereignty to every other state, all conflict should have been avoided. Since none would seek to interfere in the affairs of other states or take action which violated their sovereignty, all might contentedly live at peace with one another. In practice this happy state of affairs was far from being realised. Each ruler was more concerned with the sovereignty demanded for his own state than he was with that demanded by others. All were in bitter competition with the rest. And this led to a widespread belief that any action, if it promoted the interests of the state, was justified. This was the doctrine of *raison d'état*.

In the *Memoires* he wrote for his son, Louis XIV declared that *raison d'état* was "the first of all laws by common consent", and that those actions of kings which they "seem to do sometimes against the common law", could be justified on that basis.[25] Similarly in the preface to the original edition of his *History of My Time* (1743) Frederick the Great declared that private morality was not applicable to international politics for there the "interests of the State"* were

---

* The insistence of Frederick, like others in his day, in spelling "state" always with a capital letter (even though he wrote in French, not German) was an indication of the reverence which was so widely accorded to the idea of the state at this time.

alone decisive, and a ruler must be prepared, if necessary, to break his word. These sentiments followed ideas that had been frequently expressed over the previous century or so: in the works of such writers as the Duke de Rohan, Gabriel Naudé and Courtilz de Sandras, most of which were widely known.[26]

Frederick, who had declared himself to be above all "a servant of the state" was, inevitably, especially inclined to believe that state interest could justify almost any action he wished to take. In his view, trickery and self-interest were the essential features of political life; and every ruler was bound to adopt such policies if only in self-defence; that is, to preserve the interests of their own state. In the same foreword he wrote:

> It is very hard to maintain purity and uprightness if one is caught up in the great political maelstrom of Europe. One sees oneself continually in danger of being betrayed by one's allies, forsaken by one's friends, brought low by envy and jealousy; and ultimately one finds oneself obliged to choose between the terrible alternatives of sacrificing one's people or one's word of honour.

It would be hypocritical, he declared, to pretend that statesmen in that situation would always choose the course of honour. "One can safely say that the fundamental rule of government for all states, from the smallest to the biggest, is the principle of extending their territories." This passion was "as deeply rooted in every ministry as universal despotism is in the Vatican". The passions of rulers had no other curb but the limits of their power. "Those are the fixed laws of European politics in which every politician submits. If a ruler were to tend his own interests less carefully than his neighbours, then the latter would only grow stronger; and it would leave him more virtuous but also weaker".[27] Since it was a prime rule that a ruler should not allow himself to become weaker, it was evident that he would sometimes be required to be less virtuous.

The belief that personal morality was irrelevant to state affairs was demonstrated in the conduct of the rulers of the day. The actions of Peter the Great in allowing his son, who he believed to have betrayed state interests, to be tortured to death; or of Frederick William of Prussia in having his son (Frederick the Great) arrested and sentenced to death for a minor offence,* of Elizabeth of Russia in

---

* Even the British king, George I, had his son arrested in 1717 for insulting behaviour toward the Lord Chamberlain.

usurping the throne and imprisoning Ivan, the rightful Tsar; and of Catherine II in colluding in the overthrow and (probably) the murder of her own husband to acquire power for herself, all demonstrated that belief in action. It was seen equally in the diplomatic history of the age: in the actions of Louis XIV in carefully preparing an unprovoked aggression against the United Provinces in 1672; of Charles II in deceitfully co-operating in that aggression (against a country with which he had only recently allied himself); of Peter the Great in emphatically assuring the Swedish king in 1700 of his peaceful intentions, and signing a treaty for "eternal peace" at a time when he was engaged in active preparations for war against him; of Frederick the Great in seizing Silesia and twice attacking his neighbour Saxony, on each occasion without warning; or of the three Eastern powers in joining together on three separate occasions, in the ruthless and deliberate destruction of Poland. Such actions provide the most concrete evidence of the level of international morality that prevailed in this day.

Truth was one of the first casualties. Frederick the Great, in the same breath as declaring that a statesman should not allow himself to acquire a reputation for untruthfulness, frankly admitted the advantages of deception on occasion. He declared openly that "dissimulation" was an element in the policy of great princes.[28] In appointing ambassadors it was essential to choose people "capable of dissimulation".[29] Louis XIV, too, emphasised the advantages of deception. He believed that "plans that are devised long before can be handled so subtly and under so many pretexts that, in spite of all warnings and all the suspicions about them, they can still hardly ever fail to cause surprise".[30] That strategy he put into effect in planning his own war against the Dutch in 1672, carefully prepared in secret for the previous four years. And he openly prided himself on the way he had, five years earlier, duped the people of Franche-Comté by talking to them about ways of preserving its neutrality while in fact planning to seize the territory, telling his son that he "believed that this negotiation was good for keeping them occupied while I made my preparations for the invasion".[31]

But it was not only a matter of occasional untruths. The needs of the state might, it was believed, demand more serious deviations from the morality of everyday life. Sometimes it might require a deliberate breach of treaty obligations. Frederick the Great believed that it was alright to break treaties so long as it was for "important" motives: for example, if an ally appeared likely to make a separate peace; if lack of money made it difficult to continue a war; or if "important advantages demanded it" (though he did accept that this was the sort of thing you should do "only once – or at most twice – in a lifetime").[32] Allies too could be betrayed if necessary, since "the ruler must always be guided by the interests of the state": for example,

> if one's ally neglects his obligations; if he is thinking of deceiving you and you have no choice but to forestall him; if you are obliged by *force majeure* to break the treaty; and finally if you lack means to continue war. . . . The interest of the state is their law [that of rulers] and this law may not be infringed.[33]

And, once again, it is the history of the period which provides the clearest evidence of this morality in action, showing innumerable instances where states decided to abandon their allies, change alliances, deceive other states, or negotiate a separate peace.

The overriding demands of state interest meant that a ruler should not hesitate to make war if necessary. "When war is necessary to [defend national honour]", Louis XIV declared, "it is an injustice not merely permitted but commended of kings. It is an injustice, on the contrary, when one can dispense with it and obtain the same thing by milder means."[34] So too Frederick the Great declared that "aggressive wars, though detestable if waged for inadequate reasons, are justified if made necessary by the real interests of the state".[35] He believed that "at all times it was the principle of great states to subjugate all whom they could and to extend their power continuously".[36] Louis XIV believed that his aggressive war against the United Provinces in 1672 had enabled him to "instil fear into my antagonists, cause astonishment to my neighbours and despair to my enemies".[37] If war was necessary for these purposes, then the sooner it was made the better. As Frederick the Great wrote:

> A prince ought rather to engage in offensive war than wait till desperate times come on. . . . It is a certain maxim that a prince should rather prevent than be prevented: great men have always been successful when they make use of their forces before their enemies take such measures as tie their hands and suppress their power.[38]

And he himself put this axiom into practice in initiating wars against his opponents in 1740 and 1756.

This cheerful justification of aggressive war was accompanied by an equal willingness to condone widespread brutality in its conduct. Though this may never have quite sunk to the depths achieved in the Thirty Years War just before our age began, war was often undertaken with considerable ruthlessness. The widely expressed belief that this was an age of moderation in warfare has no basis in the historic record. France's two devastations of the Palatinate; the ravaging of Livonia and other occupied territories by Russia during the Great Northern War; the devastation of Bavaria by the troops of the Grand Alliance in 1704; the hardships, financial and other, imposed on Saxony during its occupation by Frederick the Great's forces in the Seven Years War; the sacking of Memes by Russian forces in the same war; not to speak of the vast suffering and losses imposed by Napoleon on his own and other lands (half a million men were lost, in battle, disease, cold or desertion in Russia in 1812) all these demonstrated that the costs of promoting state interest by the means these statesmen advocated were often heavy. These costs were generally seen as unfortunate but inevitable. Few efforts were made to humanise the conduct of war and its effect on civilians. And these for long had, in the view of one historian, "no direct efforts that we can trade. . . . It does not appear . . . that there . . . was any important movement towards the humanising of war or towards limiting its political aims".[39]

The doctrine of *raison d'état* – that the overriding concern of rulers should be with promoting, at any cost, the interests of their own states – thus implied a considerable ruthlessness in the means employed. The belief of the philosophers and lawyers in the emergence of a European community, in which each state recognised obligations to its neighbours in the interests of the greater welfare of all, had little perceptible influence in moderating the policies which were pursued by their rulers. The preoccupation with the interests and independence of individual states which the doctrine of sovereignty promoted far outweighed concern with moral principles and the welfare of the community of states as a whole. The general view was that expressed by the Prussian diplomat, Bielfield in 1760: "One must disabuse oneself of the speculative ideas held by ordinary men about justice, equity, moderation, candour and the other virtues of nations and their rulers. In the end everything depends on power."

LIMITATIONS OF SOVEREIGNTY

But though the idea of sovereignty was increasingly accepted during this period, there was no general agreement about what it implied. In practice its scope was often restricted. State frontiers were not yet allowed to become the impenetrable walls which that theory held them to be. Actions continued to be taken in the territory of other states which were wholly incompatible with the principle of sovereignty as it was later to be understood. The "sovereign equality" which Vattel and the other writers asserted was not usually admitted in practice.

First, non-sovereign entities, though without the influence which they had once enjoyed, continued to play a significant role. Even the popes remained figures of some consequence on the international stage: Alexander VII and Innocent XI, for example, played major roles in organising the wars against the Turks of 1663–4 and 1683–99. The emperors continued to exercise some authority, at least in Germany. They claimed to negotiate on behalf of other German states at Ryswick and Rastott; and during the Great Northern War. Charles VI, acting on behalf of the empire, called a conference to halt the war and if possible neutralise German territory. Though the larger German states were fully independent, the smaller states were, until almost the end of this period, not usually considered to enjoy full sovereignty and had no diplomatic relations with larger states. Tartars and Cossacks each played a significant role till almost the end of the period, representing a substantial military threat even to powerful states. For much of the period, therefore, substantial parts of the continent were still under the control of non-sovereign rulers, frequently owing an acknowledged allegiance to others.

Such rulers were not treated in the same way as those recognised as "sovereign". The relationships they undertook were unlike those undertaken among independent sovereign states (often they were far more complex). Thus the rulers of the principalities of Transylvania, Moldavia and Wallachis, though in practice enjoying an almost totally independent existence, had to purchase this by the payment of regular tribute, sometimes to the emperor, more often to the Turkish sultan, and occasionally to both at once. The city of Ragusa on the Adriatic coast was under the protection of Venice, yet thought it prudent to pay tribute to the Turkish sultan. The duchy of Courland, though recognised to be under Polish "suzerainty", was in practice under the control of Russia, before it passed formally into Russian hands at the end of the eighteenth century. The Barbary states of North Africa, though to all intents and purposes sovereign (signing treaties with the major west European states, for example), continued to recognise the vestigial authority of the Turkish sultan. Substantial parts of Italy were firmly under the control of local rulers or even foreign ones, yet were claimed as "fiefdoms" by pope or emperor (and occasionally, as in the case of Naples and Sicily, by both),[40] with their rights of succession therefore restricted. The age of feudalism was taking a long time to die, and for much of this period its vestiges remained. The system, in other words, remained transitional. A world of fully sovereign states did not come into existence until the period was almost ended.*

This meant that the more powerful states were able to treat some territories in ways wholly inconsistent with the normal rules of sovereignty. Thus the French kings, while they continued to acknowledge in theory the traditional status of Lorraine, progressively eroded its independence. Under the Treaty of the Pyrenees (1659), France was to evacuate French troops from the duchy (which had occupied it during the Thirty Years War), but Mazarin was unwilling to forgo access to the strategically important territory. In 1662, therefore, French forces again occupied strategic points and highways on the grounds that these were essential to French military requirements. In 1670, in preparation for Louis' war against the Dutch (originally expected to begin in the following year) a more full-scale occupation took place, regardless of the fact – indeed provoked by it – that the new duke was not an ally but one of France's most outspoken enemies.[41]

The Duke Charles V, who ruled from 1675, never entered his own territory because of the degree of French control that was maintained there. This control was often maintained with the consent of other powers, including the duke's allies. Under the Treaty of Nymegen of 1678 the duchy was in theory to be returned to its duke, but only on conditions that were quite unacceptable to him: for example, its strategically situated capital, Nancy, was to be given to France (in exchange for Toul which was of no interest to the duke): a humiliation

---

* In the early part of the period many frontiers remained uncertain because of the persistence of ancient feudal relics, having the effect that the immediate overlord owed allegiance to some external sovereign. For a discussion see Clark, *War and Society in the Seventeenth Century*, pp. 141–2: "If a neighbouring sovereign owned an inlying enclave, or an inconveniently intrusive salient . . . the assertion of sovereign rights against him would probably become a matter of high politics."

he was, not surprisingly, unwilling to accept. Similarly under the Treaty of Ryswick (1697) it was agreed that, though in theory the duchy was to be restored, including parts which Louis had purloined through his "reunions", four strategic highways were to be left under French control (which enabled France to reoccupy the duchy without difficulty at the beginning of the War of Spanish Succession five years later). As a result of these arrangements the duchy was for many years under the direct physical control of France, despite the fact that it was nominally independent and its rulers entirely hostile to that country. French control was further strengthened as a result of the War of Polish Succession, when the ruling duke Francis (now married to the Austrian heiress) was prevailed on to hand over his territories to Leszynski, the French king's father in law, with reversion to France on his death. Only when he finally died, in 1766, did the duchy finally come under full French sovereignty. For nearly a century, therefore, though the status of the duchy remained formally unchanged, in practice its independence was progressively eroded, and its territory frequently used by France for her own strategic purposes.

There were many other cases where the normal right of a ruler to control the military situation in his own land was denied. One concerned the Holstein-Gottorp territories. The situation there was even more complex than in Lorraine. The dukes were independent rulers, in continual conflict with their neighbours, the rulers of Denmark. One of the territories, Holstein was a part of the empire, while Schleswig was not; yet under a declaration of 1460 the two territories were supposed to be eternally linked. In addition the lands were not continuous but mixed up, higgledy-piggledy, with those of the Danish king, some of which were crown lands, while some belonged to the Danish state. Because of their strategic importance, threatening his own, the Danish king demanded to control the freedom of the dukes to fortify their own territories: he claimed that under treaties reached during the 1650s he enjoyed a *jus armorum*, that is a right to veto the fortification of the territories.[42] It was on these grounds that in 1697 he occupied the territories with his forces and demolished the duke's fortresses. And it was on the same grounds that when the duke presumed to rebuild these fortifications, with Sweden's support, the Danish king once more sent in his troops, so precipitating the Great Northern War (1700–21).

Military limitations of this kind did not even need always to depend on a feudal relationship. They could be imposed on states which were

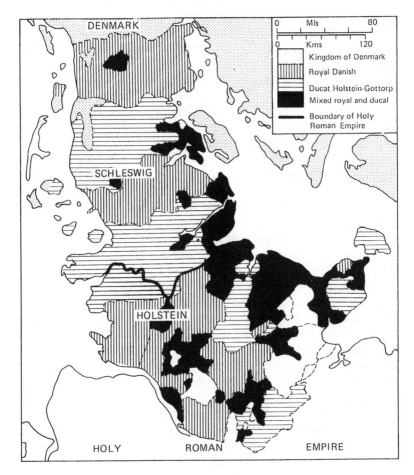

MAP 1   *The duchies of Schleswig and Holstein (showing territories of the king of Denmark and the duke of Holstein-Gottorp)*
SOURCE: R. M. Hatton, *Europe in the Age of Louis XIV* (London, 1969) p. 223.

nominally sovereign. Thus in 1716, and again after the first partition of 1772, Poland, though still universally regarded as a sovereign state, was obliged by a treaty with Russia to limit the size of its armed forces to suit the latter's strategic requirements. In other words, its weakness deprived it of the normal attributes of sovereignty.

Strategic concerns caused other restrictions on sovereignty. One of the most bizarre examples occurred in the southern Netherlands.

From the middle of the seventeenth century Dutch leaders had been continually concerned about the vulnerability of their lands to attack from France across that usually poorly defended territory (then under weak Spanish rule): a nervousness increased after the blatant French aggression in 1672. During the Nine Years War the Dutch, having occupied the territory, built fortifications there; and they were then unwilling to lose the strategic advantages they provided. Soon after the war was ended, therefore, in 1698, they reached agreement with the Spanish king, then an ally, to be allowed to garrison fortresses in the territory in peacetime as well. But after the Bourbon succession in Spain two years later, the Dutch garrisons were quickly evicted by the French. It was then agreed within the Grand Alliance that to safeguard the United Provinces, a new barrier would be restored on the conclusion of the subsequent wars. Although there were serious differences, both among the allies and between the Dutch and the Austrians, about the exact scale and situation of the barrier, in 1715 agreement was finally reached for the construction of a string of fortresses, to be manned by Dutch troops, across the territory.[43] By this agreement Austria (which inherited Spanish rights in the southern Netherlands) was placed under an obligation to allow foreign forces to occupy strategic positions within her own territory. She also had to devote a third of the territory's entire revenue to defraying the costs of maintaining them. She had to agree to maintain a very low tariff on goods imported from her neighbour to the north. Finally she was obliged to agree (as Spain had done before) to keep the river Scheldt, the territory's principal waterway on which the trade of Antwerp would otherwise have travelled, permanently closed to traffic. Those restrictions, at heavy cost to the people of the territory as well as to Austria, were designed to suit the military and commercial convenience of the Dutch. And though Austria made a major effect to end them, even briefly attempting to use armed force for the purpose in 1784–5, these extraordinary restrictions of sovereignty remained unchanged until the French revolutionary forces liberated Belgium in the following decade.

Another widespread breach of the normal rights of sovereignty, also serving the military needs of outside powers, was the practice of crossing, or occupying for a considerable period, the territory of neutral states, with or without permission. This had occurred in the age before (for example, during the Thirty Years War) imperial forces had occupied the territory of neutral Brandenberg for substantial periods. It now became common practice. At the beginning of his war against the Dutch in 1672 Louis XIV marched his forces without authority across the Spanish Netherlands, at a time when Spain was in no way engaged in that war. Russian troops, from the time of Peter the Great onwards, habitually crossed Polish territory to reach the West, whether or not Poland herself was engaged in the war in question. International lawyers sometimes accepted such a right: Grotius, for example, accepted the right of *transitus innoxius* (harmless passage), so long as local residents were protected and compensation was paid for damages if necessary. But military occupation took place for other reasons, regardless of the wishes of the ruler concerned. Under the Treaty of Seville of 1729, France and Britain agreed that Spain should send forces to occupy Parma, as a guarantee that the territory would subsequently be handed over to a Spanish prince, even at a time when the previous ruler was still alive and without regard to his views; and Spanish forces occupied Tuscany (with British assistance) in 1731, to ensure that that territory too should pass on the death of its ruler to the same Spanish prince.

There were other reasons why a state's sovereignty might be limited. In some cases external powers demanded and obtained the right to "protect" particular religious minorities. Although in general, as we have seen, the assumption was made in this age that individual rulers and governments had the right to determine the religion which would be practised by all their subjects – a principle not only enshrined in the Peace of Westphalia for Germany but put into effect in practice in other places, such as England, France and Spain, not affected by those provisions – external powers, if strong enough, often sought to protect the right of particular religious minorities elsewhere. They were able sometimes to extract undertakings defining the obligations of the weaker state. For example, under the Perpetual Peace reached between Russia and Poland in 1686, Poland accepted the obligation to grant religious freedom to her Orthodox subjects, and the right of the Russian tsar to ensure that that freedom was protected: a right which Peter the Great exercised by sending a commission to Poland to report on the religious freedom of the Orthodox population there in 1722. Russia also secured the right to intervene on behalf of Orthodox believers within the Ottoman empire. She first demanded that right, without success, during the negotiations for the Treaty of Constantinople in 1699–1700. She renewed the demand at the conclusion of her successful war against Turkey in 1768–74. And as a result, under the Treaty of Kutchuk-kainarji she secured for herself the right to protect the

Orthodox church "and those who serve it" in Constantinople. Sometimes more than one external power agreed together to intervene in that way. Thus in treaties of 1703, 1705 and 1707 Prussia and Sweden agreed together to act to protect the rights of Protestants in Poland. In other cases territories were handed over only on condition that a particular religion was protected. Under the Peace of Nymegen, Maastricht was returned to the United Provinces by France only on the condition that the Catholic faith was re-established there. And at the conclusion of the following war she returned the "reunion" territories in Alsace to the emperor only on condition that Roman Catholicism should be the dominant religion there: a provision entirely acceptable to the emperor but not at all welcome to his Protestant allies.*

A still more drastic limitation of sovereignty occurred where a state's right to determine its own constitutional system was limited by external powers. In 1667, for example, Sweden and Brandenberg entered into a treaty pledging both powers to maintain the existing constitutional system in Poland (that is, a constitution which, by virtue of the *liberum veto*, would keep Poland weak). In 1675 the Russian tsar and the emperor signed an agreement pledging them to oppose any restrictions of the rights of the nobles in Poland (rights which the Polish king, John Sobieski, was seeking to limit). In 1686 two new treaties were agreed, between Sweden and Brandenberg and between Sweden and the emperor, for the same purpose. This tradition of oversight was renewed in the next century. In 1720, in the first of a series of such treaties, Peter the Great and Frederick William of Prussia agreed to act to maintain the existing Polish constitution (which provided for an elected king and the *liberum veto*, that is a veto for every single delegate in the Polish parliament, so effectively paralysing it).[44] After the Polish civil war of 1767–8

---

* It would be tempting to see these interventions on behalf of religious minorities as anticipating those undertaken on human rights grounds in recent times. The motives, however, in this age had little to do with religious freedom (which was rarely accorded by the intervening powers themselves). Almost invariably the concern was with one faith only. Louis' concern in the case of Alsace was to secure recognition of the Catholic faith, not toleration (for which he was hardly renowned). Russian concern in the Ottoman empire was confined to the Orthodox faith. Nor was the latter's concern entirely for religious motives. Greater toleration was accorded within the Ottoman lands than anywhere else in Europe and, as Western observers correctly understood, both then and in the 1850s, Russia's motive was not so much to influence the practice of the Orthodox faith but to acquire a justification for continuing influence at the Ottoman court.

Russia secured for herself under treaties of 1768 and 1775 a recognised right of intervention to maintain the constitution. And when she intervened on a massive scale in 1792 to overthrow a new and more liberal Polish government, established under a reformed constitution, she explicitly justified this action on the basis of that provision.[45]

The right of Sweden to alter her constitution was limited in the same way. Under the Treaty of Nystag of 1721 which brought the Great War of the North to an end, Russia "guaranteed" the Swedish constitution of 1720 which provided for a parliamentary system of government in Sweden and limited the power of the king. It was generally accepted that the purpose of this guarantee was to keep Sweden, so often a danger to Russia in the past under their powerful Vasa kings, weaker than she would have been under a royal ruler: Frederick the Great clearly acknowledged this motive when, in his second *Political Testament*, he declared that it was better for Sweden's neighbours if a "republican" (that is, parliamentary) government remained in power there "because there is more vigour in a government run by one person than one run by many". On these grounds he expressed the view (in his first *Political Testament*) that a coup to restore royal rule could only take place when Russia was distracted by war, since otherwise "the sovereign would risk seeing himself dethroned by the opposition party, supported by Russian arms".[46] In this case, too, more than one government was sometimes involved in maintaining the restrictions: thus in a treaty of 1667 Denmark joined Russia in guaranteeing the existing Swedish constitution. Such constraints did not always work. Gustav III did succeed in restoring autocratic rule in 1772 (in precisely the circumstances recommended by Frederick, since Russia was involved with war against Turkey at the time), and was then determined to bring the arrangement to an end. A major objective in his war against Russia in 1788–90 was to secure a renunciation of her alleged right to "guarantee" Sweden's constitution. And though the war failed in other respects, he did succeed in the subsequent treaty in inducing the Russian government to abandon that right and to recognise his own absolutist constitution of 1772.

The United Provinces was another country in which political change was limited by external powers. That country had traditionally alternated, as in Sweden, between periods of relative autocracy when a dominant influence was held by the Orange family, holding the position of Stadtholder, and others when power was more widely dispersed. Her powerful neighbour Prussia, and to a lesser extent

Britain, both preferred rule by the House of Orange, seeing such rulers as the most likely to resist French influence. When the Patriotic Party, under strong French influence, acquired political power in 1787–7 and overturned the Stadtholder, the Prussian king issued an ultimatum demanding his return to power (the Stadtholder's wife was his sister). He then proceeded to invade with 25,000 men. In consequence he was able, with British support, to ensure the restoration of the Stadtholder and of the previous constitution. In a Treaty of 1788 the two governments agreed that they would act together to maintain the "form of government" in the United Provinces "against any attack or enterprise, direct or indirect", in total disregard of that country's sovereignty. Once again two external powers agreed among themselves what type of government they would permit to hold power in a third.

In all these cases, therefore, external powers demanded the right of veto over constitutional change in neighbouring countries, often seeing major political change as a threat to their own security interests (much as super-powers were to intervene to prevent political change two hundred years later). They therefore reserved the right to intervene where necessary to restore the type of constitution that best suited their own interests. It is difficult to conceive of a more radical violation of the doctrines of sovereignty than this represented.[47]

Rights of sovereignty were also breached when intervention occurred on questions of succession. Here too neighbouring powers sometimes sought to exercise the right to veto successions which were unacceptable to them. The War of Spanish Succession was fought to prevent Spain from having the heir to the throne which her former king had designated and the one the majority of the Spanish people manifestly preferred. The War of Polish Succession was fought to prevent Poland having the king who had been elected by the Polish parliament under due constitutional procedures. The War of Bavarian Succession was fought to prevent the Elector of Bavaria being allowed to make arrangements for his succession which he had entered into of his own free will. At the conclusion of her war with Sweden in 1743, Russia demanded an explicit veto over succession to the throne there. In other words, questions concerning succession, which in other ages had been seen as falling entirely within the sovereign rights of the people concerned, in this age were believed to be of significant interest to other states as well, if only because they could affect the balance of power in the continent as a whole (see Chapter 6 below).

But the most frequent violation of sovereignty was of a kind which (unlike most of the others described) was to remain frequent in later ages: intervention to assist a revolutionary movement. This was recognised as contrary to the recognised rules of the system (we have seen the horror with which Louis regarded revolution against a legitimate ruler), and was sometimes rejected on these grounds: thus British ministers declined to accept Marlborough's proposal to provide substantial assistance to the revolt in the Cévennes during the War of Spanish Succession, on the grounds that this would be a breach of sovereignty. More often such scruples were thrown aside, especially when two countries were at war. Louis XIV had no hesitation in providing every possible assistance to the Portuguese rebels in Spain, both before and after he himself had made peace with Spain. He sought to assist rebel factions in England when he was at war with that country in 1666.[48] He gave lavish assistance to the Hungarian rebels against the Austrian emperor, both in 1678–82 and in 1702–10. And he helped James II in his unavailing efforts to recover his throne in Ireland in 1679–80. Later, Jacobite pretenders in England were assisted by the governments of France (several times from 1707–8 to 1745), Spain (1716), Sweden (1718–19) and other countries. The emperor supported Hungarian rebels against Turkey in 1661–2, just as the Turks assisted Hungarian rebels against the emperor twenty years later. Russia helped Cossack rebels against Poland in 1653–4, just as Poland helped them against Russia a few years later.

Such activities were frequently explicitly prohibited in the treaties of the period.[49] Louis XIV had to agree in the Peace of Utrecht not only that he would not recognise the claims of the Stuarts in Britain (as he had already done in the Peace of Ryswick) but that he would give them no assistance. The Ottoman Turks had to agree under the Treaty of Passarowitz (1718) not only that they would not assist the Hungarian rebel leader, Rakosi, but that they would ensure that he was kept away from the frontier of Hungary. These were understandable precautions by threatened governments. But such undertakings were rarely observed. Louis XIV promised in the most explicit terms under the Treaty of the Pyrenees that he would provide no assistance to Portuguese rebelling against Spanish rule, even agreeing that the Spanish king could take any French ship found within 50 miles of the Spanish coast. But, after describing these undertakings in his *Memoires*, he detailed the ways in which he had proceeded to flout them and freely admitted to his successor that he did not feel in any way bound by them. He claimed that the Spanish themselves "however profoundly we have been at peace with them . . . have never failed to foment our domestic discords and our civil wars" (they had done so in a small way during the Fronde, but the two countries had then been at war) and said he "could not doubt that they had been the first to violate the Treaty of the Pyrenees in a thousand ways". He produced no evidence of this, however, and concluded, with dubious logic: "The more extraordinary, reiterated and ringed with precautions were the clauses that prohibited me from assisting this still shaky crown [Portugal's], the more this indicated that I was not expected to comply."[50] Most other rulers found little difficulty in finding equally compelling reasons for violating their treaty obligations.*

Interventions of other kinds were no less common. It was normal for governments to seek to influence political affairs in other states. Often they had, as we saw, many prominent politicians directly in their pay. France was the most often able to influence events in that way: a substantial number of politicians in Sweden, the United Provinces, England (including the Stuart kings) and other countries received regular payments from her. The British were active in some countries: both Catherine II before she became empress, and Bestuzhev, the most powerful Russian minister, were in British pay during the 1750s. Occasionally alliances could be disrupted and ministries overturned by direct approaches to local politicians. Thus, according to one historian, the "decisive influence" in causing England to abandon her alliance with France and make peace with the United Provinces in 1674 was "a campaign of clandestine Dutch intervention in English domestic politics": a campaign that "established a pattern of intervention by rival European powers that continued until 1688".[51] The French government intervened equally actively in the reverse direction: to ensure that English politicians did not decide to

---

* There was however a sense in which the principles of sovereignty none the less triumphed. The assistance that was given to minorities in this way was wholly self-interested: designed to cause the maximum embarrassment to a foreign ruler, especially in time of war. It was rarely believed, and quite possibly not intended, that a rebel faction would actually succeed, and that a legitimate ruler should be overthrown altogether. Thus, in the peace treaties which were signed at the end of each conflict, the minorities who had been so enthusiastically supported during the preceding wars were forgotten altogether: the Hungarian Catholics, the Catalan autonomists, the Jacobite pretenders, the Huguenot rebels, who had been so strenuously assisted, were ignored and occasionally explicitly repudiated. They were thus left to face inevitable retribution, sometimes savage (as all these were to discover). In the final resort they were expendable. The principles of sovereignty once more prevailed.

go to war against them. They established "clandestine connections with leaders of the Country opposition, bribing some of the most active to wreck Danby's policy of pressing for entry into the war against France", and later assisted opposition leaders to make a "lethal attack" against Danby which caused him to be dismissed.[52] Later Louis "systematically and regularly intervened in the politics of other western European states: French diplomats encouraged and subsidised opposition groups to obstruct government policy that conflicted with those of France. . . . The technique of intervention varied. . . . The giving of "presents" to minor rulers and ministers everywhere was a matter of routine and accepted as legitimate."[53] Not only monarchs, through their diplomats and other agents, but also politicians of other kinds would seek to influence foreign governments. For example in 1710 the States-General of the United Provinces presented a memorial to Queen Anne, asking her not to dissolve the British parliament: though this caused some indignation in England it was by no means exceptional by the standards of this day.

The notion of "sovereignty" which emerged in this period was thus not clearly defined. It provided no exact measure of the degree or type of independence which a state could expect to enjoy. There continued to be many political entities which were not regarded as "sovereign". Even in those that were, intervention of many kinds was still habitually undertaken. In theory the establishment of sovereign states, each independent, and each free from interference or attack from outside, might have served to create a more stable and peaceful international community. But because sovereignty was not clearly defined, and because it certainly was not always respected, no such ordered system was established.

BOOKS

Contemporary works

J. J. Bodin, *Six Books of the Republic* (1576), English trs. (Oxford, 1755) esp. Book I, ch. 10 and Book II, on sovereignty and royal power.

J. B. Bossuet, *Politique tirée des propres paroles de l'Ecriture sainte* (Paris, 1709) esp. Book IV, on royal authority.

T. Hobbes, *Leviathan* (London, 1651) especially chs XVIII–XX on sovereigns and sovereignty.

N. Machiavelli, *The Prince* (1532), English trs. (London, 1935).
Duc de Rohan, *Intérêts et maximes des princes d'etats souverains* (Paris, 1640).
J. Rousset, *Les intérêts presens et les pretensions des puissances de l'Europe* (Cologne, 1685).

Modern works

P. Anderson, *Lineages of the Absolutist State* (London, 1974).
A. G. Bruun, *The Enlightened Despot* (New York, 1967).
F. Hartung, *Enlightened Despotism* (London, 1957).
F. H. Hinsley, *Sovereignty* (London, 1966).
Alan James, *State Sovereignty* (London, 1988).
F. Meinecke, *Machiavellism: The Doctrine of Raison d'État and its Place in Modern History* (New Haven, Conn. 1957).
A. Sorel, *Europe and the French Revolution, 1885–95*, vol. 1: *The Political Traditions of the Old Regime*, English trs. (London, 1969).

5 Status

One of the most deeply felt concerns of rulers in this age was to win status. Such a concern was not, of course, new. But in earlier centuries, in a period of dynastic competition, it was the status of the rulers themselves, and of their royal houses, which had been at stake. It was this which was disputed during the thirty-year rivalry between Charles V and Francis I, in the competitive display of Francis and Henry VIII at the Field of the Cloth of Gold, in the long struggle between Angevins and Aragonese rulers in Italy. In the age we are concerned with, though personal standing was rarely forgotten, it was not the essential prize which was in dispute. The central concern was with the positions occupied by the *states* with which the rulers increasingly identified themselves. As Louis XIV put it: "The virtue of the good ruler is always aiming at . . . the greatness and the glory of his state".[1] Frederick the Great equally, the self-declared "first servant" of his own state, wrote of his concern that Prussia might "cut a fine figure among the great powers of the world".[2] Similar ambitions were shared by even the most insignificant rulers of the day. Even the minor rulers of Germany and Italy vied with each other to assert their rank and prestige within their own lesser world. All were equally concerned to establish the standing they (and therefore their states) enjoyed among their peers.[3]

Personal glory was still important if only because it could win glory also for the state. So Louis XIV advised his successor that he should not shun the limelight: "The first thought . . . of rulers must be what may or may not win the adulation of the public. The kings, who are born to possess everything and command over everything, must not be ashamed to accede to renown."[4] This ambition must therefore be a constant concern, since "a lofty heart . . . cannot be fully satisfied except by glory".[5] Frederick the Great, too, was concerned with the reputation of his royal house as well as that of his state: he told his foreign minister that he had "made it a point of honour to have contributed more than anyone to the aggrandisement of my House".[6] But this search for glory, whether for the sovereign or his state, meant that new triumphs had continually to be won. Glory, Louis declared, was "not a mistress who can be neglected, nor is one even worthy of her first favour if one does not always wish for new ones".[7] Only through ever-new successes could a reputation, once acquired, be maintained: "it is not enough to have acquired it without constantly seeking for its protection".[8]

But it was not sufficient for a state to be glorious: it was important that it should be *more* glorious than others. Reputation was inevitably seen in comparative terms. As Louis commented about the most conspicuous rivalry of his age, between the Bourbon and Hapsburg dynasties, "the state of the two crowns of France and Spain is such today . . . that it is almost impossible to raise one without humbling the other", for between them there was "an essential jealousy" and a "permanent enmity".[9] Each "in working against the other, is less conscious of harming another than of sustaining and preserving itself".

This meant that one way to win standing for one's own state was to bring about the maximum humiliation for another. Louis himself specialised in actions designed to achieve this. In 1662, after a fracas between the pope's Corsican guards and servants of the French ambassador in Rome, he not only occupied the papal enclave at Avignon and threatened to send an army into Rome, but compelled the pope to send his brother, Mario Chigi, to Versailles to deliver an abject apology. Not content with this, he secured a promise from the pope that he would never again employ Corsican guards and a commitment to erect a memorial in Rome commemorating the triumph Louis had secured.[10] In the early stages of his war against the Dutch he demanded, as a condition of peace, that the republic should send an annual mission to his court, bearing a gold medal, offering their people's heartfelt thanks for allowing them to retain their independence.[11] In 1684, after the republic of Genoa had defied his demand that it should cease its traditional contacts with Spain (with which France was at war), he subjected the city to a severe bombardment and compelled the aged Doge to travel to Versailles to perform a solemn act of repentance and beg the king for forgiveness for having incurred his anger. Other states were only a little less vindictive. In 1746, after Genoa had dared to join Austria's enemies during the War of Austrian Succession (on the not-unreasonable grounds that Austria was planning to transfer some of Genoa's territory as a reward to her ally Savoy) the Austrian commander, having conquered the city, proposed that the Doge and six senators should repair to Vienna to implore forgiveness, and that four senators should be delivered as hostages for the fulfilment of this demand. (Eventually Maria Theresa contented herself with demanding the payment of a substantial fine.)

The competition for status could take many forms. Rulers would vie in the comparative splendour of royal palaces and other public buildings. Once again the pattern was set by Louis XIV. In the vast sums he spent (to the consternation of Colbert, his Minister of Finance) in building – simultaneously – the splendours of Versailles and the Louvre, he asserted the pre-eminence of *le roi soleil* among the monarchs of Europe and of France among its states. In constructing the huge palace of Schönbrunn the emperor Leopold was partly motivated by the express desire to match the scale and glory of Versailles; and his successor Charles VI, in transforming the Kloster-neuburg Abbey near Vienna into a palace, was explicitly concerned to rival the Escorial of his arch-rival, Philip V of Spain. Frederick Wilhelm of Prussia, in constructing his own lavish palace at Potsdam, was equally concerned with establishing his place among the rulers of Europe. Even the lesser states of Germany could not afford to be altogether left out in this competition. In the twenty years after the completion of Versailles, palaces comparable in style and scale were built at Stuttgart, Mannheim, Munich, Berlin and Rastatt. As Frederick the Great pointed out, "there is no prince, down to the younger member with an apanage, who does not imagine himself to be a Louis XIV: he builds his Versailles, has his mistresses, and maintains an army".[12] Or they could compete, more usefully, in the munificence of their patronage of the arts, the renown of their opera houses, or the design of their royal parks.

A more coveted source of prestige was the renown of a state's armed forces. Even if they were not used, these could impress opponents and allies alike. Louis recommended to his successor: "Always be in a position to inspire fear by your arms, but employ them only if necessary"[13] (so anticipating the famous aphorism of Theodore Roosevelt, another statesman concerned with the standing of his country in the eyes of the world). The standing armies, which were everywhere created in this age, thus needed to compete, not only in military effectiveness but in the smartness of their apparel and the splendour of their uniforms. Regiments of glittering hussars, gleaming artillery and well-drilled infantrymen could do much to enhance the status even of relatively small and impoverished states. The Duke of Württenburg, determined to imitate Prussia's much-admired army, tripled the size of his small force, provided them with magnificent equipment and drilled them so severely that the English traveller, Burney, compared them to clocks; and he placed them under the command of 18 generals, 22 colonels, and so many lieutenants that, according to Burney, "one met only officers in the street".[14] The Elector Palatine, though by no means wealthy, at one time possessed 30 regiments, of which a quarter of the manpower consisted of officers; and, though without a seaboard, boasted a Grand Admiral commanding a few small craft which he sailed up and down the Rhine.[15] And the Emperor Francis I spoke for many in declaring, on being asked by his wife for his opinion about the future conduct of Austrian policy: "The best means to win the respect of adversaries . . . keep friends and gain new allies are a beautiful large army and the funds to maintain it ready for operation."[16]

But the surest way for a state and its ruler to win status was through success in war. Louis XIV acknowledged this in declaring that "if I sometimes inclined ever so slightly towards war, this was because it was undoubtedly the most brilliant way to acquire glory";[17] and even admitted that he would "always . . . have preferred conquering states to acquiring them [by negotiation]".[18] Sometimes war was a duty: "when war is necessary, it is in justice not merely permitted, but commended of kings. It is an injustice on the contrary when one can dispense with it and obtain the same thing by milder means".[19] The brother of Pomponne, the foreign minister who Louis dismissed for not securing sufficiently advantageous terms at the conclusion of his war against the United Provinces, fully recognised the attractions of successful war for the ruler seeking prestige: "There is the greatest pleasure for a prince in love with glory", he wrote, "in seeing himself at the head of a victorious army, able to carry his conquests where he pleases"; and he accepted that undoubtedly Louis "rose to greater fame because the war continued".[20] Frederick the Great, after his conquest of Silesia in 1740, admitted that he had done it partly from a "desire for glory. . . . The satisfaction of seeing my name in the papers, and later in the history books, seduced me".[21] This belief in the unique prestige to be acquired by success in war probably partly accounts for the frequency with which rulers themselves appeared at the head of their armies in the field during this age. Apart from Louis himself (whose presence was symbolic rather than functional), the kings of Sweden, Poland and England (William III) led their forces in battle during the seventeenth century. In the next century the kings of Sweden and Russia both took personal command of their troops during the Great Northern War; while in the War of Austrian Succession the rulers of France, Prussia, Britain, Sardinia, Naples, as well as the emperor and his brother, all took the field with their forces. All in consequence were able to enjoy a significant share of the glory when they were successful.

It was, of course, recognised, that there was a price to pay for glory won in this way. Thus, after commenting on the glory that Louis had secured in his war against the Dutch, the brother of Pomponne remarked: "If we consider how much blood and how many millions this glory cost us, there may be a few to hold it bought most dearly."[22] Even Louis himself was willing at the end of his life to accept that he "had perhaps loved war too much" and advised his great-grandson on his death-bed that he should "always choose peace before the dubious fortunes of war, and remember that the most glorious victory is too dearly bought if it must be paid for in the blood of your subjects". Maria Theresa reproached herself for having made "war out of pride",[23] and she did everything possible to frustrate her son's desire to acquire Bavaria by war in 1777–8, emphasising the likely cost and the precarious balance of forces.[24] Such sentiments, however, were scarcely typical of the age. There was usually little reluctance to commit a state to war-like action if gain was to be expected, especially where prestige was believed to be at stake. Both the rulers and the great ministers who served them saw this as one of the most favourable ways to establish the reputation of their own states, and if necessary cast humiliation on their rivals. In this way, it was hoped, they could make unmistakably clear the relative position which each enjoyed in the eyes of contemporary international society.

PRECEDENCE

The easiest way to establish the status each state enjoyed was by the creation of a recognised order of precedence. For a state to be admired it had to be self-evidently greater, more glorious, of higher status, than its rivals. A visible pecking-order was required to register this.

The search for such a pecking-order was manifested above all in the continual disputes which took place about "precedence": as shown, for example, in the honours accorded to the ambassadors of the different rulers on ceremonial occasions. Just as, among the citizens of a single state, there always existed an order of precedence indicating the courtesies that were to be accorded to each, and the order in which they should be placed at a dinner-table or pass through a doorway, so among the diplomatic representatives of different states a similar order of precedence needed to be established. For this purpose few accepted the myth, as propounded by Vattel, for example, of "sovereign equality" among states. It was generally recognised that some were more powerful and important than others, and some rulers therefore more prestigious.*

It was widely accepted that the Holy Roman Emperor ranked higher than any other ruler.** This derived from the ancient lineage of the empire, tracing its ancestry to Charlemagne, its association with the established church, and its continuing influence in Germany, as well as the extent of the domains which the existing emperors ruled directly.[25] Even this widely accepted tradition, however, was not acknowledged by Louis XIV. He disputed the notion that the existing German empire was in any way comparable to the empire of Charlemagne. The Hapsburg emperors who had "appropriated" the dignity were, he declared, "in no way comparable and should be considered merely as heads, or captains-general, of a republic, rather than by comparison with any other state".[26] He deplored the fact that the popes had "gradually given precedence at the court of Rome to the ambassadors of the emperor over all the others and that most of the courts of christendom have imitated this example". He claimed that there were tenth-century treaties naming the kings of France before the emperor, and he would not "in any way tolerate anything new by which these princes might affect to assume the least superiority over me". This view about the relative status of the two sovereigns led to a major incident at the court of the Turkish sultan. When the Grand Vizier, Ahmed Köprolu, received an imperial ambassador with great honours in 1667, the French ambassador demanded that he should be accorded still greater ceremony. When the Grand Vizier did not immediately agree, the French ambassador, bearing in mind his instructions, became so enraged that he threw down his role of capitulation (of which he was seeking a renewal) in front of the Grand Vizier: the latter, claiming that he had been struck, caused the

---

* A rough idea of the relative standing of the principal European states is provided by William Penn's *Scheme for a European Federation*, published in 1691. This awarded 12 delegates to the empire, 10 to France and Spain, 8 to "Italy", 6 to England, 4 to Sweden, the United Provinces and Poland, 3 to Portugal and Denmark, 2 to the Swiss cantons, and 1 each to Holstein and Courland.

**In 1504 Pope Julius II had composed a table of precedence, in theory based on the antiquity of the states concerned, under which the emperor ranked first, the king of France second, the king of Spain third, followed by the rulers of Burgundy, Portugal, England, Savoy and so on.

ambassador to be detained for a short while and nearly caused a total rupture of relations. Given the importance for Louis of the Turkish connection, the incident is a striking indication of the importance attached to such matters.[27]

At least as important to the French monarch was his competition for precedence with the Spanish king. All over Europe ambassadors of the two countries competed to be accorded the higher place by the governments to which they were accredited: for example, in the scale of the honours accorded to them or the positions which they were allowed to occupy on ceremonial occasions. An indication of the importance attached to the struggle is given by an incident which took place in London in 1661. One of the main ceremonial occasions when questions of precedence arose was the arrival at the court in question of a new ambassador. In that year a new Swedish ambassador arrived in London. Louis XIV however, was determined not to accept the compromise frequently adopted to avoid conflicts on such matters, under which no other ambassadors attended such occasions, so that an unseemly battle for precedence could be avoided (see below). He specifically instructed his ambassador that " he should not fail to send his coach to him and procure the first rank". The ambassador accordingly brought with him from France four or five hundred men from his own and his son's regiment; while the Spanish ambassador, not to be outdone, had (according to Louis) "armed more than two thousand men and spent about five thousand livres" to secure his own supporters. The English king, fearing a disturbance, had stationed guards, as well as issuing instructions to the people of London not to take any part in the proceedings. But despite this there was a substantial battle and many were killed on both sides. Louis took the opportunity to break off diplomatic relations and (having only recently concluded a successful war with Spain) sent an envoy to the Spanish court to demand an abject apology. So important was the question to him that, if necessary, he told his son, he would have "found cause for satisfaction in a legitimate war where I could acquire honour at the head of my army". After prolonged negotiations the Spanish government capitulated. It agreed to send an ambassador extraordinary to Louis to announce that Spain's diplomatic representatives all over Europe would "abstain from competition with my [Louis'] ambassadors and ministers in all public ceremonies that my ambassadors and ministers might attend". Louis made the ambassador read out this humiliating undertaking in the presence of all the ambassadors, residents and envoys of other states at Versailles and asked the latter to communicate the contents to their masters, so that they might know "that the Catholic King had issued orders for his ambassadors to cede the precedence to mine on every occasion". He commented to his successor that he did not know "whether anything was transpired since the beginning of the monarchy that is more glorious for it", having received the homage "of king to king, crown to crown, which could not leave even our enemies any longer in doubt that ours is the first of all Christendom".[28]

Even a century later similar incidents occurred from time to time. In 1768 the French ambassador in London, seeing that the Russian ambassador had preceded him at a court ball in a front seat next to the Austrian ambassador, climbed over the benches to insert himself bodily between them: an action that caused such affront that it gave rise to a duel in which the Russian ambassador was seriously wounded.[29]

Because of the difficulties such conflicts caused there was often a willingness, and even a desire, among ambassadors not to attend ceremonial occasions where disputes over precedence were likely to arise. Charles II personally asked ambassadors not to attend at the entry of other ambassadors to his court in order to avoid incidents, and this course had been adopted in London at the entry of the Venetian ambassador in 1660. On other occasions ambassadors themselves decided to stay away for the same reason. Louis' own ambassador, d'Estrades, had recommended this course of action on the occasion of the entry of the Swedish ambassador in 1661, but had been overruled by Louis. Louis commented that ambassadors, because of "their station, their age, their inclinations and their purposes" were often timorous on such matters and likely to be a "little more afraid of war than I was".[30] If other ambassadors stayed away, this was, in his mind, a triumph: he prided himself that, since he had secured precedence throughout Europe, it had been "a long time since the Spanish ambassadors either in Rome or in Venice had been present at the public ceremonies that mine attended". This demonstrated that "at no time, not even in the most flourishing state of their monarchy, had it succeeded in establishing the equality to which it aspired".[31]

Somewhat similar conflicts occurred on the question of naval salutes. It became common for the naval vessels of one state to demand that those of another should dip their flags as a mark of respect when they met at sea. This had given rise to disputes for many years and there had been serious incidents between France and

England in 1603. Richelieu, in his *Testament politique*, had proposed a sensible compromise. French vessels meeting English ones off the English coast would give the first salute and lower their flags; English vessels would accord the same honours to French ships off the French coast; elsewhere neither would do so. Alternatively, the larger fleet would be saluted by the smaller one. It did not matter which course was taken, he pointed out, so long as there was equality of treatment.[32] Neither had been adopted, and disputes continued to arise. One of the major issues in the first two Anglo-Dutch wars in the middle of the seventeenth century was the demand of England that Dutch ships should dip their flags when meeting English ships off the coast of England: a question resolved in England's favour at the end of the the first war in 1654 and confirmed at the close of the second in 1667.

But it was, once again, France which was particularly insistent on such questions: as Colbert correctly reported, Louis was "extremely jealous about salutes and points of honour". In his *Memoires* he prided himself on the fact that, when a French fleet carrying a French bride for the Portuguese heir to the throne met a Spanish fleet on the way, the French ships refused to respond when the Spanish commander lowered his pennant. He displayed a similar attitude to disputes with the United Provinces on the matter (even at a time when the two countries were allies against England) in 1666–7.[33] And he had conflicts with England on the same question. A French diplomat provisionally reached an agreement, somewhat on the lines proposed by Richelieu, giving precedence to the English in the North Sea provided the English showed similar respect to the French in the Atlantic. But Louis would not accept this, and the agreement was disowned. As a result, for some time the two navies deliberately avoided each other (even when they were allies) in order not to precipitate the issue. In 1678 Louis sent a French squadron into Genoese waters to demand the first salute, and when this was refused proceeded to bombard the city. In 1687 a French fleet compelled a Dutch vice-admiral to salute him and in the following year a battle took place between the two countries over the same issue. But it was, once more, above all with Spain that such disputes occurred. In 1679–80 French admirals were instructed to pursue Spanish ships and challenge them if they did not salute first. In 1685 a French fleet demanded the salute from a Spanish fleet and attacked it, causing many casualties.[34]

There were somewhat similar disputes over gunfire salutes. These too were seen as a manifestation of respect from one ruler to another, demanded especially by a stronger state from a weaker one. Thus, in a treaty with the ruler of Algiers in 1681 France demanded, and obtained, an assurance that any French vessel anchoring in the harbour of Algiers would not only be saluted, but that it would be saluted with more guns than the ships of any other country. The demand for such salutes could be used, therefore, not only to indicate the respect shown to the French monarch by a foreign ruler, it could demonstrate the *relative* respect shown to France, compared with all other states. France claimed after all, as Colbert proudly declared, "that all other nations must bow down to her at sea and at the court of Kings".

There were, therefore, a number of ways during this age in which the relative ranking of states could be publicly demonstrated. In an age when huge importance was attached to such questions, the great rulers and their ministers devoted considerable activity to ensuring that the marks of respect accorded to their own states corresponded to the status which they had no doubt they ought to be accorded.

TITLES

One of the effects of competition for status was the competition to secure honorific titles. These themselves gave some measure of relative rank. An "emperor" was higher than a "king"; a "king" was higher than an "elector"; an "elector" than a "duke"; a "duke" than a "marquis". And so on. The titles of rulers, it was generally believed, affected the rank of the states they ruled. In accordance with this doctrine, republics, having no "crowned head", were normally ranked lower than monarchies (even where the monarchs were elected)[35] and, under some views, even than Electorates.[36] Finally, even if there was agreement about these rankings, there could be disputes concerning whether or not a ruler was entitled to *claim* any particular title: a subject that became the source of many other conflicts.[37]

The fact that a clear hierarchy existed inevitably led to pressure to acquire more honorific titles. As we have seen earlier, there was a general understanding that the Holy Roman Emperor was of higher status than other sovereigns. This may have been one reason why ordinary kings now sometimes aspired to style themselves "emperor".* For example, Louis XIV, in a treaty with the ruler of Algiers of 1681, styled himself as the "emperor" of France. Peter the Great sought to underline the significance of the title of "tsar" (originally adopted by Ivan III a century and a half earlier) by having himself styled, at the request of his senate in 1721 as "Imperator", emperor of all the Russias (as well as "Father of his country" and "the Great"). But it was not enough to make a unilateral claim to a title. Thus other rulers were not willing to concede to Peter a higher status than their own. The king of Denmark, Frederick IV, refused to recognise Peter as emperor and this led to a major breach between the two countries. His successors' claim to the imperial title continued to cause controversy throughout the century. The emperor Joseph I would not concede the title to Catherine the Great, implying an equal status with his own; and this was the main reason why, despite his desire for an alliance in 1786, no formal treaty between them was signed (requiring a recognition of titles) but only the informal exchange of letters of 1780–1. Britain was equally unwilling to recognise the claim; when, after prolonged negotiations she did finally recognise it, it was specifically laid down that this was without prejudice to existing conventions concerning ceremonial and precedence: in other words it was not a recognition of any higher status for the Russian monarch. (It was not until the following century that rulers of France – the two Napoleons – Britain and Germany laid claim to imperial titles themselves.)

Just as kings sought to be recognised as "emperors", Electors sought recognition as "kings".[38] Here too it was generally accepted that the title could not be taken unilaterally. The German states were still theoretically a part of the "empire"; it was therefore accepted that any change of status required the explicit recognition at least of the emperor, and perhaps of other imperial institutions. If a German ruler acquired territory outside the empire, no great problem need

---

* One way to acquire the title, of course, was to be elected Holy Roman Emperor. It was by no means taken for granted in this age that the emperor must be a Hapsburg. Louis XIV was regarded as a serious candidate in 1658 and again in the 1670s and 1680s. In 1702 the Elector of Bavaria, governor of the Spanish Netherlands recognised the Bourbon succession there in return for a promise that the French would support him at the next election as emperor. Since it was still sometimes possible to buy the votes of the electors, or at least exercise substantial pressure on them, this was by no means an empty hope (the same Elector's son was able to secure every vote at the election following the death of Charles VI, when Austria's power was minimal: even the British king, as elector of Hanover, though an ally of Austria, gave him his vote).

arise. So when, in 1697, the elector of Saxony was elected king of Poland, there was no objection to him securing a royal crown, even though he was the ruler of a German state (he remained Elector, not king, in Saxony).[39] Similarly, when the future elector of Hanover, at roughly the same time, was designated by William III as heir to the throne of England (after his mother) should the immediate successor, Anne, die without heirs, this caused no concern to the emperor. Their elevation did, however, arouse resentment among other German rulers and stimulated comparable ambitions. The elector of Brandenburg, Frederick III, in particular was determined to acquire a crown for himself. The emperor would not accord this, however, except in return for substantial political concessions. He finally agreed to grant the royal title only when a new war against Louis XIV seemed imminent in 1700, in return for an undertaking by the elector to provide a contingent of 8000 highly trained Brandenburg soldiers for the expected conflict. Even then the concession was hedged about: the elector was not able to call himself king of Brandenburg, his principal territory, but only of Prussia (one of the most barren and least important of his lands) which was outside the empire; and even then he was to be known as king *in* Prussia rather than of it. Frederick in retaliation demonstrated his independence of the emperor by personally crowning himself and his wife (so anticipating Napoleon's famous gesture) rather than admit his reliance on the emperor or on any spiritual power.[40]

This success inspired a similar ambition in yet another elector, that of Bavaria. The Wittelsbach dukes of that country, who had only secured the title of elector at the beginning of the Thirty Years War (when the honour was transferred to them from the disgraced rulers of Bohemia), did not relish being outdone by their fellow-electors. When Max Emmanual, who had been made governor of the Spanish Netherlands by the king of Spain, his wife's uncle, transferred his support to France at the time of the Bourbon succession in Spain, he demanded in return that France should recognise his claim to a royal title (as well as the territory of the southern Netherlands): under a treaty of 1702 France undertook to recognise the elector as "king" and to do everything possible to ensure that he was so recognised by the other powers of Europe. France's failure in the war frustrated that hope. But he renewed the claim during the negotiations for the Peace of Utrecht in 1713. The British negotiator, Bolingbroke, fearing that the United Provinces might agree to Bavarian sovereignty in the southern Netherlands at great risk to Britain's security, proposed that the duke should instead be awarded Sardinia and enjoy a royal title there. But the emperor was especially hostile to Max Emmanual for having defied his authority during the war, and opposed this: he agreed to the duke recovering even Bavaria itself only on condition that he gained neither Sardinia nor the royal title. But later Bavarian electors were not to be shaken from their ambition. The elector Charles Albert, on the death of Charles VI in 1740, claimed the Hapsburg succession and hoped to be elected emperor. In 1741, to seduce him from the coalition against her, Maria Theresa herself offered him a crown as king of the southern Netherlands. The elector, who now had every chance of becoming emperor, was not then interested. But later, expelled from his own electorate, he again sought to win the promise of a crown, this time from the Maritime Powers, in return for renouncing his claim to the Hapsburg lands. He then died, however, before the proposal could be seriously considered. But the demand for a royal title was raised yet again by a later elector in 1784. When the emperor Joseph broached the possibility of an exchange of his own territory in the southern Netherlands for the Bavarian lands, the elector was willing to consider this only on condition that he was given a royal title there. Eventually because of the opposition of other powers (and the elector's heirs), this proposal too was not proceeded with. So unlike his fellow lay electors in Brandenburg and Hanover, the rulers of Bavaria for long failed to acquire a crown. He finally secured one, at the hands of Napoleon, in 1806, to be followed by Saxony a few years later: titles that were confirmed at the Congress of Vienna.

Another ruler who for long had aspirations to be recognised as "king" was the duke of Savoy. When the duke, Charles Emmanuel II, sent assistance to Venice during her long war with the Turks for Crete (1645–69) he hoped as a result to secure at least equality of treatment with "crowned heads".[41] Though that attempt failed, the ambitions of the family were not appeased. Thirty years later, in 1696, one of the conditions demanded by Victor Amadeus for changing sides during the Nine Years War was recognition by France of his claim to a royal title (stimulating almost immediately a similar demand by the Grand Duke of Tuscany).[42] He reiterated this claim at the opening of the War of Spanish Succession in 1702; and it was in part its rejection by Philip V of Spain which caused the duke once more to change sides and join the anti-French coalition. The issue became live again at the end of that war. Various territorial arrangements were then considered which might have been combined with a royal title for the duke. And though it was somewhat against his will that he was eventually allotted Sicily in 1713, this at least secured for him the crown of that ancient kingdom. And even when, in 1720, he was obliged to exchange that territory for Sardinia, he managed to retain a royal crown in that island. Thus, just as the ruler of Brandenburg became known as the king of the remote and relatively backward territory of Prussia, the ruler of Savoy, though still based in his capital in Turin, was known for the next century and a half as the king of a wild and backward Mediterranean island.[43]

Just as the electors wished to become kings, the lesser German rulers sought to become electors. Traditionally, until the Thirty Years War, there had been three ecclesiastical electors: the Archbishops of Mains, Trier and Cologne; and four secular ones: the rulers of Bohemia, Saxony, Brandenburg and the Palatinate. Even after the Reformation this arrangement survived for a century despite the fact that at one time in the 1580s (when the Archbishop of Cologne himself turned towards Protestantism) there were more Protestant than Catholic electors.[44] The Thirty Years War led to the creation of an eighth elector: the rights of the ruler of Bohemia were transferred to Bavaria, but later the electoral right was restored to Bohemia (now ruled by Austria) though the Austrian rulers undertook not to exercise it. Towards the end of the seventeenth century the ruler of Hanover, the most significant German state that was not an electorate, began to campaign for the creation of a ninth elector. The emperor used this demand, as he had done that of the elector of Brandenburg for a crown, to win concessions in return. The ruler of Hanover, like Frederick William, was therefore obliged to offer military support, and to agree to vote for a Hapsburg candidate as emperor and support the creation of yet another elector in future in return for being made elector himself. This elevation aroused the fury of less favoured German rulers who, in the following year, established an association of German princes to oppose the elevation and the way it had been effected, so severely weakening the authority of the emperor in Germany for the next decade or so: an indication of the strength of feeling such questions could arouse.

But the competition concerned not only the particular titles accorded but the honours that should be done to those who held them. One subject of dispute concerned the right to the appellation of "majesty". In many states it was customary to style a king as "majesty". But the emperor, jealous of his own rights, was reluctant to accord this title to a mere king, offering only the term "*serenitas*".

Such disputes could lead to serious diplomatic wrangles. Louis XIV appointed no ambassador to Vienna for a time, rather than accept the indignity of being denied the honour of *"majestas"*. The first English ambassador sent to Vienna by William III became involved in a prolonged dispute on the question.[45] A suggested compromise – that the issue of letters of accreditation by the emperor's chancery could be dispensed with, so that the emperor had only to accept the style used by British officials, rather than make use of it himself – was not accepted. And, to avoid, such difficulties, Britain for many years sent no ambassador to Vienna at all.[46]

Everywhere, therefore, there was deep concern about titles and the honours that went with them. Account was taken not only of the standing of the major titles held, but the number of titles claimed (since a ruler who was duke of one territory, might claim to be margrave or count of numerous others). Often the lesser rulers were even more concerned about such questions than those of major states.[47] As a French observer of the states of Germany pointed out, "there is no small sovereign in the empire with less than three times as many titles as the king of France". So quantity could sometimes be made a substitute for quality. None could hope to compete with the superb roll-call of titles claimed by the Hapsburg rulers.* But even lesser mortals could put together fairly impressive lists, especially if (like the Hapsburgs in their own catalogue) they continued to use titles to territories they had long ceased to control: so the rulers of Sweden styled themselves as "Count Palatine of the Rhine, Duke of Bavaria, Julich, Cleves and Berg", just as the English king, until the very end of our period, called himself "king of France". Even when rulers explicitly renounced a foreign throne they sometimes made arrangements to continue to use the title during their own lifetime: as the king of Poland was allowed to do (except on certain

---

* In 1724 they styled themselves (in their proclamation of the Pragmatic Sanction) as: "Emperor of the Romans, ever August, King of Germany, Castile, Leon, Aragon, the Two Sicilies, Jerusalem, Hungary, Bohemia and Dalmatia; of Croatia, Sclavonia, Navarre, Granada, Toledo, Valencia, Galicia, Majorca, Seville, Sardinia, Cordova, Corsica, Murcia and Jaen, the Algarve, Algeciras, Gibraltar, the Canary Isles, the East and West Indies, the Islands of the Mainland and the Ocean Sea; Archduke of Austria; Duke of Burgundy, Lorraine, Brabant, Limburg, Luxemburg, Gelderland, Milan, Styria, Carinthia, Carniola, Württemberg, Upper and Lower Silesia, Athens and Neopatras; Prince of Swabia; Margrave of the Holy Empire, Burgau, Moravia, Upper and Lower Lusatia; Count of Hapsburg, Flanders, Artois, Tyrol, Barcelona, Ferrete, Cybourg, Gorizia, Roussillon and Cerdagne; Landgrave of Alsace; Marquis of Oristan, and Count of Geceano; Lord of the Slavonian March, Port Naon, Biscay, Moline, Salins, Tripoli and Malines, etc.".

occasions) when he renounced the Swedish throne in the Peace of Oliva. No clearer evidence could be given of the value attached to titles than this determination to cling to them, even when the reality of power had totally evaporated.

Conflicts of this kind reflected the values that prevailed within the system. In an international society in which a very high importance was attached to status, both of states and of sovereigns (the status of the two could scarcely be distinguished) it was inevitable that disputes over such questions should be frequent and acrimonious. States were involved in a competition for prestige in which perceptions were almost as important as reality. The place which each state occupied in the pecking order, and was seen to occupy, was not regarded as a matter of indifference.

CEREMONY

Disputes over rank and title were inevitably reflected in conflicts over ceremonial questions.

One of the main duties of ambassadors abroad was to demonstrate the status of their sovereigns by representing them with as much splendour as possible. They would often need to spend large sums of money – frequently their own – to be able to create the kind of impression required. De Callières, in his famous treatise on diplomacy, declared that "to uphold the dignity of his position the negotiator must clothe himself in liberality and magnificence. . . . Let this magnificence appear in his attendants, in his livery and in his whole outfit. . . . Let him frequently give banquets and diversions in honour of the principal persons of the court in which he lives, and even in honour of the prince himself."[48] This requirement inevitably produced keen competition in magnificence. The ambassador might be judged according to the splendour of his carriage, the number of his horses, the attire of his attendants, the size of the receptions he gave, and even the number of dishes served at a banquet. No ambassador would wish, whatever the cost involved, to be compared unfavourably with the ambassador of a rival state in these respects.[49] This might cause him considerable difficulty. When Kaunitz, who had no great personal fortune, was sent as Austrian ambassador to Paris in 1752, he was obliged to delay his formal entry to the court for eighteen months because he could not afford the great cost required for the ceremony. Eventually his sovereign, Maria Theresa, had to send him a special remittance of one hundred thousand florins to pay for the ceremony, to ensure that it was undertaken with adequate grandeur.[50]

Few court ceremonies occurred at which problems of precedence or etiquette did not arise. Apart from questions concerning the positions to be occupied by ambassadors of different powers (see above), there were many others concerning the form which such ceremonies should take. When the first English ambassador to the imperial court at Vienna was appointed after the revolution of 1688, he postponed his audience until he had established what honours were normally offered at the imperial court for a diplomatist of his rank; and when the audience did take place he expressed his deep dissatisfaction with the ceremonial that was offered in his case.[51] British representatives in Venice had repeated disputes about the reception offered them in the early eighteenth century. Successive residents protested that during their formal audiences the doors should not have been closed but left open (believed to be the practice in receiving envoys from the more important courts); and later residents declined to have formal audiences at all in order to avoid such difficulties.[52]

Similar conflicts arose about the position in which an ambassador received guests: whether at the top of the stairs or at the foot. The Prince de Conti, a prince of the royal blood in France, was so angered at the failure of the British ambassador of the time to come to meet him at the foot of the stairs that he refused to make his call.[53] And the honours which should be done to a prince of the blood by an ambassador continued to be a major point at issue between the two governments. There was controversy on whether or not an ambassador should give his hand to envoys of other states when receiving them in his own house: another question seen as so important that formal instructions on the question were given to all British ambassadors before they set out for their posts.[54] The size of equipages for carriages was another source of contention. During the negotiations for the Peace of Ryswick (questions of protocol were always taken especially seriously during such negotiations) it was agreed that the guards should admit to the conference "none but those who come in coaches with six horses". This had the effect that the minister of Lorraine "was excluded till some minister with a better equipage came by and took him up".[55] There were many disputes about the order in which courtesy calls were made by and to ambassadors, and about the scale of the honours to be done when new ambassadors arrived. The master of the ceremonies in Britain had to determine, for example, whether a particular ambassador should be introduced at the court by earls and be attended by three trumpets (a privilege which was accorded only to the representatives of crowned heads).*

Disputes on etiquette might be especially acute between countries that were in a state of enmity. Countries which were at war, for example, did not wish to appear to be the first to seek terms, and wished to ensure that the other appeared in the role of "*demandeur*". Louis recounts how, when he and Charles II both wanted to end their war in 1666, "the king of Great Britain . . . maintained that since he had declared war against him first, I should also send off to his domain first to negotiate the peace", and he congratulates himself for having refused this demand.[56] Louis sought to resolve the question in his favour for a time by proposing that the house of Henrietta Maria, the widow of Charles I, should be used for the negotiations, a solution that would have represented a victory for himself since her house lay in France. The issue was finally settled by an agreement that the peace talks should take place in neither country, but in Breda in the United Provinces.

Similar conflicts could affect the conduct of a war. During the war for Crete (1645–69), in which Venice was supported against the Turks by various Christian forces, the commander of the papal fleet and that of the Knights of Malta, preparing for a sea battle against the Turks, each demanded to hold the place of honour, which was on the right of the line of battle. Because they were unable to resolve the question, both fleets weighed anchor and returned home without participating in the battle.[57] There were often conflicts between commanders of allied powers in the field about which exercised superior authority. During the War of Spanish Succession, for example, this was the cause of substantial disputes on both opposing sides. The Dutch would not accept Queen Anne's husband, Prince George, as the commander-in-chief of allied armies (though they were quite willing to accept Marlborough); while on the opposing side there

---

* Questions of protocol of this kind were almost as intensely fought out even when no foreign representatives were involved. Louis XIV records in his *Memoires* his brother's persistent, but vain effort to get Louis to allow his wife to sit on a chair with a back while in the presence of the queen; and explained how important it was that he had refused this request, since it was not right that he should "permit anything that might seem to approximate him to me", stressing "how careful I had to be of rank, how ill-founded his claim, and how useless it would be for him to persevere" (Louis XIV, *Memoires*, p. 143).

were conflicts between French and Bavarian commanders. Sometimes special arrangements had to be reached to resolve such questions. Thus in the agreement made between France and England before the Dutch war of 1672 it was provided that the commander of the English auxiliary corps was to have precedence over all French lieutenant-generals.[58]

Where two sovereigns or their representatives were competing for an honour, compromise became almost impossible since whichever side yielded would have been deemed to acknowledge the superior status of the other. It was on these grounds that it was often felt wiser, rather than risk defeat in such a battle, to avoid it altogether by not participating in the event in question. Ambassadors would, as we saw, quite frequently absent themselves from particular functions altogether, rather than undergo the possibility of humiliation or a major altercation. That is why, when the English king proposed that no ambassadors should attend at the entry of the newly appointed Swedish ambassador in 1661 to avoid controversy, this was accepted by all the diplomatic community, including (initially) the ambassadors of France and Spain. That is why, when the British were unable to secure the honours they believed appropriate from the emperor in Vienna, they left the post unfilled rather than suffer a further rebuff; just as British residents in Venice avoided formal audiences at that court for similar reasons. That course was even sometimes recommended by text-books of international law. Martens's *Law of Nations*, one of the most famous text-books of the day, in treating of disputes over precedence, suggested a number of alternative procedures for overcoming the difficulties, including attending the occasion incognito – a somewhat bizarre way of avoiding trouble – yielding the precedence while insisting that no precedent was created, and avoiding attending ceremonies altogether.[59] Disputes about the order in which the signatures of different states' representatives should appear on a peace treaty were resolved by similar devices. For example, alternative copies of the treaty could be used, in which signatures would appear in a different order (the *Alternat*); or the treaties could even be drawn up in a circular form, so that all the signatures would appear at the same level.[60] At Nymegen the Dutch even specially constructed a house with doors so arranged that the Spanish and French delegates would simultaneously reach the table where they were to sign their copies of the treaty. It was only at the Congress of Aix-la-Chapelle in 1818, just after the end of our period, that it was eventually agreed that states should sign treaties in alphabetical order, in order to end the innumerable wrangles which had so long taken place on this question.

Disputes of this kind, which appear petty and even ridiculous when recounted today, had considerable importance to the rulers of this age and the ministers who served them. For they saw themselves as engaged in a bitter struggle, among rulers and their states, for pre-eminence if possible, and at least for superiority over immediate rivals. Questions of status, honour, ceremony and precedence were at the heart of that struggle. So long as status was the main object of concern, it was not altogether irrelevant to attach importance to the ways in which, within the society of states to which all belonged, it was publicly measured.

BOOKS

G. Butler and S. Maccoby, *The Development of International Law* (London, 1928) esp. ch. 1 on precedence and status rivalries.

Jean Dumont, *Corps universel diplomatique du droit de gens* (Amsterdam, 1735) esp. parts of the supplement concerning ceremonial, dignities and titles.

A. Fauchier-Magnon, *The Small German Courts in the Eighteenth Century*, English trs. (London, 1958).

A. Goodwin (ed.), *The European Nobility in the Eighteenth Century* (Manchester, 1953).

D. B. Horn, *The British Diplomatic Service, 1689–1789* (Oxford, 1961) esp. ch. XI: "Ceremonial and Privilege".

Sir E. Satow, *A Guide to Diplomatic Practice* (London, 1917) esp. ch. 5, on titles and precedence, and ch. 6, on maritime honours.

6 Succession

SUCCESSION AS AN INTERNATIONAL ISSUE

Another important cause of conflict in this period were questions relating to succession.

A large proportion of the wars of the age were mainly or partly concerned with succession. These included not only the four generally known as wars of succession – in Spain (1702–14), in Poland (1733–5), in Austria (1740–8) and in Bavaria (1778–9). A number of other wars of the age were at least partly concerned with that question. The first Dutch war between England and the United Provinces (1652–4) was aggravated by English concern about the power of the Orange family in the republic and Dutch concern about the fate of the English king, closely related to that family. The First War of the North (1655–60) was the conclusion of a sixty-year struggle resulting from the claims of Polish rulers to the Swedish throne; and the renunciation of that claim was an important part of the final settlement. The War of Devolution (1667–8) was fought by Louis XIV to promote the dubious succession claims of his wife in the Spanish Netherlands. The Nine Years War (1688–97) was precipitated by his effort to promote succession claims in the Palatinate and in Cologne; while another major issue was the succession in England after the overthrow of James II. The Great Northern War (1700–21), though mainly about territory, was also concerned for a time with rival claims to the Polish throne. The War of Spanish Succession was concerned with succession in England as well as in Spain. Spain's war against Austria in 1717–20 was concerned with rights of succession in Italian territories acquired by Austria a few years earlier. The War of Polish Succession was about succession in Lorraine as well as in Poland. Sweden's war against Russia in 1741–2, though originally territorial, could be ended only by agreement on the succession to the throne in Sweden. The Seven Years War continued the struggle over rights in Silesia that began in 1740; and so on. In all these cases, which include most of the major wars of the era, a central issue was: which monarch had the right to rule in a particular country? The frequency with which wars took place on the point gives an indication of the importance it had in the minds of contemporary rulers and statesmen.

TABLE 2:   European wars mainly or partly concerned with succession,
1648–1815

Date	Participants	Issue	Outcome
1667–8	France–Spain	Succession of French queen (Spanish princess) in Spanish Netherlands	Claim withdrawn
1689–97	France–England	Succession of William and Mary in England[a]	Succession accepted by France
1702–14	England, Austria, United Provinces, etc. – France, Spain	Succession of Bourbons in Spain	Succession accepted if French throne renounced
1704–7	Saxony–Sweden	Right of Saxon elector to Polish throne	Augustus compelled to renounce Polish crown
1718–20	Spain–Austria, Britain, France	Right of Spanish royal family in Sardinia and Sicily, and of Austrian emperor in Spain	Claims renounced.
1733–5	France, Spain, Poland–Austria, Russia, Saxony	Succession in Poland, Lorraine, etc.[c]	Succession in Poland for Russian candidate; Lorraine to pass to France
1740–8	Prussia, France–Austria, Britain	Succession of Maria Theresa in Austria[b, c]	Maria Theresa succeeds but loses Silesia
1741–3	Sweden–Russia	Succession in Sweden	Sweden accepts heir demanded by Russia
1778–9	Prussia, Saxony–Austria	Proposed transfer of part of Bavaria to Austria	Transfer prevented

[a] This also partly concerned succession in the Palatinate and Cologne.
[b] This also partly concerned succession to the Empire (to which Charles Albert of Bavaria was elected after Austrian setbacks in 1742, to be succeeded by Francis, husband of Maria Theresa, in 1745).
[c] The wars of Polish and Austrian succession also concerned succession in the Italian duchies (Parma, Tuscany and Naples and Sicily).

It was not self-evident that succession issues should be of international concern at all. Under the principle of sovereignty now so widely acknowledged, succession to the throne of a particular country should have been of concern only to the government and people of that state. However fiercely different claimants or factions *within* that country might dispute the succession, other powers should have remained totally disinterested. Where issues of that kind were concerned, however, the principle of sovereignty was, rarely observed. The general feeling was (as in the age of ideological competition of recent years) that who acquired power in one state could have important repercussions on others: it must therefore become a matter of international concern. The growing sense that Europe had become a community, the members of which were closely interrelated (see above), meant that governments were not prepared to distance themselves from developments, even internal ones, which could have important consequences for the continent as a whole. In other words, the principle of sovereignty, however, passionately it was advocated, here came into conflict with another principle, perhaps even more influential: the principle of the balance of power. In some cases, it was felt, the former principle, that of the essential political independence of each state, had to be subordinated to the latter.

There were a number of reasons why, it was felt, succession in one state could affect the legitimate interests of others. These reasons were different from those that had stimulated intervention on the same question in earlier days. In the age of dynastic competition of the later Middle Ages intervention had normally been on a bilateral basis: it was the means by which the ruler of one state asserted a dynastic claim to succession in another. So English rulers fought for over a hundred years for the throne of France; the Aragon and Angevin families fought each other for succession in Naples. In the age of religious conflict from 1559 to 1648, intervention had occurred because it was believed that a particular succession could determine which faith was likely to be practised, or tolerated, in another state; that was the main reason why Philip II put forward dynastic claims in England in 1588 and in France a year or two later; why a number of governments intervened over succession in Cleves-Julich in 1609–10; why Spain intervened in the Valtellina of Switzerland in 1620–3; and why Austria intervened in Bohemia in 1618, causing war throughout the continent. Neither of these motives were significant in the wars of intervention which took place during our age. Rulers almost never now put forward claims on their own behalf to rule elsewhere. Wars were fought to *prevent* another ruler succeeding, not to promote a personal claim. Nor were religious motives decisive. Religious factors were significant in promoting *domestic* concern about succession in England in 1680–8, but were not the main motive why William III accepted the invitation to intervene there in 1688, nor why Louis opposed him. And while religion was one factor causing France and other countries to support the Jacobite cause in England over the next fifty years, it was not the only reason, and rarely the most important.*

The reason that external powers now felt concerned to intervene on such questions was that the type of succession which took place was believed likely to have an important effect on the balance of forces within the continent as a whole. In each state the sovereigns exercised such dominant power that who succeeded could be of decisive political importance both at home and abroad. The ruling families of the continent had become so closely inter-married in the dynastic interests of each, that succession in one state could bring to power a ruler closely related to the royal family of another. Even if no direct union of the crowns was likely to occur (and it was recognised that normally such a union would now no longer be tolerated by other powers), close alliances might be established: as was believed likely to occur in Spain, even without a direct union of the crowns, as a result of the Bourbon Succession in 1701–2. Even if a succession was likely to bring no direct dynastic affiliations of this kind, it might none the less have important foreign policy consequences: like the expected Polish succession in 1733–5 (which could determine whether Russia or France had a dominant influence there) or the proposed Swedish succession in 1742 (which was of acute concern to Denmark and Russia). Or again it could produce major territorial changes: like that proposed in Bavaria in 1777–8 (see below). In any

---

* It was still believed, rightly or wrongly, that dynastic marriages were sometimes undertaken for religious purposes. S. Pufendorf, in his *Introduction to the History of the Principal States* (Frankfurt, 1684), trs. J. Krull (London, 1697) p. 421, declared that the Pope, in trying to "reduce the protestants to this obedience . . . flattereth the protestant princes and takes care that many of them may marry Roman Catholic ladies". With or without the help of the pope, Charles I, Charles II and James II in England had all married Catholic ladies, and the latter thereafter became converts to the Catholic faith. This, far from converting England, was a major factor in bringing about the fall of James II and the succession of a new and firmly Protestant line. But while Protestant rulers sometimes married Catholics (creating a Catholic line of succession), the reverse virtually never happened; and it was for this reason that the balance of religions on the electoral college in Germany shifted in favour of the Catholics. Despite this, generally speaking religion was not the main reason for concern about succession. On the contrary, religious conversion now took place for *political* reasons (as when the Elector of Saxony adopted the Catholic faith to enable him to become king of Poland), rather than political intervention being undertaken for religious reasons, as before.

of these ways succession could have important consequences for the family of European nations as a whole. And it was on these grounds that, it was believed, external states had a right to a say in the type of succession which occurred elsewhere.

But it was not any succession that precipitated international action. The straightforward passing of a crown from father to son or nephew, according to the normal rules of succession, would hardly ever cause controversy. For there was little reason why this should affect the balance of advantage among other states. It was, typically, where there was some deviation from the normal procedure that outside powers were tempted to intervene. It was when a ruler was over-thrown, as in England in 1688, and replaced by another, installed by revolution; when a ruler died without direct heirs, as in Spain in 1700, and a controversial succession occurred in defiance of previous understandings; or when a ruler died, as in Austria in 1740, having made questionable arrangements governing the succession before his death (preferring his own daughter to those of his elder brother); on when a ruler, like the Elector of Bavaria in 1777, had been persuaded to make special arrangements for the benefit of a particular neigh-bour: it was in such circumstances that opposition from other states was likely to occur. Where the kings were elected, as in Poland, almost any succession could be regarded as controversial (if only because it could be suggested – often with every justification – that those who had elected him had been influenced by bribery) and so frequently stimulated foreign interest of some kind. It would of course be naive to suggest that the purpose of intervention in these cases was simply to replace an illegitimate ruler with a more legit-imate one. Almost always there were other, more self-interested reasons why intervention was thought desirable. But it would be wrong to suggest that the unorthodox character of the transition was irrelevant. It might not, alone and in itself, be enough to bring about action by neighbouring powers. But equally, without it intervention would usually not take place at all.

But the fact that a succession was controversial, though it might be a necessary condition for intervention, was not a sufficient one. It was necessary in addition for other states to feel that their interests could be seriously damaged by the fact that one ruler or family rather than another came to power in the state in question. This is indicated by the fact that if the state concerned was remote (like Russia or Turkey) or unimportant (like the German mini-states), even the most controversial succession did not bring about intervention, or even objection from elsewhere. Almost every succession which took place in Russia from the coming to power of Peter the Great in 1696 to that of Catherine the Great in 1762, was controversial in one sense or another.[1] Yet none of these brought any intervention from elsewhere, nor any thought of it; nor did the continual armed conflicts over succession in the Ottoman empire almost every time a sultan died; nor did the hotly disputed claims to the throne of Sweden in 1619–20. None of these, whatever their domestic significance, sufficiently affected the balance of power in Europe as a whole to make intervention necessary. And it was that balance which, as we have seen, was of primary concern to every government of the day, and therefore most likely to stir them to action.

PRINCIPLES OF SUCCESSION

Intervention over matters of this kind was made easier because the rules governing succession were by no means simple. They could thus easily become the subject of controversy.

This was not only because they varied from one country to another. States were quite often willing to interpret the rules which they believed should be applied elsewhere. Louis XIV and the emperor Leopold were quite willing to agree among themselves the principles which should govern the distribution of Spain's territories should Charles II die without issue, as seemed likely when they negotiated the partition treaty of 1668, with scant regard to Spanish laws of inheritance. Many of the principal states of Europe expressed their opinion on the principles that should govern inheritance in Austria in 1740 (despite having previously accepted principles enunciated by the emperor himself). Nor was consistency on such matters regarded as essential. Louis XIV was quite willing in 1668 to ignore the principles of divine right and "fundamental law", which in 1701 he was to declare excluded a partition of Spanish lands. Leopold was quite willing at that earlier time to accept a division of Spanish territory which, during the War of Spanish Succession, he was to declare contrary to the traditions and interest of the Spanish state.

Sometimes the rules recognised in different states diverged sharply. An obvious case concerned the right of female succession (which itself differed from the right of succession through the female line). Even in a single state the principles were not always clear. In Russia there had been no female tsar before the death of Peter the

Great, and at one time succession by a woman would probably have been regarded as impossible. Yet in the next 40 years four women ascended the throne, and between them ruled the country for 65 out of the next 70 years. Formally succession in Russia was determined by each tsar before his death. But this could not determine the position if one died, as Peter did, without naming an heir. (Peter is believed to have been about to name a successor at the moment of his death.) Whether or not a woman could succeed there in practice depended on the attitude of powerful figures at the court and in particular in the armed forces. Often there was an attempt to impose conditions on succession: thus Peter II had to undertake to marry the daughter of Menshikov, the most powerful figure at his accession, while Anna originally agreed to the Privy Council's demand that she should obtain their consent before, *inter alia*, marrying, choosing an heir and making important appointments. Some therefore probably believed that women were more desirable successors, being more likely to submit to such conditions. But they came to the throne mainly because of the deliberate elimination of a series of weak or inadequate male heirs who were by one means or another pushed aside (Peter's son Alexei, the child Ivan VI, and the weak-minded Peter III) in favour of stronger and more competent women.

The uncertainties concerning the rules on this point had more serious international consequences in Austria. Here there had been no female ruler before 1740. A will made by Ferdinand I before his death in 1564 had asserted that his own descendants should inherit his brother Charles V's possessions if no direct legitimate heir remained; but it did not (as was subsequently contended by Charles Albert of Bavaria in 1740) specifically exclude female succession. In 1703 the emperor Leopold laid down that each of his sons and their male heirs should succeed the other in the territories he ruled. This made clear that Charles should succeed Joseph in Austria and the related Hapsburg territories if the latter died without leaving a son, but not whose daughter should succeed if both died without male heirs (though it was generally assumed that in that case the daughters of the elder brother Joseph had the prior right). In fact neither Joseph I, who succeeded in 1705, nor Charles VI, who succeeded in 1711, had male heirs. As a result when Charles succeeded, he found it necessary to make special arrangements – the so-called Pragmatic Sanction – under which his own daughter, Maria Theresa, and not the daughters of Joseph, was to succeed if he died without male heir. He then spent most of the rest of his life securing assent to this, first from the estates of the various Hapsburg lands, and later from the governments of other European countries (to each of which he was obliged to make substantial concessions in return). No clearer recognition could have been given that such questions were not exclusively domestic but matters of *international* concern. The arrangements he made none the less remained controversial; and all his efforts did not prevent a major effort to overturn them on his death, even from governments which had recently given their explicit assent. At that time both Bavaria and Saxony, whose rulers had married daughters of Joseph I, put forward claims to the entire Hapsburg heritage, while Prussia, Spain and France each claimed various parts of it. Here too, therefore, the controversial character of the succession, and the absence of incontrovertible rules to judge its legality, facilitated the challenges which were to be raised to it.*

Disagreements also frequently occurred as a result of the renunciation of rights of inheritance, which were frequently made in this age. When the ruler of one country or the heir to a throne married into the royal family of another country, they were often required to renounce rights of inheritance in their native land, so eliminating the danger of a union of the crowns, which could procure preponderant power for a particular state. Both the mother and the wife of Louis XIV, each daughters of a Spanish king, made such undertakings on their marriages. Similarly Philip V of Spain, in order to secure

---

* These were not the only problems resulting from the female succession in Austria. Though the crown of Hungary was supposed to have been made hereditary in the Hapsburg line after the conquest of that country in 1687, female succession was even more unacceptable there than in other Hapsburg lands. The Hungarian diet only agreed to accept the Pragmatic Sanction in 1723 in return for firm promises that Hungary would only be ruled according to her own laws and not after the pattern of other provinces, and that traditional freedoms and rights would be respected. This strengthened the hands of the Hungarians when they wrested still further concessions in coming to Maria Theresa's rescue in 1704–1 (when they habitually referred to Maria Theresa as "king": *rex*).

There were also considerable complications for the empire. Since Maria Theresa could not herself be emperor, she could only seek to secure the election of her husband, Francis. But his position was anomalous since the power of previous emperors had derived from their being also rulers of the Austrian hereditary lands, and without them he was little more than a figurehead. Even when their son Joseph succeeded as emperor in 1765, the anomaly was not removed. Though he became, like Francis, "co-regent" in the Hapsburg lands, the division of authority continued to weaken him in both his roles. This division had caused no difficulties while Francis lived, since there was no doubt that his wife was the accepted Hapsburg ruler. But the situation when she shared power with her son Joseph was more ambiguous and led to many disputes between mother and son.

recognition of his rights in that country, was required, in the Treaty of Utrecht, to renounce his rights to inherit in France. Under the treaty of Vienna of 1738 his son Don Carlos was allowed to acquire the throne of Naples only on condition that his rights would pass to his second son, so preventing a union if he were to succeed in Spain (as he eventually did in 1759).

Renunciations of that kind, however, did not in practice do away with the threat to the balance of power that they were designed to remove. They could subsequently be challenged on the grounds that they conflicted with the "fundamental law" of the state in question, or with the "divine right" of kings. For even if it was accepted that a ruler, or an heir, could renounce on behalf of himself, it was sometimes suggested that they could not do so on behalf of their heirs. This controversy arose over several of the successions of the age. Though in theory the wife of Louis XIV had renounced all claims to the Spanish throne on her marriage, this was subsequently challenged by Louis and his supporters, not simply on the grounds that she had not brought with her the dowry promised on her marriage but, more fundamentally, because it was not open to any member of the royal family to sign away their own rights and that of their descendants in this way.[2] This contention became a major issue on the outbreak of the War of Spanish Succession. Similarly, at the conclusion of that war, there were many, both in France and in Spain, who held that the renunciation by Philip of his right to succeed in France, should the child Louis XV not survive (as seemed quite likely), was also not valid on the same grounds: again a cause of acute disquiet and a potential cause of war.[3] The same issue became of crucial importance at the outbreak of the War of Austrian Succession in 1740. Then once again it was argued that the renunciation of the Austrian throne which had been made by the daughters of the emperor Joseph were invalid in that they conflicted with the fundamental law governing inheritance in the Hapsburg lands. Similar controversies could take place when a ruler was dethroned. Such a usurpation, as in England in 1688, could be denounced as contrary to fundamental law and divine right and recognition of the new ruler refused on those grounds: this was the argument used by Louis XIV for supporting James II and later the Old Pretender between 1688 and 1713.[4]

A related question concerned the rights of parliaments to determine rules of succession. In many countries the accession of rulers traditionally had to be confirmed by estates or parliaments; and often that assent had been given only in return for pledges by the new ruler

concerning, for example, their willingness to respect traditional liberties, to grant immunities from taxation to nobles and other privileged
groups, to consult about declarations of war, and so on. In this age of
absolutism, the right of parliaments to impose conditions of that kind
was increasingly discounted; the doctrine of divine right implied that
no elected body could interfere with a succession which was ordained
as well as by the "fundamental law" of the state. But in some states
that assumption was in direct conflict with the new doctrines concerning the sovereignty of parliaments. In the United Provinces, for
example, the traditional view had little influence, except among some
supporters of the Orange cause, since it was recognised that the
power of the stadtholders derived from the votes of parliaments in
the individual provinces and the republic as a whole. In Sweden the
power of the parliament to determine succession questions was
explicitly asserted in the constitution of 1720, and was put into effect
when Ulrike, the younger sister of Charles XII was made queen in
preference to her older sister; when she was prevailed on to abdicate
in favour of her husband in the following year; and when in 1643
Frederick was chosen as heir (under strong pressure from the Russian
tsarina) in preference to his cousin, the Duke of Holstein-Gottorp.[5]

But it was in England that the doctrine of parliamentary control
over succession was most explicitly asserted. In the Act of Settlement
of 1701 the English Parliament implemented that right, naming the
dowager Electoress Sophia as the successor to Anne. In the years
that followed it was the major aim of English governments to secure
unqualified foreign acceptance of this succession and of Parliament's
right to determine it. Thus they demanded and secured the inclusion
of an additional clause in the Grand Alliance of 1701 under which
recognition of the Protestant succession was made a principal war
aim of the allies (a pledge understandably given with some reluctance
by the Catholic emperor).[6] A similar commitment was secured from
the United Provinces in the two Anglo-Dutch treaties of 1709 and
1713 (given in return for agreement by Britain to a barrier in the
southern Netherlands). And a comparable undertaking not to disturb
the succession established by the British Parliament was secured from
all the parties to the Treaty of Utrecht in 1713; from the parties to the
Triple Alliance of 1717 and the Quadruple Alliance of 1718 a few
years later; and finally in the Treaty of Aix-la-Chapelle of 1748.
There was even an attempt to get the principle of parliamentary
authority applied in other countries. It was laid down in the Treaty of
Utrecht, for example, that the succession arrangements established

in the treaty for France and Spain should be officially registered by the French parliament and Spanish *cortes*.[7] So a new source of a ruler's legitimacy began to be asserted, in conflict with traditional constitutional doctrines: parliament, being ultimately sovereign, had the right to determine succession questions.

There was another source of uncertainty concerning rules of succession. Precisely because of the hostility to be expected from other states if a ruling monarch put forward a direct claim to a throne elsewhere, those claims were sometimes asserted only on behalf of younger sons or nephews. This concession to the needs of the balance of power became more common as the age progressed. Thus in the first treaty for the partition of Spanish territories in 1668, Louis XIV and the emperor, though each was willing to concede to the other a part of the expected legacy, none the less claimed their own shares on behalf of themselves and their states: which would have led in both cases to a huge aggrandisement of already very powerful countries. Thirty years later both were more cautious. In the partition treaty of 1698 the territories were to go, not to themselves nor to their direct heirs, but to a younger grandson and a younger son, neither at the time expected to inherit in their own lands. It is true that the emperor never accepted the treaty, but this was because it did not bring to his younger son Charles the territory he most desired (in Italy), not because the territory would fall to Charles rather than himself.[8] And though under the partition treaty of 1700 the Dauphin was due to inherit the Bourbon share, this was for a relatively modest part of the whole: only the Italian lands; and the major legacy would still have gone to Charles, a younger son.[9] On similar grounds, later Spanish claims in Italy were also put forward on behalf of younger sons: the sons of Elizabeth Farnese, who were not expected to inherit in Spain itself. When one of these, Don Carlos, became ruler in Naples and Sicily in 1738, it was provided that he too should be succeeded only by a younger son so that is should not go to Spain if he inherited there (as he did). In the same way Tuscany, which went to the Duke of Lorraine at the same time, was also acquired in secundogeniture, so that it would be inherited not by his elder son (later the emperor Joseph) but by a younger son only. Finally Parma too, which was handed to the brother of Don Carlos at the same time, was also to be held only in secundogeniture, for the same reason.

Such provisions, though intended to minimise conflict, did not prevent it. For example, a prince of the cadet branch might remain under the powerful influence of the family and state from which he originally came: as Philip V appeared to be under the influence of his grandfather during his first years as king of Spain. The result was that, even though as a result of his succession, France herself acquired no territory at all, it appeared to the other nations of the continent far too favourable to that country. Or a younger brother might unexpectedly succeed his elder brother if the latter died without heirs: as Charles III of Spain was to do in Austria in 1711, so wholly upsetting the calculations on which the Grand Alliance had fought the War of Spanish Succession, and the expected balance of power at its conclusion. Or a younger prince who was accorded one territory might unexpectedly inherit in another: as Carlos, king of the Two Sicilies, did in Spain in 1759, so leaving in doubt the independence which his successor, even though a younger son, would enjoy. Or a teritory which was to be transmitted only through the cadet branch of a family might in practice be, to all intents and purposes, absorbed among its other territories: as Tuscany was in practice by Austria. Although, therefore, arrangements of this kind represented an understandable attempt to reduce the threats to the balance of power which might result under normal rules of inheritance, they by no means did away with all the controversies and conflicts which could occur over questions of succession.

There were many other ways in which the rules of succession could lead to conflict. Obscure local laws of inheritance might be, exploited to promote a particular claim: as the rules applied in Brabant were used by Louis XIV to justify his claims on behalf of his wife in the Spanish Netherlands in 1667, and the claim he put forward on behalf of his sister-in-law in the Palatinate in 1688. Ancient claims of dubious legality dating from many years earlier could be resurrected: like that concocted by Frederick the Great to parts of Silesia in 1740 (which dated from 1675, related only to parts of the province, and which had anyway been formally renounced by Prussia). A territory could be held to be a "fiefdom" which came under the ultimate control of a distant suzerain who could still control its disposition: as the emperor claimed to be in the case of Milan at the opening of the War of Spanish Succession and of Parma when Charles VI occupied it in 1731. A "guarantee" of a particular constitution could be used to justify intervention on behalf of one claimant rather than another: one of the reasons given by Russia for intervention over the Polish succession in 1733. Where a ruler was elected, the eligibility of a candidate could be contested, as was that of the French nominee,

Cardinal Fürstenberg, in Cologne in 1688, ruled invalid by the Pope.

The only principle on which there was widespread agreement in this age was the total irrelevance of nationality to a right to succession. Whatever other justifications might be put forward on behalf of a particular candidate, those that were totally disregarded were race, culture and language. Thus when there was intense discussion throughout Europe about the succession in Spain at the end of the seventeenth century, the three main candidates discussed were French, Austrian and Bavarian, with the Duke of Savoy as a possible reserve: no Spanish candidate was even considered. When the Polish throne was contested in 1733–5, one candidate was Portuguese, while the successful candidate was a German who had no connection with Poland, spoke no Polish and is said to have disliked the country (his success had the result that Poland was ruled for nearly 70 years – from 1697 to 1763 – by Saxon kings). England was ruled in turn by Scottish, Dutch and German dynasties. Most of Italy was ruled by Spanish or Austrian princes. Sweden had German kings from 1721 onwards and a French ruler thereafter. Russia was ruled from 1762 by a German grand-duke and his German widow, and subsequently by their progeny. There is little evidence that the ministers who served these monarchs, still less the public generally, were concerned about these questions. Rulers could enjoy a substantial measure of public support regardless of their origin or nationality; as William III in England, Philip V in Spain and Catherine II in Russia demonstrated. Often they became more devoted to their country of adoption and its interests than they had been to their own, and more effective champions of its interests than native rulers had been.

In other words, it was the interests of the state, not of the family or individual ruler, which was the decisive factor. And it was on the basis of that interest, not the abstract principles of succession laws, that each government considered questions of succession, whether in their own country or elsewhere.

SUCCESSION AND THE BALANCE OF POWER

Thus whether or not a particular succession occurred in this age did not ultimately depend on genealogy, rules of inheritance or legal arguments. Such principles were not altogether irrelevant. At least they provided the arguments on which a claim could be based, and no claim was likely to succeed which could not produce any justification at all.* But they were not decisive. The decisive factor was the constant struggle for power and territory among the rulers of the day and the concern which this induced among them for the balance of power.

The concern for the balance could decide, in the first place, whether a claim was put forward at all. It was generally recognised that any succession which might produce a radical alteration in the balance of power should not be allowed to occur. Thus the Frenchman, Fénelon, had asserted that though on the death of Charles II France would have a legal right to the succession in Spain (since the French queen's renunciation was void), this would bring such an accretion of power to France that "all Europe" would then "have a right to concur in excluding us from the succession".[10] The Grand Alliance of 1701 declared, as a reason for forming the alliance, that as a result of Louis' acceptance of Charles II's will, France and Spain had virtually become "one and the same kingdom" and could "within a short time become so formidable to all that they may easily assume to themselves the dominion over all Europe".

When Charles VI abandoned his claim to the Spanish throne in 1720 he said that it was done in order to maintain "a balance of power and equitable apportionment of forces among the European rulers", and declared that a union of the crowns of two major European states "should be deemed unlawful". Similarly, when he reaffirmed this renunciation in the Treaty of Vienna in 1735 he declared that he did this "in order to maintain the peace of Europe and the balance of power". When the first Bourbon family compact between France and Spain was entered into in 1733 one of the justifications was that the succession of Maria Theresa in Austria, together with her projected marriage to Francis of Lorraine, bringing that territory to Austria, threatened the European balance.[11] And when Maria Theresa did succeed seven years later the British Secretary of State, the Duke of Newcastle, told the House of Lords that

---

* Louis XIV published a long memorandum under his own name setting out the legal arguments for his wife's claims to parts of the Spanish Netherlands in 1666 (*Traité des droits de la reine Marie-Thérèse sur divers états de la monarchée espagnole*); while Frederick the Great got his foreign minister Podewils to prepare a similar document giving the legal grounds for his claim to Silesia (which he commended as the "work of an excellent charlatan").

the only attachment we have to the court of Vienna is on account of preserving the balance of power in Europe. . . . The preservation of the balance of power and liberties of Europe does not so much depend upon preserving entire the dominions of the house of Austria as in taking care that none of these dominions shall devolve to any potentate in Europe whose power by that accession may become dangerous to the public liberty.[12]

During the war that followed it was widely recognised that the approach to be adopted to the conflict should depend on the likely effect on the balance of power. A writer of the time explicitly asserted that the legitimacy of the claims which France, Spain and Bavaria had put forward to particular Hapsburg territories must depend on their effect on the European balance. "This was a question of the public interest of all Europe, to which, under international law and the law of nature, the particular interests of any state or ruler had to be sacrificed".[13] Another writer of the period agreed that legitimacy was not the most important consideration: even "the most legitimate Masters should sometimes renounce their rights in order to preserve the balance".[14] Whether or not a particular succession could be accepted, was recognised to depend ultimately not on the rules governing succession alone but on its expected effect on on the European balance. Where a succession was both controversial and was likely to affect the balance, it was always liable to challenge. The effect of this was seen in each of the succession wars.

The succession likely to occur in Spain on the death of Charles II was inevitably controversial because there was no obvious heir; and it would affect the balance of power because of the number and significance of the Spanish territories, including valuable lands in Italy, the Low Countries and the Americans, over and above the Spanish heartland itself. That is why it was at first accepted by all concerned that the territories should not pass en bloc to another European state. And that is why Louis XIV, for all his intense ambition, was long willing to negotiate a compromise under which he would sacrifice a substantial part of his claim: both in the partition treaty he negotiated direct with the emperor Leopold in 1668, and later in those he negotiated with William III (who claimed to act on behalf of Europe as a whole) in 1698–1700. On the same grounds, even after those proposals had been rejected by the emperor, he remained willing to accept the transfer of the whole to his grandson, as proposed in Charles II's will, without the expectation that any part would fall to France. That solution, had it been handled differently, might even have been accepted by most other states as compatible with the European balance: England and the United Provinces both temporarily acknowledged Philip V as king of Spain in the aftermath of his succession. But it was always clear that Spain under a Bourbon ruler was likely to be closely aligned with France. And, by sending French forces into the southern Netherlands and evicting the Dutch garrison there, by securing for France the valuable *asiento* affording her the right to trade slaves to South America, and by despatching a horde of French advisers, and even troops, to Spanish territories in Philip's wake, Louis himself accentuated those fears. He thus gave every appearance that Spain was to be made a satellite of France, so that the balance of power on the continent would be tilted decisively in his favour. It was this which caused other major states to believe it was necessary to undo Philip's succession. Though each had their own particular interests to assert – to secure recognition of the Protestant succession for England, to win a new and stronger barrier in the southern Netherlands for the United Provinces, to win territories in Italy for Austria – the *common* interest they shared was in preventing France from acquiring excessive benefits from the succession. And it was this aim which they were eventually able to achieve, even after some of their more exorbitant demands had been abandoned.

It was a similar concern which brought conflict over the succession in Poland. Every election of a Polish king brought competition among external powers to secure the election of their own candidate and so to win influence. But for all of them it was as important to *prevent* the crown being won by a powerful rival as to *gain* it for their own candidate. In 1669 and 1674 France and the Hapsburg emperors each sought to secure the election of their own favourites – the prince de Conti and Charles of Lorraine – despite the fact that publicly both were committed to a compromise candidate, William of Neuburg. Though neither succeeded in his own campaign each prevented the other from prevailing. Later France and Russia became the two main rival king-makers. France traditionally saw Poland, with Sweden and Turkey, as an element in her anti-Hapsburg alliance structure, while Russia increasingly saw her as a client state. In 1696-7 Russia was particularly concerned to prevent the election of the French candidate (the same one as before). She used her influence to bring about the reversal of the original election and so secure the succession of Augustus I of Saxony (Augustus II of Poland). On the death of Augustus in 1733, a similar contest took place. France sought to promote her interests by supporting the claims of her own king's father-in-law, Leszcynski. Russia and Austria, having originally supported a Portuguese candidate (on the grounds that he was weak enough to submit to their own influence), now switched their support to the son of the former king, the future Augustus III. They overturned the election of the Polish parliament and went to war to impose their own candidate. Again motives were largely negative: while Russia and Austria sought to prevent the French candidate from winning control of Poland, France fought to prevent a dominant Russian influence. And because the former were successful, at least in that sector of the war, it was their candidate who finally secured the throne. The question of who ruled Poland was therefore fought out, as in the case of Spain, not by the people of the country mainly concerned (the Polish parliament had voted decisively for Leszcynski) but by external powers having little knowledge of Polish affairs but with interests of their own to pursue. And the outcome depended not on the balance of opinion among the Polish people or parliament, but on the result of the struggle among external forces. Ultimately it was, once again, concern about the balance of power within the continent – not about the interests of Poland – which determined the question.

The attitudes adopted towards the succession in Austria five years later were similar. Here too the primary consideration (as the above quotations show) was the effect which the settlement might ultimately have on the European balance. When Charles VI died in 1740, a threat to the balance seemed imminent. The Prussian seizure of Silesia, and the claims put forward by half the nations of Europe to various Austrian territories, seemed likely to overturn it. But it was precisely the probable effect of these claims, and of the corresponding loss to Austria, which caused other powers to resist them. The reaction of Britain was particularly decisive. Though at first her policy, like that of the others, was purely self-interested – designed to bring Austria to a settlement with Prussia, even at the cost of Silesia, so as to release Prussia from her close alliance with Britain's enemy, France – she soon saw, especially with her Hanoverian eyes, the importance of the struggle for the continental balance. In creating a "pragmatic army" to support Maria Theresa she was concerned to maintain Austria's place as a major component in the European balance and the "old system" of alliances. Even Frederick the Great became increasingly concerned about the balance: France should not gain excessively from the war, nor Austria be too much weakened.

Three times he deserted his French allies to secure an accommodation with Austria,[15] and largely for that reason declared his readiness to guarantee the remaining Hapsburg territories to Maria Theresa if she would accept the loss of Silesia. Russia too, in allowing her forces to be used for the defence of the United Provinces and in renewing her alliance with Austria in 1746, recognised the danger to her of too decisive a French victory. Although, therefore, the policies of each state were partly motivated by immediate self-interest, underlying them was a more general concern that the balance of the continent should not be too much disturbed.

The same motives were at work in the succession dispute in Bavaria in 1777–84. Again it was the effect on the European power structure which mainly determined the attitudes of external powers; and again it was the attitude of the external powers which finally decided the question. The Elector of Bavaria (the only Bavarian who had any say in the question) was quite content, for his own good reasons, with an arrangement which would hand over all or much of his electorate to the emperor Joseph. The emperor was, for obvious reasons, equally satisfied with some plan of that kind: either the acquisition by Austria of the most immediately valuable parts of the electorate in return for financial compensation (as planned in 1778); or the exchange of the entire electorate for the Austrian Netherlands (as planned in 1784). Neither arrangement, however, was acceptable to outside powers, Prussia and other German states, especially, believed it far too advantageous to Austria. Even Austria's purported allies, France and Russia, were indifferent or hostile. What the people of Bavaria thought about the question was not considered. The opposition of the external powers was eventually enough to prevent any transfer of the kind contemplated from taking place. The effect of the arrangement on the balance of power in Europe, and especially in Germany, was here too far more important in determining the outcome than any other factor, including the internal effects in Bavaria itself.

There were other ways in which concern about the balance of power affected the attitudes taken towards claims to succession. Support for a claim by another state was sometimes given as a means of securing in return support for some other question. Britain agreed to support Prussia's claim to Berg-Julich in 1725 in order to win her adhesion to the alliance of Hanover against Russia, Austria and Spain (although the United Provinces, which did not want Prussia to acquire this territory ajoining her own frontiers, forced Britain to abandon the commitment when she too joined the alliance in the following year). During the years between 1725 and 1740 most of the other states of Europe were able to gain concessions from Austria in return for supporting the Pragmatic Sanction. Conversely, sometimes a claimant state would make concessions to win support for its own claim. Thus in 1743 Denmark offered to help Sweden to reconquer Finland if she would accept her crown prince as successor to the throne. Sometimes there was an exchange of commitments concerning succession. Thus at the end of the Seven Years War Frederick the Great agreed to support Joseph's claim to become king of the Romans (and therefore future emperor) as well as Austria's claim to succeed in Modena, in return for final recognition of his rights in Silesia.

Finally, concern for the balance of power affected attitudes towards dynastic marriage in this age. These were no longer undertaken, as in earlier periods, with the simple aim of acquiring a title to new territories elsewhere (the means by which the vast Hapsburg inheritance, for example, had been put together). It was often recognised that even if a claim could be acquired in that way, it might not be possible eventually to make it good: the reason for the renunciations of titles mentioned earlier. Dynastic marriages were now made mainly for diplomatic rather than for territorial purposes. Thus Peter the Great married his daughter and two nieces to the ruling families of important Baltic states not with a view to being able to put forward claim to those territories in the future but as a way of increasing Russia's influence in the area. William III married Mary Stuart not because he anticipated at that time that he might eventually acquire the English crown but because he hoped to counteract the dangerously pro-French stance of English policy (and the marriage was followed the next year by an Anglo-Dutch alliance). Frederick of Sweden married the sister of Frederick the Great not because he hoped to acquire rights to succeed in Prussia (where Frederick had no direct heir), but because of the diplomatic benefit to Sweden from such an alliance. The dukes of Holstein-Gottorp married into the royal families of Sweden and Russia not because they expected to win the rights of succession there (though they did finally succeed in both places) but because they needed the diplomatic support of those countries against Denmark.[16]

Concern about questions of succession and concern about the balance of power were therefore closely interrelated. And it was rarely, if ever, that policy concerning the succession in one country could be determined on the basis of that country's own interests alone. The decisive consideration was the effect it might have on the balance of power in the continent as a whole.

THE INTERNATIONALISATION OF SUCCESSION QUESTIONS

Because this effect was so widely recognised, the settlement of such matters came to be internationalised.

This was shown, first, by the degree to which the claimant states themselves believed it necessary to win international support for their positions. The reason that Louis XIV, despite his own intense ambitions, was willing to negotiate the partition treaties of 1668, 1688 and 1700, was precisely that he recognised that the Spanish settlement would so deeply affect the balance of the continent that only an outcome which secured some international consent was likely to be durable.[17] The reason that Charles VI was willing to make concessions to virtually every state in Europe to secure their consent to the Pragmatic Sanction was his knowledge that without international recognition conflict was likely to result. The reason that British leaders sought, and won, the explicit recognition of the other major states of Europe to the Protestant succession in England was that they were aware that otherwise continued foreign intervention was likely to occur. The reason that Louis XV was finally willing to abandon the excellent claim of his father-in-law to the Polish throne in 1735 was that he recognised that that claim would continue to be unacceptable to the major states which were immediate neighbours of Poland (and that this was the price of winning significant advantages for himself in Lorraine, and for his ally Spain in Italy). And the reason that Austria agreed to abandon her designs for the succession in Bavaria in 1784 was that it had been made evident to her that this solution, however agreeable to the ruler of that land, was totally unacceptable to other major powers in the region.

An even clearer recognition that such questions were legitimate matters of international concern was the frequency with which they were the subject of international agreements. Sometimes these were bilateral agreements between the state directly affected and some other nation. The treaties between England and the United Provinces, by which the latter recognised the Protestant succession in England (in 1709 and 1713) were of this sort. So were the treaties of Breslau (1742) and Leipzig (1745) in which Prussia accepted the succession arrangements in the other Hapsburg lands in return for the retention of Silesia. These were voluntary commitments. But sometimes such a recognition was *imposed*, usually on the conclusion of a war. So Louis XIV was made to recognise the succession in England, first in the treaty of Ryswick of 1797 and again, in a still more unequivocal form, in the Treaty of Utrecht of 1713. More unusually, the Swedish government was obliged in 1743, at the conclusion of an unsuccessful war with Russia, to accept for their *own* country succession arrangements which were imposed on her by Russia, and were contrary to that which her Estates had originally planned;[18] just as the United Provinces was obliged after the first Dutch war not to appoint a member of the house of Orange as Stadtholder or Captain-General.

In some cases bilateral agreements were entered into concerning succession in a *third* state. The three partition treaties concerning succession in Spain were of this sort: they were specifically rejected by the Spanish king, court and people, who objected to any division of their lands (the 1668 treaty was secret but would certainly have been rejected by them had it been known). Similarly in 1732 Prussia and Russia signed a treaty agreeing to exclude either the sons of Augustus or Leszcynski to the Polish throne, and undertook to send troops in to prevent this if necessary. In 1762 the same two countries again agreed among themselves (without reference to any Pole) on the person who should become the next king of Poland (Catherine's former lover, Poniatowski), even though he was in theory to be elected.

Most significant, however, were *multilateral* agreements concerning succession questions. In the Treaty of Utrecht all the parties undertook a mutual recognition of the succession in Spain and in England. The signatories undertook to accept the Protestant succession in England, as provided for by parliament; and to recognise the right of Philip V to rule in Spain, subject to the condition that he could not also become king of France (they recognised too, in that case, not merely the authority of the present ruler, but the succession which should take place if he were to die without heir: namely, that the succession should then fall to the Duke of Savoy). As a result of the treaty, therefore, a considerable proportion of the major states of the continent became committed to a particular solution to two previously contested succession disputes.

But a still more comprehensive international agreement of this kind was the treaty of Vienna of 1718.[19] The treaty of Utrecht, despite its explicit character, was unsuccessful in resolving finally even the two succession questions, concerning Spain and England, which had been the major issues of the preceding war and which it purported to resolve; still less those which soon emerged concerning the successions in Austria and France. Between 1713 and 1720 succession conflicts in these four states became the principal issues of European politics. In France, as we have seen, there were still some who hoped (or feared) that Philip V of Spain could become claimant despite the renunciation contained in the treaty of Utrecht, and this caused considerable insecurity, both to the regent of France who was himself hoping to succeed if the present king died, and to other powers of the continent. In England, the Jacobites' cause had been by no means abandoned; and France, Spain and Sweden all gave direct practical assistance to promote that cause between 1715 and 1719. In Spain Austria had not finally abandoned the claim to that throne which she had fought the war of Spanish Succession to promote. And in Austria, conversely, Spain continued to harbour claims of her own, which she proceeded to assert by attacking Austrian territory in Italy. In these circumstances there was an attempt to secure wider and firmer undertakings to recognise the succession in all four states, and so to restore stability to the continent.

That desire was especially evident in those governments which felt most threatened and so most insecure. Thus Britain and France, now in unexpected partnership, took the lead in securing a multilateral agreement. They began that process with a purely bilateral understanding. This was the Anglo-French treaty of 1716: Britain recognised the succession of the regent in France should Louis XV die, while the French government reaffirmed the existing succession arrangement in England, so again repudiating the Jacobite cause. This was supplemented in the following year in the Triple Alliance between the two countries and the United Provinces which contained similar undertakings. In 1718 in the Quadruple Alliance Austria agreed to recognise Philip's claims to rule in Spain. But the vital adherence of Spain was still lacking. Finally in 1720 after the Alliance powers had successfully defeated Spain's adventure in Italy, she too was brought into the arrangement. Under the treaty of Vienna she recognised for the first time Charles VI's right to the Hapsburg lands, including those acquired in Italy; while Charles conversely recognised Philip's rights in Spain. No clearer recognition could have been given than this wide multilateral arrangement, which included mutual guarantees and provisions for backing those guarantees by collective armed action (see below), that succession questions were seen as matters of international concern.[20]

Less than 20 years later another widely supported treaty also contained a multilateral pledge to respect succession settlements: this time in Austria and Poland. Under the third treaty of Vienna of 1738, which finally concluded the War of Polish Succession (the war itself had ended three years earlier), the signatories all committed themselves to accept the right of Maria Theresa to succeed in Austria. The treaty also recognised the right of Augustus III to the throne of Poland. It also resolved the long-disputed question of rights in Lorraine: the duchy was granted temporarily to Lezcynski, the unsuccessful candidate in Poland, but was to pass on his death to his son-in-law, the king of France, enabling France finally to absorb that long desired territory. These provisions were made multilateral in a wider sense than the treaty of Vienna and all conventional peace treaties. For they were signed not only by the participants in the war, but by other states as well. Thus in April 1739, the two maritime powers, Britain and the United Provinces, though not involved in the war, added their signatures to the treaty, so pledging their support to the arrangements which had been arrived at. In consequence virtually all the major states of the continent became committed to the settlement they contained: a settlement which was not, in its essentials, undone as a result of the major European conflict which broke out the following year.

The treaty of Aix-la-Chapelle, concluding that succeeding war, contained another multilateral agreement of succession rights: this time in Austria and England. Under the treaty France, which had renewed active support for the Jacobite cause in Britain during the 1745 rebellion, yet again guaranteed the protestant succession in England and undertook to expel the Stuarts from her shores. At the same time the parties undertook to accept Maria Theresa's rights to all the Hapsburg territories except Silesia (which she had already ceded to Prussia three years earlier). Thus those states which had previously laid claims to Hapsburg lands – Bavaria, Saxony and Spain – in signing the treaty renounced those claims and accepted the Hapsburg succession. At the same time in agreeing to "guarantee" Silesia in Prussia's hands, the parties made a multilateral commitment to non-succession in that case: in other words they endorsed the transfer of territory which had been acquired by armed force and recognised a new succession.

The settlement of the conflict over Bavarian succession in 1778–84 was also, in effect, the subject of an international decision. In this case there was no formal multilateral treaty; but here too the states which were not themselves directly concerned, namely the states of Germany, made clear that they were not willing to countenance the kind of solution which Austria had devised in her own interest, and demanded the right to a voice in the question. Since the territory concerned belonged to the empire, there was a clear basis for demanding a multilateral solution of the question. In sending Prussian forces to prevent the proposed arrangement, Frederick the Great could claim to be acting on behalf of the German states as a whole in defence of the the empire. And when Joseph renewed his efforts in 1783–4, now proposing an exchange of the Austrian Netherlands for Bavaria, Frederick again presented a multilateral opposition, in the form of the so-called League of Princes (*Fürstenbund*) which he then established. Yet again it was shown that major European states were not willing to see issues of this kind, even though apparently purely internal, settled on a unilateral basis. They were regarded as of more general concern, and so needed to be resolved within a wider framework.

This belief in multilateral settlements, however, though widely accepted, was never formalised. It was, for example, left unclear which states had the right to participate. Thus in 1669, not long after the conclusion of the first Partition treaty between Louis XIV and the emperor Leopold concerning Spanish succession, the United Provinces proposed that the two should agree to negotiate with the Republic as well about the problems surrounding that succession.[21] Similar questions arose over the second and third Partition treaties of 1698 and 1700. These were negotiated principally between France on the one hand and England and the United Provinces on the other (both represented by William III). But the latter two states had no direct interest, since neither made any claim to the succession. The emperor, however, who was very directly involved (both as a claimant and because some of the Spanish territories, such as Milan, were regarded as imperial fiefdoms) was not a party, and indeed strongly opposed the arrangements. The Duke of Savoy too, another potential beneficiary, was equally indignant at being left out of the discussions and especially at the fact that the second treaty allotted Milan to the Duke of Lorraine rathen than to him.[22] The same problem arose during the discussion of succession arrangements before the treaty of Utrecht: the Duke of Savoy was again annoyed that, without any consultation, he should have been offered Sicily in which he had little interest, rather than Milan which had been his original objective throughout the war.[23]

Although, therefore, during this age there were many disputes about succession, there was an increasingly widespread recognition that they were not to be resolved by unilateral action or by force of arms alone. Ultimately the arrangements made for a succession, even if they were of primary concern to a single state and its people, needed to be endorsed by other states, if only to ensure that it did not too seriously damage their interests or security. The bilateral agreements that were made on this question, and still more the multilateral arrangements frequently entered into, demonstrated a recognition that the states of the system shared a common interest in what were apparently domestic affairs. Succession in one state was seen as important by all the others because it could affect the balance of power in the continent as a whole.

7 Territory

THE IMPORTANCE OF TERRITORIAL OBJECTIVES

An essential element in the task of state-building, to which the rulers of this age devoted themselves, was the acquisition of territory.

There was nothing new in an appetite for territory. A large proportion of the wars of the age of dynasties, in the years before 1559, had been fought by the rulers to assert dynastic claims to particular lands they coveted. In the age of religious struggle that followed there continued to be a widespread desire to acquire control of particular territories, though now often to ensure that particular religious faiths were practised there: it was this that had mainly motivated Spain's wars on England and France in the 1580s and 1590s, the rival claims pursued in Cologne (1583–9) and Cleves-Julich (1609–10), and the struggle for Sweden from the 1590s, as well as many of the contestants in the Thirty Years War.[1] But after 1648 there was a major change in the nature of territorial ambitions. Territory was no longer desired by rulers for the benefit of their own houses; nor to promote their own religions. It was desired to promote the purposes of *states*, with which they themselves now increasingly identified themselves. For this reason it was no longer any territory to which they might be able to put forward a dynastic claim, or where their own religion was under threat, however remote or disparate from those they possessed already, that was desired. It was *particular* territories, believed to be of special value to the state concerned.

Dynastic claimants had been eager for territory to add honour to the royal name, to add to the list of titles, properties, crowns and styles on which they could pride themselves. The huge assemblage of lands put together by the Hapsburg rulers (see above) and the more modest acquisitions of the English kings in France or of the French kings in Italy, were thus personal possessions of the royal line, akin to the extensive estates which might be put together by well-married families within states. They were claims to loyalty and allegiance, rather than to direct control. There was little attempt to create unified administrations in the territories put together in this way. Usually each territory continued to go its own way, with its ancient institutions and customs little disturbed. Often the ruler had to pledge himself not to interfere with time-honoured traditions, even to speak the language of the territory in question (as even a ruler as powerful as Charles V had to agree to do in inheriting in Spain in 1515).

The interests of states were quite different. The territories which were desired by the rulers of our age were those that would promote the power, strategic and economic, of their kingdoms. Often they had no compunction in admitting these territorial aims. Louis XIV, in his *Memoires* for his successor, listed a number of territories which he hoped to acquire: including Lorraine, Franche-Comté, Jersey and even the Isle of Wight. Frederick the Great was equally frank: "The first concern of a prince", he declared, "is to sustain himself, the second aggrandisement."[2] Aggrandisement could come about in two ways: "by rich successions or by conquest".[3] He gave as one of his reasons for preferring alliance with France to any alternative the fact that "if joined with France, we could hope for acquisitions".[4] In the first of his *Political Testaments*, written in 1752 (also for his successor), he too listed the various lands he hoped to secure. These included not only some smaller German territories to which he believed he had legitimate dynastic claims, including Baireuth, Ansbach and Mecklenburg (though he had to admit that in the last case there were eight living princes who stood between him and his hoped-for inheritance), but much larger and more important lands, such as Saxony (which he proceeded to invade and occupy four years later), Polish Prussia and Swedish Pomerania.[5] The dukes of Savoy never concealed their determination to acquire territory in the Milanese, even if it was necessary to nibble at it "leaf by leaf, like an artichoke": an aim in which they secured substantial success, largely by selling their support to each major power in turn. Elizabeth Farnese, the Italian-born wife of Philip V of Spain, openly declared her ambition to obtain territories in Italy for her two sons: an aim in which, by persistent efforts, she too ultimately succeeded. Both Russia and Prussia, long before the Polish partitions took place, had decided on those Polish territories they hoped to secure when Augustus III of Poland died.[6] And maritime powers, such as Britain and the United Provinces, though having less appetite than their neighbours for territory in Europe, were equally willing to name the various territories overseas they wished to win. It was, in a word, generally accepted that all states were engaged in a competition for lands; and none saw any reason to be shamefaced about that ambition.

The purposes for which territory was required were now more clearly defined. The most important reason was to create readily defensible and powerful states. Many states had grown piecemeal as a result of acquisitions through inheritance and conquest. They usually had little geographical or strategic logic. Still less were they based on any ethnic or linguistic ties among their peoples, a factor rarely considered in this age. There was thus now a desire to round frontiers to create more self-sufficient units.

There was a special concern to consolidate divided territories. Frederick the Great, for example, deplored the discontinuity of Prussia's scattered lands,* a strip of wholly detached territories stretching from East Frisia near the North Sea to East Prussia at the other end of the Baltic, and openly declared the need to acquire the lands that would fill the gaps.[7] He needed to acquire Saxony, he declared, to "round out our boundaries and create a mountain barrier to separate Silesia from Bohemia".[8] Swedish Pomerania and Polish Prussia were also described in his two *Political Testaments* as desirable acquisitions, which could help to join Prussia's divided lands into a single stretch of territory. Louis XIV's declared aim to acquire Lorraine and Franche-Comté were motivated by a similar desire: to round France's boundaries to the north-east and protect her newly acquired territories in Alsace. Sweden had an urgent strategic need to secure Scania, which lay on her own side of the Baltic but was occupied by Denmark; just as Denmark needed the Holstein-Gottorp lands, mixed higgledy-piggledy with her own on her side of the Sound, placing her in constant military danger when the Duke of Holstein-Gottorp was aligned (as he usually was) with Sweden. Augustus, Elector of Saxony and king of Poland, two totally detached territories, inevitably wished to join them together; in 1698 he discussed with the Elector of Brandenburg an exchange of territories that, by linking them, would have made them more defensible. A similar desire for contiguous territories caused Austrian statesmen to consider many times the exchange of her distant outpost in the Austrian Netherlands for immediately adjacent territory, in Bavaria (see below). In this way territorial objectives became more specific than in earlier times: it was not expansion for its own sake that was desired but the acquisition of particular places of special value to the state.

This aspiration led eventually to the somewhat vague concept of

---

* Prussia was not alone among German states in being divided in this way. Bavaria, for example, had enclaves in Swabia, Franconia, the Upper Rhine, Alsace and even the southern Netherlands.

"natural boundaries". French rulers saw the Pyrenees in the south as a natural boundary of France (which did not prevent her from intervening several times during this age in Catalonia, beyond those mountains). In the south-east they saw the gateway into Italy as the natural boundary, to which they continually aspired. And in the east the Rhine became, in popular mythology, France's "natural boundary", and so the object of national ambitions for two centuries. Russian rulers saw the Baltic and Black Seas as representing legitimate natural borders to which Russia should expand. It was more difficult for them to find any visible natural boundary with Poland; and in practice that border was moved continually towards the west as Russian power increased. Major rivers, such as the Danube and the Vistula, were sometimes claimed as natural dividing points between contesting states. But neighbouring countries rarely agreed on where their "natural" boundaries lay. And the claim by the Convention in France, after the French Revolution, that France had a "historic right" to all territory within the area bounded by the Alps, the Rhine and the Pyrenees was one factor making war with other European states finally inevitable.

Territory of strategic value was always particularly coveted. This is shown in the way in which statesmen themselves described their objectives. In describing his desire to acquire Franche-Comté, for example, Louis XIV said that it was naturally "part of his kingdom", not only by "its location, its language and all rights"; but especially because it opened "a new passage to Germany for me, while at the same time closing the kingdom to my enemies".[9] In the same way he said of Lorraine that "it would be very advantageous and desirable for me to control it: it was a passage for my troops to Germany and Alsace and some other areas that already belonged to me", while in the hands of others it was "an open door to foreigners for invading our domains".[10] Jersey appeared "advantageously situated for me, both for war and for commerce"; it was "easy to defend because of its proximity to Brittany", and he therefore "thought of means to seize it at the first opportunity".[11] In the same way he had, he said, "for long been interested in seizing the Isle of Wight, which is well situated to survey the entire entrance to the Channel, so that my ships will continually give chase to those leaving the English ports".[12] Frederick the Great, too, often gave strategic motives for his territorial ambitions. The reason that Saxony would be a valuable acquisition was that it would "push back our frontier and make Germany more defensible by making possible a defence of the Elbe and the

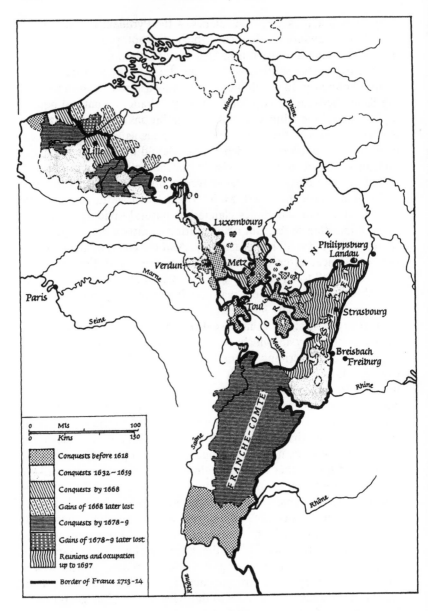

MAP 2   *The expansion of France, 1648–1714*

SOURCE: R. M. Hatton, *Europe in the Age of Louis XIV* (London, 1969)
p. 221.

mountains separating it from Bohemia".[13] Polish Prussia, which split his Baltic lands (dividing his possessions in Prussia and East Pomerania) was also strategically important: in foreign hands it made the former difficult to defend from an attack from the Vistula or the Baltic by the superior Russian navy.[14] The acquisition of Polish Pomerania would "suit us best after the other two", because it separated Prussia from his other possessions and made it hard to defend the former effectively.[15] Strategic interest underlay Denmark's concern to acquire the Holstein-Gottorp lands, which threatened her from close quarters. Russian leaders from Peter the Great onwards acknowledged the strategic importance of access to the sea: in the Baltic (achieved in 1721 after the Great Northern War), in the sea of Azov (achieved provisionally in the settlement with Turkey in 1700), and in the Black Sea (achieved in 1774). And strategic motives lay behind the British desire to acquire such places as Gibraltar and Minorca in the Mediterranean, as well as positions in the Caribbean and North America.

These strategic motivations were reflected in the wars that were fought, and the settlements reached at their end. As a result of his early wars Louis XIV was able to acquire a whole series of strategically valuable accessions, including the vital "gates" of his country (as he himself described them): Roussilon and Cerdagne controlling the entry from Spain, acquired in 1659, Casale, controlling the entry to Italy, acquired in 1683; positions controlling the crossings of the Rhine, such as Breisach (on the right bank) and Philippsburg acquired in 1688, both lost in 1697; Strasbourg, annexed in 1681 and retained; Lorraine, occupied in 1661 and on and off thereafter till finally absorbed in 1766; Luxembourg (acquired in 1684 but lost again in 1697); and a whole series of fortresses on the southern Netherlands border. In the same way Austria acquired in the treaties of Carlowitz and Passarowitz important fortresses in Hungary and Transylvania, even, for a time, Belgrade, opening the way to the Balkans. Russia won forts on the Baltic; Smolensk and Kiev controlling the Ukraine; and, eventually, positions on the Black Sea, including the Crimea. Sweden and Denmark fought for Wismar and Zeeland, controlling the Sound and the islands of Gotland and Osel. Britain won in successive wars a series of positions in the Mediterranean, including at different times Gibralta, Minorca, Malta and even, at the end of the period, the Ionian islands.

But the territorial objectives of one state inevitably often clashed with those of another. The strategic ambitions of France in the southern Netherlands, for example, clashed diametrically with those of the United Provinces and England in the same area: and it thus became an important strategic interest for both countries to prevent further French expansion there. In the same way France's advance into Alsace appeared to the German states, and especially the emperor, as a threat to the German empire; while her positions on the Alpine border in the south were a threat to Savoy and to Italy generally. It was the perception of this threat which made the containment of France such an important objective of other states in this period. This was expressed in the demand for "barriers"; that is, strings of fortresses, which could bar the way to further expansion. In the settlement of the Spanish Succession War, for example, it was planned to create new barriers of that kind: in the southern Netherlands (see above), on the Rhine and in the southern Alps.[16] France herself at one time wished to create a barrier on the Rhine and sought a close relationship with the Rhine states, especially Cologne, Munster and the Palatinates, as well as with Bavaria, to maintain it. The extension of Russian power to the west during the Great Northern War (1700–21) stimulated a similar concern, among the states that felt threatened, to bar her progress by neutralising German territory or allying with Scandinavian powers (as France had long sought to do by recruiting allies in the east of Europe.

The desire for territory was also in some cases stimulated by economic motives. Russia, Sweden, Poland and Prussia vied for ports in the southern Baltic, because they were the outlets through which grain and other exports could be sent abroad. The North Sea ports of Bremen and Verden continually changed hands, and Hamburg was constantly under threat from Denmark, because of the commercial importance of these flourishing trade centres providing access to the North Sea. One reason why Silesia was so much desired by Prussia, and its loss so mourned by Austria, was that it was economically the most advanced among the Hapsburg territories.[17] Trieste was an important acquisition for Austria because of the access it provided for Mediterranean trade. The commercial value of territories acquired outside Europe was even more self-evident, providing as they did valuable commodities – sugar, spices, silks, precious metals and naval goods – both for home consumption and for export elsewhere.

There was one particular economic advantage to be had from acquiring territory which was peculiar to this age. The general practice for troops to live off the country meant that they could be an expensive burden at home, and could more profitably be stationed elsewhere on somebody else's land. Thus Louis XIV, when weighing the relative benefits of war against Spain or England in 1666 gave as one argument for preferring war against Spain that "it would be more convenient for me to thrust them [his troops] upon the domains of Spain than to feed them constantly at the expense of my subjects".[18] One reason for Sweden's war against Poland in 1655 was to enable Charles X's army, which he could not easily pay, to live off the lands which they conquered.[19] By invading Saxony at the beginning of the Seven Years War, and leaving a significant part of his forces there, Frederick II not only secured important strategic objectives, but placed the burden of maintaining them on Saxony rather than on his own impoverished lands. And one of the reasons for the expansionary policy of France after the Revolution was the opportunity it gave to shift some of the expense of maintaining her large forces on the countries she invaded, such as Belgium and Italy.[20]

Whatever the motivation, the territorial acquisitions made during this age brought a substantial change in the shape of the major states. Maps 3 and 4 show the difference between their frontiers in 1648 and 1815. A systematic process of consolidation occurred. The scattered territories of Prussia were now brought together in a single stretch of land. Austria finally gave up control of the distant southern Netherlands, acquiring instead substantial territory, adjacent to her own, in Hungary, Transylvania and northern Italy. France had swollen to something like her present boundaries (which, unusually in this age, with a few small exceptions corresponded approximately to her linguistic borders). Spain lost huge amounts of territory, especially in The Netherlands and Italy, acquired in the days of her military pre-eminence, and was once more confined (in Europe) to a single block of territory within the Iberian peninsula. Sweden and Denmark each shed lands on the further side of the Baltic and acquired some on their own. Russia was the country most transformed. While she had possessed, when the age began, no port other than Archangel, closed by ice for much of the year, and no outlet on the Baltic or the Black Sea, by its end she controlled Finland, a large stretch of the Baltic coast, most of Poland, the Ukraine, and a huge area in the south stretching to the northern shore of the Black Sea. There continued to be entire peoples – Germans, Italians and Poles – who were divided and without a state of their own. There were others still submerged within multinational empires. But, in consequence of the

MAP 3   Europe, 1648

EUROPE IN 1648

——— Holy Roman Empire

Brandenburg Prussian Possessions

Austrian Possessions

Spanish Possessions

Swedish Possessions

RUSSIAN EMPIRE

Moscow

LITHUANIA

POLAND

Warsaw

EAST PRUSSIA

COURLAND

LIVONIA

ESTONIA

INGRIA

SWEDISH EMPIRE

NORWAY (DANISH)

DENMARK

Copenhagen

BRANDENBURG

GERMAN STATES OF THE EMPIRE

SAXONY

BAVARIA

AUSTRIAN EMPIRE

Vienna

HUNGARY

Budapest

TRANS—SYLVANIA

MOLDAVIA

WALLACHIA

CRIMEA

Black Sea

Constantinople

OTTOMAN EMPIRE

SICILY

NAPLES

Naples

PAPAL STATES

Rome

TUSCANY

MODENA

PARMA

SARDINIA

CORSICA

Mediterranean Sea

VENETIA

Milan

SAVOY

SWITZERLAND

FRANCHE COMTE

FRANCE

Paris

SPANISH NETHERLANDS

UNITED PROVINCES

London

ENGLAND

UNITED KINGDOM

SCOTLAND

Edinburgh

North Sea

IRELAND

Dublin

Atlantic Ocean

SPAIN

Madrid

PORTUGAL

Lisbon

0   100   200   300 mls

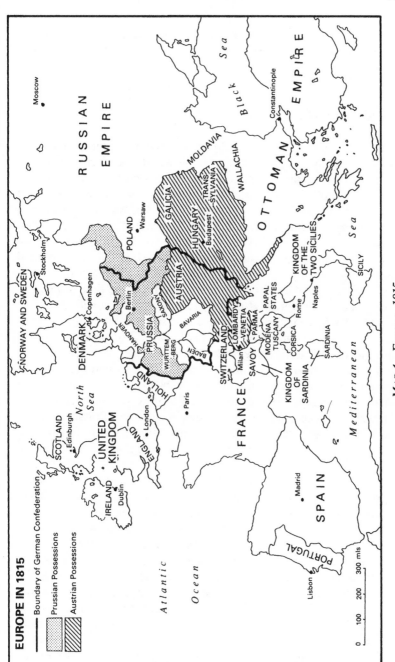

MAP 4 *Europe, 1815*

SOURCE: *Atlas of World History* (Nelson, 1965).

territorial changes achieved in this age, by the close of the period something more closely approaching the national states of modern times began to be established.

MEANS OF ACQUIRING TERRITORY

A territory that was desired could be acquired by a number of means. It was generally accepted that the simplest and most decisive way was by the use of military force. It was recognised that this could be expensive, both in blood and treasure, but it was rarely suggested that its use for such a purpose was wrong. War was recognised as a normal way of achieving that. Louis XIV recounts how in 1666, when he was able to choose between making war on England or Spain, he "envisaged with pleasure the prospect of these two wars as a vast field that could create great opportunities for me to distinguish myself, and fulfil the great expectations that I had for some time inspired in the public".[21] Frederick II of Prussia was equally candid about the need to use force for this purpose if necessary. It was not sufficient, he told his successor in the first of his *Political Testaments*, simply to indicate the territories one wishes to acquire; it was necessary to "propose the means of acquiring them". He described precisely the circumstances which would be favourable for Prussia to acquire Saxony: for example, at a time when Saxony was in alliance with Austria, a breach of relations between Austria and Prussia could be made the pretext for "invading Saxony, disarming its forces, and fortifying the country".[22] He even indicated the exact routes by which his invading army would enter the country, the forces he would employ and the strategic feints he would use (very much the strategy he proceeded to use in invading Saxony at the opening of the Seven Years War four years later). If Austria came to the assistance of Saxony, further moves would be necessary: "having subjected Saxony it would be necessary to carry the war into Moravia", where a decisive battle would make it possible to threaten Bohemia and the Austrian capital. If Britain appeared menacing, France could be induced to occupy Hanover. At the subsequent peace Prussia would arrange an exchange of territory: he would generously return Moravia to Austria, but would secure Saxony in return, while if necessary compensating the Saxon Elector with Bohemia at Austria's expense.[23]

This was not mere talk. A large proportion of the wars of the period were launched with clear territorial objectives in view, often openly avowed. Sweden attacked Poland in 1655, with the aim of

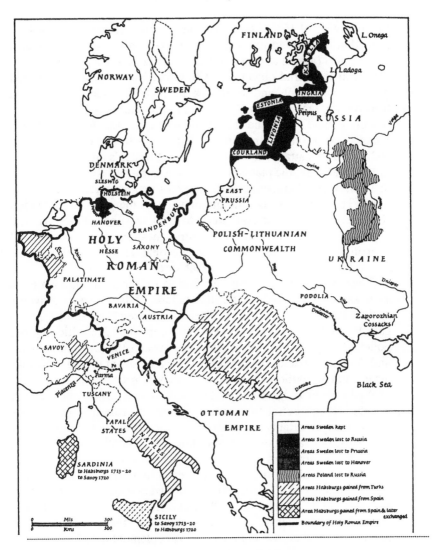

MAP 5 *Territorial changes east of the Rhine, 1648–1721*

SOURCE: R. M. Hatton, *Europe in the Age of Louis XIV* (London, 1969)
p. 220.

securing a further stretch of Baltic coast. Brandenburg participated in
the same war (on both sides in turn) with the aim of acquiring full
control (sovereignty) in East Prussia; while Russia participated (also
on both sides in turn) in the hope of acquiring Livonia and Riga.

France's wars of 1667–8 (aimed at the Spanish Netherlands), of 1672 (aimed at the United Provinces), of 1681–4 (aimed at Luxembourg) and of 1688 (aimed at Cologne and the Palatinate) were all directed mainly at territorial objectives. The Great Northern War, launched by Russia, Saxony and Denmark in 1700, was designed to win territory for each of them (Ingria and Estonia for Russia, Livonia for Saxony-Poland, and the Holstein-Gottorp lands for Denmark). Spain's assault on Sardinia and Sicily in 1717–18 and on Gibraltar in 1627, Turkey's attack on Venice in 1714, Sweden's attacks on Russia in 1743 and 1788, the planned attack of Austria and Russia on Prussia in 1756, were all launched in the hope of making territorial acquisitions. Territory was also the major issue in the wars of succession (Chapter 6 below); and all were to lead to substantial territorial adjustments, over and above the central question of succession (itself a territorial matter). War had indeed become sanctified as the normal means for fulfilling ambitions of that sort.

There were some who were willing to recognise the human costs such assaults involved. After the failure of her own endeavours against Prussia in 1756, Maria Theresa opposed the use of force to gain territory. She wrote to her son Joseph in 1772 criticising the policy of "trying to profit by the war between the Ottoman empire and Russia to extend our frontiers and gain advantages of which we never thought earlier":[24] "even were they to procure me the district of Wallachia or Belgrade itself, I should always consider them dearly bought". It was better to seek to "escape . . . from this unfortunate position as creditably as possible, without thinking of gains for ourselves, but rather of re-establishing our reputation and our good faith".[25] And six years later, when her son was willing to risk war for the sake of gaining Bavaria, she was even more outspoken: "even if our claims on Bavaria were more confirmed and more solid than they are, one should hesitate to kindle a universal blaze for the sake of a particular convenience. . . . We should lose the public credit so happily established: we should have to supplement it by force and we should never enjoy tranquillity, peace and the happiness which follows on good faith, credit and public confidence". Such matters, she believed, should be arranged

by the conciliatory way of negotiations and decency but never by the way of arms or force, which would rightly raise all the world against us from the first, and would lose us even those who would have remained neutral. I have never seen such an enterprise

187

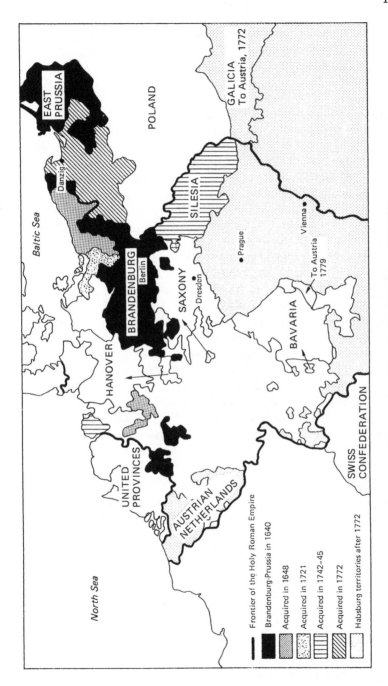

MAP 6   The growth of Brandenburg-Prussia, 1648–1772
SOURCE: Geoffrey Treasure, The Making of Modern Europe, 1648–1780

prosper, except for one against me of 1741, which resulted in the loss of Silesia. The invasion of Saxony, Spain's of Portugal, ours of 1756, not one succeeded; they totally ruined all who undertook them.[26]

Even less pacific rulers recognised that war should be the last resort. All would have preferred to acquire territory peacefully if that option were open. Even Frederick the Great declared that "acquisitions made by the pen are preferable to ones made by the sword".[27] Louis XIV admitted ruefully that "hope of victory usually draws both sides into the fight and yet one of them is always defeated";[28] and he was to warn his great-grandson on his deathbed that "the most glorious victory is too dearly bought when it must be paid for in the blood of your subjects". In discussing how he could acquire Polish Prussia, one of the territories he most desired, Frederick the Great admitted that he "did not think the way of arms was the best means of doing so";[29] it would be better to try to take advantage of the situation of the instability that would occur on the death of the Polish king to intervene discreetly, so that Prussia might acquire "now a town, now another district, until all is eaten up"[30] (a fairly accurate anticipation of the first partition of Poland twenty years later). For Swedish Pomerania, the third major territory he coveted, the best way might be to await a conflict between Sweden and Russia for Livonia: Prussia might then offer to support Sweden in return for the cession of the territory in Swedish Pomerania.[31] In the same way, Louis XIV was willing, in a series of treaties of partition, to seek to acquire by negotiation a reasonable share of the Spanish heritage rather than seek to win everything at the risk of confrontation.

Negotiations alone, however, were unlikely to succeed unless a ruler had something – often other territory – to bargain with. That is why Frederick the Great believed it might be necessary to seize Bohemia in order to exchange it subsequently for the territory he really desired, Saxony. Similarly, to acquire Polish Prussia the best option would be "a situation where Russia might have a pressing need of our assistance": there might then "be the possibility of securing the cession of Thorn, Elbing and a neighbouring place to secure communication from Pomerania to the Vistula".[32] Later "some other morsel", could be obtained in the same way, he suggested, for example by offering Rhine territories, such as Julich or Berg, in exchange for Saxony: "however it is accomplished this acquisition is necessary if this State is to be given the consistency it

lacks".[33] And his minister was later to propose a complicated exchange of German territories, involving Austria, Prussia, Saxony and
the Palatinate, to satisfy the territorial needs of each state.[34] Concessions of other kinds could be made in return for territory. In 1668
Louis XIV offered to recognise Spain's claim to Portugal if Spain
would give him the Spanish Netherlands in return. In 1686 Russia
offered to join the war which Poland and Austria were waging against
the Turks if Poland would finally cede her Kiev. Charles XII of
Sweden, at his weakest moment in 1713–14, was willing to consider
ceding Swedish territory in return for equivalents elsewhere, or at
least military assistance in acquiring them.[35]

In some cases a combination of diplomatic and military pressure
was necessary. An example is the persistent campaign launched by
Elizabeth Farnese, the queen of Spain, and her husband Philip V, to
acquire territory in Italy for their two sons, Carlos and Felipe, after
the War of Spanish Succession. The first step was the war Spain
launched in 1717–18 to recover Sardinia and Sicily, given up at the
end of that war a few years before. The failure of this attempt was
followed by a series of pressures, bargains and negotiations. The
duchy of Parma, from which the Spanish queen had herself originally
come, became the next target. The emperor Charles VI declared that
territory an imperial fief, which he would assign only when the
present ruler died without heirs. Under international pressure, however, he did agree in 1720 that Swiss troops should be admitted to it,
as a guarantee that the desired transfer would take place when the
time came. Soon the Spanish rulers were demanding that the Swiss
should be replaced by Spanish troops, as a safer guarantee that the
transfer would take place. The emperor at first rejected this and,
when the ruler finally died in 1731, occupied the duchy with his own
forces. Under pressure, however, he did eventually agree (in return
for Spanish acceptance of the Pragmatic Sanction) to allow Spanish
troops to enter, enabling Don Carlos to take up the succession. But
the Spanish rulers still wanted territory for the younger son and
secured powerful support for this claim from France. Under the
second Bourbon Family Compact of 1733 France agreed to support
both a claim for Don Felipe to acquire Naples and Sicily (the
kingdom of the two Sicilies) and that of Don Carlos to acquire
Tuscany (in addition to Parma). As soon as the War of Polish
Succession broke out later that year Spain accordingly occupied
Naples and Sicily. At the end of the war, therefore, she was able to
strike a new deal: the emperor now had to agree to give the more

valuable Naples and Sicily to Don Carlos, while he himself regained control of Parma. But the result was that Don Felipe still had nothing, so that Spain's appetite was still not satisfied. When she joined the War of Austrian Succession in 1740, she revived the demand for Parma and Tuscany, this time for Don Felipe, offering in return to guarantee Austria's remaining lands. That proposal was rejected by Austria. But at the end of the war, in which Austria was less than successful in Italy, Spain finally regained Parma, awarding it this time to the younger brother, while Tuscany passed into Austrian hands. In this case, therefore, the alternation of war and diplomacy yielded substantial territorial gains for the Spanish rulers.

Austria herself combined diplomatic and military claims in an attempt to acquire control of Bavaria. During the negotiations at the close of the War of Spanish Succession, some Austrian statesmen believed that the territory of the defeated elector of Bavaria would represent a more valuable acquisition for Austria than the distant Spanish Netherlands. The emperor himself rejected that view, however, and such an exchange was not pursued at that time. But there were continuing Austrian attempts to secure Bavaria by a number of means during the course of the century. Charles VI himself at one time hoped to marry his daughter Maria Theresa to the Elector of Bavaria, so winning the territory through a dynastic union: the Elector would have become emperor but Bavaria would have been joined to the Hapsburg lands. During the War of Austrian Succession Austrian forces invaded and occupied Bavaria and at one time Maria Theresa was interested in securing the electorate on a long-term basis. When, because of subsequent military reverses, she was not able to achieve this, Austrian statesmen began to consider alternative arrangements. In 1755–6 Kaunitz considered, for example, an exchange of the Austrian Netherlands for territories in northern Italy. After Maria Theresa's son Joseph became emperor in 1765, he too began to look seriously at ways of acquiring Bavaria, an aim he openly avowed. He persuaded the new Elector, who succeeded in 1777, to sign an agreement transferring Lower Bavaria, strategically the most important part, to Austria (with the possibility of a further transfer later), in return for a promise to provide for the Elector's large brood of natural children. But this aroused opposition both from the Elector's heirs and from other German states. To prevent the transfer Prussia, having won the support of other German states, invaded Austrian territory, and Joseph had to be content with acquiring only a small area of south-east Bavaria. However, his enthusiasm for a more substantial acquisition was not dampened. In 1784 he made a new proposal: the ruler would hand over the electorate to Austria, being given in return the Austrian Netherlands, where he would be made king. But again Prussia and other German states strenuously opposed this proposal, as did the Elector's heirs, and again the idea had to be dropped. Finally, in 1792 an exchange of the same kind was mooted yet again, but could not be proceeded with because of the loss of Belgium to the French revolutionary forces.

Another means of acquiring territory was by purchase. This was by no means uncommon in this age. Louis XIV bought Dunkirk from England in 1661 for four million livres. Twenty years later he purchased the important fortress of Casale from the Duke of Mantua. And in the following century, in 1768, France effectively purchased the island of Corsica from Genoa. Hanover bought Bremen from Denmark in 1715 for thirty thousand thalers. Prussia in effect bought Stettin and part of Pomerania from Sweden in 1720, agreeing to pay two million ecus in return for retaining them; while in the following year Peter the Great similarly agreed to pay two million thalers to the same country in return for acquiring Livonia. Genoa bought Finale from the emperor Charles VI in 1730; Denmark bought St Croix from France in 1732. Denmark made a payment of cash (in addition to two small territories) in return for the final renunciation, by the Holstein-Gottorp family and their Russian heirs, of their rights to their lands in 1767. Occasionally a territory could be acquired as the dowry of a royal bride: England acquired Tangier and Bombay as part of the dowry of the Portuguese Infanta, Catherine Braganza, in 1662. So normal was the idea of the transfer of territories through a cash transaction that even bribery, it was believed, might be of assistance in some cases: Frederick the Great suggested that if Prussia were to negotiate to acquire Swedish Pomerania (at a time when Sweden was in pressing need of money) "it might not be impossible to succeed by corrupting a few senators".[36]

Traditionally the simplest and cheapest way of acquiring territory had been through well-judged matrimony. This was the means by which in earlier days the major territorial acquisitions had been acquired (enabling the Hapsburgs, for example, to put together their vast empire). There was, however a strict limit to what could be acquired in that way during this age. Precisely because of the effect such arrangements could have on the distribution of territory (and so on the balance of power) dynastic marriages were now often hedged with explicit renunciations and limiting clauses. When Louis XIV married the daughter of the Spanish king, she had to make a specific pledge that in doing so she renounced all her rights to inherit in Spain (which did not prevent Louis from manufacturing bogus claims to the Spanish Netherlands based on his wife's rights in 1667). Similarly, the marriage of Maria Theresa to the Duke of Lorraine could not bring that duchy permanently to Austria, as the emperor would dearly have liked, because France ensured at the end of the War of Polish Succession that it should pass to France eventually. Even if no explicit reservations of this kind had been made, there were other difficulties. As we shall see in the next chapter, other states were now increasingly willing to intervene to prevent any succession which seemed likely to upset the balance of power. Thus, even where well-founded claims based on heredity could be made, they were often not put forward. Both Louis XIV and the Austrian emperor might have demanded the right to the entire Spanish inheritance (both had married daughters of the Spanish king); but both were willing to negotiate for a compromise settlement, renouncing at least part of their rights and assigning even these to cadet branches. The nieces of Charles VI had a better claim to inherit in Austria than his daughter, yet they were willing to sign away their rights in her favour. In these and many other cases the disposition of territory was often determined by negotiation rather than by any attempt, as had been normal in earlier times, to apply strictly traditional rules of inheritance.

There was thus a wide range of means available for securing territory in this age. Which was adopted depended largely on the capabilities of states. Those that were powerful – France in Louis XIV's day and again after 1789, Prussia in the middle of the eighteenth century, Russia throughout most of the period, Britain beyond the seas – were often able to acquire the lands they wanted by armed force. The weaker states could not resort to that method: needing to rely on diplomacy alone, they found themselves more often losers than gainers of territory. Sometimes territory could be won from weaker nations, but not from stronger ones. Austria could win huge amounts of territory from Turkey, but conceded it to Prussia in Germany; Sweden could win territory from Denmark, but lost it to Russia. Overwhelming power was not always necessary. Sometimes even small states, such as Savoy, could, by skilful diplomacy (including changing sides at crucial moments), make small but significant territorial gains. But it was generally recognised that force was the surest means of securing territorial adjustments; and few states hesitated to make use of it when they had the chance to win the territory they prized.

RECOVERY OF TERRITORY

Because territory was such a prized objective its loss was bitterly resented. Often there were prolonged efforts to regain the lands that had been taken. A significant proportion of the wars of the age resulted from the efforts by one state to recover territory that had been lost in earlier encounters.

One example concerned Alsace, which was to become a source of conflict between France and her German neighbours for three hundred years. The Peace of Westphalia contained deliberately ambiguous provisions concerning this area. While it unequivocally transferred ten major towns to France, most of the rest continued to be governed according to traditional feudal arrangements. It was still seen in Germany as a part of the empire, as it had been for centuries. By the so-called reunions of 1680 – rulings by specially appointed law courts – Louis XIV secured judgments recognising France's right to previously contested areas. The emperor and other German rulers were determined to reverse these judgments.[37] One of the main purposes of the League of Augsburg, formed in the following year, was to resist and if possible reverse the encroachments. Although the emperor agreed, because of his preoccupation with war in the east, to a temporary truce in 1684, as soon as the Nine Years War began four years later Austria insisted that a key element in the peace settlement was the restoration of the status quo established in the Peace of Westphalia. The war was indecisive. But at the Peace of Ryswick in 1697 France was obliged to evacuate Breisach and Phillippsburg and other important points; fortification on the Rhine were to be destroyed (though she retained Strasbourg); and the other territories she had acquired through the reunions were to be restored. At the end of the following war, in 1714, France had to give up possessions on the right bank of the Rhine and islands in the middle of the river. But again she retained Strasbourg, with Landau and most of the rest of Alsace on her own side. The Austrian emperor therefore remained unsatisfied. He was determined to recover these territories: the official document sworn at the emperor's election continued to refer to his duty to recover Alsace until the Hapsburgs briefly lost the imperial dignity in 1742. But they were not successful enough in the wars of Polish and Austrian succession to achieve their aim. The Rhine continued to prove an impenetrable defence against revanchism; and it was not until the following century that German states were once again able to recover the former imperial lands – Alsace and Lorraine – which they continued to regard as their own.

The seizure of Silesia by Frederick the Great in 1740 led to a similar struggle for repossession by Austria. Eventually this was to prove equally unsuccessful. Having taken possession of the province, Frederick, believing that he had established a *fait accompli*, immediately offered to guarantee the new Austrian queen in all her other territories if she would accept the loss of Silesia. But Maria Theresa, though young and inexperienced, was determined to recover the lost territory. Having won the support of the Hungarian nobility, she mobilised all the resources of her enfeebled state in a war of re-conquest. With only half-hearted support from her allies, however, she was unable to achieve her aim, and twice concluded peace treaties surrendering Silesia to Frederick. In her own eyes these represented only truces in a continuing struggle. She entered into a treaty with Russia in 1746, including a secret provision referring to the recovery of Silesia. And though Frederick was able to secure, in the Treaty of Aix-la-Chapelle, guarantees for his possession of Silesia by the other signatories, she proceeded to prepare for a new war to recover the territory. In her eyes the question was not whether the war would be renewed, but with what allies she would fight. Eventually she accepted the strategy proposed by her minister, Kaunitz, to secure the alliance of France (in addition to that of Russia, Saxony, Sweden and other German states) for that purpose. Even with the help of this vast coalition however she was again unsuccessful, and was obliged at the end of the war once more to acknowledge Prussia's control of Silesia. But she still remained unreconciled to the loss and was constantly seeking "compensation" for it elsewhere (for example, Bavaria or Alsace-Lorraine). One of her justifications for seizing Zips from Poland in 1669 was that this represented some compensation for the loss of Silesia. And one of her reasons for resisting the first partition of Poland three years later was that, since Prussia would benefit at least as much as Austria, she would still not get the *quid pro quo* she deserved for the loss of Silesia.

Denmark, likewise, fought a series of wars to regain territories she had lost. In 1657, she joined the First War of the North for the express purpose of recovering from Sweden the territories she had lost in 1645 after her previous war. Though she failed on that occasion she did not abandon hope of securing her revenge. Determined to recover Scania, she engaged in war once more in 1675–9, but was compelled by French intervention to restore the previous status quo. She made continuing efforts to acquire the lands of the duke of Holstein-Gottorp, who was in league with Sweden. In 1700 she joined in an alliance with Russia and Saxony-Poland against Sweden, immediately attacking the Holstein-Gottorp lands. Once again she was defeated, this time still more quickly, but ten years later resumed the struggle. At its end though she did not recover Scania, she had the satisfaction of securing control of the Holstein-Gottorp lands in Schleswig, which had been for her a prime objective in the war.

From this point it was Sweden, having lost substantial territories in 1721, which became involved in wars of recovery. The main objective of the anti-Russian "Hat" party in launching war against Russia in 1741 was to secure the recovery of some of the Baltic territory lost twenty years earlier. All she achieved was the loss of further territory, this time in Finland, to Russia. So now there were still more lands to be reclaimed. After Gustavus III restored autocratic rule in 1772 he too proceeded, when he had assembled sufficient forces, to launch a new war in the hope of recovering these Finnish lands (1788–90). Again he was militarily unsuccessful; and only the preoccupation of Russia with war against Turkey in the south saved him from losing yet more territory. Even then Sweden's hope of recovering territory was not totally extinguished. She launched yet another war in 1808–9 but this was equally unsuccessful: the only result was that Russia secured most of the rest of Swedish Finland.

Turkey was another power which suffered substantial losses of territory, first to Austria and Venice and later to Russia, and was to fight a number of wars of recovery. She surrendered huge amounts of territory in the Treaty of Carlowitz of 1699 (see below). By her victory over Peter the Great on the Pruth in 1711, she recovered Azov and fortresses on the Dnieper which she had lost in 1700. In 1714 she attacked Venice in order to recover the territory in Greece and Dalmatia she had lost in 1699 and secured much of it. In 1735–9 a new war with Austria and Russia provided the opportunity of recovering territory; and as a result she regained Wallachia and Serbia (including Belgrade), lost to Austria in 1718. In 1768 a violation of Ottoman territory by Russian troops was used as the pretext for a further war, in which she hoped to recover territory north of the

Black sea; defeated however, she was compelled instead to yield further lands and to grant independence to the Crimea. Finally, in 1787 she launched yet another war, designed to recover the lands lost fifteen years earlier. Again she only suffered further losses, yielding the fortress of Ochakov, and being compelled to recognise the Russian annexation of the Crimea.

Spain was another country which lost substantial territory during the period, especially at the end of the War of Spanish Succession, and made repeated efforts to recover it. Though her invasion of Sardinia and Sicily in 1717–18 failed in that purpose, she persisted, as we have seen, in seeking, through a combination of diplomatic and military pressures, to recover territory in Italy for Spanish princes. She was even more determined to regain Gibraltar. After the failure of negotiations to that end (in which she was at one time assured that Britain would return the territory) she attempted to achieve it by war in 1727–8; and renewed the siege of the Rock in subsequent wars (for example, in the long siege of 1779–82). She had more success over Minorca. This was acquired by Britain in 1713, taken by France in 1748, regained by Britain in 1763, and finally recovered by Spain, after the War of American Independence, in 1783. On the other hand her efforts to retake the Falkland Islands, which she regarded as her own, were unsuccessful: though she sent a naval expedition which expelled the British from Port Egmont in 1770, threatened with a major war and without support from France she was compelled eventually to return it to Britain.

Overseas territories moved back and forth particularly rapidly, sometimes being passed from hand to hand at the end of each successive war. New York, founded originally by the Dutch in the early seventeenth century, was captured by Britain in 1667, retaken by the Dutch in 1773 and was handed over finally to Britain in the following year. Trinidad was successively in Spanish, Dutch, French and British hands. St Lucia, at first British, was made "neutral" in 1713, ceded to France in 1763 and reacquired by Britain during the Napoleonic wars. The French fortress of Louisbourg was captured by Britain in 1745, recovered by France in 1748 and taken again by Britain in 1759 and held, this time permanently, in 1763. Florida, originally Spanish, was taken by Britain in 1763, recaptured by Spain in 1783, and finally sold to the US in 1819. Louisiana, for long French, was handed over to Spain in 1763 and sold by Napoleon to the US in 1803. The French colony of Senegal was handed over to Britain at the end of an unsuccessful war in 1763 but was recovered by her again after a more successful one 20 years later.

TABLE 3: Patterns of warfare: traditional antagonists, 1648–1815

Opponents	Wars	Opponents	Wars	Opponents	Wars
France–Austria	1673–9	France–Spain	1635–59	France–Britain	1665–7
	1688–97		1667–8		1689–97
	1701–14		1673–9		1701–13
	1733–5		1683–4		1740–8
	1741–8		1689–97		1756–63
	1792–7		1793–5		1778–83
	1798–1801				1793–1802
	1805				1803–15
	1809				
	1813–15				
Britain–United Provinces	1652–4	Denmark–Sweden	1657–60	Russia–Sweden	1656–61
	1665–7		1675–9		1700–21
	1672–4		1700		1741–3
	1780–4		1709–20		1788–90
			1788–9		1808–9
		Russia–Turkey	1677–81		
			1687–1800		
			1710–13		
			1736–9		
			1768–74		
			1787–92		
			1806–12		

What is striking is that in all these cases efforts at recovery, though persistent, were unavailing. Normally territory had been lost because one nation was stronger in the first place. That relationship did not alter in the succeeding period. The state that had lost before – Austria against Prussia, Sweden and Turkey against Russia – continued to lose. And the lost territories were therefore not recovered.

It was partly because of these rivalries for particular territories that the same countries often fought each other over and over again. Pairs of antagonists were established. France and Spain fought each other five times between 1648 and 1697, after which (with a change of dynasty in Spain) they were for long at peace. England and the United Provinces fought each other three times between 1652 and 1674, after which they were continually at peace until 1780. Sweden and Denmark fought each other three times between 1657 and 1700. In the course of the whole period Sweden and Russia fought four wars against each other. Britain and France seven, Russia and Turkey six. As the period progressed, however, the pattern changed slightly – the traditional rivalry between Bourbon and Hapsburg, which had dominated European politics for so long, was replaced by new rivalries, reflecting new territorial conflicts: between Austria and Prussia in Germany and between France and Britain overseas. The diplomatic revolution of 1756 vividly demonstrated that change. While the age-old antipathy between France and Austria was finally set aside, the two new rivalries survived the change, and were fought out with equal passion, with new partners, in both wars.

Revanchist sentiments were encouraged by the fact that existing frontiers rested on no logical foundation. Because the borders did not reflect any clear linguistic, ethnic or cultural divisions, any ruler could believe himself to have an equal claim to territory elsewhere. If it was normal for Sweden to rule large areas inhabited by German-speaking people on the south side of the Baltic, there was no reason why Denmark should not rule Swedish-speaking areas on the Swedish side. If Austria claimed authority in distant Belgium, why should not Spain claim it in distant Italy, or Britain in Gibraltar or Minorca. Since dynastic rights counted for less and less and territories were freely swopped around to suit the convenience of governments, one state had as good a reason to claim a particular territory as another. German-speaking Silesia could as logically be controlled by German-speaking Prussia as by German-speaking Austria; Italian Naples by non-Italian Austria or non-Italian Spain. The urge to regain lost territory might be made especially powerful by long historical associations (Alsace); by geographical factors (Gibraltar); by the economic significance of a territory (Silesia); or by dynastic rivalries (Sicily, Parma). But ultimately the most important factor was pride of possession, the mutual jealousy of rulers, each unwilling to suffer loss at the hands of another. Often, it was believed, the next war might provide the occasion for avenging a past wrong, for regaining a treasured property which had been unjustly stolen by another.

TERRITORY AND THE BALANCE OF POWER

But whether or not substantial territorial gains could be made depended ultimately on a different factor: the balance of power.

Efforts by one state to aggrandise themselves excessively always brought efforts by others to prevent this. The successive acquisitions made by Louis XIV – from Spain in 1659 and 1678, and in Alsace, Casale and Luxembourg in the following years – caused other states of the continent to join together to prevent any further gains (and even to take away some which had already been made). When Sweden, already hugely enlarged in 1648, made further acquisitions in 1660 and began to increase in power still further early in the following century, a growing group of states came together to prevent further gains; and succeeded in depriving her in 1720–1 of many of the acquisitions previously made. When Russia in turn appeared likely to profit excessively from Sweden's defeat, advancing even into North Germany, a significant number of states joined to limit her acquisitions (see below). When the Prussian king, having acquired one Austrian province, proceeded in 1756 to invade another German state, a powerful coalition, including the three largest states on the continent, joined together to restore the status quo. Finally, when France once more seemed likely to acquire a still greater domination after the revolution there, the other states of the continent, after many hesitations, finally combined their efforts to cut her back to size. Thus there was always a limit to the gains which could be made by any one state: a limit that was set by the balance of power mechanism.

It was unilateral action which was particularly objectionable. Unilateral steps by France to secure the Spanish Netherlands in 1667–8 provoked a multilateral response: the creation of the Triple Alliance of the United Provinces, Sweden and Britain to compel her to desist. Unilateral acceptance by France of Charles II's will in 1701, in defiance of the multilateral arrangements reached in the final partition treaty agreed only a year earlier, stimulated a combined effort by the Grand Alliance to compel her to relinquish the gains she had made. Austria's efforts to acquire Bavaria through private arrangements with its elector (even when these were peaceful) had to be prevented by the joint action of other states. The six partition treaties of the age relating to Spain and Poland were a visible manifestation of this effort to substitute multilateral for unilateral action.[38] The treaties relating to Spain, agreed between the rulers of France and Austria in 1668, and among a wider group in 1698 and 1700, aimed to prevent excessive gains being made by any one state. The treaties relating to Poland between Russia, Prussia and Austria in 1772, 1793 and 1795, were designed to prevent any one of them acquiring an excessive amount of Polish territory in relation to the others.[39] It was above all the fear that one particular power might be stealing a march on others for its own advantage which promoted collective action to keep it in check (or at least ensure that the spoils were shared).

Similarly, alliances were often designed to ensure an equal sharing of territorial benefits. Their provisions often included understandings about the distribution of gains at the end of a contemplated war. Thus the Dover treaty between England and France of 1670 provided that England should win territory around the Scheldt estuary, which she needed for commercial reasons (in addition to a subsidy), while France would acquire the gains she desired elsewhere in the Republic. The alliance between Prussia, Saxony and Denmark for war against Sweden of 1698, specified what each was to expect from the exercise: Ingria and Estonia for Russia, Livonia for Augustus and the Holstein-Gottorp lands for Denmark. The Grand Alliance of 1701–3 specified the gains to be acquired by each member of it: a string of fortresses for Portugal, Montferrar and parts of Lombardy for Savoy, the Spanish Netherlands and "just satisfaction" in Italy for Austria, and so on. The alliance created against Austria in 1740–1 specified the precise partition of Austrian lands and the gains to be made by each party: Bavaria, Prussia and Saxony were each to secure juicy morsels of Hapsburg territory in Bohemia, Silesia and Moravia, Spain lands in Italy, France in the Austrian Netherlands, and Sardinia in the Milanese (leaving Maria Theresa only eastern Austria and Hungary). The alliance against Prussia in 1756 provided for a similar share-out of her territory: Silesia and Glatz for Austria, eastern Prussia for Russia, eastern Pomerania for Sweden, Cleves and Wesel for France. Nor need any ruler rest content with the promises made by one set of partners. By switching alliances, a state could sometimes maximise its gains: so by changing sides Brandenburg secured a recognition of its sovereignty in East Prussia from Sweden and Poland in turn in 1655–60; while Savoy, by changing sides twice (in 1696 and 1702) during the two wars against Louis XIV, maximised the profits she acquired.

But alliances also had dangers. Though they might reduce the threat from one direction, they might create a new one elsewhere. It was no use preventing one power aggrandising itself if the effect was to allow an ally to do so just as much. This partly accounts for the frequency with which alliances were deserted during this age (see below). During the war against the Dutch of 1672, many in England became more concerned about the growth of French power which might result than with the traditional rivalry with the Dutch, and quickly demanded a separate peace or even a change of sides. In 1710–11, Tory leaders in Britain became worried that by fighting for the total destruction of French power in Spain, they might merely replace it with an enhanced Austrian power (a danger made even more acute when Charles II of Spain became also Charles VI of Austria in 1711). Frederick the Great, having secured his own objectives against Austria in 1740–1, deliberately allowed Austria to make a recovery (while purporting to remain at war with her) rather than see France win too pronounced a victory. It was these ambiguous attitudes which ensured that the territorial settlements reached at the end of wars rarely provided for a totally clear-cut result. They nearly always represented compromise, in which no power got as much as it had hoped. At Nymegen Louis got far less than he set out to acquire, mainly because of the defection of England and Brandenburg. At Ryswick, on the other hand, he suffered a less serious defeat than he might otherwise have done, because Savoy changed sides to join him. At Utrecht he was spared more humiliating losses because Britain abandoned her allies for balance of power motives. Austria was unable to recover the territory she hoped for in the Seven Years War because Russia withdrew from the contest. Even in 1814–15, though at least there was a decisive winner, France came reasonably well out of an unqualified defeat because of the mutual jealousies of the victorious powers and their concern to maintain a balance in Europe: so France was able, even after the Hundred Days, to keep the boundaries of 1790. As a result of this constant search for balance the territorial changes resulting from war in this age were much less than would otherwise have been the case.

It was the same concern with the balance which led to the principle of "compensation", appealed to so widely in this age. It came to be widely accepted that a gain, especially of a territorial kind made by one state, had to be matched by corresponding gains by others. Sometimes this principle was applied even where a territory had been lost in war. Thus for decades after the loss of Silesia in 1740 Austria continued to argue that she should be awarded alternative territory to make up for this loss. She would have been content, for example, during the War of Austrian Succession, to accept territory in North Italy (Maria Theresa described it as a "*dedommagement*") for that purpose,[40] and her ally Britain proposed that either Bavaria or an area of Italy might be suitable substitutes. Or a ruler who had lost in one area was compensated elsewhere: so during the negotiations for the ending of the War of Spanish Succession Philip V of Spain was offered one Italian territory after another to reconcile him to the loss of Spain itself.[41] More often compensation was demanded, not for losses incurred but for the gains which had been made by others. So during the Polish partitions each new demand by one party would stimulate a further demand by another.[42] And in the negotiations at the end of the Napoleonic wars any acquisition which promised to one victor power had to be matched by corresponding gains for another.[43] Precise calculations came to be made about the area, population, resources and strategic value of each territory, in order to be able to match it with others elsewhere.[44] And at the Congress of Vienna a "statistical" committee was set up precisely to undertake such calculations and comparisons: to ensure that a reasonable balance was achieved among the major powers in the allocation of territories.

To achieve this, territories were shuffled around, swopped and bartered in unscrupulous fashion. Under the Treaty of Utrecht, Sicily, for long ruled by Spain, was handed over to almost equally distant Savoy; while Sardinia was awarded to Bavaria, even more remote. Eight years later Sicily was once more transferred, this time to Austria, while Sardinia was now transferred to Savoy in compensation. In 1738 Sicily was handed over yet again, this time to the son of the king of Spain, and joined with Naples in the kingdom of the Two Sicilies. Parma, which had been briefly ruled by the same prince from 1732, was six years later transferred for a short time to Austria, and finally handed over to another son of the king of Spain in 1748. In 1738, when the Saxon Elector was recognised as king of Poland, Lorraine was given to the unsuccessful candidate for the throne of Poland as a consolation prize. And so on. Transfers of that kind, designed to secure a balance among the powers, bore no relationship either to the rules of inheritance, to historical rights, or to geographical logic; still less to cultural or linguistic ties; and least of all to the loyalties and desires of populations. They were crude bargains, designed to suit the convenience of the rulers who held power, to secure an accommodation among them. In every case the people concerned acquired a foreign ruler, and almost always it was one who had no previous connection with the state concerned, and was therefore usually totally ignorant of its laws and customs.

One consequence of the competition for territory among the larger powers was the progressive elimination of the smaller ones. At the beginning of this period there still existed several hundred political entities in Europe, including, besides fifteen or so significant states, a considerable number of principalities, duchies, margravates, free cities, archbishoprics and other ecclesiastical territories. During the course of this period a significant number of these smaller states were swallowed up. Sometimes this occurred because a ruling family died out and became subject to a claim from a powerful ruler elsewhere; sometimes because they were conquered or absorbed. Among the states which disappeared from the map as a result of this process was Poland; Venice (occupied by France in 1797 and added to Austria in 1814–15); Transylvania (semi-independent until conquered by Austria in 1683–99); Moldavia and Wallachia (principalities brought under increasingly close control by Turkey); Courland (finally absorbed by Russia in 1785); Schleswig and Holstein (absorbed by Denmark in 1721 and 1767); Corsica (acquired by France in 1768 after a period of semi-colonial rule by Genoa); Genoa itself (absorbed by Sardinia in 1815); not to speak of large numbers of lesser states in Germany and Italy. The states of Germany were drastically reduced through the forcible mergers introduced by Napoleon and maintained or adjusted at Vienna. Smaller states were increasingly unable to maintain a genuinely independent existence, and were thus sacrificed to the remorseless demands of the balance of power. In his *First Political Testament*, Frederick the Great commented on this process. Even in his own time, he wrote, he had seen Frisia absorbed by Prussia, three small territories by Saxony, Hanau joined to Hesse and Saxe-Lauenburg to Hanover. Hanover now seemed likely to acquire Osnabrück, while Prussia (he hoped) would get Mecklenburg and Franconia (each of them large areas which would greatly enhance Prussia's resources). Some of the free cities too, he believed, would be absorbed by their neighbours (as Augsburg had been by Bavaria, Hamburg by Denmark, Erfurt by Saxony, Ulna by Württemburg, Frankfurt-am-Main by the Palatinate, Lübeck by Hanover).[45] As he later stated, in commenting on the emperor's efforts to absorb Bavaria: "everybody will want to round their frontiers, the strong at the expense of the weak. Woe to the abbeys, or imperial cities which find themselves at the mercy of a neighbour strong enough to take possession of them".[46]

The competition for territory was inevitably one in which the larger states were likely to benefit most. But even the strongest powers could not win unlimited gains. They were checked, not, as in the age that followed, by the power of nationalist sentiment challenging the claims of autocratic rulers of different race, language and culture, but by the rival ambitions of other states, each with their own pretensions, and each determined that none should profit excessively from the competition in which all the main states were engaged. This concern for balance thus ensured that, at least among the larger states, territory was not shared out too unequally.

8 Trade

PROFIT AND POWER

One of the principal concerns of governments in this age was to increase their own country's share of the foreign trade that was available. This represented an important part of the general competition for prestige and power which took place among the states of the system. Trade was seen not as a mutually advantageous activity, which could bring benefit to all who engaged in it, but as a form of competition. That competition took place not merely between the individual merchants: it was a contest above all between the states to which they belonged, each seeking to acquire a greater share of the total amount of trade which was to be won.

It was generally believed that the total quantity of trade available was finite. An increase in the trade of one state must therefore involve a reduction in the trade of others. Colbert, for example, believed that "one nation could improve its commerce, its merchant marine, or its manufactures, only by taking away something from the trade, the shipping or the industry of another country".[1] This belief, which was widely derided in later ages, may not have been so naive or irrational as it was sometimes made to appear. Total available purchasing power was limited (there were constant complaints of the "shortage of money" which constrained trade); and with primitive banking systems and metallic currencies, it could not easily be increased. Credit was tight. Tradeable commodities were in limited supply. A large proportion of the population lived largely outside the money economy.[2] As Colbert himself argued:

> The discovery of new trade is very uncertain . . . and even if it did occur, it would not bring about new consumption of necessaries or luxuries. At the most it could make it easier for one nation rather than another to attract those goods which are already consumed and which constitute a part of the consumption of all Europe.[3]

That belief, whether rational or not, led to the idea that the states of the continent were engaged in continual competition to acquire a larger share of the limited quantity of trade. The ultimate objective was to win the largest share of the available money of the continent: what Colbert described as a "war of money". As he put it:

> There being only a given quantity of money which circulates in all Europe . . . one cannot succeed in increasing it . . . without at the same time taking the same quantity from other states, a fact which causes the double elevation which had been seen . . . in the last few years, one augmenting the power and greatness of your Majesty, the other effacing that of his enemies . . .[4]

Victory in that contest was important, he asserted, "because it is only the balance of money in a state that makes the difference in its greatness and power".[5] To add to the nation's stock of money was therefore to "increase the power, the greatness and the plenty of the state".[6] John Locke shared this belief. The war for money was not merely a competition to acquire more money, he held, but to acquire more than other states.

> Riches do not consist of having more gold and silver but having more in proportion than the rest of the world, more than our neighbours, whereby we are enabled to procure for ourselves a greater plenty of the conveniences of life than comes within the reach of neighbouring kings and states, who, sharing the gold and silver of the world in less proportion, want the means of plenty and power and so are poorer.[7]

This belief that it was *relative* wealth that counted was supported by the German cameralist (financial adviser), B. W. von Hörnigk, who wrote that "whether a nation be today mighty and rich or not depends not on the abundance of its powers and riches, but principally whether its neighbours possess more or less than it. For power and riches have become a relative matter."[8]

Concern with the volume of bullion that entered or left the country was nothing new; it had been a dominant preoccupation of rulers and their advisers throughout the later Middle Ages. There was, however, the beginnings of a change in attitudes on this question; it was now no longer generally believed that the best way to achieve that aim was by physical controls on the movement of bullion, or regulations requiring merchants who sold abroad to hand over to the king's agent the precious metals they acquired. Direct controls over the export of bullion were now relaxed. No such controls were maintained in the United Provinces from the time it secured its independence. They were lifted in England in 1663, and in other countries similar relaxations took place, or what regulations existed were not strictly enforced.[9] In this new age the aim was increasingly to secure the surplus by trade alone. As the English writer Thomas Mun put it (in defending the East India trade, in which he was engaged, against those who denounced it for losing silver to the East): "all nations which have no mines of their own are enriched with gold and silver by one and the same means . . . which is the balance of their foreign trade".[10]

Thus the "balance of trade" became almost as important a concern of every government as the "balance of power". Because it dictated the balance of money, this would determine, it was believed, whether a nation was rich or poor. As one writer put it: "If the exports of Britain exceed its imports, foreigners must pay the balance in treasure and the nation grows rich. But if the imports of Britain exceed its exports, we must pay the foreigners the balance in treasure and the nation grows poor."[11]

There were two ways of improving the balance. One was by cutting down on imports. It was widely suggested that they should be restrained by prohibitions or high tariff, or even that consumption should be held back, for example by sumptuary laws to penalise conspicuous consumption, because of the adverse effect on the balance of trade. So Thomas Mun warned of the dangers of excessive consumption: "if England were to consume more than it earned it will fare in England in short time as it doth with a man of great yearly living, that spendeth more yearly than his own revenue and spendeth of the stock besides".[12] John Locke expressed himself similarly: "we have seen how riches and money are got, kept or lost in any country; and that is by consuming less of foreign commodities than what by commodities or labour, it pays more".[13]

The second way to improve the balance was to increase exports. There was a general sentiment that selling was better than buying: that it was not a balance but a surplus that was needed. As Mun put it, "we must ever observe this rule: to sell more to strangers yearly than we consume of theirs in value".[14] And the German writer J. J. Becher, was even more explicit on the point: "it is always better to sell goods to others than to buy goods from others, for the former brings certain advantages and the latter inevitable damage".[15] And Charles Davenant in Britain was equally convinced that exports were superior to imports: "by what is consumed at home one loses only what another gets and the nation in general is not at all the richer; but all foreign consumption is a clear and certain profit".[16]

Because of this effect on the balance of treasure, trade was seen as a question that must be a major and constant concern of governments. As Bolingbroke, previously the leading minister of an English administration, put it, "The wealth and power of all nations depending so much on their trade and commerce . . . good government . . . will be directed to make the most of every advantage that can procure towards the improvement of trade and commerce".[17] It was not therefore a question that could be left simply to the efforts of individual merchants pursuing their own interests. For their interests, as was often noted, were different from those of governments. As Josiah Child observed, the eyes of the merchants are "so continually fixed . . . upon what makes for their peculiar gain or loss that they have not leisure to expatiate or turn their thoughts to what is most advantageous to the kingdom in general". They were therefore "not always the best judges of trade and its relationship to the profit on a power of a kingdom".[18] It was for governments to judge what was to the "advantage of the kingdom in general". In making those judgements they generally acted on the assumption that (as Child himself observed on another occasion) "profit and power ought to be jointly considered".[19] In devising the particular policies which should govern that trade they were usually at least as concerned about their effect on the power of the state as they were about their consequences for the economic welfare of their citizens.

THE WAYS OF PROMOTING NATIONAL TRADE

The governments of the period devised a number of means for winning for their own countries a larger share of the total trade available.

It was generally recognised that one essential condition of success was to have a substantial shipping fleet. Colbert bewailed the dependence of France on the shipping of other countries, which increased the cost of her imports and reduced the value of her exports, and so produced a loss of precious metals.

> The commerce of all Europe is carried on by ships of every size to the number of 20,000, and it is perfectly clear that this number cannot be increased, since the number of people of all the states remains the same, and consumption likewise remains the same. . . . The Dutch fight at present, in this war [of trade], with 15,000–16,000 ships . . .

the English with 3,000–4,000 . . . the French with 500–600. These two last cannot improve their commerce save by increasing the number of their vessels, and cannot increase this number save from the 20,000 which carry all the commerce, and consequently by making inroads on the 15,000–16,000 of the Dutch.[20]

Since the total volume of trade was limited, so too was the amount of shipping that could be used to carry that trade, and any increase in France's share would only be won at the expense of other countries. He therefore set about building (in addition to a substantial navy) a substantial fleet of merchant ships, providing subsidies for building and buying ships, and even seeking to attract Dutch and English shipwrights to France.[21] He also placed a heavy tax on foreign shipping to deter its use.[22] As a result he substantially raised the amount of trade which was carried in French shipping. English governments showed a similar concern. Under the Navigation Act of 1651 no goods from Asia, Africa or America were to be imported in foreign ships. From Europe goods must be carried either in English vessels or in ships of the country of origin, while the coasting trade was to be reserved entirely for vessels owned by Englishmen. Though these measures were modified in the Navigation Act of 1660, the main objective was the same: to ensure that as much as possible of English trade was carried in English ships, so increasing the country's potential naval strength and reducing freight charges.[23] In addition, in most countries colonial trade was reserved for the shipping of their own country. In all these ways governments managed to reduce their dependence on foreign shipping, so damaging other states – especially the hated Dutch – as much, they hoped, as their own.

Another widely used way of winning an increased share of trade was by the establishment of trading corporations, often with official support. Trading companies of this kind had existed from long before our period began. English companies had been established to develop trade to Muscovy (1555), the Eastland (Baltic) trade (1559), the Levant (1581) and Senegal (1586). From the beginning of the seventeenth century they were established in several countries, often as a result of direct state action: for example, the Danish East India Company (1612), the Swedish East India Company (1626), the Swedish Africa Company (1630), the Swedish South Sea Company (1630). Others, such as the Dutch East India Company (1602) and the Dutch West India Company (1621) resulted from the combined action of interested traders, though often with some degree of official encouragement. But with the intense competition to win overseas trade which took place in our period new efforts of that kind began to be made. In England the Company of the Royal Adventurers was set up in 1660 to exploit trade in Africa, the East India Company in 1664, while Charles II personally set up the Canary Company. Colbert was determined that France should be in a position to compete in this field. In his eyes such companies were an important weapon in the war for trade: he congratulated his master that he had "formed companies which attack it [Dutch trade] on all fronts, like armies".[24] In 1664 (the same year in which the English East India Company was formed) he set up an East India and a West India company, granting each a monopoly of trade to France from these areas. Other governments followed suit. In 1667 the emperor Leopold set up the Eastern Company of Vienna, though within twenty years it had collapsed: scarcely surprising given Austria's lack of shipping or experienced seamen (not to speak of coastline). Despite these drawbacks in 1719, Charles VI, established a new Eastern Company, as well as seeking, unsuccessfully, to set up an Ostend Company for the purpose of reopening the Austrian Netherlands to foreign trade. Spain created a series of such companies, of which the most successful was the Caracas Company founded in 1728, and the Royal Philippine Company which grew from it at the end of that century.

The most successful of these companies became far more than trading organisations, since they were often compelled to undertake substantial administrative functions and, in the case of the Dutch and the British East India Companies, to undertake extensive military campaigns to maintain order and establish political control. While they were often given some naval and other support by their own governments; they were usually granted a substantial degree of authority in the lands where they operated, for example they signed treaties with local rulers and deployed their own armed forces.[*] In all

---

[*] Cf. E. L. J. Coornaert, "European Economic Institutions and the New World: the Chartered Companies", in *The Cambridge Economic History of Europe*, vol. VI, (Cambridge, 1957), p. 248: "The state habitually delegated to the company a part, large or small, of its sovereign power. . . . To establish themselves and to order their trade the companies were instructed to make treaties with the established rulers. They had to be able to defend themselves against their European enemies or against foes roused by their intrusion into economies that were already established: they had to guard their posts and fortifications and to be ready to defend them. And they armed themselves, signed conventions, raised soldiers, furnished warships, contracted alliances, and became involved in all the complexity of inter-state diplomacy. For the administration of the territories, they had to exercise a jurisdiction which was at first confined to their own nationals, but which spread slowly to include the natives as well."

this their most important objective was to win for themselves and their countries a dominant control of the trade in the communities for which they competed. No wonder Colbert described the French companies as "armies" which would help his sovereign to win control of a larger share of the available trade.

But a still greater success could be secured by winning a monopoly of trade in a particular region or a particular commodity. Among their own nationals particular *companies* had a monopoly of trade in the areas where they operated. The Dutch East India Company, for instance, was granted a monopoly of trade between the Cape of Good Hope in the West and the Straits of Magellan in the East; while the Dutch West India Company was granted all trade on the Atlantic seaboard of the American continent and from the Tropic of Cancer to the Cape of Good Hope. The entire world was thus partitioned between these two companies.[25] The monopolies granted to the companies were given for a period of at least a dozen years and sometimes, as by the French government, for forty or fifty; each time the monopoly was renewed the state could secure for itself higher payments and more favourable conditions.[26] But for governments what mattered were not monopolies for companies but monopolies for states. So Spain claimed a monopoly of the trade to South America and the adjoining region, including the Philippines, and reserved navigation to herself in the adjoining seas. In the same way Venice claimed a monopoly of navigation in the Adriatic to safeguard her control of the trade of that area (she was only persuaded to relinquish this claim by Charles VI after the latter had helped her to defeat the Turks in the war of 1716–18). The United Provinces defended her trade in the East Indies by ejecting with military force any others who attempted to establish trading stations there (as when she ejected English merchants from Amboyna and attempted to do so at Pula Run). In the final resort the ability of any state to maintain a monopoly depended on its capacity to defend it by force. Thus Portugal lost her monopoly position to the Dutch in many places. And Spain, for all her claims, could not effectively maintain her monopoly of trade in South America since she was not able to supply all the needs of her own colonists and could not prevent widespread smuggling to the area from the Caribbean. But the attempt was still made. Even when the monopolies granted to the *companies* were, during the course of the period gradually withdrawn (the monopolies of the Eastland Company, the Merchant Adventurers and the Royal Africa Company in England in the last quarter of the seventeenth century, and that of the Levant Company in 1773), the monopoly maintained by the *states* in particular areas – above all in their own colonies – was maintained. For whatever the benefits of greater freedom of trade among nationals of the same country, there was none to be had, it was generally assumed, by according that freedom to the merchants of other states.

Almost as valuable as the control of particular areas was the domination of trade in particular *commodities*. Most favourable of all was the position of the Spanish who controlled the main source of gold and silver and so, it was generally believed, of "wealth". This had the effect that other countries, notably England and the United Provinces, were obliged to promote trade with Spain to acquire the precious metals they needed to undertake their trade elsewhere. The Dutch were almost equally fortunate in securing effective control of the East Indies; for from there came some of the most highly valued commodities which were traded at this time – above all, spices, such as nutmeg, cinnamon, cloves, pepper and others – which could often be sold in Europe at something like a hundred times their cost of production. The control of the sugar trade brought almost equal profit to a succession of states. It was largely in the hands of the Portuguese in the second half of the seventeenth century, when Brazil and Madeira were the principal sources; passed temporarily to the Dutch when they controlled parts of Brazil; to the English in the latter part of the seventeenth century, when they acquired Jamaica and other Caribbean islands (together with the technique of cultivation which the Dutch transmitted to them); and finally in the eighteenth century was dominated by the French through their control of St Domingue, Martinique and Guadeloupe, the richest sugar islands. The Dutch controlled much of the trade with the Baltic, including many strategic commodities – the so-called "naval goods" (hemp, tar, pitch, timber and flax) as well as the valuable trade in salt and grain. Finally, the English, by winning control of the greater part of the Indian trade, acquired a dominant share of the trade in calicoes and other textiles produced within the sub-continent.

Almost as valuable was the control of trade *routes*. By acquiring a string of trading posts in West Africa, the Cape, Ceylon and the Malabar coast of India, the Dutch were able to maintain control of the valuable trade route to the East Indies. British possessions in Bermuda, the Leeward Islands, New England and Arcadia enabled her to protect the trade to the Caribbean and North America; just as her acquisitions in Minorca, Malta and (eventually) the Ionian

Islands helped her to protect her trade in the Mediterranean. Venice was able, through her control of the Adriatic and Aegean Seas, to safeguard her own trade to the Levant. Denmark, through her control of the Sound, could maintain a stranglehold over all trade to the Baltic, which she was thus able to tax to her own advantage; while the United Provinces, Sweden, Russia and even England all used their navies at different times to safeguard their own share of this valuable trade, which had a strategic as well as commercial importance.

Governments were concerned not only to acquire benefits for their own trade but to damage that of their opponents.[27] The simplest way of doing this was to prohibit them from enjoying particular types of trade. Thus during the 1650s, when the Dutch were seen as England's main trade rivals, the latter prohibited the export to the United Provinces of those products which were believed to be most valuable to her – wool, woollen cloth, fullers earth, pipe clay and other products which she needed for the production of textiles. Even this was not considered enough: for a time there was serious consideration of seeking to cut off Dutch imports of wool from Spain as well, by buying up Spain's wool exports, not because England needed them (she had only too much of her own) but to deprive the Dutch of a vital raw material.[28] The Dutch retaliated in kind: for a time they prohibited the import or sale of cloths finished in England, England's most important export to them. In some cases governments prohibited the import of manufactured products from other countries (which were the more valuable) and allowed only that of the raw materials which they were able to use for their own production. Thus, for example, Colbert prohibited the import of silk manufactures from Italy, allowing only raw silk to be bought there. Conversely, Savoy in 1722 banned the *export* of raw silk to Britain, since it was used to make manufactured products which competed with her own, and banned the import of woollen cloth products for the same reason.[29] When relations were particularly bad such measures were intensified. In 1672, at the height of her trade war with France, but before war itself broke out, the United Provinces banned almost all trade with that country, an embargo that was quickly reciprocated by France. Similarly, in 1678 England banned the import of many French products, and these measures were intensified in 1689 after the outbreak of war between the two countries.

Even if no outright prohibition was imposed, imports from trade rivals could be penalised by high tariffs. Thus Colbert in 1664 and again in 1667 imposed penal duties on imports, primarily those from the United Provinces, which he saw as France's chief trade rival. This precipitated an escalating trade war between the two countries. The United Provinces threatened to impose similar tariffs on French manufactured goods, wine, brandy and salt and warned the French government of the damage which this would do to their own interests. Colbert, believing that the Dutch themselves would be more severely damaged by the reduction in trade (since they used many imports from France to trade elsewhere), refused to withdraw his measures. Accordingly the Dutch introduced their own higher duties in 1671, causing the French to raise their own duties yet again later the same month. During the war that followed the withdrawal of France's 1667 tariff was a major war aim for the Dutch; and it was one in which they were to succeed in the Peace of Nymegen in 1678. Conversely, more favourable trading arrangements were sometimes made when political relations were favourable. Thus after Portugal abandoned the French cause and renewed her alliance with Britain under the Methuen Treaty of 1703 England was granted access to Portuguese markets for many of her products in return for giving access to Portuguese wine to England. Similarly, English trade with Savoy was promoted as a result of an alliance with that country in the War of Spanish Succession.[30]

A major concern was to reduce dependence on imports of manufactures from elsewhere. As Colbert put it, the aim was "to prevent money from going out by means of the establishment of all sorts of manufactures . . . and to make it come in by means of all sorts of commerce and by facilitating the export of all our goods and manufactures".[31] The same dual approach was favoured by Frederick the Great in the following century: "Two things", he wrote, "are conducive to the welfare of the country: one to bring money in from foreign countries: this is the function of commerce; two, to prevent money from leaving the country unnecessarily: this is the function of manufacture".[32] Thomas Mun wrote that England should seek to "gain so much of the manufacture as she can" in order to improve the balance of trade.[33] There was widespread jealousy of the Dutch who undertook the processing of imported raw materials and then exported them to other parts of the continent. Many governments were concerned to share in this trade. So the governments of the age sought to develop their own manufacturing capabilities to reduce dependence on imports. Bounties (subsidies) were granted for exports and drawbacks (tariff rebates) for re-exported items. Local production of luxuries, silk textiles, tapestries, furniture, porcelain and soap production was promoted: Colbert in France, Frederick the Great in Prussia, and Charles III in Spain all set up state or state-aided factories for this purpose. They were particularly concerned to develop local processing production, previously monopolised mainly by the Dutch for linen manufacture, tobacco curing, sugar refining, brewing of beer, cloth manufacture and the curing of herrings. Finally, there were attempts to develop local production of the so-called "naval goods": Britain, for example, sought to develop alternative sources of supply in her North American colonies.[34]

Many of these changes were undertaken by state action. Even if not directly managed by the government (and many were), the new industries were minutely regulated by state officials: as by the army of inspectors whom Colbert appointed to supervise the minutest details of production in France. This was merely one of the many ways in which governments in this age expected to intervene to safeguard the state's commercial interests. The state was believed to have an interest in commercial success which was quite distinct from that of the merchants themselves. As Josiah Child argued: "If our trade and shipping diminish, whatever profit particular men make, the nation undoubtedly loseth; and on the contrary, if our trade and shipping increase, how small or low soever the profits are to private men, it is an invariable indication that the nation in general thrives."[35]

To enable the state to exercise these functions new institutions were created. So in Sweden a College of Commerce was established in 1651, under the supervision of the chief minister Oxenstierna; in England parliamentary committees for trade and plantations were set up in 1661, followed by an official Council of Trade and Navigation, with representation of merchants as well as parliamentarians and officials, and in 1696 a Board of Trade and Plantations; in France Colbert established a Council of Commerce in 1664 to supervise necessary measures to promote trade and industry; though this fell out of use after a dozen years it was replaced by a new one in 1700. A number of German states established "Colleges of Commerce" in similar institutions to perform the same type of function. Through such bodies governments organised and promoted trade, both at home and abroad. They organised convoys and other forms of protection for their merchant shipping. They created free ports (as in Marseilles, Trieste and Fiume). They established, like Colbert in France, the legal and financial framework within which trade, both foreign and domestic, was to be conducted;[36] organised assistance in commercial insurance;[37] and even set up transportation companies to ship goods to and from the ports from which they were traded, or between the principal urban centres.[38] All of these measures were designed to promote the governments' overall objective of state-building. They sought, in other words, to increase their independence of other states for shipping, processing, manufacturing and above all trade. Improvement in any of these areas would promote the further objective: improving the "balance of trade" and preventing the outflow of precious metals. In this way they might be enabled, so they believed, to prevail in the "war of money" in which all were so strenuously engaged.

THE WAR FOR TRADE

But to succeed in that competition the kind of measures which we have been describing were not always regarded as sufficient. Sometimes, it was believed, more forceful action was required.

The statesmen of the age, as we have seen, habitually described the struggle for trade in military terms. Thus Josiah Child called it "a kind of warfare". Colbert described commerce as a "perpetual and peaceable war of wit and energy among all nations".[39] Trade, he declared, caused "perpetual strife, both in time of war and peace, to decide which should have the greater share".[40]

Sometimes the use of such phraseology was metaphorical only. All that was meant was that there was among the states of the system a continual and intense competition for trade. What the words demonstrated was the almost universal belief that one nation could acquire trade only at the expense of another. This meant that each state was believed to have an interest, not only in increasing its own trade, but in damaging that of its rivals. On these grounds Colbert, writing to his master in 1670, rejoiced that in the "war of money" in which all states were engaged, Louis had "already vanquished Spain, Italy, Germany, England and several others whom you have cast into the direst poverty and need, and from whose spoils you have grown rich"; and he exulted that "even the vanquished cannot conceal their losses, which they proclaim in their merchants continual complaints of lost trade".[41] And in the next century William Beckford, an English merchant trading to the West Indies, welcomed the prospect of the new war against France on the grounds that "our trade will improve by the total extinction of theirs".[42]

But sometimes the talk of a "war for trade" had a more literal meaning. It was not merely competition that was intended. Merchants and politicians alike believed that trade had in some cases to be fought for in the most literal sense. During the 1650s and 1660s, there were many in England who believed that English trade could flourish only if that of the Dutch was damaged. So Pepys in his diary quotes the words of a leading British merchant: "The trade of the world is too little for us two, therefore one must down."[43]

Sometimes it was the merchants themselves who became involved in armed conflict with their rivals, with only marginal participation by their governments. So Dutch and Portuguese merchants fought against each other for favourable trading positions in Angola, in Brazil, Ceylon, the East Indies and elsewhere. So too English and Dutch merchants fought for control of Amboyna, Pula Run and Bantam in the East Indies, and for New Amsterdam in North America.

In other cases the conflict was mainly among governments. The earlier Anglo-Dutch war of 1552–4 had resulted from sharp differences between the two countries concerning questions of trade and navigation.[44] The First Northern War of 1655–60 resulted partly from differences concerning the control of commerce in the Baltic. France's war against the United Provinces in 1772 was even more clearly stimulated by commercial rivalry: though its original cause was the resentment of Louis XIV against the Dutch for helping to frustrate his war against the Spanish Netherlands four years earlier, he and his minister Colbert were also deeply concerned to reduce Dutch dominance of international trade and to acquire some part of it for France. The prize of victory in such a war, Colbert wrote to his master in 1670, would be "the spoils of the most powerful republic since the days of Rome"; in consequence the power of the Dutch, together with their commerce, "will diminish year by year" and in a few years time "you will reduce them to the direst straits".[45] And soon after the war began he wrote again to the king, pointing out that if the war was successful he might think it well "to divide the advantages of this commerce by cutting down a part of that of the Dutch so as to transfer it into the hands of the French".[46] The Dutch merchants equally (though they recognised that normally peace best suited their interests) sometimes demanded warlike action: the English ambassador at the Hague reported that, when their government proposed returning to the English ships that the Dutch had captured during a dispute in 1658, "the Directors of the [Dutch] East India Company declared plainly that it were much better to have a war with

England than to restore their ships".[47] Conversely, Clifford, the leading English minister in 1672, favoured war against the Dutch at that time principally as a way of winning trade from them.[48]

Commercial issues remained important in later wars of the period. During the Nine Years War, though England and the United Provinces were primarily concerned to curb French military power, both wished to use the opportunity to secure a reduction in French tariffs (raised once more in 1687). At its end the Dutch won a favourable commercial treaty, including a commitment by France to restore the tariff of 1664; while the English negotiators were originally instructed to secure a similar treaty but never pressed for this (on the grounds that "the balance of trade, as it now stands, is evidently on the English side").[49] At the beginning of the War of Spanish Succession the English government, particularly concerned at the trade privileges given to France by the new Spanish government,[50] made it clear that it regarded access to Spanish trade to South America as a major war aim; and in the settlement Britain demanded and secured the right to the valuable *asiento*, that is the right to sell slaves in the area, and the right to send an annual trading voyage. She also took the opportunity to negotiate a new trade agreement with France (though this was finally rejected by the English parliament as being insufficiently favourable). The United Provinces was equally concerned in that war about commercial questions (including the new tariff introduced by France in 1702), and she too won a new trade agreement with Spain at its conclusion. The war between Britain and Spain which began in 1739 even more clearly resulted mainly from commercial differences. The agreement reached at the end of the previous war had led to continual disputes. The Spanish government was concerned at the illegal trade with her South American colonies carried on by British traders and the excessive trade that they claimed was being undertaken by the annual trading voyage. The British merchants were equally concerned at the action of Spanish coastguards in stopping and searching English merchant vessels, sometimes without due cause. They were supported by British politicians who demanded war to end such indignities, and in some cases demanded the seizure of Spanish colonies so that trade to them could be undertaken equally profitably but with less interference.

Commercial motives were a factor in other wars. Frederick the Great was well aware of the economic benefits which Silesia could bring his relatively poor kingdom when he seized that province in 1740; and its economic value was probably a factor in strengthening

Maria Theresa's determination to recover it in 1756. The struggle between Britain and France in Canada, India and the Caribbean were undertaken largely for commercial reasons. France and Spain were partly concerned with winning colonial and commercial advantages when they joined the War of American Independence against Britain in 1778–9.

Thus a number of the wars of the period were fought at least partly for commercial reasons. Conversely, trade sanctions were sometimes used as a means of winning wars. Trade was not automatically cut off when two countries went to war; often much commercial activity continued. Dutch merchants were particularly reluctant to abandon altogether their trading activities, even with enemies, because a state of war existed: their government had to be cajoled by its allies into taking stronger action against them during the wars against France in the second half of the seventeenth century. Even at the end of the period, at the height of the Napoleonic wars, British ministers could take pride in the fact that some of Napoleon's army were still being clothed in cloth which had been sold to France by Britain. But in many cases governments now made a deliberate effort to cut off all trade to their enemies when war broke out. Britain used her sea power to cut off much of France's maritime trade during the War of Austrian Succession and the Seven Years War. And she reduced France's trade with the world beyond Europe to a minimum during the Napoleonic wars. Napoleon himself, in turn, unable to halt Britain's imports from across the sea, tried through his Berlin decrees to cripple British commerce by preventing sales to the European continent.

Thus it was generally accepted during this age that one way by which trade was to be won was through war. Even when not deliberately launched with commercial aims in mind, wars fought primarily for other reasons could be used to extract important commercial benefits. Success in war could in this way be used to promote success in trade. Profit and power, in other words, continued to be closely interrelated.

TRADE AND THE BALANCE OF POWER

The relationship between profit and power was in fact reciprocal. Not only could power help to win trade: success in trade could promote power.

It was the latter which was most widely recognised. Queen Anne accepted the relationship in declaring, in a speech from the throne in 1714, that "it is in the nation's interests to aggrandise itself by trade". There were many ways in which an increase in trade, could, it was believed, promote the power of the state. It would, for example, promote shipbuilding and the training of seamen, which would increase a nation's naval power in time of war. Thus, at the very beginning of our period in 1649, Lord Shaftesbury declared that "it is trade and commerce alone that draweth store of wealth along with it and potency at sea by shipping, which is not otherwise to be had".[51] Josiah Child pointed to the contribution of the East India trade to Britain's strength in that it employed "great warlike English ships that may carry fifty to seventy guns apiece", and insisted that "though the dominion of the sea may be obtained by our arms in fortunate battles . . . it can never be retained, preserved and maintained but by the excess and predominancy of foreign trade".[52] Charles Davenant declared that a loss of trade for England "would ill consist with our being great at sea upon which . . . all our safety and certainty depend".[53] Similarly, successful trade could safeguard the supply of needed raw materials, including the prized "naval goods", that were so essential to security. One reason that the United Provinces, Britain and other countries attached so much importance to protecting their Baltic trade was that it safeguarded supplies of this sort: Josiah Child in his *Discourse on Trade* pointed to the benefits which, for that reason, Britain's trade with Norway and Denmark brought not only to the "private gain" for traders but to the "public profit of the kingdom in general".[54] Overseas trade could also win valuable supplies of precious metals, which themselves were vital to success in war. Thus Colbert declared that "trade is the source of finance, and finance is the vital sinew of war".[55] And a constant argument of English writers such as Mun, Child and Davenant (all involved in the East India trade) was that foreign trade, by reducing a surplus of precious metals, was vital to the welfare of the nation: for this reason France, the United Provinces, England and other countries especially valued trade with Spain and Portugal since it could be the means of winning supplies of gold and silver which were needed to purchase other goods and to increase the national "wealth". Finally, trade was believed to increase a nation's power simply by promoting its prosperity generally. This would be so whether or not individual merchants benefited. As Josiah Child put it:

if our trade and shipping diminish, whatever profit particular men make, the nation undoubtedly loses; and on the contrary if our trade should be increased, how small or lowsoever the profits are to private men, it is an infallible indication that the nation in general thrives.[56]

For these reasons success in trade was believed by many to represent an integral part of the general balance of power between states. Charles Davenant certainly thought so: "Is power to be compassed and secured but by riches? And can a country become rich anyway but by the help of a well managed and expended trade?"[57] In the next century, during the Seven Years War, John Campbell argued similarly: "We may safely say that the balance of power . . . was created by trade, and must continue to be the object . . . of trading countries as long as they preserve their commerce and their freedom."[58] J. V. Moreau, writing at about the same time, declared that "the balance of trade in America is like the balance of power in Europe . . . The two balances are one".[59] Choiseul also felt that the traditional assessment of the power balance was outmoded: "the true balance at present exists in trade and in America. The war in Germany, even if conducted more successfully than it is, cannot prevent the ills to be feared from the great superiority of the English at sea."[60]

But if it was widely held that trade was the source of power, it was equally well recognised that, conversely, power could promote profit. This was clearly the belief of all those English merchants who clamoured for war with the Dutch in the 1650s and 1660s, or with the Spanish in the 1730s. It was demonstrated in the wars which took place for favourable trading posts and colonies in the Caribbean, the Americas and Asia. It was in that belief that an English pamphleteer in 1745 argued that "our commerce will in general flourish more under a vigorous and well-managed naval war than under any peace which would allow an open intercourse with those two nations [France and Spain]".[61] And a similar point was made by the elder Pitt during the Seven Years War: "Our trade depends upon a proper exertion of our maritime strength: that trade and maritime force depend upon each other."[62] Daniel Defoe declared that "to be masters of the marine power is to be masters of all the power and all the commerce in Europe"[63] while a French pamphleteer a few years later wrote that "the power which is strongest at sea must necessarily be the strongest commercially and thus the most formidable".[64]

Sometimes commercial and naval strength were seen as almost synonymous. Thus the elder Pitt, denouncing the lenient terms granted to France after the Seven Years War, declared that by returning two valuable West Indian sugar islands to her, the government had "given her the means of recovering her prodigious losses and becoming once more formidable to us at sea".[65] Similarly Louis XV, justifying French intervention in the War of American Independence, declared that this had been done "not with any idea of territorial aggrandisement, but solely as an attempt to ruin [England's] commerce and to sap her strength".[66]

In fact it is doubtful if the relationship between commercial and military power was as close as was generally believed. The United Provinces was the most successful trading nation of the continent during the first century of our period, but her military power declined steadily during that time; and it is arguable that her strength in trade, by increasing commercial pressure to avoid wars, or to end them quickly once begun, in fact weakened rather than strengthened her. Conversely, Sweden was a major military power until 1721, without being a particularly significant trading nation. Prussia and Russia both became great powers during the course of our period, without achieving any great commercial success. France was at the peak of her military power at the end of the seventeenth century and at the beginning of the nineteenth, but these were not periods of pronounced commercial success for her: her trade grew most strongly during the first half of the eighteenth century when she was militarily unsuccessful. The only power for which some such correlation might be found is Britain; and even in her case it is not clear which was cause and which effect, or indeed if there was any direct relationship at all. Maritime strength could help a country to be successful both in commerce and in naval warfare. But it was possible to be a successful maritime power (like the United Provinces in the eighteenth century) without having a very powerful navy; and it was possible to have a strong navy (like France at the end of the eighteenth century) without having a notably vigorous overseas trade.

Whatever the effect on its power a nation's trading position could affect its whole approach to international conflict. A country that depended heavily on trade could be expected to be disposed towards peace and to seek to avoid war. Thus de la Court, in describing the interest of Holland was insistent that "nothing is more necessary to us than peace with all men" because "there is more to be accomplished by us in times of peace and good trading than by war and the ruin of trade".[67] The Grand Pensionary de Witt in negotiating with a hostile France in the period before the war of 1672, said that the Dutch required "tranquility . . . to preserve the state of their trade".[68] Dutch merchants were often a powerful influence in favour of restoring peace (like their English opposite numbers)[69] when their country had been long at war: as in 1696 and 1710–13. And it was largely on commercial grounds that Dutch governments sought to avoid involvement in the War of Austrian Succession and the Seven Years War. But not all trading nations adopted the same attitude. The British were traders as much as the Dutch (Catherine the Great said that they were "first and always traders" long before Napoleon called them "a nation of shopkeepers"). Yet in their case their commercial interests sometimes influenced them in favour of war. The interest of a maritime nation which was also a strong naval power and an island was not necessarily the same as the one that was relatively weak and had highly vulnerable frontiers (such as the United Provinces). Though the two states were frequently labelled together as the "maritime powers", therefore, their situation and interests were often different. The interests of other trading nations, with moderate overseas trade and limited naval power, were different again. Though willing to risk war if their interests demanded it, they expected that, if they chose not to be involved, their trade could continue, unaffected by the unwelcome attentions of the British navy. These were the countries that supported the Dutch slogan of "free ship, free goods", and formed the successive "armed neutralities" of the period (see below).

Differences of interest in relation to trade were shown even more clearly in divergent attitudes towards trade liberalisation. In the early years of our period Dutch writers and statesmen were the most outspoken in calling for the removal of restrictions on international, and indeed on all trade. Thus de la Court advocated many of the same policies which were later to be propounded at greater length, and with greater sophistication, by Adam Smith and for similar reasons: the ending of monopolies, subsidies and other privileges, a reduction to the minimum of all taxes on trade and manufacture, the removal of impediments on foreigners wishing to establish themselves in trade or manufacture, the ending of the restrictive practices of guilds, and above all an equal concern for the interests of the consumer as for those of the producer.[70] There were a few English merchants of the same period, interested in the expansion of trade world-wide, who advocated similar policies. For example, Child in his *New Discourse on Trade* declared that "if we would engage other nations in trade with us, we must receive from them the fruits and commodities of their country as well as send them ours"[71] and he too favoured a reduction in taxes on trade and in the privileges of trading monopolies. But it was particularly after England had made herself, from the middle of the eighteenth century, an even more successful trading and manufacturing nation than the United Provinces, that her writers began to demand the same liberalisation which Dutch commentators had called for earlier. So Hume, in his *Jealousy of Trade*, and Adam Smith, in his *Wealth of Nations*, began to preach the common interest of all nations in increased trade (against the earlier notion that by competing for the same trade they had opposite interests) and so the benefit to all of removing restrictions which might inhibit that trade. Nor were such ideas confined to theoretical writing. British statesmen, sometimes directly influenced by Adam Smith, such as Lord Shelburne, who had studied and admired his works, proceeded to seek (for example in negotiating the Eden Treaty with France in 1786) precisely the type of trade liberalisation which Adam Smith advocated.

Thus a change in attitudes to foreign trade developed. It was now the balance of economic power between the more and less advanced, rather than the balance of military or naval power, which determined the policies pursued. Those with a developed manufacturing capacity had a different interest from those that were still beginning to develop their manufacturing industry; and they therefore sought new ways of developing their trade, by preaching the liberalisation of trade and the abandonment of protectionism, and opening up a market from which they were the most likely to benefit. The majority, however, whether they were militarily weak or strong, had a different economic interest; and they generally remained protectionist in their attitude. Either way, profit and power began to appear less closely interconnected. Governments no longer went to war (in Europe at least) for economic purposes. It began to seem possible that nations had a common, rather than a conflicting, interest in trade.

But the doctrines which had prevailed for most of our period were not instantly blown away by Adam Smith's new thinking. Many aspects of the old policy continued to be practised well into the nineteenth century (when the theories of Friedrich List gave a new lease of life to some of them). Even Britain made significant steps towards liberalisation only in the 1820s, and only abandoned protectionism in 1860, while the majority of European states moved, still more hesitantly, in the decade that followed. Only slowly, as it began to be perceived that trade could be of mutual benefit and that a reduction of barriers might benefit more than one party, did a new set of policies begin to be advocated. Eventually the "balance of trade", in the sense of a continuing surplus leading to an inflow of precious metals, began to seem more dubious as an end of policy; the "balance of power", though as ardently pursued as ever, no longer seemed so dependent on economic factors. The promotion of economic strength finally came to be pursued by specifically economic means, rather than, as in much of this age, by means that depended on a superiority of military power.

BOOKS

Contemporary works

N. Barber, *A Discourse of Trade* (London, 1690).
F. Brewster, *Essays on Trade and Navigation* (London, 1695).
——, *New Essays on Trade* (London, 1702).
J. Child, *A Treatise Concerning the East India Trade* (London, 1681).
——, *A Discourse about Trade* (London, 1690).
——, *A New Discourse of Trade* (London, 1693).
C. Davenant, *Discourse on the Public Revenues and Trade of England* (London, 1698).
M. Decker, *An Essay on the Causes of the Decline in Foreign Trade* (London, 1739).
T. Mun, *England's Treasure by Forraign Trade* (London, 1664).
M. Postlethwayt, *Great Britain's Commercial Interest* (London, 1759).

Modern works

P. W. Buck, *The Politics of Mercantilism* (New York, 1942).
The Cambridge Economic History of Europe, vol. VI: *The Economy of Expanding Europe in the Sixteenth and Seventeenth Centuries* (Cambridge, 1967).
E. M. Carus-Wilson (ed.), *Essays in Economic History* (London, 1954 and 1962).
C. W. Cole, *Colbert and a Century of French Mercantilism* (New York, 1939).
D. C. Coleman, *Revisions in Mercantilism* (London, 1969).
R. Davis, *The Rise of the Atlantic Economies* (London, 1973).
——, *A Commercial Revolution: English Overseas Trade in the Seventeenth and Eighteenth Centuries* (London, 1967).

——, *English Merchant Shipping and Anglo-Dutch Rivalry in the Seventeenth Century* (London, 1975).

L. A. Harper, *The English Navigation Laws* (New York, 1939).

G. E. Heckscher, *Mercantilism*, English trs. (London, 1934).

W. E. Minchinton, *The Growth of English Overseas Trade in the Seventeenth and Eighteenth Centuries* (London, 1969).

A. Small, *The Cameralists, the Pioneers of German Social Policy* (Chicago, 1909).

N. Steersgard, *The Asian Trade Revolution of the Seventeenth Century* (New York, 1975).

J. de Vries, *The Economy of Europe in an Age of Crisis, 1600–1750* (Cambridge, 1976).

C. Wilson, *Profit and Power* (London, 1957).

9 Colonies

Another type of contest in which the states of this period engaged was the competition for colonies.

The desire for colonies resulted directly from the desire for trade. Colonies were wanted for the products they could supply. Europeans did not settle in remote foreign regions out of a desire for conquest, but to secure access to particular commodities which could be profitably traded in Europe: gold and silver from South America, slaves from Africa, tobacco and sugar from the Caribbean, spices from the East Indies, silks and calicoes from India. Except in the Americas, permanent settlement was not usually intended, still less the detailed administration of local populations. Often only small trading stations were established at first. Colonies were thus not an end in themselves but simply a means to a widely desired goal: a more extensive trade. As Montesquieu put it: "The end of their establishment is not the foundation of a town or a new empire but the extension of commerce".[1]

This did not mean that colonies were of concern only to the traders who got profit there. Trade, as we saw in the last chapter, was seen as the business of governments, and not just of merchants. For that reason colonies also became the business of governments. Just as trade, even if undertaken by merchants and their companies, was supported and encouraged by governments in the interests of the state, so too the acquisition and defence of colonies, even if first undertaken by traders, came to be supported and encouraged by governments in the interest of the state. If explorers such as Columbus, Cortes and Pisarro first discovered and conquered the Americas, they did so only because they had the backing, financial and military, of the Spanish crown. If Henry the Navigator, Vasco de Gama and Magellan explored the coast of Africa and Asia, they did so only because they had the encouragement and support of Portuguese kings. If the Dutch and English trading companies established trading posts and settlements in the Caribbean, Africa and the East Indies they did so with charters and monopolies granted by the rulers of their countries. Governments may not have been the initiators of such enterprises, but they were closely involved from the beginning. For they were always well aware of the value that these settlements could have for the states which ruled them.

For this reason they ensured that such places were held under the control of the state from which their traders came. Sometimes, as we saw earlier, they might delegate sovereignty to the companies which they themselves had chartered. But ultimately it was the sovereignty of the state that was asserted in that way. From the time our period began this state control was made closer. So in 1650 the Parliament in England declared that her colonies are "and ought to be subordinate to and dependent upon England . . . and subject to such laws and orders as are or shall be made by the parliament of England". So Colbert in France ensured that Canada, once administered by the Company of New France, was brought directly under royal control, and that other colonial enterprises received the direct support of the state, including the defence of royal ships and royal armies where necessary, and were administered by military governors appointed by the crown. In the United Provinces colonial policy was formulated by the States-General, and its two great trading companies had the closest links with the provincial and national governments.[2] The colonies of Spain and Portugal were from the beginning held by the crown, and trade to them was undertaken only under strict royal control.

If colonies were so cherished by their governments, it was not at that time because they were seen as military assets. From the strategic point of view they were regarded as liabilities rather than assets. They had to be defended by the mother country, sometimes at considerable cost. Even if they were not garrisoned (as few were) expensive expeditions had to be sent out from the mother country whenever they were threatened by a foreign power. If the local people were employed for such purposes, this too could be an expense, direct or indirect. What is more, such forces could become uncomfortably powerful (at one time the British East India Company had an army of 150,000, far greater than that of Britain itself, as well as its own navy). Long before the American Revolution English writers were warning of the dangers that might finally result if the colonists were provided with the capability of arming themselves effectively.[3] For this reason Charles Davenant warned that "wise countries never teach their colonies the art of war".[4] And Josiah Child declared that "there is nothing more prejudicial and . . . dangerous to any mother kingdom than the increase of shipping in their colonies, plantations or provinces".[5]

If colonies were regarded as an asset to the state, therefore, it was not for military reasons but because of the contribution they could make to the nation's balance of trade. As Sir Arthur Young pointed out, "the difference between purchasing a commodity of a foreign country or of a colony is immense: in the first case it is paid for probably with cash; but in the latter manufactures are exchanged for it".[6] One of the reasons why Colbert attached value to colonies was because they were "a market for French goods and a source of needed products".[7] Pieter de la Court demanded the creation of colonies by the United Provinces because they were "so generally profitable to the land and inhabitants of Holland".[8] In England Charles Davenant declared that, so long as they complied with the English laws, through the trade they created colonies would bring great benefit to the motherland: "the stronger and greater they grow, the more the crown and the kingdom will get from them".[9] And towards the end of the period Edmund Burke declared that by colonies you "not only acquired commerce, but you actually created the very objects of commerce; and by that creation raised the trade at least four fold".[10] Even Josiah Tucker, later a strong critic of the colonial system, believed in his earlier years that "the trade to our colonies and plantations must appear to be of the utmost consequence to the power, strength and prosperity of Great Britain".[11]

Nor were the advantages to be had from colonial trade merely the rosy dreams of enthusiastic writers. They were demonstrated by the record of the growth of such trade in this period. Already in 1715 trade with the North American colonies represented almost 20 per cent of all British overseas trade; by 1785 it had reached 34 per cent. British trade with Africa and Asia, mainly to colonies, was 7 per cent of the total of 1715, but had increased to 19 per cent by 1785. The increase in France's overseas trade, primarily to her West Indian colonies, was comparable. By the 1780s over half of all Britain's foreign trade and over a third of that of France was being done with areas outside Europe, almost entirely their colonies. Almost half of Portugal's trade at the end of the eighteenth century was carried on with her colonies in America, Africa and Asia.[12]

But the state's interest in the commercial value of colonies was not the same as that of its merchants. The value the colonies could have for the merchant was self-evident: the trade they engendered could bring him profit. The value they could have for the state was different, and sometimes conflicting. The value of the colony to the state was that, being under its sovereignty, its trade could be directed and controlled to ensure that it contributed to a favourable trade balance. This required different policies from those that would bring the maximum benefit to the merchant. The latter might benefit by purchasing goods in a foreign country, or in a foreign country's colony, and then selling at home. But this would adversely affect the national balance of trade, and so the interest of the state. Because it was they who controlled policy governments were able to ensure that it was the interest of the state rather than that of the merchants (still less that of the consumer) which prevailed.

To secure this objective there was one overriding principle which was universally applied by all the European powers. Colonial trade was always reserved to the home country and its nationals. As Montesquieu put it: "It is a fundamental law of Europe that all trade with an overseas colony is regarded as a pure monopoly."[13] Almost without exception (and these usually only temporarily*) all a colony's imports had to come from the mother country; and all its exports had to be sent only to that country. So the English Navigation Acts of 1651 and 1660, and the Staple Act of 1663 reserved to English traders the trade to and from English colonies. So Colbert in France ensured that all trade to Canada and the French West Indies was undertaken only by French merchants who alone were accorded the passports which were required for undertaking that trade.[14] He ordered that "with no exception whatever, all foreign ships were to be excluded from trade with the islands" and even that the colonial authorities should "sink all foreign ships that come thither".[15] Nor were French ships permitted to take foreign goods to the islands; a regulation that the French navy was instructed to enforce stringently. The Spanish government had similar regulations; they fought a continual (and losing) battle against foreign traders and smugglers seeking to sell their goods to the Spanish colonies. Other countries enforced similar laws. The wisdom of such policies was, for most of the period, taken for granted. Josiah Child, for example, believed that "all colonies or plantations do endamage their Mother-Kingdom" unless "the traders of such plantations are . . . confined by severe laws . . . to the mother kingdom".[16] And Charles Davenant insisted, even more firmly, that "the principal care should always be to keep [colonies] dependent on their mother country and not to suffer those laws [the

---

* For example, Portugal, when still engaged in fighting for its independence from Spain, and therefore desperate for support from elsewhere, agreed when making peace with England in 1654 and the United Provinces in 1662 to allow their merchants the right to trade in Portuguese colonies, in return for recognition of Portugal's sovereignty within those colonies.

Navigation Acts] on any account to be loosened whereby they are tied to it, for otherwise they will become more profitable to our neighbours than to us".[17]

This overriding concern for the balance of trade meant that if necessary the interests of the colonists, like that of home traders, might have to be subordinated to those of the mother country. As an English writer put it: "the colonies were acquired with no other view than to be a convenience to us; and therefore it could never be imagined that we are to consult their interests preferably to our own."[18] And Lord Carmarthen told the British House of Commons: "for what purpose were [the colonists] suffered to go to that country unless the profit of their labour should return to their masters here? I think the policy of colonisation is highly culpable if the advantages of it should not redound to the interests of Great Britain."[19] Although, therefore, the colonists themselves would have benefited from a freeing of trade, so that they could purchase their requirements from the nearest and cheapest source, and sell them to the most profitable market, they were not permitted to do so. So French producers of rum and molasses in the French sugar islands were not permitted to sell them in the English North American colonies, in exchange for much-needed meat, livestock and provisions, even when they could find no reasonable market in France.[20] So the inhabitants of the Spanish colonies were forced to rely on expensive and unreliable exports from Spain rather than secure what they needed from eager English, Dutch and French merchants in the Caribbean. So the English colonists of North America were not supposed to do business with French and Dutch territories in the West Indies, even though they represented a far better market for some of their goods than the distant mother country.

In particular the colonists were everywhere deterred from developing manufacturing or processing industries which would compete with those at home. Lord Dartmouth, a British Commissioner of Trade, complained in 1702 that the North American colonies "instead of confining themselves to the production of such commodities as are agreeable to the true design and intention of these settlements . . . have improved their skills to such a degree that . . . as good druggets are made in those countries as any in England".[21] And Charles Davenant complained that "it cannot be for the public good of a kingdom . . . when the product of such colonies is the same as the kingdom's and so rivals the kingdom".[22] Such activities, whether or not in the interests of the colonists, were held to be against the interests of the mother country and so forbidden.

Still less were the interests of the indigenous peoples to be taken into account. The Indians of North America could sometimes be useful allies against a rival colonial power, but it was never supposed, either in France or England, that a colonial power had a moral obligation to ensure that their interests, economic or political, were safeguarded, or their lands preserved from seizure if desired by the settlers in Canada or North America. The people of the East Indies could be useful suppliers of pepper, cloves and other valuable spices, but it was never believed in the United Provinces that the government of that country, in extending its claims there, undertook any special responsibility for their welfare; and in practice they were subjected to an increasingly ruthless system of tribute and forced deliveries at derisory prices.[23] Settlements in India were established for the purpose of promoting trade in its products but those who did so felt little concern for the welfare of those who supplied these products. In Africa, the local people were themselves treated as commodities to be trafficked and sold into slavery for the profit of those who undertook the trade. Nor was there much thought whether Europe's exports were beneficial to the places where they were traded. Since Europe had little else which was in great demand and usually had a large trade deficit, firearms, strong spirits and opium were widely regarded as the most suitable commodities to exchange for those that were bought.

Only towards the end of our period, in the second half of the eighteenth century did there begin to be serious questioning within European countries about the morality of the colonial system as it was then developing.[24] For the most part colonies were seen in essentially instrumental terms. They were desired not for themselves but as a means by which certain important state interests could be promoted. As a committee set up in the Netherlands to consider Dutch colonial policy in 1802 declared: "the colonies exist for the mother country, not the mother country for the colonies". Colonies were seen as assets by which the mother country might be placed in a more favourable position than its rivals. The gain or loss of such assets could therefore be a significant factor in determining the balance of advantage among the states of the system.

THE VALUE OF COLONIES

The benefits which colonies were thought to procure for the states that acquired them were of several kinds.

First, they could be the source of important materials needed in the mother country which might otherwise have to be imported from elsewhere. Thus Hakluyt had rejoiced, even before our period began, that the discoveries in America could "afford us . . . either all or a great part of the commodities previously bought more dearly or more dangerously elsewhere". A widespread hope in the early days was that colonies could represent, as they had for Spain and Portugal, a wondrous source of precious metals and so of "wealth": El Dorados which would enrich the nation. They would thus provide the means to purchase goods from elsewhere and to improve the trade balance. The charters of the trading companies often emphasised particularly this potential source of wealth. For example, the charter of the Royal Africa Company of 1663 gave pride of place to the right it accorded to "all mines of gold and silver" in the territories covered.[25] The French colonists of Canada in the early days had high hopes of discovering similar riches, though Colbert eventually reconciled himself to the fact that it was more likely that only less exciting minerals, such as iron and copper, would be found.[26] The early English settlers in Virginia also had hopes of finding rich supplies of precious metals, but soon realised that these were unlikely to be fulfilled.[27] But even when the dream of buried treasure faded, it continued to be the hope that colonies could supply other minerals, as well as timber, tobacco and various foodstuffs that could not be produced in Europe.

Secondly, it was hoped the colonies could be a source of strategic materials, the so-called "naval goods" essential to maintain shipping: timber (for masts and planks), hemp (for ropes), flax (for sails), copper (for guns), pitch and tar. For most European countries the traditional sources of supply had been the Baltic states. But there was a widespread desire to reduce dependence on this hazardous source of supply, which could easily be cut off by the hazards of war or shifts in alliance policy. As one English politician declared; "While we fetched our naval stores from Russia, it was in the power of the Tzar not only to set what price he pleased, but even to prevent our having them at all . . . Therefore since these commodities were so absolutely necessary to our navy, it was not fitting we should lie at the mercy of a foreign prince for them."[28] On these grounds Colbert hoped that New France (Canada) might be a source of timber, shipping, and even a centre for shipbuilding.[29] English governments too for long sought to develop alternative supplies from its North American colonies, supplies that would be reliable because under their own control,[30] though there were some who warned of the dangers of making the colonists too powerful in the processes.[31] Nor was this the only strategic value of colonies. It was often pointed out that the trade engendered by colonies, mainly the slave trade, provided excellent training, and a source of supply, for sailors who might be urgently required in war: it was in other words, as so often proclaimed, "a nursery of seamen".[32]

Thirdly, colonies could be the source not only of precious metals, raw materials and strategic goods for the mother country but of a favourable trade balance. There was at this time a growing demand in Europe for a number of commodities that could not be obtained within that continent: precious spices of various kinds, especially pepper, ginger and cloves, for which high prices and huge profits could be obtained (some spices sold in Europe for a thousand times what it cost to procure them), beverages such as tea, coffee and cocoa, sugar, tobacco, silk, calico and other textiles. Even if sold only in the home market they could bring substantial profit. But if they were sold in other countries they not only brought profit to the merchants but substantial benefit to the state, since they improved its balance of trade. So Colbert saw, as one of the chief values of colonies, that they were a "source of goods for trade".[33] In England Sir Arthur Young held that

"the wealth resulting from the colonies ought certainly to arise from the cultivation of staple commodities; that is from the production of those articles which a mother country must purchase of foreigners if her own settlements did not yield them. . . . What a prodigious difference there is between paying to the French a million sterling for sugars, or exchanging a million's worth of our manufactures for the same commodities from our own colonies."[34]

Colonial trade could thus be above all a means of import-saving: so in the British House of Commons Sir John Selwyn proclaimed that the new colony of Georgia (acquired in 1733) would "be able to produce as much raw silk as will save the nation upwards of 300,000 pounds which is now yearly sent out of England to Italy and other countries for that commodity".[35] And forty years later the Earl of Sandwich told the House of Lords that "by encouraging the English sugar plantations, and making it a matter of state to do so, we might in short space of time engross that manufacture to ourselves . . . doubling at least the balance of trade we now enjoy by the same". One of the reasons for developing production of naval goods in the colonies was that this too would benefit the balance of trade: Erasmus Philips pointed out that by securing naval stores from New England Britain "might save a great part of four or five hundred thousand pounds per annum in these commodities which we bring from Denmark, Sweden and the east countries".[36] And this colonial produce could not only be procured without any outflow of precious metals, it might even, it was believed, because of the use of slave labour, be cheaper than similar materials obtained elsewhere.[37]

But colonial goods were not only of benefit to the home country in saving imports from elsewhere and so reducing the outflow of precious metals: they could also be re-exported to other countries. This would bring a double benefit to the balance of trade: not only the saving in the precious metals otherwise spent on imports but a *source* of precious metals acquired from sales abroad. According to one English writer, "tobacco, ginger, sugar, indigo, rice and the rest of the plantation goods have brought us (besides what was necessary for our consumption) a balance from France, Flanders, Hamburg, Holland and the east countries of about six hundred thousand pounds a year".[38] Burke too emphasised this advantage: "those [sugar islands] who supply the home consumption purvey to our luxury; those who supply the foreign market administer to our wealth and to our power".[39] There was a further benefit: the saving in freight. As Charles Davenant pointed out, by re-exporting colonial goods, England could "make Europe pay us good freight which is pure gain".[40] Overall, as a result of import-saving, additional exports and saving in freight charges, the overall benefit to the balance of trade would, it was believed, be huge.

This did not exhaust the benefits which colonies were thought to procure. They would provide a favourable market for the manufactures of the mother-country. Because other traders were not allowed to sell there, they offered a safe, protected market that would help home manufacturing industry to develop. One of the merits which Colbert saw in colonies was that they provided French manufacturers and merchants with captive purchasers. Spanish governments persistently sought to shield their own colonies from the exports of other countries in order to provide Spanish producers with a safe market. In England Daniel Defoe pointed to the advantage the colonies provided in offering a safe "vent" for English products at a time when they faced increasing competition and protectionism from elsewhere: if Europe ceased to buy, we should . . . make markets of our own in which the whole world would not supplant us. . . . The world is wide, there are new countries and new nations who may be so planted, so improved, and the people so managed, as to create a new commerce; and millions of people call for our manufacture who never called for it before.[41]

Bolingbroke made a similar point: it was a special merit of trade to the colonies, in his view, that they were "entirely our own": therefore it was "highly in our interests to encourage and improve them, since they may be useful to us and a considerable support to the nation when other branches may possibly fail us through the designs and contrivances of our rivals in trade".[42] And Sir John Wentworth, the governor of Canada, congratulated Pitt on the conquest of Canada because "it must be of inestimable value to Great Britain, as the peopling of this continent cannot fail of creating a full employ in the manufactures of our mother country".[43] It was even held that one of the benefits to be gained from the slave trade (over and above the high profits it was said to produce[44]) was that it could increase the number of consumers of European products in the West Indies. Matthew Decker, for example, argued that an increase in the trade would be a "transplanting of men for our benefit by taking them from one climate where by its heat they wanted no clothing, and carrying them to another where they cannot live without, nor be supplied by any but ourselves".[45]

There were other more peripheral benefits which were said to be produced by colonies. Some argued that those employed in the colonies were more productive than the equivalent number employed at home (partly because of the low price paid for slave labour there): Charles Davenant calculated that in the southern colonies of North America and the West Indies every settler, employing perhaps six others, "negro, slave or European strangers" was "as profitable as seven heads would be in England".[46] Moreover, because they offered a market for the mother-country's goods, they provided employment at home as well as abroad. Thus Josiah Child argued that England's "plantations, spending mostly our English manufactures . . . and employing near two-thirds of all our English shipping", provided employment for "maybe two hundred thousand persons here at home".[47] They also provided a useful outlet for surplus population: this was the view expressed by the Earl of Selkirk among many others in England[48] (though there were others who argued equally forcefully that they drained the mother country of many useful workers). In any case the colonies provided a field for the profitable investment of surplus capital: Brougham held that

> when a nation has so greatly increased its wealth and industry that its trading profits are small its capital would seek every sort of outlet . . . and surely the security of the capital employed in colonial speculation is infinitely greater than that of the capital lent to merchants or princes of foreign states.[49]

Finally, by reducing dependence on other states, colonies made a country more self-sufficient and therefore stronger.

Not all, however, were so convinced of the benefits of colonies. Frederick the Great, in his *Second Political Testament*, expressed considerable scepticism about their value. As time went on, he believed, their populations would increasingly demand their independence. He correctly foresaw revolts in Britain's North American and Spain's South American colonies, and believed this would "disabuse the sovereigns about the benefits they have promised from these distant possessions". If one tried to calculate what such possessions cost, including the wars they engendered and the expenditure undertaken to sustain them, "one would have to conclude that the only advantageous possessions are those which are immediately adjacent to a state".[50] Though this view may have contained an element of sour grapes, reflecting Prussia's lack of colonies and Frederick's anti-British feeling at the time, it was a view that began to be shared by some even in those countries which had substantial colonial possessions. Critics in Britain, for example, began to argue that the manufactures being developed in the colonies would become an increasing threat to those produced at home; that re-exports of colonial goods to other countries benefited the recipients more than the exporting countries; that the capital and enterprise devoted to plantations and other colonial activity would have been more profitably employed at home or in developing fisheries which required no permanent settlement; that colonies imposed an unacceptable defence burden on the home country, so that at least their territory (for example in North America) should be limited; that the colonists would become in time too strong and thus eventually a source of weakness; and that colonial goods were often more expensive than those which could be obtained from other sources.[51]

In a few cases these criticisms led to downright condemnations of the entire colonial system. For example, Josiah Tucker in Britain held that "the planting of colonies with a monopolising or exclusive trade" was nothing but a "cheat". Britain could well benefit from trade with the colonies even if they were independent: "the very best system (best I mean in behalf of England) would have been to have thrown up all foreign dominions at once; and to have trusted solely to the goodness and cheapness of our manufactures".[52] Even if the colonies developed their own manufacturing industries this would only place them in the same situation as the foreign countries with which Britain already had a flourishing trade. He therefore rejoiced at the independence of the North American colonies and hoped to see the separation of others elsewhere. Similarly Jeremy Bentham urged all colonial powers to "emancipate your colonies"; and claimed that "it is not in the interest of Great Britain to have any foreign dependencies whatsoever".[53] Adam Smith was less categorical in demanding total decolonisation, but presented the most cogent and influential critique of the system of tying the trade of colonies to the mother-countries. He showed that the apparent gains this policy brought were only short-term and illusory: "By rendering the colony produce dearer in all other countries, it lessened its consumption, and thereby cramps the industry of the colonies, and the enjoyments and interests of all other countries."[54] The distortion of trade and of capital movements meant that costs were raised and consumers penalised. Industry became over-dependent on a single market. The costs of defence meant that "all the European colonies have, without exception, been a source rather of weakness than of strength to their respective mother countries".[55] As a result such colonies have been "the source of expense and not of revenues to their mother countries". The retention of colonies could only be justified if the monopoly of the home merchants and manufacturers was withdrawn. It was probably unrealistic to "hope for the total separation of colonies from the motherland – such a measure . . . never was and never will be adopted by any country in the world"; but if it was, the country would be

immediately freed of the annual expense of the peacetime establishment of the colonies, but might settle with them such a treaty of commerce as would effectually secure to her a free trade more advantageous to the great body of the people, though less so to the merchants, than the monopoly which she at present enjoyed.[56]

Such views, however, remained those of a minority. There was little disposition among the states which possessed them to "emancipate their colonies", nor even to introduce the reforms advocated by Adam Smith. Even in Britain, where free trade ideas had the greatest influence and were most obviously in the national interest, the opening of colonial trade had to wait until halfway through the next century. In other countries exclusive or preferential trade was retained far longer. Generally speaking colonies were still seen as a source of strength rather than a weakness. John Cary argued in Britain that they

> take off our products and manufactures, supply us with commodities which may be either wrought here or exported again, or prevent fetching things of the same nature from other places for our home consumption, employ our poor and encourage our navigation.[57]

Certainly the European governments showed no decline in their attachment to their colonial possessions. Trade with the colonies increased more rapidly than overseas trade in general.[58] In 1763, 1783 and again in 1815 the victorious powers were as eager as ever to acquire new colonial possessions from the countries they had vanquished. Generally speaking, in other words, colonies continued to be seen as important assets in the competition for advantage and prestige in which the states of the system were engaged.

THE WAR FOR COLONIES

Because colonies were, for these various reasons, highly valued, they became a major source of conflict. The competition for colonies did not involve all states, nor all colonial territories. Non-maritime states took little or no part in it. Even some countries which established companies that traded overseas, such as Sweden, Russia and (briefly) Austria, had not sufficient interest in that trade, nor adequate maritime strength, to compete effectively in the quest for colonies. And some that did acquire overseas territories – such as Denmark, Prussia (which, under the Great Elector, bought from Denmark a trading post in the West Indies and briefly established a factory in the Gold Coast before selling it to the Dutch West India Company for only six thousand ducats), Austria (which bought a trading post in India from the Great Mogul) and the tiny duchy of Courland which acquired Tobago for a time, were scarcely serious competitors. The struggle was therefore one which took place primarily among the five principal maritime countries of Western Europe: Spain, Portugal, the United Provinces, Britain and France.

Until 1600 only the first two of these were significant colonial powers. Both had embarked on colonisation in the fifteenth century, and a century later still faced no significant competition. Spain controlled Central and South America and most of the Caribbean, and Portugal a still more widely flung empire straddling Brazil, parts of West Africa, Ceylon, and places in India, the East Indies and even China, while no other power had established any significant foothold outside Europe. Only after 1600 did their position come to be challenged. At that time (between 1580 and 1640) the two countries were joined, at least in theory, under the same king. But this scarcely affected their colonial possessions: Spain gave no effective military support to Portuguese colonies when they increasingly came under threat from the Dutch who, engaged in their eighty-year war against Spain, took the opportunity to threaten the Portuguese colonies she claimed to rule. Using their maritime skills to promote both their own profits and the interests of their country, Dutch traders challenged the Portuguese in many of the places where they had established themselves: in Brazil, Angola, West Africa, Ceylon, India and Indonesia. The Portuguese, themselves rebelling against Spain from 1640, succeeded in restoring their position in Brazil and Angola. But elsewhere, in the Guinea coast of Africa, in Cochin in India, in Ceylon, in Malacca and the Spice Islands, the Dutch succeeded in dislodging them permanently.

From about the time when our period began, instead of scuffles and skirmishes among groups of traders seeking to extend or defend their own positions, these conflicts increasingly became affairs of state: elements in the wider competition which took place among the nations of the system. Colonisation itself became increasingly, as we saw, a deliberate act of state policy. Governments sought to extend their own "sovereignty" to lands where their colonists settled (though this occurred later in Asia and Africa than in the Americas and the Caribbean). Increasingly the distribution of colonial territory ceased to result from the varying enterprise or valour of private venturers. It was the outcome of wars undertaken between states; and it was defined in peace treaties reached between states at the end of those conflicts. Thus the fifty-year conflict between the Portuguese and the Dutch in many parts of the world, beginning early in the century, culminated in open war in Europe in 1657, which was concluded by a formal peace treaty between them in 1662. Under this it was agreed that Portugal should keep all her colonies in America and Africa, except parts of Guinea. But elsewhere the Dutch secured title to the other places they had acquired (as well as a large indemnity and the right to trade in Portuguese territories). England, which also fought a war with Portugal from 1650 to 1654, won a similar right to trade with Portuguese colonies; and with the marriage of her king to Catherine of Braganza in 1661 was also given control of her settlement in Bombay. Both countries had in effect profited from Portugal's weakness at a time when she was still fighting to win her independence from Spain, to secure colonial gains, and to extract trading privileges that were never normally offered to outside countries by colonial powers.

The Dutch and the English too came into conflict in their colonial territories. This occurred both in the east and in the west. In the East Indies the Dutch were as anxious to expel the English traders, seeking to share in the prosperous spice trade, as they had earlier been to expel the Portuguese. Already in 1622 they had ejected the English from Amboyna, murdering ten English merchants who had dared to aspire to participation in the spice trade there. Now, in a period of repeated warfare between the two countries in Europe (in 1652–4, 1665–7 and 1672–4), the Dutch used the opportunity to establish their position more permanently. At the end of the second war they won the cession of Pula-Run, and in the following years, by conquering or subverting native rulers in the Moluccas, Maccasar and Mataram (in Java), they secured the expulsion of the English and all other foreigners from these valuable territories: the English East India Company was finally expelled from Bantam in Java in 1682.

The same two countries clashed in North America and West Africa. In North America the fur trade was the major cause of conflict. At the beginning of the century the Dutch had established themselves at New Amsterdam (New York), an enclave among the English North American colonies. In 1664, even before the second war between the two countries broke out in Europe, English colonists seized the Dutch settlement, setting up in its place the colonies of New York and New Jersey. At the peace settlement in 1667 the United Provinces recognised this cession in return for English recognition of Dutch sovereignty in Surinam in South America, where the two states had also clashed. In 1673, during the third war between the two countries, the Dutch once more captured New York but restored it again at the peace in the following year. In the Caribbean too each country attacked the colonies (as well as the shipping) of the other. The island of St Eustatius changed hands ten times between 1664 and the final peace of 1674, after which it became, with Curacao (which the Dutch took from Spain in 1634), an important centre for entrepôt trade. In Africa a similar struggle took place. England captured the Dutch slaving station at Cape Coast in 1664, but restored it at the peace of 1667. After the final peace of 1674, and especially after the two countries came into alliance in 1688 (for a time under the same ruler), such conflicts largely ceased. There were no further exchanges of colonial territory between them for over a century. As a result, the Dutch were left in possession of the East Indies with their spice trade, and of settlements in India, the Cape, the Caribbean and Surinam; while they in turn recognised the English colonies in North America and the Caribbean.

More bitter and long-lasting was the conflict between England and Spain. Neither made any serious attempt to challenge the other in its principal colonial possessions: in England's colonies in North America or in Spain's in the south (though some in England demanded an attack on the latter (see below). But in the peripheral areas they were continually in conflict. This occurred above all in the Caribbean. Spain originally controlled all the four largest Caribbean islands: Cuba, Hispaniola, Puerto Rico and Jamaica, as well as Trinidad near the South American coast (though she did not prevent an earlier attempt at settlement by England in the last place). But she lost Jamaica to England at the end of their first war against each other in 1659 (just as she lost the western part of Hispaniola, St Domingue (later Haiti), to France at the end of the Nine Years War in 1697). England had some hopes of acquiring Spanish territory in the War of Spanish Succession: under the terms of the Grand Alliance she reserved the right to retain any Spanish colony she might win in the course of the conflict. In the event, though there was sporadic fighting in the Caribbean, there was no permanent transfer of territory in that area. In Europe, however, England acquired the important Spanish territories of Gibraltar and Minorca. From that point these two places were at the centre of the colonial struggle between the two countries. Gibraltar was besieged by Spain in almost every subsequent encounter, notably in the long siege of 1779–83, but was never taken. Minorca remained in British hands after the War of Austrian Succession, but was taken by France (while Spain was still at peace) at the beginning of the Seven Years War, returned to Britain at its end, and finally restored to Spain at the end of the War of American Independence in 1783.

There was also conflict between the two countries in the border areas between their colonies. The establishment of a new British colony in Georgia in 1733 led to a border dispute with Florida, then still under Spanish rule. In Central America, in present-day Honduras, English settlers from the Caribbean established settlements to cut and sell logs for the dyeing industry. These were seen by Spain as an illegal encroachment on their territory, and were attacked by Spanish forces in the early 1750s. However, as a result of her victory over Spain in 1762–3, Britain secured permanent recognition of the log-cutters' rights. In the same peace settlement Britain secured the cession of Florida, which was only thinly settled and was needed to protect the southern flank of the English colonies, while Spain received Louisiana from France in compensation.

At the same time there was an increasingly bitter conflict between the two countries about trade to Spain's South American colonies. The system by which the trade of colonies was reserved to the mother-countries could only work effectively if that country was in a position to satisfy the needs of its own colonists. This Spain was unable to do. Increasingly, therefore, especially from the beginning of the eighteenth century onwards, part of the needs of Spain's South American colonies were regularly met through illegal trade by other countries, either from the Caribbean or direct from Europe (French ships regularly traded, contrary to Spanish laws, direct to the Pacific coast of South America). But it was Britain which was most anxious to benefit from this trade. After the War of Spanish Succession when she won the contract to trade slaves to South America as well as the right to send an annual trading voyage to the area the conflict intensified. British traders, especially those based in the Caribbean, not content with the new opportunities, persisted in illegal trade. The efforts of the Spanish *costa-gardas* to prevent this, and the frictions which resulted (the *costa-gardas*, paid a commission on their takings, frequently stopped innocent ships), led to war between the two countries in 1739–48. Many in Britain demanded that the opportunity should be taken to acquire colonial territories from Spain: one speaker in the British Parliament declared that "it is by conquests in that part of the world [Spanish America] that we can most effectually secure or enlarge our navigation, and it is there that they can least resist us".[59] But during the war British operations in the Caribbean were generally unsuccessful and Britain secured no territory from Spain: only a brief renewal of the increasingly unprofitable *asiento*. Spain in turn planned to make colonial conquests on her belated entry into the Seven Years War in 1761, planning attacks on Jamaica and the West African slaving stations, as well as Gibraltar; but her failure in the war meant that it was she and not Britain which was obliged to part with territory (Florida).

But the fiercest and most persistent contest for colonies was that between England and France. The two countries contended, first, for the territories controlling the fur trade in North America. The English Hudson's Bay Company, having secured a royal charter in 1670, sought to monopolise the fur trade in the area between Hudson Bay and the Great Lakes. But they were challenged by French traders in the area and this led to armed clashes between the two groups in the 1680s (at a time when the two countries were at peace in Europe). During the Nine Years War (1688–97) further skirmishes took place. Colonists on either side seized settlements belonging to the other in the St Lawrence, Hudson Bay and Newfoundland areas. For the most part, the gains of one side were cancelled by the gains on the other, and at the war's end the previous status quo was restored. But a few years later in the War of Spanish Succession (1702–13) the hostilities were resumed. This time the English captured the French base at Port Royal in Acadia (Nova Scotia), and at the end of the war that territory was handed over to Britain, together with fur-trading posts in the Hudson Bay area. France also had to cede sovereignty to Britain in Newfoundland, though French fishermen were allowed to continue drying their catches along its coast. In the following years the French proceeded to build a substantial fortress at Louisbourg on Cape Breton Island, commanding the Gulf of St Lawrence. During the War of Austrian Succession (1740–8) a British force besieged and captured this strategically important fortress; but to secure the return of Madras, which had been taken by the French, it was returned at the end of the war.

Increasingly the conflict concerned, not the right to fishing and other economic assets, but the security of England's North American colonies. Already before the end of the previous century French fur-traders, missionaries and soldiers had penetrated out of their original area of settlement in the St Lawrence area to the Great Lakes and south down the Ohio Valley. By 1700 they had reached to the Gulf of Mexico. From that point, moving along the Alabama, Tennessee and Mississippi valleys they had established fortified posts at Fort Louis (1702), Fort Toulouse (1703), Fort Assomption on the Mississippi (1739) and, eventually, Fort Duquesne (1753) opposite the English colony of Pennsylvania and Fort Cumberland (1754) on the east side of the Appalachians. This string of forts barred the expansion of the English colonists to the west and was seen by them as an increasing threat. From 1750 onwards there were frequent clashes between the two sides. During 1754–5, while the two countries were still at peace in Europe, substantial military clashes occurred. For the first time British regular forces, under the command of General Braddock, were sent to North America, but at first suffered serious reverses. The contest was intensified after war broke out in Europe in 1756. Pitt saw victory in Canada as an essential war aim for Britain, both for economic and security reasons: the means of winning control of the fisheries and fur trade, as well as securing the safety of the North American colonies. In 1758 Louisbourg was again successfully besieged. This was followed by the capture of Forts Duquesne and Frontenac, and, in the following year, of Quebec, Fort Niagara and Ticonderoga. In consequence the French position was destroyed and in September 1760 the French forces surrendered. Under the Peace of Paris the whole of Canada, with the exception of the tiny islands of St Pierre and Miquelon, became British.

The same two countries competed in the Caribbean, especially for the valuable sugar islands there. In earlier times Portuguese territories had been the main source of the sugar consumed in Europe: successively Madeira, Sao Tome and Brazil. But by the end of the seventeenth century these were no longer able to satisfy the rapidly growing European taste for sugar, and there was an increasing interest in the use of the Caribbean islands, previously mainly the source of tobacco, indigo, rum and other products for the purpose. In the early eighteenth century, Jamaica and Barbados were the principal centres of production in English hands, while France held the more productive islands of St Dominique, Martinique and Guadeloupe. In the War of Spanish Succession both sides raided the islands of the other, but neither could challenge the other successfully in its larger possessions. The British captured the French part of St Kitts (the island had previously been shared) and retained it at the peace settlement. During the War of Austrian Succession (1740–8) both countries sent large fleets to the Caribbean. The English planned raids on Martinique and Guadeloupe, while France proposed an attack on Jamaica. These were, however, not carried out and there was stalemate. At the war's end the two countries agreed to "neutralise" Dominique, St Lucia, St Vincent and Tobago, but there was no transfer of territory. In the Seven Years War (1756–63) on the other hand, the British succeeded in taking Guadeloupe (1759) and Martinique (1762). But they disappointed their own planters by refusing to destroy the plantations or evict the cultivators, who were allowed to trade within the British empire and to continue to live under French law and customs. There were many in Britain who believed that at least Guadeloupe should be kept permanently, pointing out that its exports were worth £600,000 a year, while those of Canada, the prize most generally desired, were worth only £14,000. Most of the British planters had no wish for this, since, confined to the British market, the new production would compete with their own and would severely depress prices. It was thus finally returned to France, with St Lucia, also occupied in the war, which was held to be essential in its defence (though Pitt believed this was all the more reason for keeping it). Britain therefore contented herself with securing Grenada and the "neutral" islands (Dominique, St Lucia, St Vincent and Tobago).

There were also conflicts between the two countries for places in West Africa. These were mainly important as sources of slaves, or at least as stations from which the trade in slaves could be conducted and defended. But in some areas – Senegal and Gambia – there was also significant trade in other commodities: gum, gold-dust and ivory. In 1677 the French West India Company had acquired the mouth of the Senegal, capturing the islands of Goree from the Dutch, and they retained this at the Peace of Nymegen in the following year. About the same time the English Royal Africa Company became active at the mouth of the Gambia, a little further south. For eighty years the two companies operated in close proximity, with little friction. But during the Seven Years War, Britain occupied the French positions in Senegal, including Goree (Pitt was anxious to acquire control of the gum trade[60]), and though she returned the latter she held the positions in Senegal. She was, however, obliged to return them at the end of the War of American Independence in 1783. As a result the general position in West Africa was restored: France remained active on the Senegal river and Britain on the Gambia.

The final area of conflict between the two countries was India. Here the principal interest of the European powers was to bring home silks, calicos, indigo, saltpetre and coffee; and since there was little market for European goods in India they usually had to pay for these in precious metals. Both countries had established trading posts in the sub-continent during the second half of the seventeenth century: the British primarily in Bombay, Madras and Calcutta, the French on the Malabar coast in the south-west, Pondicherry, south of Madras, and Chandragore, north of Calcutta. In both cases their trade was in the hands of their East India Companies, each of which had been granted monopolies by their governments. During the first half of the eighteenth century the trade of both increased sharply: that of the French company increased ten-fold between 1728 and 1746, though it remained only half as large as the British company's. They did not at first compete for territory, seeking only small settlements from which they could trade. As a result, during the War of Spanish Succession both agreed to maintain an informal truce, and there was no fighting in India. At the beginning of the War of Austrian Succession the French, still far weaker, proposed a similar arrangement. This might have been accepted by their opposite numbers, but the British government had already sent a naval force from England. The two companies then determined to do everything in their power, by use of their own local forces, to weaken, and if possible eliminate their rivals. The French were the more successful, capturing Madras in 1746, defeating an Indian ruler who came to the aid of the British, and frustrating a British effort to take Pondicherry. At the end of the war, however, they had to agree to return Madras in order to recover Louisbourg in Canada. The status quo in India was therefore restored.

The struggle was quickly resumed. Both sides now sought to strengthen their own positions by winning influence among local Indian rulers to whom, in return for patronage, they offered military assistance. Again the French had the greater success at first. They won power for their own candidates in the principal states of central and east India (the Deccan, Hyderabad and the Carnatic) but in 1751 Robert Clive, supporting a new contender for the throne of the Carnatic, won a major victory: a reverse which led to the recall of Dupleix, the leading French official in India in 1754. In the same year a temporary accommodation was reached, defining the spheres of influence of each power. The main area of competition now moved north to Bengal, the richest area of the sub-continent. In 1756, the year that war again broke out in Europe, Calcutta, Britain's principal trading station, was seized by a rebel Indian Nawab. Having reconquered the town the British proceeded to move against the neighbouring French settlement at Chandernagore. In the south, although the French with superior forces were able to take a number of British positions, their attempt to besiege Madras was this time unsuccessful. The French fleet, based in Mauritius, was prevented by superior British naval strategy from providing assistance from the sea. Meanwhile the French position in central and east India was steadily weakened and finally overrun. In 1761 the French garrison at Pondicherry was forced to surrender. At the Peace of Paris of 1763, though the French were permitted to retain the trading stations they had held in 1749, they had to agree not to fortify their position in Bengal (leaving it permanently vulnerable to British forces) and to recognise the British-supported rulers in central and eastern India. In effect the British had established their domination of the sub-continent. French power, as in Canada, was largely eliminated.

So a new balance of colonial power had been established. The distribution of colonial territories, and the trading opportunities they provided, had been determined ultimately by the balance of military, and especially of naval, power among the contenders.

COLONIES AND THE BALANCE OF POWER

The struggles we have been examining so far were primarily one element in the overall competition for trade which we examined in the previous chapter. It was because of their economic value that colonies were fought over so bitterly. But even at that time trade was sometimes valued partly for non-commercial reasons: because it could promote the power, as well as the wealth, of the state. So, for example, Marshal Vauban of France, who could claim some expertise in matters of military power, argued at the close of the seventeenth century that France should no longer seek territorial expansion in Europe, but should henceforth concentrate on maritime warfare against England and the United Provinces, since it was only by colonial expansion that France could become a real world power.[61]

The increased trade which colonies could provide was seen as an important contribution to its power, and so affected the balance of power among states. An English writer even declared that "the balance of trade, I cannot too often repeat it, is in fact the balance of power".[62] William Pitt had a similar view about the importance of trade, and so of the colonies that created it, in the overall balance of power. Already in the War of Austrian Succession he had declared, "When trade is at stake it is your last entrenchment; you must defend

it or perish."[63] And fourteen years later in the Seven Years War
when his main aim was to win control of major trading areas in
Canada and India. His criticism of the term of the Peace of Paris was
based on the view that the British ministers who had agreed to return
valuable colonial possessions to France had ignored British interests
in destroying France's "maritime and commercial power".[64] He
argued that "the trade with these colonies is of the most lucrative
nature and of the most considerable extent: the number of ships
employed by it are a great resource to our maritime power: and what
is of equal weight, all that we gain by this system is made fourfold to
us by the loss which ensues to France".[65] Pitt's opposite number in
France, Choiseul, had an essentially similar view:

> In the present state of Europe it is colonies, trade and in conse-
> quence sea-power, which must determine the balance of power
> upon the continent. The House of Austria, Russia, the King of
> Prussia are only powers of the second rank, as are all those which
> cannot go to war unless subsidised by the trading powers.[66]

From about the middle of the eighteenth century, however, this
view that colonies affected the balance of power only indirectly, by
their influence on the trade which each state could command, began
to give way to a rather different appreciation. Increasingly, it came to
be seen, colonies could have a *direct* influence on the balance of
power because of their own strategic importance. Instead of being
seen as economic assets which could contribute to military power,
they came to be seen rather as military assets which could maintain or
defend economic power.

There were a number of reasons for this change of emphasis. First,
the wars which had already occurred, above all the Seven Years War,
had demonstrated the strategic significance of certain colonies, and
the threat which could be posed to others. The French position in
Canada had threatened the position of the English colonies in North
America; the English position in Madras and Calcutta had threatened that of the French in Pondicherry. The spectacular results of the
war demonstrated the importance of effective military action in these
remote regions; vast areas in Canada and India had been lost and
places of almost equal value – Guadeloupe, Havana and Manila –
had changed hands temporarily through war-like action. It was
increasingly obvious that, whether desired for their economic or
military value, existing colonies needed to be effectively defended or

plans had to be made, by those who had lost then, to conquer them again (as both France and Spain prepared to do after 1763). Whether for defence or reconquest, adequate military preparations had to be made and appropriate alliances established. As Lord Brougham pointed out: "If a state values its colonies and is unable at all times to defend them, or to reconquer them when lost, it may, by uniting its interests with another power . . . both immediately prevent its own loss of territory and in general curb the enemy's strength."[67] Either way military power was necessary to retain control of colonies.

Secondly, as a result, the vision of the colonial powers now became increasingly global rather than local. In the early part of the period each colonial theatre was seen as separate and distinct. The skirmishes that took place were essentially local and limited. They were undertaken mainly by the settlers themselves, with the limited forces at their disposal, for essentially parochial purposes. From the middle of the eighteenth century governments at home took over the responsibility. While in the War of Austrian Succession the capture of Louisbourg had been undertaken for Britain by North American militias, in the Seven Years War its capture, and the subsequent conquest of Canada, was undertaken by troops from the mother country. While in the former war the struggle for India was undertaken almost entirely by local forces, in the latter both governments sent major battle-fleets to Indian waters to play a decisive part in the final outcome. Increasingly, too, the outcome in one area was balanced and adjusted by the outcome in another. So in 1748 Madras was exchanged for Louisbourg; in 1763 Guadeloupe for Canada, Manila for Minorca. The battle for colonies was increasingly a single, interrelated struggle. It was in recognition of this interconnection that Choiseul, after the Seven Years War, warned that in future France would never allow Britain to found new colonies in distant parts of the world without insisting on her right to match them with corresponding French acquisitions.[68]

Thirdly, it was increasingly recognised that campaigns in the colonies directly affected the European balance of power. If Canada could be conquered in Germany, as Pitt maintained, it was equally the case, as the Seven Years War and the War of American Independence only too clearly demonstrated, that colonial campaigns could have a decisive effect on the outcome in Europe, if only by diverting substantial forces. The importance of this factor was increasingly recognised. So Brougham maintained that, although Britain might be unable to conquer France on the European mainland, she "generally had the superiority in the colonies both of the West and East Indies; and when she availed herself, during war, of this superiority, France could never, by direct invasion of Great Britain, hope to regain her lost colonial possessions."[69]

This recognition of the strategic importance of colonies was reflected in policy. It was shown first in the action now taken to acquire greater knowledge of remoter territories, previously largely unexplored, which could have strategic significance. In earlier times most exploration had been undertaken by traders and explorers, acting mainly on their own initiative even if with some official backing. Now increasingly it was governments themselves, often their navy departments, that took the initiative in organising such expeditions. These were now explicitly intended to explore and map out new areas and if necessary to claim them. So, the British Admiralty sent out William Dampier to explore the Pacific in 1699; launched Anson on a worldwide voyage in 1740; dispatched Byron in 1764, Wallis and Cartaret in 1766 and Captain Cook in 1769 to explore the South Seas and if possible find the rumoured southern continent there; finally sent Captain Cook to explore the North Pacific, including a possible western exit of the Northwest Passage. So too France undertook a series of expeditions in the Pacific area, including those of Bouvet and Bourgainville, to visit Samoa, the Solomons and New Britain. So too the Spaniards sent expeditions to Easter Island and Tahiti, for essentially similar purposes.

But the new attitude was demonstrated above all by the choice of colonies which the governments now sought to acquire. Already at the Peace of Paris the importance of strategic motives had been demonstrated: the controversial preference for barren Canada over rich Guadeloupe, of tiny Minorca over the potentially productive trading areas of Cuba or the Philippines. From this point that motive became increasingly powerful. The balance of power in these remote parts of the world, it began to be felt, was as vital as the balance of power in Europe and intimately connected with it. Thus an English writer maintained that if the North American colonies "should ever fall into French hands, it would not be possible . . . to maintain a balance of trade and power in America. And who will imagine that he could maintain them, after that, in Europe."[70] And the same writer commented: "if it be needful to maintain a balance of power in Europe, why not in Asia among the European powers established there? Will not the rise or decline of their trade and power in the Indies affect that of their particular states in Europe?"[71]

Certainly from this point there was a special interest in those acquisitions – often only small islands – which had strategic value. So France, having already acquired Mauritius (previously abandoned by the Dutch) in 1721, acquired Réunion and Madagascar in 1768, because of their strategic importance rather than for any economic importance they might have. So Britain acquired Gibraltar, Minorca for a time, and later Malta and the Ionian Islands in the Mediterranean for similar reasons. In Asia the same motives were evident. After she had established her dominance in eastern India in 1763 Britain looked for naval bases in that area and beyond (during the Seven Years War she had had to rely on her base in Bombay): so she acquired, if only briefly, Balambang off the north coast of Borneo in 1764; Negapatam in eastern India (from the Dutch) in 1784; Penang in 1786; and occupied Trincomalee (as well as Padang on Sumatra) during the War of American Independence, and subsequently negotiated to share its use.[72] Both France and Britain were interested in acquiring positions in Burma (the British East India Company held the port of Negrais for a few years and the French operated a shipyard at Rangoon for a similar period after 1766). And Spain, France and Britain were all interested in the strategically placed island of Tahiti, sending ships to visit it at different times.

Often the new acquisitions made by one power aroused the fear and hostility of others. It was partly France's acquisition of Mauritius, and the dangerous use she made of it during the Seven Years War, which caused Britain to seek new acquisitions in the region (and to take the island during the Napoleonic Wars). In the same way it was Britain's increasingly powerful position in the Pacific which aroused Spain's apprehension concerning the security of her American colonies. Spain had been unwilling to allow any foreign power to establish itself too close to those territories (the Spanish ambassador in London told the British government that "all those countries [in the Pacific region] are the king's and no one may settle in them".[73] She was thus highly suspicious of Britain's interest in the Falkland Islands. After his voyage in 1740 Anson had reported on the potential strategic importance of these islands and Britain became seriously interested in establishing a base there. Lord Egmont, First Lord of the Admiralty after the Seven Years War, described the islands as "the key to the whole Pacific Ocean" because of their position. In 1763–4 both France and Britain, unknown to the other, sent expeditions and established positions there. In 1767 France handed over her posts to her ally Spain, whose interest was more immediate.

Thereupon in 1770 Spain launched an attack on the British position at Port Egmont and expelled the British garrison. This caused deep anger in Britain and war seemed imminent. But France was unwilling to give Spain the support she needed if she was to have any prospect of success, and the latter was therefore compelled to restore the western Falklands to Britain. The British garrison was temporarily re-established but withdrew for economic reasons six years later.

Spain was equally nervous about threats to her territories from the North American continent. In the second half of the eighteenth century, Russia, Britain and Spain simultaneously demonstrated an increasing interest in the North Pacific area. Russia, having discovered the Bering Strait in 1728, fifteen years later began exploring from Alaska towards the south. Britain sent Captain Cook to the region in 1776. And about the same time Spain, concerned at the threat which either of the others might represent to her California territory, sent an expedition north from there (she had already in 1775 reached and claimed Alaska). In 1789 a similar Spanish expedition reached and destroyed a settlement which had been established by a British trader in Nootka Sound. Again war appeared imminent. And once more only the inability of the French, preoccupied by political crisis at home, to give her any support, compelled Spain to back down. The British settlement remained and Britain won recognition of her right of access to the coastline between Alaska and California and to fish for whales in the Pacific; but, to meet Spanish apprehensions, she undertook not to set up her new colonies in either the "eastern or western shores of South America".

But the colonial balance of power was not only affected by the discovery of new territories. The balance could be turned by helping to evict a rival power from the territories she controlled. So in 1778–83 France and Spain welcomed the opportunity to assist the American colonists to expel British power (though Spain was always apprehensive about the effect this would have on their own position in the south). As a result of their efforts, they were able to win concessions in other parts of the world: the recovery of Minorca and Florida by Spain, and of Senegal and Tobago by France. Britain in turn, thirty years later, gave every encouragement to the South American revolutionaries in their effort to free themselves from their Spanish masters. Similarly, in 1793 Britain assisted French settlers in St Domingue to maintain their independence from the French revolutionary government, and subsequently gave some help to the local revolutionary leader, Toussaint, the former slave, against Napoleon's efforts to reimpose French rule.

The Napoleonic wars provided new opportunities for pursuing this competition for strategically valuable territory. The French revolutionaries were as well aware of the value to their country of overseas possessions as the royalist ministers who preceded them. In 1797 Talleyrand wrote an essay, which he read before the Institut de France on the advantages of establishing new colonies.[74] One of the territories which had been widely seen in France over the previous twenty years as an especially desirable acquisition was Egypt, with its strategically vital location on the route into the east (plans for a Suez Canal had already been discussed at the time). In the year following Talleyrand's lecture, Napoleon sought to realise this dream by invading Egypt. He was however prevented by British action from holding it.[75] Here, as elsewhere in the world, British sea-power proved ultimately decisive. It was this which enabled Britain to take Tobago and St Lucia from France in the early years of the war; and later French Guiana, Senegal, Martinique and St Domingue (1809), Guadeloupe, Mauritius and Réunion (1810). Nor was it only from France that she seized colonial territories. She took Trinidad and other smaller Caribbean territories from Spain in 1796–7. And she occupied the Dutch colonies in Ceylon (ceded to her at the Peace of Amiens in 1802); Surinam; a number of Caribbean territories; the Cape of Good Hope (occupied briefly in 1795 and again in 1806); Curacao (1807); part of the Moluccas (1808); Amboyna and Banda (1810); and Java (1811). And once again the settlement in 1814–15 demonstrated which type of colonies were now most valued. It was everywhere the strategically significant places that were retained by Britain: St Lucia with its valuable harbour; Ascension Island in the Atlantic; Heligoland in the Baltic; Malta and the Ionian Islands in the Mediterranean; Aden (occupied in 1802 and annexed in 1838); the Cape of Good Hope and Mauritius protecting the vital sea-routes in India and beyond. Between 1793 and 1815 the total number of British colonies increased from 26 to 43; and the majority of these were relatively small territories taken because of their strategic value. Against this, territories that were commercially far more significant, larger and more populous, she was willing to return: Java, the Maluccas, Amboyna, Banda and Curacao to the Dutch; the prosperous sugar islands of Martinique and Guadeloupe, and populous Réunion, to the French; West Indian territories to Denmark. These could provide some economic benefits to the country that held them, but not what was now most valued: military power. And it was the effect on the balance of power not, as a century before, on the balance of trade, that was now believed to be most important.

The value that was attributed to colonies thus changed significantly during the course of this period. Colonies had been sought at first primarily for trade, and it was on the basis of the trade they could procure that their value was assessed. As the period progressed these benefits, though certainly not despised, appeared less significant. Colonies of substantial economic importance were restored to their former owners. Colonies were now acquired mainly for a different reason: because they could contribute to the defence of the empires of which they formed a part, and so, indirectly, assist in maintaining the balance of power in Europe.

BOOKS

Contemporary works

J. Anderson, *Considerations on Colonial Policy* (London, 1813).

Lord Henry Brougham, *An Inquiry into the Colonial Policy of the European Powers* (London, 1803) 2 vols.

F. Hall, *The Importance of the British Plantations in America* (London, 1731).

Sir W. Keith, *The History of the British Plantations in America* (London, 1738).

M. Postlethwayt, "Colonies", in *The Universal Dictionary of Trade and Commerce*, 4th edn (London, 1774).

T. Pownall, *The Administration of the Colonies* (London, 1765).

J. Tucker, *A Series of Answers to Certain Objections Against Separating from the Rebellious Colonies* (Gloucester, 1776).

A. Smith, *The Wealth of Nations* (Edinburgh, 1776) esp. Book IV, ch. vii "Of Colonies".

Modern works

J. C. Beaglehole, *The Exploration of the Pacific* (Stanford, Conn., 1966).

G. L. Beer, *British Colonial Policy, 1754–1765* (New York, 1907).

——, *The Old Colonial System* (New York, 1912).

C. R. Boxer, *The Dutch Sea-borne Empire, 1600–1800* (London, 1965).

——, *The Portuguese Sea-borne Empire: Four Centuries of Portuguese Expansion* (London, 1969).

The Cambridge History of the British Empire, vol. I: *The Old Empire* (Cambridge, 1929).

H. H. Deschamps, *Les Méthodes et les doctrines coloniales de la France* (Paris, 1953).

C. H. Haring, *The Spanish Empire in America* (New York, 1947).

V. T. Harlow, *The Founding of the Second British Empire, 1763–93*, 2 vols (London, 1962, 1964).

D. B. Hertz, *The Old Colonial System* (Manchester, 1905).

K. Hotblack, *Chatham's Colonial Policy* (London, 1917).

K. Knorr, *British Colonial Theories, 1570–1850* (Toronto, 1944).

C. L. Lokke, *France and the Colonial Question, 1763–1801* (New York, 1932).

R. Pares, *Yankees and Creoles: The Trade Between North America and the West Indies* (London, 1956).

——, *War and Trade in the West Indies* (London, 1963).

J. H. Parry, *The Spanish Sea-borne Empire* (London, 1966).

——, *Trade and Dominion: European Overseas Empires in the Eighteenth Century* (London, 1971).

H. I. Priestley, *France Overseas through the Old Regime* (New York, 1937).

R. L. Schuyler, *The Fall of the Old Colonial System* (Oxford, 1945).

G. Williams, *The Expansion of Europe* (London, 1966).

J. A. Williamson, *A Short History of British Expansion*, vol. I: *The Old Colonial Empire* (London, 1965).

10 Alliances

THE SEARCH FOR ALLIANCES

The states of this system were generally, as we have seen, self-seeking and competitive. They saw every other state as a rival which could easily become an enemy. None was always a friend. The major states of the system were at war, at one time or another, with almost every other. But despite this – and even because of it – they sometimes found it advantageous to establish alliances with one or more other states, if only to be able to make war more effectively against whichever was the greatest threat at the time. As the French diplomat de Callières put it: "There is indeed no prince so powerful that he can afford to neglect the assistance offered by a good alliance in resisting the forces of hostile powers which are prompted by jealousy of his prosperity to unite in a hostile coalition."[1]

This advice was almost universally followed. No state was so powerful that it could afford to dispense altogether with such arrangements. Whatever their own strength, they knew that, since their enemies might themselves be able by combining with others to outmatch their capabilities, they too must sometimes take similar steps to keep pace with them. Even Louis XIV at the height of his powers, even Napoleon with Europe at his feet, did not scorn to seek alliances that could assist them against their enemies.

Such arrangements were particularly important in this age because few wars were likely to remain bilateral affairs. In the nineteenth century most of the wars of the major powers were fought on a one-to-one basis (and even in the single exception – the Crimean War – only one side included more than one partner). They were fought out in relatively restricted areas over brief periods (several were over in a few weeks and the longest lasted little more than two years). In this age all the major wars were fought out within the continent as a whole (and often beyond it), lasted years, and sooner or later involved several states on either side. Every state therefore needed to be prepared to fight a conflict against several other states simultaneously; and one which might involve several different regions – eastern Europe as well as western, the Baltic as well as the Mediterranean, the Rhine as well as the Danube. This made the assistance of friends elsewhere essential. Britain could not fight France in Germany without the help of Austria or Prussia; Spain could not fight Austria in Italy without the help of France; Saxony/Poland could not fight Sweden in Livonia without the help of Russia; and so on. On these grounds all the major wars of the period were fought out between groups of states, joined together in more or less uneasy partnership.

Some of the alliances were genuinely defensive in character: formed out of fear that some other state or group of states might threaten the peace in the future. The League of Augsburg, first created in 1681 among Sweden, the United Provinces and a few German states, and broadened to include the emperor and Spain in 1686, was intended to counter the increasingly aggressive conduct of Louis XIV. The Quadruple Alliance, established by Britain, France, the United Provinces and Austria in 1718, was intended to preserve the settlement reached at the conclusion of the previous conflict and committed the parties to joint action against attempts (such as that of Spain currently being undertaken in Italy) to undermine that settlement. A good many alliances – such as those between Britain, France and Spain of 1721 and between Russia and Sweden of 1724 – were explicitly described as "defensive". The Treaty of Westminster, concluded between Britain and Prussia in 1756, committed the two countries to "neutralise" Germany and so to protect that region against attack from France or Russia. The alliance established between Russia and Prussia in 1764 was explicitly described as "defensive" in its purpose: it was designed not to threaten other states but to reassure each party, previously declared enemies, against attack from other powers, and particularly to protect Prussia from a revanchist war by Austria.

In other cases, however, alliances were overtly *offensive* from the start. When Louis XIV made up his mind to make war on the United Provinces in 1668–9 he proceeded to conclude alliance treaties with England (1670), Sweden (1671), Munster, Cologne, Bavaria and Saxony among other states, to assist him in that endeavour. The alliance established between Prussia, Saxony/Poland and Denmark in 1698–9 was for the express purpose of making war against Sweden. The coalition put together by Austria in 1756–7 was formed with the aim of making war against Prussia and the recovery of Silesia (and though it was eventually Frederick the Great who precipitated the conflict this was only because he knew that the coalition planned to attack him in the following year: see below). The Convention of Aranjuez of 1779 between France and Spain united those countries in a war on Britain to recover territories lost in previous conflicts.

But though alliances were often explicitly designated as "defensive" or "offensive", it was not always easy to classify them neatly in that way. Sometimes they were formed only after the war had already broken out, and their purpose was not simply to defend territory under attack, but to carry the war to the enemy as well. Thus the terms of the treaty between the emperor and the United Provinces of May 1689, in which the Grand Alliance was founded, stated that it was "not only a defensive but also an offensive alliance between the contracting parties". Similarly the alliance formed between the emperor and Poland in May 1657 (subsequently joined by Brandenburg) to resist the assault on Poland of Charles X of Sweden was described as "offensive" (though it was established to resist an attack) but the same states signed simultaneously a "defensive alliance". The second Grand Alliance of 1701, though no doubt seen by its members as defensive in intention, in fact preceded a general outbreak of war and committed them to war aims which went far beyond the maintenance of the status quo. The League of Nympenburg of 1741, entered into a year after the outbreak of the War of Austrian succession and the second Bourbon Family Compact of 1743, proposed sweeping political gains for the countries which participated. And more generally, because there was often no agreement on which *action*, and therefore which country, was responsible for precipitating war, it was also not always easy to distinguish which alliances, however they were designated, were genuinely "offensive" or "defensive".

The most striking feature of these alliances, and what most distinguishes them from those of other international societies, for example in the nineteenth century, still more in the twentieth century, is the fact that, whether offensive or defensive, whether entered into before war broke out or after, they were nearly always seen as short-term in character. As soon as circumstances changed they could quickly be abandoned and alternative partners chosen (see below). Often they were formed for the purpose of fighting a particular war, and were frequently abandoned, tacitly or explicitly, as soon as that war was completed. They were in any case seen as understandings between rulers rather than between states and depended on the will of each individual ruler. Thus when a ruler died, the alliance might have to be renewed with his successor; or the new ruler might, like the tsar Peter III on ascending the throne in Russia in 1762, adopt an entirely new policy, which involved abandoning former allies and reconciliation with former enemies. Even the establishment of a new government, like that of the Tory government which came to power in Britain in 1710, might have the effect that allies were abandoned and a separate peace with their common enemy concluded. Short-term alliances of this kind were thus not in any way comparable to those of the late nineteenth century: for example those between Germany and Austria (1879) and between France and Russia (1891–4) – or of the late twentieth century – which persisted regardless of changes of ruler or regime, and lasted sometimes for three or four decades.

But though formal alliances were normally short-term affairs, more lasting understandings between states did sometimes emerge, even if they were not solemnised in formal treaties. These resulted from a number of causes. Sometimes they rested simply on common interests and the traditional associations which resulted. Thus, for example, England and the United Provinces, after the conclusion of their three brief wars (1652–4, 1665–7 and 1672–4) remained for the next fifty years or so in a close partnership, sufficiently stable for the two countries to be commonly bracketed together as "the Maritime Powers". With these two Austria, inspired by unequal enmity to France, was frequently joined (for example in the two major wars between 1688 and 1714); and this too was a grouping sufficiently consistent to be identifiable, in Britain at least, as the conventional alliance pattern: the "old system", as it was frequently called. There were other habitual groupings, sometimes but not always formalised in alliance treaties: between France and her eastern partners, Sweden, Poland and Turkey, united mainly by common hostility to Russia; between Russia and Denmark (consolidated in a formal alliance in 1768) resulting from their common hostility to Sweden; and between Austria and Russia, who engaged in formal alliances in 1726, 1746 and 1781 and were frequent partners in war (for example in 1686–99, 1733–5 (in Poland), 1736–9 (against Turkey), 1756–62 and 1787–91).

Often such long-term relationships were the effect of equally long-term antagonisms. The intense hostility between France and Spain before 1700 (the two countries fought five wars against each other in 52 years); between England and France (evidenced in eight wars between 1665 and 1815); between Denmark and Sweden (three wars between 1657 and 1721); between Austria and Prussia (two wars between 1760 and 1763), stimulated the alliances each antagonist formed with like-minded states against its chief enemies. So it was common hostility to France that brought England, the United Provinces and Austria together; and their common hostility to Britain that held France and Spain together in the eighteenth century. It was common hostility to Sweden that brought Russia, Denmark and often Poland together, and common hostility to Prussia which brought Russia and Austria into alliance for much of the period between 1726 and 1814.

Sometimes long-term partnerships had a dynastic foundation.[2] France and Spain, which fought against each other so often when ruled by rival dynasties (seventeen times in the two centuries before 1700), became consistent allies after the Bourbon succession in Spain in 1700. That close association was expressed in the three Family Compacts of 1733, 1743 and 1761 (and the later treaty of 1779); and the two countries fought together in every war of the century until the French Revolution. They were joined by two Bourbon rulers, those of Naples and Parma after they succeeded in those territories: both were parties to the third Bourbon Family Compact of 1761. Family connections helped to cement relations between the United Provinces and Britain at the times when the Orange family, closely related to the English royal family, held power in the former country: for example in 1672–1702, after 1747, and after the Orange restoration of 1787. The dynastic links which Peter the Great deliberately established by marrying his daughter and two nieces into the ruling families of Holstein-Gottorp, Mecklenburg and Courland ensured, as intended, that those states were usually closely tied to Russia's cause. Bavaria and Cologne, under closely related Wittelsbach rulers, were nearly always closely allied. Foreign policy was, of course, still more closely aligned when two states had a common ruler: like England and United Provinces (in 1689–1702), Britain and Hanover (after 1714), and Poland and Saxony (1697–1763), though even in those cases policy differences sometimes occurred: there were considerable divergencies in the policies to be pursued by Britain and Hanover when George I ruled both, and in 1715–17 he was at war with Sweden as ruler of Hanover but still neutral as king of England.*

Religious ties, on the other hand, so often the source of long-term partnerships in the previous age, were now rarely decisive. Common hostility to the non-Christian still played a part in the early years of

---

* Connections through the female line had less influence on policy. Louis XIV was the husband and the son of Spanish princesses yet the two countries were, before 1700, continually at war. The marriage of the Duke of Savoy to Louis XIV's niece, and of his daughter to Louis' grandson, did not prevent the duke from allying himself more often with Louis' enemies than with his uncle-in-law. The marriage of Frederick the Great's sister to the king of Sweden did not prevent Sweden from declaring war on Prussia in the Seven Years War.

the period, uniting Christian rulers, even those normally in conflict, against the Turks in 1663–4 and 1683–99. Occasionally Protestant rulers preferred to join with others of the same faith. The formation of the Triple Alliance between England, the United Provinces and Sweden in 1668 was eased by their common Protestant belief. And there were many in Britain who welcomed the fact that in the Seven Years War their country was allied to a Protestant ruler rather than, as in previous wars, with a Catholic one. But religious sentiment was no longer powerful enough to be the decisive factor in determining alliances. Over and over again alliances crossed the religious barrier. So Catholic Austria could happily ally itself with Protestant England and Protestant United Provinces; Protestant England with Catholic Savoy, Portugal and (before 1700) Spain; Catholic France with Lutheran Sweden and Prussia – and even Moslem Turk. Conversely, Lutheran Sweden fought Lutheran Denmark while Catholic France fought Catholic Austria.[3] Occasionally religion caused friction among allies (as within the Grand Alliance over the terms of the Peace of Ryswick relating to religion in returned territories and recognition of the Protestant succession in England for example). But it did not dictate which power was allied with which.

Ideology was still less significant. At the beginning of the period England and the United Provinces, with parliamentary, non-monarchical systems and a common hostility to autocracy in addition to their Protestant faith, had far more in common with each other than with any other states of the system; but this did not prevent them from fighting three wars in twenty-odd years. Parliamentary Britain was frequently allied with autocratic regimes in Austria, Prussia, Russia and even (in 1716–31) with France. Conversely, the autocratic monarchies of the continent, for all the similarity of their political institutions, were not deterred from fighting successive wars against each other. Even in the Napoleonic wars, though political belief certainly played a part in the opening stages, this quickly ceased to be of much account in determining policy. The rulers of Spain, Prussia, Austria and Russia, whatever their initial hostility to the revolution, had little difficulty in coming to terms with it when their national interests demanded this; and were even willing to make war against their former ally Britain in association with the French emperor.

Occasionally geographical factors influenced the formation of alliances. In 1726–7, the three eastern states of Austria, Russia and Prussia were allied against the western powers, Britain, France, the

United Provinces, Denmark and Sweden, though it is doubtful if geographical considerations played much part in determining these alignments. There was possibly a more genuine geographical factor at work in the War of Polish Succession a few years later: the eastern states, Russia and Austria, as neighbours of Poland, had a common interest in preventing the French candidate from acquiring power in that country; while France and Spain as western countries had a corresponding interest in expelling Hapsburg power from Lorraine and Italy. In a few cases there were deliberate attempts to create alliances on a geographical basis. In the years after the Seven Years War, the Russian foreign minister, Panin, sought to establish a "northern system", including Russia, Prussia, Poland/Saxony, Sweden and Denmark and possibly Britain, while France was allied with the southern states of Austria, Spain and Spain's satellites in Naples and Parma. This was, however, an unusual configuration. Alliances were not usually formed of compact geographical blocks. Often it was close neighbours who were the most implacable enemies: Sweden and Denmark, Spain and Portugal, Austria and Savoy, Russia and Turkey – antagonists of this sort often had an interest in seeking alliance with a distant partner, who could help to encircle their opponents. Alliances, therefore, more often straddled the continent than established single cohesive blocks of territory of the kind seen in the twentieth century.

Each of these long-term factors, therefore, had some part to play in influencing alliance policy, but none was decisive. The most striking feature of the age is precisely how catholic each state showed itself in its choice of allies. Those who were friends in one war were enemies in the next, and vice versa. There were indeed some in positions of power who explicitly advised against any long-term commitments. Walpole declared that it was his policy "to keep free from all engagements as long as we possibly can". Frederick the Great in his second *Political Testament* insisted that

> in politics you should have no predilections for one people or aversion against another. It is necessary to follow blindly the interests of the state and unite with the power whose interests at that time fit most closely with Prussia's. . . . The wisest policy is to await the opportunity to see then in what circumstances you find yourself and to profit from them insofar as they can favour us.[4]

The general opinion of the age was that alliances should be short-term arrangements, tailor-made to benefit each state in the particular situation in which it found itself at the time, not long-term commitments based on a common viewpoint or related national interests.

THE TERMS OF ALLIANCES

Whether a particular alliance would be found advantageous obviously depended on the precise terms laid down. Great care was devoted to the drafting of alliance treaties and tough bargaining took place, sometimes over several years[5] on the obligations to be met by each party.

Some alliance treaties were severely practical, being mainly devoted to specifying the precise contributions in men or money to be made by each party. The many subsidy treaties of the age were mainly straightforward business arrangements of this sort, specifying how much would be paid by one state to another in return for forces which the latter would supply. Britain which, with a small standing army, often had a need for additional forces and, by the end of the seventeenth century, an efficient financial system which generated substantial revenues to pay for auxiliaries, specialised in treaties of this kind. She made repeated arrangements with smaller German states, such as Hesse, the Brunswick duchies and, occasionally, Saxony under which, in return for financial payments, they provided contingents to fight for Britain, not only on the European continent but elsewhere: Britain used Hessian forces, for example, in North America during the War of American Independence. Agreements were also sometimes made not for the direct supply of troops, but according the right to recruit forces directly from the territory of another state: for example France's treaty with the cantons of Switzerland of 1663 gave her the right to raise troops in that country to fight under French command when required. Occasionally more than one power agreed to share in providing a subsidy. In both the Nine Years War and the War of Spanish Succession England and the United Provinces (at that time under the same ruler) believed that the alliance of Savoy was vital, tying down French troops on her south-east border. They accordingly agreed to pay Savoy an initial subsidy of 100,000 écus, with 80,000 a month thereafter: of this England was to pay two-thirds and the United Provinces a third.

These arrangements were not always with the smaller states. Alliance treaties between the major powers also often provided that one state should contribute financial assistance to another in return

for the offer of military forces. Once again it was Britain which, for
the same reason, most often purchased forces from such a partner.
Her long negotiations with Russia in 1753–6, for example, concerned
the precise amount of money which she would pay in return for what
level of commitment of forces by Russia. Britain originally hoped to
hire Russian forces that could be used to resist an attack on Hanover,
whether by Prussia or France (just as Russian forces had been
employed to defend the United Provinces in the War of Austrian
Succession a few years before). There was prolonged haggling,
especially about the size of the British subsidy. It was eventually
agreed that Russia should provide a force of 55,000 troops in return
for a subsidy of £100,000 if the force remained on Russian territory
(for example in Livonia threatening East Prussia), or £500,000 if they
needed to be sent elsewhere.[6] The arrangement was never finally
fulfilled because, by concluding a subsequent treaty with Frederick
the Great providing for the neutralisation of Germany, Britain
robbed the alliance of any value in Russia's eyes. But Russia then
undertook similar negotiations with other allies. In April 1756 she
offered to provide 60,000 troops to Austria (under their alliance of
1746), and later raised this to 80,000 in return for the offer of a
subsidy of a million roubles a year, together with an offer by Austria
to provide a force of the same size. For Saxony, a vulnerable state
with inadequate resources of her own, Russia herself became the
paymaster, providing a subsidy of 100,000 roubles (together with a
similar sum to its chief minister as "expenses").

There were comparable negotiations between Austria and France
in the same period. When first approached for an alliance in 1755,
France was willing to enter into a defensive arrangement only,
unlikely to involve her in onerous commitments elsewhere while she
was at war with Britain: under the Treaty of Versailles of May 1756
both countries agreed to provide a force of 20,000 to assist the other
if it were attacked. A year later, however, after the outbreak of the
Seven Years War, France became willing to commit herself more
fully: then, as the wealthier state, she agreed to make the main
financial contribution. She undertook to pay Austria a subsidy of
twelve million florins, as well as providing a force of 105,000 men to
fight in Germany (with 10,000 mercenaries), in return for the cession
of most of the Austrian Netherlands to Spain and four cities of that
territory for France herself. Two years later, however, when she
came under greater military pressure she negotiated a reduction in
this commitment, offering only 100,000 men in Germany and a

halving of the subsidy. Two years after that she was unable to pay even this reduced subsidy, and Austria was accordingly compelled to reduce the size of its army by 20,000.

Generally speaking, therefore, the poorer and less-well-organised powers, such as Russia and Austria, made their contributions mainly in the form of forces and were net recipients of financial help. Against this the wealthier and better-organised states to the west of the continent were the main providers of finance to each alliance. Britain, in particular, was willing to accept ever-increasing financial commitments as a means of securing success in war. She recognised that, however great her dominance at sea, to be able to prevail in Europe she must dispose of adequate land forces, or rely on those of others who were her allies there. Thus in the War of Austrian Succession she was willing, while avoiding full-scale participation on the continent, to offer Austria not only a financial subsidy but to pay the cost of 12,000 troops, to be hired from Denmark and Hesse, which would fight on behalf of Austria (though eventually she kept these forces for herself to defend Hanover). In the Seven Years War she undertook to pay to Frederick the Great from 1758 onwards a huge subsidy of £670,000 a year (in addition to establishing an "army of observation"), to sustain Prussia's war effort and so to "conquer America in Germany". This tradition of British munificence to her allies was maintained in the Napoleonic wars. Her financial contributions then reached unprecedented levels: in 1813 alone British subsidies, mainly to Russia, Prussia and Sweden, amounted to £11 million, and in the course of the entire war they reached nearly £50 million: a vast sum by contemporary standards.

However, alliance treaties did not necessarily contain any commitments for the payment of subsidies. More normal were the commitments by all the parties to provide a certain level of forces to the common effort, whether equal or unequal. In the treaty between Britain and the emperor of 1716 both rulers agreed to provide 12,000 men (8000 foot and 4000 horse) or, if appropriate, ships of war of equal value. Similarly, in the Quadruple Alliance two years later the three larger powers (Britain, France and Austria) agreed to provide 12,000 men (8000 foot and 4000 horse) and the United Provinces half that figure; or, alternatively, ships or money (calculated at 10,000 Dutch florins to 1000 foot soldiers or 30,000 florins for 1000 horse). The contributions demanded often reflected the differing capabilities of the powers. Under the Treaty of Hanover of 1725 Britain and France were to provide 12,000 men (8000 foot and 4000 horse) but

Prussia only 5000 (3000 foot and 2000 horse): a clear recognition of Prussia's inferior strength at that time. Under the treaty of Vienna of 1725 between Spain and Austria it was laid down that Spain would provide fifteen ships of the line and 20,000 men (including 5000 horse) in defence of Austria, while the latter, which had no navy, was to send 30,000 men (including 10,000 horse) to defend Spain. In this and other treaties it was provided that the ruler being attacked would undertake the cost of providing winter quarters for the forces of the other. The alliance of Hanover of 1719 between the emperor, Saxony/ Poland and Britain/Hanover went into even greater detail on this point: it not only provided that the country being assisted should meet the cost of providing food for horses, but even laid down the amount of hay and oats to be given to each horse (Article III). There was sometimes a limitation on where the forces being provided could be used by those being assisted. For example, that same treaty stipulated that the forces being provided by Britain/Hanover could be used only in Germany and not in Hungary: in other words it was made clear, though not explicitly stated, that the treaty was designed to protect German territory from Russian incursions, not to protect the Hapsburg domains against threats from other sources – for example Turkey.

There were other points to be decided besides the geographical areas covered. A crucial one concerned the circumstances in which the alliance commitments would become operational: in other words what was the *casus belli*. Each party to a defensive alliance agreed to defend the other if it was attacked; but it was not always self-evident whether a particular country had been attacked or whether it had itself initiated a conflict. Thus when Austria, which had signed an alliance treaty with Britain only two years earlier, found herself at war with France and Spain in 1733, she understandably expected to receive support from her ally. But the pacific Walpole contended that the treaty was not applicable because Austria had brought the conflict on herself by intervening in Poland to overthrow the elected monarch there. In other cases the wording of the treaty was even more open to conflicting interpretation. For example, under the first Bourbon Family Contract of 1733 France and Spain agreed that they would each secure "prompt satisfaction . . . by force of arms if necessary", if the other were "attacked, molested or insulted by any person whatsoever". Such wide conditions made it possible for the treaty to be invoked in almost any circumstances, and could therefore give rise to considerable conflict among the parties. Some treaties contained a provision explicitly intended to prevent disagreements of this kind: the alliance treaty between Spain and France of 1796 specified that a request for forces by either ally must be met, whatever the circumstances, and "all discussions of whether the war envisaged . . . be of its nature offensive or defensive, shall be declared of no validity whatsoever".

Alliance treaties, besides specifying the contribution in men or money to be made by each party, sometimes spelt out the way their operations would be co-ordinated if war broke out. For example they might provide for the establishment of a "council of war", composed of the military commanders of each power, to discuss their common strategy: a provision of this kind was included, for example, in the alliance between the emperor, Poland/Lithuania and Brandenburg of 1657 and in the Holy League established between the emperor, Poland and Venice in 1684. Sometimes the arrangements called for went further than this. Under the third Bourbon Family Compact of 1761, France and Spain undertook to "discuss and agree upon all tactics before putting them into operation" and to "establish working agreements especially tailored to the particular demands of the war". By this means they would be able to "decide on their respective tasks . . . and as to . . . the strategy for all their mutual undertakings". In the alliance of Hanover of 1719 between the emperor, Saxony/Poland and Britain/Hanover, the parties pledged themselves to agree on the "place and manner of uniting their forces, and the general command and conduct of the army and for supplying the same with provisions and . . . on the direction and execution of the military operations" (Article XII). The Alliance treaty between Russia and Austria of 1760 provided (Article III) for the co-ordination of their actions through the exchange of plans and the appointment of generals from each state to serve on the council of war of the other. In other cases the machinery for consultation was not laid down in the alliance agreement but developed only later. Thus in the Nine Years War the parties to the Grand Alliance of 1689 decided in the following year to establish a standing "congress" which met at the Hague each winter between campaigns to discuss strategy and objectives.

But allies needed to reach agreement not only on the forces or subsidies to be provided and the co-ordination of strategy but on *ends*: their political objectives or war aims. It was by no means easy to agree on these and they were for this reason not even mentioned in many alliance treaties. Different allies often had very different concerns. Frequently the only objective they genuinely shared was the destruction of the common enemy. Thus the three principal members of the Grand Alliance, though they shared a common hostility to France, had otherwise widely differing objectives. Austria was concerned to win territory in Italy and, if possible, to gain the Spanish succession; the United Provinces to secure new trading arrangements and a barrier in the southern Netherlands; Britain to win commercial concessions in Spain and her colonies and recognition of the Protestant succession. The Grand Alliance Treaty of 1701 offered some recognition of each of these aims: for the emperor "equitable and reasonable satisfaction" of his "pretensions to the Spanish succession"; for Britain and the United Provinces "sufficient security for their . . . dominions and for the navigation and commerce of their subjects", together with the right to "seize by force what lands and countries they could belonging to the Spanish dominions in the Indies". But these generalised statements were not sufficient to prevent disagreements at a later stage about precisely how, or how far, the aims were to be achieved. When the war was at its climax the differences among the allies came out into the open. At that time Austria might have been willing to let France have the southern Netherlands or Spain's South American colonies, neither of which were of much interest to her, but this would have been totally unacceptable to the Maritime Powers; conversely while the latter would have been willing for France or even Spain to have territory in Italy, this would have been totally unacceptable to Austria.[7]

Even when there were only two parties to an alliance the problem was only a little less difficult. When Austria and Russia entered into alliance in 1781, their main objectives were wholly different: Austria wanted support against Prussia, Russia against Turkey. This created problems. Russia refused to give her support to Austria over the Bavarian issue in 1784 (see above); conversely, although Austria, reluctantly and after six months delay, agreed to join Russia when she was attacked by Turkey in 1787, her heart was never in the undertaking and she withdrew in 1790, returning to Turkey almost all the territory which she had by then gained. Only when two countries had a genuinely similar viewpoint would they wholeheartedly agree to support the political objectives of the other. In the three Bourbon Family Compacts, providing for their co-operation in three major wars (the War of Polish Succession, Austrian Succession and the Seven Years War), France and Spain had for that reason little difficulty in reaching agreement on their principal war aims: for example, the return of Gibralta and Minorca to Spain, the return of Italian territory, handed over to Savoy in 1713, to France, and common action to deprive Britain of Georgia and of the right to the *asiento*.

Where allies disagreed on war aims, however, it was not difficult for a skilful enemy to exploit the differences between them. So France, by negotiating separately with Britain in 1711–13, was able to split the coalition against her: in this way she avoided making to Austria and the United Provinces concessions as great as might otherwise have been required. So too Charles XII of Sweden, by negotiating separately with Russia and Britain in 1717–18 was able to maximise distrust between them and reduce, if only marginally, the overwhelming defeat which would otherwise overcome his country. Virtually no alliances in this age were so cohesive as to make it impossible for an enemy, even on the verge of defeat, to salvage something from the wreck. The universal concern with the balance of power meant that there were usually some who would rather save an enemy from the worst humiliation than see an ally unduly advantaged.[8]

For this reason, however carefully their terms were drawn up, the alliance treaties of the age were unable to keep allies to a common course of action unless their interests precisely coincided. In most cases no such identity of interests existed. There was as much concern that an ally should not become too powerful as there was to defeat the common enemy. Whatever their terms might state, therefore, few alliances proved long-lasting.

THE OPPORTUNISM OF ALLIANCES

The impermanence of alliances resulted partly from the fact that they were based on little more than immediate short-term interests. If they had been based on a common political viewpoint or religious attitude they might (as in the age of conflicting religious faiths between 1559 and 1648, or that of conflicting ideologies in recent times) have remained fairly stable over a considerable period. But, as we have seen, these factors were of little influence. As a result each state felt itself free to change partners at short notice as opportunity offered, sometimes switching alliances almost from year to year. By

The Balance of Power

that process a former enemy was suddenly made into an ally, and an ally could as rapidly become an enemy.*

An example of this phenomenon can be seen during the early years of the period in northern Europe. In 1654 Russia declared war on Poland in support of the Cossack revolt in that country. In the following year Charles X of Sweden took the opportunity to declare war on Poland also, so becoming an ally of Russia. A year later, however, Russia, concerned at the growth of Sweden's power, turned and made war on her, converting her from ally to enemy. Accordingly in 1660 Sweden made peace with her original opponent Poland, so enabling her to fight more effectively against Russia, her former ally. But in the following year she made peace with Russia too, so that the latter was then able to resume its original war against Poland, which continued until 1667. Brandenburg, showed herself equally flexible during the same war. At first she joined Sweden in war against Poland (winning recognition of her claim to sovereignty in Prussia in return). In 1657, however, she switched sides, joining Poland against Sweden (so securing recognition of the same claim from Poland).

Equally rapid shifts in alliances were to be seen in western Europe a few years later. In 1665-7 England was engaged in war against the United Provinces and her ally France. A year later, following France's attack on the southern Netherlands, England and the United Provinces, so recently at war, joined together (with Sweden) in the Triple Alliance directed against France, the United Provinces' former ally. But in 1670 England joined France (her former enemy) to make war on the United Provinces (only two years previously her ally): a war which finally broke out in 1672. Two years later England again abandoned her new ally to make peace with the United Prov-

---

* Rapid shifts of alliance were made easier by the fact that alliance treaties usually remained, at least nominally, secret. It was explicitly provided in the three Bourbon Family Compacts, that they should remain "secret so long as they [the parties] deem advantageous" (to quote the words of the third). In practice they nearly always became known or were at least suspected. It was because she got wind of the third Family Compact that Britain explicitly demanded that the Spanish government should deny that she intended to join France in the Seven Years War, on pain of a declaration of war if she refused (she did). Sometimes, even if the existence of an alliance was known, a particular clause was kept secret. Thus Russia's promise to Austria in their treaty of 1746 that she would help the latter recover Silesia if Prussia attacked either Austria or Russia was contained in a secret clause. Similarly the agreement between France and Prussia in 1777 that they would prevent Austrian expansion in Bavaria and the Balkans was also contained in a secret understanding.

inces. But after the war's conclusion the English king once more became a pensioner, and in effect an ally, of the French monarch until the two countries were again at war in 1688. Sweden and Brandenburg showed equal inconstancy: Sweden, a member of the Triple Alliance against France in 1668, none the less joined France against her recent partner, the United Provinces, in the war which began in 1672. Conversely, Brandenburg, which was allied with France when the war began, in the following year abandoned her and joined the opposing alliance. Its Elector signed a new alliance with the United Provinces in 1678; in 1682 again entered into a subsidy treaty with Louis XIV; and in 1686 turned again, entering into a secret anti-French treaty with the emperor.

Similar rapid changes took place during the 1720s. In 1716 Britain, having been at war with France for most of the previous thirty years, entered into an alliance with her. Together the two countries helped Austria (France's former enemy) to resist an attack by Spain (so recently France's ally) in her Italian territories. In 1721 Spain and France once more entered into alliance, and France promised to support Spain in her ambitions in Italy. In 1725 Austria and Spain, having been bitter enemies in two wars over the previous twenty years, joined together in the Alliance of Vienna (later joined by Russia) against their two former allies Britain and France (later joined by the United Provinces, Sweden and Denmark). Neither alliance, however, provided any assistance to their respective members, Spain and Britain, during the war which the two countries fought in 1727–8. In the following year, Spain, disillusioned with the Austrian connection, joined her recent enemy Britain, together with France and the United Provinces, in the Treaty of Seville, to help her win control of the north Italian duchies (see above). Three years later there was yet another reshuffle. The fifteen-year entente between France and Britain, one of the only stable features of the previous period, was once more abandoned. Spain and France were again closely joined in the first Bourbon Family Compact of 1731, while Britain rejoined her old ally, Austria, in the second Treaty of Vienna. The wheel had come full circle and something like the earlier pattern of alliances (that of the War of Spanish Succession) had been re-established.

The fluidity of alliances was equally evident during the Napoleonic wars at the end of the period. Here was a conflict in which, it might have been expected, the revolutionary character of the new regime in France, the execution of her king, and above all the dominance she secured over the entire continent, might have provided the common interest necessary to ensure that a stable alliance was maintained against her. Yet for nearly twenty years the other principal states of the continent were unable to sink their differences and join in united action to end the French hegemony. The first coalition of 1793–4 included all the other significant states of the continent – Britain, Austria, Prussia, Russia, Portugal, the Netherlands, Sardinia, Naples and several German states. If it had persisted it should have been able to bring the war to a relatively early conclusion. But by 1795 Prussia and Spain had already reached accommodations with France and withdrew from the conflict for more than a decade. Russia, more concerned with events in Poland than with the struggle against France, made virtually no contribution. Smaller states were defeated or lost heart. Austria made her own separate peace in 1797, so that finally only Britain was left at war. Though a new coalition was formed in 1798, it disintegrated equally quickly. It was originally intended to include all the major powers other than France: Britain, Austria, Russia and Prussia. But Prussia, deciding she preferred neutrality, never joined. Russia, having won some success in Italy, suffered setbacks in Switzerland and the Netherlands, became disillusioned with her allies and withdrew in November 1799. Austria too, having suffered defeats in Italy and Germany, sued for peace at the end of the following year. Again Britain was left alone and she herself agreed a temporary peace in 1802–3. The third coalition, formed in 1805, included Britain, Austria and Russia, but was still more short-lived. Napoleon rapidly defeated Austria (1805), Prussia (1806) and Russia (1807). Each made separate peaces; and each was even induced to declare war on its former ally Britain. Austria briefly but vainly renewed the contest against France in 1809 but was again rapidly defeated and once more signed a separate peace. Even when Russia, after five years of collaboration with Napoleon, was once more forced into war in 1812, she fought at first in total isolation from the struggle being waged by Britain in Spain. Only in 1813, with the fourth coalition, was there once more a serious attempt to establish some unity of purpose among the four powers: and next year, under the Treaty of Chaumon, each committed itself to refrain from seeking a separate peace and to the general principles of the settlement to be secured from France. Even when the common interest of the major powers appeared self-evident, therefore, most were willing to seek opportunistic accommodations to protect their own interests.

One or two countries made a speciality of rapid changes of alliance. Savoy was renowned throughout the continent for her propensity in this respect. Wedged between France and the Hapsburg empire, and constantly seeking further territory to her south, she tried to achieve that aim by seeking alliance first with one side and then with the other. At the beginning of the Nine Years War her duke joined the Grand Alliance, securing an undertaking that the two French fortresses of Pinerolo and Casale threating his kingdom would be taken from France and the former handed to him at the end of the war. However, from 1691 he engaged in negotiations with France, and undertook in 1694 to remain inactive during the following campaign if the French allowed him to capture the fortress of Casale. In 1696 he switched sides altogether, in return for territorial concessions from France. At the beginning of the subsequent war in 1701 he signed a new treaty of alliance with France. But he maintained close contact with France's enemies, and in 1703 again switched sides, this time in return for the promise of territory in Lombardy and Mantua.[9] As a result of his dexterity he won in the final settlement territory in north Italy and the award of Sicily (subsequently exchanged for Sardinia), not to speak of a crown to go with it. The duke's successor enjoyed a similar success in the War of Austrian Succession, winning the promise of territorial concessions from Austria by threatening to join the enemy if he was refused.

Saxony was another state that specialised in rapid switches of alliance. She had first demonstrated this facility during the Thirty Years War when her Elector, though himself Protestant, abandoned the cause of his religion to win from the emperor the cession of Lusatia. During the period that followed the tactic was to prove less productive. At the beginning of the Great Northern War (1760–1721) Saxony was allied with Russia and Denmark against Sweden. After losing the long campaign for Poland, however, in 1702–6, the Elector capitulated to Charles XII as soon as the latter reached his own territory. He immediately renounced the crown of Poland and agreed to hand over to the Swedish king one of his principal allies, Patkul, the Livonian rebel, who was shortly put to death. When the fortunes of war changed again five years later, however, he rejoined his former allies, reclaimed the crown of Poland and sought a share in the spoils of war. But even then he continued to negotiate for alternative outcomes which might benefit the interests of his electorate, first discussing with the Crimean Tartars a campaign against his principal ally, Russia, and in 1719 joining an alliance with the emperor and Hanover against that country. As a result of his unreliable conduct he won no territory from the war, and was unable to reach a final settlement with Sweden until 1731, eleven years after it ended. In the War of Austrian Succession Saxony's inconstancy proved equally unrewarding. He joined the anti-Austrian coalition in 1740, claiming a substantial share of the Hapsburg inheritance. In the following year, jealous of Prussia's successes, he reached an agreement with Austria which he hoped would lead to the acquisition of territory at Prussia's expense. But when Austria a year later made peace with Prussia, ceding most of Silesia, Saxony gained nothing. In 1745, lured by the promise of subsidies, he switched again to the Austrian side but was immediately defeated and saw his capital occupied by Prussian forces. Once again, therefore, Saxony had secured no profit from her conduct and won no gains from either side. In the Seven Years War (1756–63) she was offered no opportunity to change sides, since she was defeated by Prussia at the opening of the war and was occupied throughout its course. Only during the Napoleonic wars did new opportunities for territorial gains arise. By offering no opposition to Napoleon, in 1809 she eventually secured a grant of territory at Austria's expense, and even a long-coveted crown. Her opportunism however, cost her dear. Occupied by Russia's troops in the last years of the conflict, she found herself at its conclusion altogether without friends and lost nearly half her territory in the final settlement. While Savoy did quite well out of selling its favours to the highest bidder, therefore, Saxony secured no returns at all.

But it was not only the smaller states that were willing to abandon their allies when they believed national interest demanded it. The larger states too habitually deserted their partners to negotiate for a separate peace if this seemed advantageous. During the Nine Years War such negotiations were undertaken almost from the beginning (from at least 1692 onwards) by the emperor, Savoy and England, regardless of the fact that regular meetings took place among them to concert common policies. In 1698–9 Austria, Poland and Venice, which had been engaged in a common war with Russia against the Ottoman sultan, secured a separate settlement, leaving their ally, Peter the Great, to make his own peace on unfavourable terms in isolation. In the War of Spanish Succession, though there was an attempt at joint negotiations in 1709, Britain two years later began independent negotiations, agreed a unilateral cease-fire in 1712, and so compelled her main allies to reach their own arrangements, in highly unfavourable circumstances, in her wake. In the War of

Austrian Succession Frederick the Great three times abandoned his ally France to make a separate peace with Austria.[10] In the Seven Years War Russia, as soon as a new ruler with a different view of her national interests ascended the throne in 1762, abandoned her allies and made a separate peace. The desertion of allies was thus the normal practice of the day.

To guard against such defections alliance treaties habitually included provisions under which the parties committed themselves not to seek a separate peace.[11] Those undertakings were consistently violated. In 1648 the United Provinces concluded a separate peace with Spain, despite having agreed with France when she joined the war in 1635 that neither would do so. In 1677–8, the same country once more concluded peace with France, even while general negotiations were still continuing, with little regard for the interests of her allies, who had entered the war in order to preserve her from defeat. During the same war Charles II was not deterred from withdrawing from the conflict in 1674 despite the fact that he had undertaken at the beginning of the war not to make a separate peace or to accept any terms which were unacceptable to his ally, France. During the War of Spanish Succession Britain's unilateral cease-fire and separate negotiations with France were not deterred by the fact that she had undertaken in the alliance treaty that "it should not be permitted to [any] party, when the war is once begun, to treat of peace with the enemy unless jointly, or with the common advice of the other parties" (Article VII). The fact that France had agreed with Spain, in each of the Bourbon Family Compacts, not to enter into separate negotiations,[12] did not prevent her from undertaking her own negotiations to protect France's interests, with only a marginal concern for Spain, in each of the peace negotiations that followed. The fact that Russia and Austria had agreed in their alliance treaty of 1756 not to seek a separate peace in no way deterred Peter III from withdrawing from their joint war in 1762. Undertakings of that kind were not sufficient, in a highly competitive state system where *raison d'état* was the prevailing doctrine, to deter resort to independent settlements when these seemed advantageous.

The unreliability of allies in this age was therefore only too obvious. It is thus not surprising that alliances were regarded sceptically. They were generally thought of as only short-term expedients which could be useful for particular purposes – for example, to make war against a particular opponent – but were to be quickly abandoned once their usefulness was exhausted. It was sometimes suggested that they were a good way of averting the danger of a powerful rival. Thus Frederick the Great suggested that it was "one of the first principles of policy to try to ally oneself to whichever neighbour could otherwise deliver the most dangerous blows against you";[13] and he gave this as the reason for Prussia's alliance with Russia (1764) which might otherwise have threatened East Prussia. Colbert expressed an opposite, and still more cynical view in his *Political Testament*, by suggesting that it was always dangerous to form an alliance with a power that was stronger than yourself. Deriding the folly of the Bishop of Munster who, in the Dutch war, had aligned himself with France (much to the latter's advantage), he declared that ultimately the strong would inevitably dictate terms to the weak. Thus "the prince of mediocre power, if he knew his business, would never commit himself to those who can deal with him as masters, who usually have no other rules for their actions than self-interest".[14]

ALLIANCES AND THE BALANCE OF POWER

As in other ages statesmen had no difficulty in finding laudable motives for the alliances they formed. In an age when the "balance of power" was such a widely revered concept, it is scarcely surprising that they were frequently extolled as the essential means of maintaining that balance. Thus Walpole declared that "by alliances . . . the equipoise of power is maintained": it was "by leagues well concerted and strictly observed that the weak are defended against the strong".[15] Frederick the Great likewise asserted that "the balance which is established in Europe by the alliance of many princes and states against the overpowerful and ambitious . . . is solely designed for maintaining the peace and security of mankind".[16]

Such tributes were not entirely hypocritical. In a sense, alliances were designed to maintain a balance of a kind. Quite often this was their explicit intention. It was because a particular state, such as France under Louis XIV and later under Napoleon, had acquired an excessive power in relation to the other states of the system that alliances were formed to keep it in check. Throughout the period coalitions were created to prevent any single state acquiring dominance. The Triple Alliance (1668), the Holy Leagues of 1664 and 1683, the League of Augsburg (1686), the two Grand Alliances, the Quadruple Alliance of 1718, Austria's grand coalition of 1756–7, the Alliance formed against Russia in 1719, the successive coalitions, however feeble, created against Napoleon – all of these are examples of alliances established for the express purpose of preventing dominance being won by a particular power. Sometimes two powers only came together for such a purpose: as when Britain and Prussia joined forces to prevent the Austrian coalition prevailing in 1756, or when, after Britain's spectacular success in the Seven Years War, France and Spain joined together to redress the balance once more;[17] or when Russia and Austria alarmed at Prussia's growing power and influence, joined in alliance against her in 1781.

In many cases such combinations succeeded in their aim. To a considerable extent the balance was preserved. France was not allowed to seize the southern Netherlands in 1667–8; or conquer the United Provinces in 1672–8; or to win, even indirectly, the whole Spanish inheritance in 1700–14. Austria was preserved from total destruction after the death of Charles VI; as was Prussia in 1756–63. Britain was compelled to give up some of the gains of 1763 twenty years later. France was prevented from acquiring a total domination of Europe in Napoleon's day. The existence of mutually hostile alliances and the fact that, as a result, many wars became continental in scope, made it harder to secure decisive outcomes in any way. As Frederick the Great commented in his *History of My Time*:

Since the establishment of a certain equilibrium between sovereigns, the largest enterprises rarely produced the expected results. As a result of the equality of forces and the alternation of losses and gains, the antagonists find themselves at the close of the most desperate war much where they were before it began.[18]

In consequence the status quo was rarely dramatically altered. Some kind of a balance at least was maintained. The composition of the alliances might change from one war to the other, but the final effect was similar. Between 1740 and 1763, for example, two major wars were fought out, both in Europe and beyond, between substantial alliances, which between them included most of the major states of the system. Their membership was wholly different in the two wars. But their final effect was similar. No major upheavals took place on the continent. Austria was not destroyed in the first war, nor Prussia in the second. Prussia gained slightly in power and prestige in the first, and Britain in the second (though even that was partly undone in the War of American Independence twenty years later). Thus the alliances, it might well have been argued, had achieved precisely the purpose attributed to them by Walpole and Frederick II. A rough balance among the major powers and the general structure of the system were preserved.

It would, however, be a gross oversimplification to suggest that it was the purpose of the alliances to achieve such public-spirited objectives. In many cases it was not the aim of an alliance to maintain the balance, but on the contrary to overturn it. The purpose of the alliance against Sweden, created in 1698–1700, was to destroy the previously existing order in the Baltic by the conquest of Sweden. The purpose of the coalition established against Austria in 1740 was to dismember the Hapsburg domains. The objective of the coalition established against Prussia in 1756 was to crush that power permanently. The purpose of France's alliance with Spain in 1796, with Prussia in 1806, with Russia in 1807 and with Austria in 1809–10 was to preserve an *im*balance: France's hegemony in Europe. In all these cases the purpose of alliance was to destroy the balance, not to protect it. The stability of the system, in other words, did not rank highly among the objectives of the states concerned.

But even if the *purpose* of alliances was not to maintain the balance (as statesmen piously asserted), this could still have been their *effect*. For the creation of one alliance, it could be held, must lead to the establishment of another whose purpose was to resist and so neutralise the first. But there was no automatic law that the creation of one alliance would be followed by the establishment of another of equal power. The alliance of Russia, Denmark and Saxony/Poland during the Great Northern War produced no matching coalition in support of Sweden to resist it: on the contrary it was joined in time by Prussia and Hanover/Britain and led not to a balance but to the total destruction of Sweden's power in the Baltic. Austria's coalition in 1756 against Prussia, including France, Russia, Sweden, Savoy and Spain, was not matched by any comparable counter-alliance. The financial assistance provided to Prussia by Britain, and the intermittent help of Hanoverian forces, in no way matched the power available to the other side, and it was only the generalship of Frederick the Great and the providential defection of Russia in 1762 which prevented the destruction of the Prussian state. Even Napoleon's domination of Europe, to which for long only rapidly crumbling "coalitions" were opposed, might not have been effectively countered but for his monumental folly in attacking his ally Russia in 1812. If, in all these cases, the balance was not so radically overturned as at one time seemed probable, it was not because of some automatic process by which an exactly equal counter-alliance was quickly formed to match the initial threat; still less because of the selfless commitment of all European states to maintain the existing status quo. It was simply because as Frederick the Great had pointed out, overwhelming victories usually proved more difficult to accomplish in the military conditions of the age than over-confident aggressors had rashly anticipated.

There was another reason why alliances often failed to perform the service attributed to them by Walpole and Frederick the Great. The victims of attack were not always in a position to create the alliance necessary to resist aggression. If they were small and weak or friendless (and sometimes the two went together), they might find that there were none ready to fly to their support when they found themselves under attack. So Venice could fight a long war against the Turks from 1644 to 1669 without securing any worthwhile support from her neighbours. Sweden could attack Bremen in 1652 and 1666, Savoy could attack Genoa in 1672–4, Denmark could attack Holstein in 1682 and Hamburg in 1686, without the intervention of substantial alliances to defend the victim. Or if an aggressive power took only one small nibble at a time (salami tactics), it might avoid stimulating any such response: so Strasbourg (1681), Luxembourg (1681–4) and Genoa (1684) might be successively seized or subdued by France without any others being sufficiently aroused to come to their assistance. Or the area attacked might be so remote that it was believed to be indefensible, or beyond the confines of the alliance system. So the Crimea (1781–2), without stimulating the formation of an alliance to resist her. So Poland might be progressively swallowed by her neighbours, without being able to call on any alliance to come to her assistance.

Again alliances were often too impermanent to prevent further assaults in the future. The Triple Alliance of England, the United Provinces and Sweden could halt France's attack on the southern Netherlands in 1668; but four years later it no longer existed to halt her attack on the United Provinces (two of its members were even willing to join the monarch against whom the alliance had been created in a war against their former partner). The Quadruple Alliance was able to halt Spanish aggression in 1717–19; but it did little to prevent a recurrence of Spanish aggression in 1727–8. The creation of the first coalition against France in 1793, including most of the states of Europe, could not ensure that similar combinations could be put together when Napoleon increased France's power still further in the following decade: on the contrary, many of the states in Europe were too cowed to put up any effective resistance at all and certainly no joint resistance. Because they were so impermanent alliances were not able to act as a standing deterrent against any new aggression. No potential attacker was discouraged by the knowledge that there already existed a powerful alliance ready to preserve the peace and come to the aid of the state under attack. On the contrary he might be stimulated by the knowledge that a hostile alliance was in process of formation and might subsequently become more dangerous: as Frederick II was stimulated by the knowledge that his enemies were planning to attack him to launch his own invasion of Saxony in 1756.[19] Moreover alliances could be made on either side: the would-be aggressor might convince himself that he could create a combination more formidable than any that was created against him, as Louis XIV was able to do in 1669–72; and Russia, Saxony and Poland in 1698–9. Because there was no general commitment to act against aggression, nor even general agreement on what constituted a "balance" (it could always be argued that one more territorial gain was necessary to establish the balance), blatant breaches of the peace might easily go unchecked. Alliances thus could not automatically keep the peace or preserve the balance. They could quite easily be used, whatever Walpole or Frederick the Great might say, to destroy it.

Alliances in this age, therefore, did not consistently act to stabilise the system. They were in most cases a short-term instrument of national policy rather than a long-term means of preserving the status quo. They were as useful to a ruler planning aggression against another state as to one seeking to defend itself against such an attack. They could not even preserve the interests of national states equally. Where there was a clear common interest among their members they could promote the purposes they shared in common. In other cases they proved extremely fragile, and one ally or another frequently abandoned its partners to secure its own ends. It was only when several nations together had a clear common interest in defeating a major threat to the system, as in the case of the Grand Alliance or at the end of the Napoleonic era, that the function of alliances was to prevent any single power from securing domination (and even in those cases they sometimes disintegrated, as in 1712–13, before a conflict had been brought to an end). There did not exist that essential basis of consensus – whether on the behaviour to be expected of states, or on the nature of the balance that was to be preserved – to make alliances into an effective instrument for maintaining stability generally within the system.

11 Institutions

THIRD-PARTY SETTLEMENT

As in all other international societies, the states of this period made use of various procedures for resolving the conflicts that occurred among them. Some of the methods used were familiar from earlier times. Others were devised during the course of our age to meet new needs.

Traditionally the most common means used for this purpose was some form of third-party settlement. Such procedures had been used in ancient China as well as among the Greek city-states.[1] In the Middle Ages mediation and arbitration, often by the pope or his representative, had been fairly common. A papal legate presided over the Congress of Arras, which sought to bring an end to the Hundred Years War. Ferdinand of Aragon in 1489 travelled to Edinburgh to mediate between the kings of England and Scotland, and in 1533 Francis I mediated peace between Henry VIII and his nephew James of Scotland. During the age of religious conflict which began about the middle of the sixteenth century ecclesiastical mediators were inevitably less frequently employed. Mediations were still undertaken among rulers of the same faith: for example, the Papal Nuncio mediated between France and Spain to bring about the peace of Vervins in 1598, and the pope himself mediated between Spain and Savoy during the war of Mantuan Succession in 1613–16. Between Protestant rulers too the same procedure was used: for example the elector of Brandenburg mediated between Sweden and Denmark to bring an end to their war of 1643–5. But the pope was no longer an acceptable mediator for Protestant powers;[2] and when the dispute was between a Catholic and a Protestant ruler a lay figure, usually a foreign ruler, had to be found. Thus, for example, the French king mediated between Spain and the Netherlands in 1609 and between Sweden and Poland in 1629.

The decline in the strength of religious feeling during our age reduced these difficulties. Mediation was now as frequently used between Catholic and Protestant rulers as between those of the same faith. Thus the Protestant king of Sweden mediated between Catholic France and Catholic Austria in 1794–7 during the Nine Years War; the Protestant Maritime Powers mediated between Catholic Austria and Moslem Turkey in 1698–9; Catholic France mediated between Lutheran Sweden and Orthodox Russia in 1711–12, and so on. The problem was now only to find a foreign ruler who would be trusted, at least to some extent, by both sides. And that acceptability no longer depended mainly on religious factors.

The mediator did not have to be a single figure or a single government. Sometimes two or three powers undertook the role. The Maritime Powers – England and the United Provinces – mediated jointly between Sweden and Denmark to secure the Treaty of Altona in 1689, and between Austria and Turkey to produce the Peace of Carlowitz in 1698–9. In these cases the two mediating powers were close partners and allies, likely to adopt a similar viewpoint in the conflict. But this was not always the case. Sometimes two countries of differing or even opposing views were chosen. Russia and France, traditional enemies, both mediated at the end of the War of Bavarian Succession in 1779 and became joint guarantors of the settlement. Occasionally even three different powers performed the task. Denmark was to have acted as a mediator at the Westphalia peacemaking in addition to the pope and Venice (she was only prevented from doing so by becoming involved in war with Sweden at the crucial moment); in 1687, during the conflict between Sweden and Denmark over the Holstein-Gottorp lands, the emperor, Brandenburg and the United Provinces were proposed as joint mediators; and the two Maritime Powers and France all sought to mediate between Turkey and Russia in 1611.

In theory mediation was a personal undertaking. It was performed by a particular ruler at the request of other rulers. But as the power of governments, secretaries of state and foreign offices increased, it increasingly became the task of diplomats rather than of the sovereigns themselves. Mediation came to be undertaken by a government or a state rather than a ruler. Whichever performed it (and in this, as in all else, the rulers increasingly identified with their own state and its interests) mediation was never totally disinterested. The mediator might deliberately favour a friend and damage an enemy: France, when mediating between Turkey, her long-standing friend and ally, and her opponents, Russia and Austria, in 1739, shamelessly recommended terms that were deeply damaging to her traditional enemy, Austria. Or the mediator could use his position to stir up trouble between opponents: thus Louis XIV expressed deep distrust of the motives of the emperor when he mediated between himself (with the United Provinces) and England in 1667, fearing that he "might find a way to incite some new dispute over the articles that still remained to be considered".[3] Or a mediator might even deliberately try to *prevent* a settlement being reached, so ensuring that a war continued: thus the French mediator, when mediating between Sweden and her enemies at the beginning of the Great Northern War, was instructed to keep the war going in case either of the opponents, released from their own war, were recruited by France's enemies in the conflict already anticipated over the Spanish succession.[4]

Even if it was not as self-interested as this, mediation could yield useful dividends. Sweden sought to acquire the role of mediator during the Nine Years War since, she believed, this might result in territorial gains for herself, or at least in guarantees for her vulnerable Baltic possessions.[5] The emperor Leopold was willing to mediate at the beginning of the Great Northern War in return for an offer of Swedish troops to help him oppose the second partition treaty.[6] At the very least, the position was generally seen as a source of prestige, and there was therefore often some competition to perform the role. Both France and her current enemy, the Maritime Powers, sought to act as mediators between Turkey and Russia in 1711–13 (and both did so at different times). And one of the reasons why the emperor Charles VI facilitated the return of the Swedish king to the Baltic in 1713 was to improve his own chances of being asked to mediate in the Great Northern War.[7]

Inevitably it was usually the states that were succeeding least well in a conflict that were most willing, and sometimes anxious, to secure mediation: while those that felt they were doing well would often scorn it. During the first few years of the Great Northern War Charles XII refused offers of mediation, believing that he could attain his ends by force of arms alone; Peter the Great, on the other hand, in 1706 when his principal allies had been defeated, actively sought the mediation of France, even at one time offering his troops to fight in the War of Spanish Succession as an inducement. A year or so later, when his own position in the latter war was desperate, Louis himself sought the mediation of Sweden or Russia to extract him from his difficulties. Nor was there any hesitation in seeking to bribe the mediators if necessary. For example, the British and Dutch mediators between Prussia and Turkey in 1711–12 (their representatives in Constantinople) had both at one time or another been in receipt of bribes from the Russians, though it is not clear that this influenced them in their proposals of a settlement.

In some cases the more formal procedure of *arbitration* was used. In this case the parties to a dispute had, in principle at least, to commit themselves to accept the decision of the arbitrator. Most states, in this as in other ages, were unwilling to take this risk, at least in political disputes: the French governor of New France (Canada) was disgraced and dismissed for agreeing to arbitration by the British governor of New York on a dispute with the Iroquois Indians in 1683–4 thereby, it was felt, throwing doubt on the French case. France proposed arbitration by the English king (at that point in her pay) of her dispute with Spain over Luxembourg in 1683–4; but this was unacceptable to Spain which considered her rights there beyond challenge. For purely legal and especially for commercial disputes, however, arbitration was more often acceptable. For example, the peace treaty between England and the United Provinces in 1654 provided for the submission of overseas commercial claims between the two countries from 1611 to 1652 to be submitted to arbitration by the Swiss Cantons. About the same time France and England agreed in the Treaty of Westminster that damages suffered by the two countries in conflicts since 1640 should be assessed by a commission of six, three from each country; and in case of disagreement the city of Hamburg would name new commissioners to reach a decision. In 1665 Brandenburg and the United Provinces agreed to submit certain disputes to the Grand Council of Malines. Sometimes arbitration to a dispute would only be agreed at the end of a war: when the attempt to solve it by armed force had already proved unsuccessful. For example, the dispute about succession in the Palatinate which led to the Nine Years War was submitted at its end (Article VIII of the Treaty of Ryswick) to arbitration (and led to a decision unfavourable to France). The Treaty of Nymegen provided that disputes between France and Spain about fortified places near their contested border would be referred to the States General of the United Provinces; while the Treaty of Utrecht provided that questions relating to the boundary between Hudson Bay and the French territories, contested by arms during the war, and claims for damages as a result of armed raids, should be resolved by arbitral commissions. Finally, ten years after the conclusion of the War of American Independence, Britain and the US agreed that remaining disputes about the boundary between Canada and the US and other matters resulting from the war should be referred to three arbitral commissions consisting of appointees of the two sides under a neutral chairman.

Both mediation and arbitration were therefore regularly used as a means of resolving inter-state disputes during this age. Arbitration was hardly ever used for important issues, though it was sometimes successful in resolving lesser ones, especially of a commercial nature. Mediation was usually attempted only after a war had already begun, in order to bring it to an end, not to prevent it breaking out in the first place. Nor is there much evidence that mediation had much effect even then in bringing peace. A country which still believed it had a chance of winning would usually refuse it. And it was only when both combatants were already exhausted that the good offices of third powers had much chance of being accepted. The growing use of a third-party settlement represented a small advance. It might occasionally allow two powers, otherwise too proud to seek an accommodation, to enter into serious negotiations for a settlement. But it cannot be said to have had a very significant effect in reducing the scale of conflict in this age.

GUARANTEES

There were other, less traditional methods that began to be used to promote the stability of the system. One of these was the increasing use of "guarantees": of territory, treaties, constitutions or successions. If used systematically these might have been able to strengthen the force of commitments undertaken in treaties and so (at least in theory) have created a greater predictability in the conduct of international relations.

The simplest type of guarantee was of territory. When one state guaranteed the territory of another, it became committed to defend it, should it be attacked. This, it was hoped, would act as a deterrent against aggression by other states.

Guarantees of this kind were frequent in this age and in almost no other. They could be both bilateral and multilateral in form. Bilateral guarantees were the most frequent, featuring over and over again in the treaties negotiated in the century or so from 1650 onwards. A great number of the alliance treaties of the second half of the seventeenth century included mutual guarantees of this kind. They became still more common in the early eighteenth century. Britain and United Provinces, for example, gave each other mutual guarantees in their bilateral treaty of 1716, as did Britain and France and Britain and the emperor in their treaties of the same year. Spain and France, in the three Bourbon Family Compacts of 1733, 1743 and

1761, agreed to guarantee each other's territories both within Europe
and outside,* and to secure "just, prompt and due satisfaction" if
they were attacked.

Such guarantees were given not only of territory already possessed
but of territory that *might* be acquired in the future. In their treaty of
1716 Britain and the emperor mutually agreed to come to the defence
not only of the "kingdoms, provinces and rights . . . which either of
them actually has and enjoys", but also of any which, while the
alliance lasted, "they should by mutual consent acquire". Peter the
Great guaranteed the Duke of Holstein-Gottorp (his son-in-law) in
his possession of Schleswig, although that territory was not then his.
In the Bourbon Family Compacts France and Spain guaranteed not
only existing territories but all those "realms and rights" which they
"may possess at any time in the future", as the 1733 treaty put it. And
in 1781 when Russia and Austria were discussing an alliance treaty
including mutual guarantees, Catherine the Great sought to have
these extended to any territory which each might acquire in future
(she was at that time contemplating the annexation of the Crimea
which took place during the year that followed).

States were naturally especially anxious to gain guarantees for
territories which had only been recently acquired, and which were
therefore the most vulnerable. So in 1715 Denmark, which had
recently recovered the Holstein-Gottorp territories, and Britain/
Hanover, which had recently acquired Verden, mutually guaranteed
those territories. Similarly, in 1719, Prussia, which had recently
acquired Stetten from Sweden and Britain/Hanover which had
gained Verden and Bremen mutually guaranteed each other's territories. After she had acquired Schleswig in 1720 Denmark secured
guarantees from Britain and France (within the same year) and
subsequently from most of the other major states of Europe. In the
Treaty of Aix-la-Chapelle Frederick the Great was able to secure
guarantees from all the signatories of his possession of recently
conquered Silesia; while Spain won guarantees in the same treaty for
the duchies acquired by Spanish rulers in the same treaty in Italy.

Multilateral guarantees, as provided in that treaty, were of course
especially valuable. The bilateral guarantees which Britain and

---

* In most other cases it was assumed that the guarantees applied only to European
 territory. Sometimes this was made explicit; for example the treaty between Sweden
 and the Maritime Powers of 1700 contained reciprocal guarantees, but only for their
 "kingdoms, states, provinces, jurisdictions and territories in Europe".

France had given each other in 1716 were made multilateral in the Triple Alliance (including the United Provinces) of the following year, and more so in the Quadruple Alliance of 1718 (to which Spain also later adhered). The mutual guarantees which the emperor and Spain gave each other in the Treaty of Vienna of 1725, in which they undertook the "reciprocal defence and guaranty" of "all the kingdoms and provinces which they actually possessed", were later broadened by the accession to the treaty of Russia, Bavaria and several of the German states. Similarly, in the opposing alliance of Hanover established in the same year, Britain, France and Prussia, under Article II, offered reciprocal guarantees of their territories both in Europe and beyond. In 1752 Austria, Spain and Sicily, then the dominant powers in Italy, joined in mutually guaranteeing the territorial settlement there; and, whether or not in consequence, Italy was kept largely free from war until the end of the century.

Guarantees were provided not only for territories but for entire treaties. In this case the signatories committed themselves to preserve not just the territorial but other provisions of treaties to which they became parties. Already in 1648 France became a guarantor of the provisions of the Peace of Westphalia relating to Germany (and so acquired a right of intervention in Germany to ensure their implementation). In 1668 the states of the Triple Alliance – England, the United Provinces and Sweden – guaranteed the settlement reached at that time between France and Spain at Aix-la-Chapelle and undertook to provide forces of a specified size to do so. France herself became a guarantor of the terms of the Peace of Oliva between Sweden and Poland in 1660 (and was vainly called on by Sweden fifty years later to take action to implement the guarantee). There were other cases where a state or states which had helped to mediate a settlement were subsequently asked to guarantee it. For example the Maritime Powers, having successfully mediated to secure the Treaty of Altona of 1689 between Sweden and Denmark, subsequently became guarantors of it (and undertook some action to fulfil the guarantee when Denmark attacked Sweden in 1700).

The states which had guaranteed one treaty would sometimes demand a reciprocal guarantee of another. For example, the Maritime Powers, having guaranteed Altona, eight years later successfully called on Sweden to match this with a corresponding guarantee of the Peace of Ryswick (for which she too had acted as mediator). And Sweden herself, at the end of the War of Spanish Succession, was only willing to guarantee the Peace of Baden and renew her guarantees of Westphalia in return for a renewed guarantee of the Peace of Oliva of 1660. Guarantees of this kind could, as in the case of guarantees of territory, be multilateral. Thus, for example, the signatories of the Treaty of Aix-la-Chapelle all offered to "afford each other reciprocal guarantees" that its provisions would be put into effect.[8]

Guarantees were also often given of rights of succession. In an age when these were in constant dispute, so that threats to an existing dynasty were an ever-present fear, it is scarcely surprising that these were often demanded. So the British government repeatedly sought guarantees of the Protestant succession in Britain: both in bilateral treaties (such as those with the United Provinces in 1709 and 1716), and in multilateral treaties, such as the Treaty of Utrecht, the Triple and Quadruple Alliances and the Treaty of Aix-la-Chapelle. In the same way the emperor Charles VI and his successors sought repeated guarantees of the succession of Maria Theresa in Austria, not only in bilateral treaties with almost every state of the continent (with Spain in 1725 and 1731, with Russia in 1726, with Prussia in 1728, with the Maritime Powers in 1731–2, with Savoy in 1723 and France in 1735) but in multilateral commitments (such as those of the treaties of Vienna of 1738 and of Aix-la-Chapelle of 1748).

Often external powers were only too willing to offer such guarantees. In return they could either secure political concessions (as almost every power in Europe did as the price of guaranteeing the Pragmatic Sanction for Austria). Or, even better, they might, they believed, win for themselves the right to intervene to ensure that the succession they favoured indeed took place: Russia made a guarantee of this kind a condition for agreeing to peace with Sweden in 1743; and she was given the right to station 12,000 Russian troops in Sweden to ensure that it took place.

Finally guarantees were sometimes given of a country's constitution. Sometimes there was a common interest between the government of the state which was guaranteed, often having no wish for a change in the existing arrangement, and that of the external power which did the guaranteeing. Thus for example, the nobility in Poland cherished its archaic constitution entrenching its power, while the parliament in Sweden benefited in a very different way from the reformed constitution of 1720 in that country, and both were only too willing to ensure that they should not be changed. Conversely Russia, believing that both constitutions weakened the two states concerned, was equally pleased to provide the guarantee which helped to preserve them. In the same way there was a common interest between the stadtholder and his supporters in the United Provinces and the external powers which sought to protect him. So after Prussia with British support intervened to overthrow the government and restore the stadtholder to power in 1798 the two governments agreed in a treaty in the following year to maintain that form of government in the United Provinces "against all attacks and enterprises, direct or indirect of whatsoever nature they might be" (Article III).

Reciprocity was a basic feature of the system of guarantees. A guarantee, especially of territory, represented an asset of value, for which corresponding concessions might be extracted. Thus in return for renewing their guarantee of Altona in 1700 the Maritime Powers were able to secure a commitment by Sweden to provide assistance against France if the latter should invade the Spanish Netherlands (of great concern to United Provinces), or support the Stuart cause (of great concern to England). Similarly when in 1742 France agreed to guarantee Denmark's rights in Schleswig she did so only in return for an undertaking that Denmark would not join her enemies in the War of Austrian Succession. Austria agreed to guarantee Denmark's possession of the same territory only in return for a guarantee of the Pragmatic Sanction. And so on.

In theory a network of reciprocal guarantees of this kind might, if they had been faithfully fulfilled – or even if it was *believed* that they would be faithfully fulfilled – have provided the basis for a stable international order. If outside states could be relied on to intervene by force to defend a territory or preserve a treaty provision, aggression might have been deterred and the peace maintained. The system failed to have this effect because the guarantees were in practice rarely implemented. In many cases there was never even any intention to implement them. For example, Augustus I of Saxony offered Sweden a guarantee of her possession of Livonia at the very moment (in 1699) when he was planning a war to seize the territory himself.[9] Austria was willing to give Prussia a guarantee of her possession of Silesia in 1748, yet shortly afterwards began actively planning to reconquer it. Spain guaranteed the Protestant succession in Britain in 1713, yet shortly afterwards gave active assistance to the Jacobite cause. In other cases, whatever the intention when the guarantee was given, no effort was made to implement it when action was most needed. So France did nothing to fulfil her guarantee of the Peace of Oliva when Sweden was attacked in 1700; the Maritime Powers did nothing to fulfil the guarantees of the Treaty of Travendal

(1700) when Denmark renewed her attack on that country a few years later. The guarantors of the Pragmatic Sanction not only did nothing to defend Maria Theresa's rights when they were threatened in 1740: they themselves took the lead in seeking to deprive her of her territories.

The truth is that there did not yet exist the mutual trust which alone would have made the system of mutual guarantees an effective way of safeguarding the peace and securing respect for treaties. When the need to implement the guarantees arose there was no difficulty in finding plentiful reasons for ignoring them. It could always be maintained that circumstances had changed in the intervening period (and even international lawyers held that the treaty provisions were binding only *sic stantibus rebus*, that is, if circumstances remained unchanged). In practice guarantees increasingly became a formality. Probably few fully believed they would be fulfilled even at the time when they were given. They added little of significance to the normal undertakings given in every treaty. States would, as before, act to safeguard their provisions only when it suited their interests to do so.

MULTILATERAL DISCUSSION

Another method used to maintain stability during this period was through organising large-scale meetings of governments to discuss the problems of the continent. It became increasingly common to convene, whether or not at the end of a war, a widely attended international conference to consider questions that were in dispute.

The precedent for multilateral conferences of this kind was set, at the beginning of the period, in the spectacular peacemaking of Westphalia (see Table 4). That settlement was discussed, because of differences between Sweden and France concerning protocol, in two different centres, 30 miles apart: Munster and Osnabruck. While the representatives of the emperor and his allies appeared at both places, Sweden negotiated only at Osnabruck and France only at Munster. The negotiations lasted for six years from 1642 to 1648, preceded by several years of abortive peace-feelers. The meetings brought together almost every state of the continent. Only Russia – not generally seen at this time as a European power – Poland/Lithuania, which had not been involved, and England, which was concerned in the war only briefly at an early stage, were not represented. But even

TABLE 4:   Principal international congresses, 1645–1815

Date	Place	Subject of discussion
1642–8	Westphalia (Munster & Osnabruck)	Thirty Years War
1660	Oliva	First War of the North
1668	Aix-la-Chapelle	War of Devolution
1676–9	Nymegen	Dutch war
1687–9	Altona	Dispute between Sweden and Denmark over Holstein-Gottorp lands
1697	Ryswick	Nine Years War
1699	Carlowitz	Turkish war
1701, 1712–13	Utrecht	War of Spanish Succession
1720–5	Cambrai	Various international issues
1727–8	Soissons	Various international issues
1748	Aix-la-Chapelle	War of Austrian Succession
1779	Teschen	War of Bavarian Succession
1797–8	Rastadt	Peace between France and the empire
1814	Chatillon	Napoleonic wars
1814–15	Vienna	Napoleonic wars

these countries subsequently recognised the validity of the treaties which thus became genuinely Europe-wide commitments.[10] It was generally recognised that the conference would not only bring an end to the war and a resolution of the immediate issue that had caused it, but would provide the framework within which the continent's affairs would be conducted for many years to come. The provisions of the treaties came to be recognised as an important part, perhaps the most important part, of the "Public Law of Europe"; and their legitimacy continued to be reaffirmed over the next century and a half (see below).

The treaties not only provided a territorial settlement but determined the character of the European system in other important ways. They recognised the effective independence of the German states, including in particular their right to conduct their own foreign relations and to make treaties. They established a new constitution for the empire, covering, for example, the rights of the estates, the power of the imperial and Aulic chambers, and the creation of a new (eighth) Elector. They determined the distribution of ecclesiastical property in the empire, disputed for over a century. They recognised the right of the German rulers over ecclesiastical as well as over secular affairs, acknowledging, as the Peace of Augsburg had not, equal rights for Calvinist rulers with Lutherans. And they formally acknowledged the independence and sovereignty of the United Provinces and the Swiss Cantons.

During the next century and a half there took place a series of large-scale meetings of governments, usually dignified as "congresses" rather than mere "conferences". Though none of these was, until the very end of the period, of comparable importance with the Westphalia meetings, they did often bring together many of the principal states of the continent to discuss questions of concern to all of them. This occurred partly because many of the wars of the period involved most, if not all, of these major states, so that they were inevitably brought together of peace-making conferences at their conclusion. Such meetings provided the opportunity for discussing not only the immediate issues which had led to war but, quite often, other major questions on which multilateral commitments were required. They too therefore could lead to multilateral understandings on major issues of importance to the whole continent:* the separation of the crowns of Spain and France, agreed in the multilateral arrangements of 1713, 1718 and 1725; the Protestant succession in England (in the treaties of 1713, 1718 and 1748); the succession in Austria (1738 and 1748); the future of the north Italian duchies (1718, 1738 and 1748). Even more significant in their consequences were the multilateral treaties reached at Vienna in 1814–15, which determined the future of the continent in almost as decisive a fashion as had the Westphalia treaty. Agreements of this kind acquired a legitimacy and a general respect which purely bilateral treaties, of the sort mainly reached in earlier days, could not expect to enjoy.

The need for multilateral arrangements was recognised in the fact that it was quite often provided that these conferences might be attended by some states which had played no part in the preceding wars. Sometimes this was because they were accepted as having a special interest in the matters being discussed. Thus, for example Britain and the United Provinces, which had taken no part in the first Northern War (1655–60) but were concerned with navigation in the

---

* These were not necessarily set out in multilateral treaties. Sometimes, as at Utrecht, the agreements that were reached were set out in a series of bilateral treaties.

Baltic, participated together with France which had also taken no part but was the recognised mediator, in the Congress at Oliva which ended it. A few years later the same two countries took part in the peacemaking for the treaty of Aix-la-Chapelle (1668) ending the War of Devolution in the Spanish Netherlands, though they had not been involved in that war, only in the attempt to end it. Even when the interests of non-participants were less direct they were sometimes admitted to a peace conference. The negotiations for the Treaty of Utrecht (1713) were attended by representatives from Poland, Sweden and a number of German states which had not participated directly in the war, and Articles XXVI and XXVII of the treaty provided that Sweden, Genoa, Tuscany, Parma and the Hanseatic cities were to be "included" in the Treaty though they had taken no part in it. In other cases outside powers were invited to accede to a peace settlement in which they had taken no part. For example, Britain and the United Provinces were invited to become parties to the Treaty of Vienna (1738) concluding the War of Polish Succession, though they had not participated in the war nor in the peace negotiations which followed. They were in this way committed to respecting the settlement in a way that they would not otherwise have been. The multilateral approach thus maximised the degree of international consensus that existed for a particular settlement, and so deterred subsequent efforts to overthrow it.

There were also cases where international conferences were called to discuss major issues even though the participants had not been involved in a war. Many European powers took part in the conference in The Hague in 1710 which the Maritime Powers convened to agree on a convention for the neutralisation of Germany in the Great Northern War. In 1712 the emperor convened a further conference in Bremen intended to secure peace in that war, which also mainly brought together states not involved in the conflict. Three out of the four powers which negotiated and signed the Quadrilateral Alliance of 1718–19 were not themselves involved in the hostilities the treaty was intended to bring to an end. At the Congress of Cambrai of 1721–5 the four members of that alliance and other interested states, such as Italy, discussed during a time of peace a wide range of issues concerning southern Europe (including the future of the North Italian duchies, the type of peace-keeping force to be established pending their transfer to Spanish rulers, the future relations between Lorraine and France, Gibraltar, the succession in Austria, and the titles which could be used by the Austrian and Spanish rulers); and though the conference failed to resolve those questions, the fact that they continued to be debated there over four years reflected a desire for the continuing discussion of contentious issues, in peacetime as well as in war. Again, at the Congress of Soissons a little later (1728–9), similar issues were discussed among the same group of nations, also at a time when no war was in progress.

The most spectacular example of multilateral diplomacy of this kind occurred at the very end of the period at the Congress of Vienna. Like the Westphalia conference at its beginning that meeting laid down the basis of the system which was to operate throughout the period that followed. It provided far more than a territorial settlement, though in this alone it was revolutionary in effect, bringing about the most sweeping rewriting of the map of Europe to take place since 1648 and even before (see below). In addition to awarding large territories in Europe to Russia, Prussia and Austria and colonial territories to Britain, it provided for the destruction of Venice, the dismemberment of Saxony, the transfer of Norway (from Denmark to Sweden), the final integration of the smaller German states (now reduced to 38 in number), merged Holland with Belgium, created semi-independent entities in Poland and the Ionian Islands (under Russian and British protection) and set up a "free city" of Cracow. But the effect of the settlement went far beyond these territorial arrangements. It created a new confederation of German states under Austrian presidency. It provided for the permanent neutralisation of Switzerland and part of Savoy. It established, for the first time, the general principle of free navigation in international rivers. It created a new regime for the management of the Rhine and similar arrangements for five other rivers. It laid down new principles concerning long-disputed questions of diplomatic precedence and procedure. And it even incorporated a commitment, vague but unmistakeable, to the abolition of the slave trade. Never had international relationships in Europe been so transformed by a single set of agreements.

But although a tradition of multilateral discussion was being slowly established, it did not succeed in maintaining the peace of the continent. For this reason there was a series of proposals for still more ambitious schemes for the discussion of its affairs. The English Quaker William Penn in 1693 put forward a plan for the establishment of a general European diet, which would bring together representatives from all the European states to discuss disputes and to reach decisions on the basis of weighted voting: the largest and most powerful state would have twelve times the vote of the smallest.[11] Twenty years later the Abbé Pierre, who had served as secretary to a member of the French delegation at the Utrecht peace-making, put forward a plan to establish a European senate, in which the 24 principal European states would be represented, each wielding one vote, to adjudicate on disputes and to take collective action to reinforce the judgments which included the use of armed force if necessary.[12] Fifty years after that Jeremy Bentham put forward a plan for a "Common Court of Judicature", that is an international court, to resolve disputes among states, supported by a European diet which would reach judgments on the matters placed before them; these judgments would be circulated throughout Europe after which, he believed, the force of public opinion should be sufficient to secure compliance.[13] Finally, in 1793 Emmanuel Kant, in his work *Perpetual Peace*, proposed that every European state should undertake that there would be no further territorial changes, whether by conquest, inheritance, exchange, purchase or gift, that it would not enter into alliances for the purposes of making war, nor interfere in the internal affairs of other states; finally that all states should adopt a republican form of government, so as to avoid the rivalries of personal rulers, and join in a federation enabling all countries to live in peace under a common and mutually accepted law.

Such schemes were regarded by most statesmen as little more than Utopian dreams. Some of them – particularly that of the Abbé Pierre – were widely discussed, but there was no serious thought that they would be put into effect. They may, however, have had some marginal influence on the conduct of affairs. Even among governments proposals were occasionally put forward for a more institutionalised system of multilateral discussion. The authors of the Grand Alliance of 1701 undertook that, when the forthcoming war had been completed, they would establish a permanent alliance to ensure that its terms were effectively implemented: which implied regular discussions among the members for that purpose. Soon after the war was over, in 1718, the Quadruple Alliance did create a type of collective security system (see below). And at the end of the Napoleonic wars, a system of regular consultation among the major powers was formally established and lasted for nearly a century.

During the period we are concerned with the system of consultation among the major powers was not as advanced as this. But the arrangements that were made none the less demonstrated a recognition that the affairs of the continent sometimes required wide-ranging discussions among all interested states. Peace conferences might be used to discuss a wider range of issues than those which had led to war. And sometimes *ad hoc* conferences could be convened, not always at the conclusion of a war, to debate important issues. The procedure was not yet fully systematised. But the habit of multi-lateral debate none the less began to be established.

COLLECTIVE SECURITY

Perhaps the most important institutional development in this age was the emergence of an embryonic conception of collective security: the idea that the states of the system ought to act together to defend the existing international order when it was threatened.

This idea was to some extent implicit in the generally respected notion of the balance of power. The main reason that an obligation to preserve the balance was so widely accepted was that only this, it was believed, would safeguard the common security of all. It was, as Fénelon declared, because otherwise "the most powerful would certainly at length prevail", that the others were called on "to unite together to preserve the balance". It was, as Vattel asserted, because dominant powers "seldom failed to molest their neighbours . . . and even totally subjugate them" that other states were justified in seeking to "prevent their designs by force of arms". The conclusion most generally drawn was that this meant that each *individual* power was justified in taking action to redress the balance. But because the threat was to many states, or to the system as a whole, it was equally reasonable to conclude that in those circumstances it was joint action which was needed. The states of the system, in other words, had not only an individual but a collective interest in opposing aggression and preserving peace.

The first need, if the peace was to be collectively preserved in this way, was to define the status quo to be defended. It was generally accepted that this definition was contained in the successive multi-lateral treaties of the age, which not only laid down the existing territorial boundaries, in more or less detail, but often defined the order in a broader sense: setting out, for example, the principles and understandings concerning rights of succession in other states, mari-time rights, the sovereignty and independence of states, diplomatic procedure and representation, and other questions. Together such treaties, it came to be recognised, had established the "Public Law of Europe". It was this public law which a collective security system was required to uphold and defend. In adhering to those treaties the states of the system committed themselves to recognise and endorse that law. And in "guaranteeing" the treaties, as in many cases they did (see above), they committed themselves to defending it (much as members of the League of Nations and United Nations at a later date committed themselves to defending the territorial integrity of fellow-members).

In many of the wars of the period the members of one alliance or the other explicitly declared that their aim was to defend the provisions of some earlier treaty; and they ensured that the peace settlements reached at the end of the war deliberately reaffirmed the earlier treaty. Thus during the Dutch war (1672–8) the alliance between the United Provinces, Spain and the emperor declared in its first Article that it aimed "above all" to put right the "infractions" of the Peace of Westphalia committed by France; and the Treaty of Nymegen at its end explicitly reaffirmed that the Westphalia settlement of 1648 represented the "foundation and basis of the present friendship and public tranquility" and would be "restored" (except where a few small changes were made) "in all and every . . . point".

That new treaty (Nymegen) was then in turn added to the definition of the status quo. So, under the Hague Treaty of 1681 between Sweden and the United Provinces, later joined by the emperor and France, the parties pledged themselves to "guarantee" both the Westphalia and Nymegen settlements.[14] The parties to the Grand Alliance of 1689 explicitly committed themselves to "vindicating" (that is, restoring) the settlements of Westphalia and the Pyrenees (the treaty of 1659 ending the long war between France and Spain), and so restoring France to her earlier boundaries; and when Sweden offered to mediate in the conflict, the alliance powers agreed only on condition that the peace should be based on the treaties of Westphalia and Nymegen. And once more the Peace of Ryswick at the end of the war ensured that, except in respect of Strasbourg, France was indeed returned to her former boundaries. Similarly, at the end of the Spanish Succession war that followed, the Utrecht Treaty between France and the United Provinces explicitly reaffirmed the Treaty of Munster (one part of the Westphalia Settlement), reached seventy years earlier, which was still seen as the "basis" for the new treaty. In 1725 the alliance of Hanover committed the parties in

Article V to secure the "maintenance and observance of the West-phalia treaties" in order to ensure the peace of the "empire in particular and Europe in general".

Thereafter each new settlement continued to reaffirm earlier treaties, and was then itself in turn added to the list of those to be defended. Thus the Treaty of Vienna of 1738, ending the War of Polish Succession, listed the Westphalia treaties and those of Nymegen, Rys-wick, Baden and the Quadruple Alliance of 1718 as the "basis and foundation of the present peace" which, except in so far as they were altered by that treaty, would be "inviolably observed" and "fully implemented". The Treaty of Aix-la-Chapelle (1748) had a still longer list: it explicitly reaffirmed the Westphalia treaties, the two treaties of Madrid between Britain and Spain (1657 and 1670), Nymegen, Ryswick, Utrecht, Baden, the Triple and Quadruple Alliances (1717 and 1718) and the Vienna Treaty of 1738: and declared that "these together represented the base and foundation of the general peace of Europe".[15] The Peace of Paris of 1763 renewed and confirmed all the same treaties, now adding not only Aix-la-Chapelle itself but the Treaty of Madrid between Britain and Spain (1750) and a number of lesser treaties relating to Portugal; and it declared once again that together these served as "the basis and foundation of peace".

These treaties were therefore recognised as representing the basis of the existing order. The security of each state and even of each alliance, was seen (at least publicly) to depend on maintaining and defending those settlements. Private war, individual gains were not worthwhile if they disrupted the general order. Even outside multi-lateral treaties individual states recognised these principles. Thus the alliance treaty between Sweden and the Maritime Powers of 1700 declared that, since "the security of their kingdoms, states, provinces, jurisdictions and territories, depends . . . on the preservation of a general peace among the Christian princes" the signatories undertook to defend the Westphalia treaties and those of Nymegen and Ryswick which had succeeded them.

But it was not sufficient simply to reaffirm existing treaties. A collective security system required that its members were willing to defend settlements by force if necessary. Quite often during the course of this period governments did commit themselves to doing this. Apart from their "guarantees" bilateral and multilateral, they sometimes took more positive steps to that end. The signatories of the Triple Alliance of 1668 – England, the United Provinces and

Sweden – bystanders of the war between France and Spain for the Spanish Netherlands, not only demanded a French withdrawal but pledged themselves to intervene by force and compel this if necessary. The members of the Holy Alliance against the Turks of 1683 committed themselves to provide forces to help the emperor resist the threat which they posed to Vienna and to the whole of the Christian world; and in their bilateral treaty the emperor and the king of Poland committed themselves to help each other recover territories lost in earlier times (Hungary and Wallachia and the Ukraine respectively). The members of the first Grand Alliance of 1689 not only committed themselves to fight to restore France to her former boundaries, but agreed, as we saw earlier, to maintain a "perpetual defensive alliance" to "safeguard the peace". The parties to the second Grand Alliance of 1701 agreed that even after they had secured their aims in a final victory, there should be "and always continue to be" between the contracting parties a defensive alliance for the maintenance of the peace (Article XII), and that any other state that had "a concern for the general peace" would be invited to join (Article XIII). And in effect when that time came they did renew their own alliance. New alliance treaties were signed between Britain and the United Provinces, and between Britain and the emperor in 1716, committing them to defend each other's territory. And in the following year France, their former enemy, joined in similar commitments in the Triple Alliance.

In 1718 something approaching a genuine collective security system was established. The basis of this was contained in the Quadruple Alliance of 1718. This was negotiated in the first place between Britain, France and Austria, and was later joined, somewhat uncertainly, by the United Provinces. In the treaty the signatories undertook to defend each other's territories, by force if necessary, and each undertook to contribute forces (12,000 men each from the three larger powers, 6000 from the United Provinces) for that purpose. If any of the parties were "invaded" or "disturbed" in the possession of its kingdom, the others would provide the forces necessary to defend it; and, if this proved insufficient, they would "without delay" undertake to send still more. In addition, they agreed under separate and secret articles to use their forces to "compel" the rulers of Spain and Savoy to accept the provisions of the settlement they proposed of the war in Italy: that is, the withdrawal of both countries from Sicily, and of Spain from Sardinia. On the basis of the treaty Britain and France did in fact make use of their own forces – off Sicily and in Catalonia –

to compel Spain to give up the territory which she had taken by force. These actions were taken in accordance with their collective decisions to restore peace and may therefore be seen as a genuine collective security operation to counter aggression.

An alternative method for promoting security was by undertaking special defensive measures in areas believed to be particularly vulnerable. This was done in a number of arrangements made during the period to create "barriers", that is, strings of fortresses, on the borders between states. At the beginning of the period France was anxious for barriers to guard "the gates" of her territories: for example, in Cerdagne and Navarre to protect her against Spain, and at Pinerolo and Casale to defend her from attacks from Italy. In the same way, much later, Napoleon's occupation of the Rhineland was intended to secure France from invasion from Germany.

The most well known barriers were created, by multilateral agreement, against France herself. The barrier in the southern Netherlands (see above) was originally established as a result of a bilateral agreement between the United Provinces and Spain the sovereign power (then France's enemy) at the end of the Nine Years War. But after the Bourbon succession in Spain, the territory came under effective French control, the Dutch garrison was removed and the barrier made useless. The creation of a new and more powerful barrier in the neighbouring territory, thus became an important war aim not only for the United Provinces but for her allies. After Austria acquired the territory at the conclusion of the war, therefore, the United Provinces negotiated with her a new agreement allowing her to establish her own fortress manned by her own soldiers, directed against France. From a military point of view the attempt was a failure: inadequately maintained, the barrier was easily overrun by French forces during the War of Austrian Succession. Other barriers created in the Utrecht settlement were no more effective. The barrier established against France in the southern Alps could not prevent Napoleon crossing into Italy without difficulty, any more than the so called barrier of the Rhine prevented him advancing into Germany. Whatever the theoretical value therefore of such barriers (which anticipated some modern arms-control methods) they did not in this age do much to improve the security of the states they were intended to protect.

Nor did the collective security established in the Quadruple Alliance prove much more durable. Changes in alliance partners in the following years meant that its provisions were largely forgotten when new European wars took place in 1733–5, 1740–8 and 1756–63. Even so, the underlying principle that the acquisition of territory by force should not be tolerated was not entirely forgotten. None of the three wars brought decisive changes in territorial boundaries in Europe since some states were always willing to fight to prevent any major changes being made. Thus the Treaty of Aix-la-Chapelle provided that "all territories conquered since the outbreak of the present war . . . shall be restored to the rightful sovereign and in its present state" (Article II);[16] and the Peace of Paris ending the Seven Years War provided similarly for the restoration of the *status quo ante bellum* in the continent of Europe. Nor were European boundaries changed in the settlement between Britain and her European opponents after the War of American Independence. The only major exceptions were the seizure of Silesia from Austria by Prussia, a change which was not reversed, and the partition of Poland, in which three of the major powers colluded together. Even in 1814–15 there was no attempt to secure major territorial changes at France's expense. But for the Hundred Days, France would actually have made gains, acquiring the boundaries of 1792 in place of those of 1789; and even after Napoleon's last bid, she was allowed to retain those of 1790. There continued to be a sense that none of the great powers should be too diminished in case the continental balance was overturned.

Indeed it is arguable that then, and perhaps earlier, major changes in the status quo were prevented not so much by a genuine commitment to collective security and the defence of the status quo, as by the balance of power mechanism itself. Any attempt by one major state to secure territorial advantage was resisted by other such powers and therefore came to nothing. But this did not prevent all territorial change, Great powers resisted encroachments at their own expense but there was less willingness to prevent the larger powers aggrandising themselves at the expense of the small, as should have occurred in a genuine collective security system. Lorraine was swallowed by France with the consent of the other powers, the Crimea, Gourland, Finland and Bessarabia (among other places) were swallowed by Russia without any effective counteraction. At the Congress of Vienna, though France's aggression was eventually undone and she was returned to her old borders, the very powers that achieved this proceeded to enrich themselves at the expense of the weaker states: so Venice was swallowed by Austria; Pomerania, the Rhineland and other German territories by Prussia; Poland newly enslaved by Russia. Any idea that the states of the continent were

committed to maintaining existing territorial boundaries, or uphold-
ing Westphalia and the series of treaties that followed, was then
abandoned. What happened was that a new status quo was now
established: one which was still more favourable to the major powers
of the continent.

Having satisfied their own interests, however, those powers did
proceed to set up a new collective security system of a sort. Under the
Treaty of Chaumont, Britain, Austria, Prussia and Russia pledged
themselves to supply a force of 60,000 men each (or in Britain's case
the financial equivalent) to be used to enforce the terms of the peace
settlement. And over the next few years a number of armed actions
were undertaken by one or more of the powers, with the express
authority of the rest (Britain sometimes dissenting) to prevent attempts to disrupt the European order. So, as in 1718, a mechanism
for preventing threats to the status quo was established, not unlike
that set up for a similar purpose in 1945; one which similarly gave the
main responsibility to the five most powerful states of the world.
And, as in the latter case, it was disagreements among the great
powers, rather than any inadequacy in the system itself, which was to
prevent it from operating as effectively as hoped.

During the course of this period, therefore, there were sporadic
attempts to establish a system for collectively considering and if
possible resolving the conflicts of the continent. There was an increasing sense that many of the incidents that arose were not simply
bilateral affairs, affecting only the states most immediately involved.
They could affect others, if only because they could disturb the
"general peace of Europe". At the very least they could affect the
European balance of power. Or they might bring about unilateral
changes to settlements that had been collectively agreed. There was,
therefore, it was sometimes held, a need for joint action to defend
the existing order if necessary.

These efforts, however, were fitful and disorganised. What was
above all lacking was any real consensus about the status quo to be
defended. A reaffirmation of earlier treaties was not enough to
achieve this. Actions that were seen as unacceptable violations of
treaty terms by one power were seen as desirable changes by another.
When a state was powerful enough to challenge the status quo there
was not enough unanimity among the rest to compel it to relinquish
its claims: to reverse the seizure of Strasbourg by France, of Silesia by
Prussia, of Poland by its three powerful neighbours. Only when a
single state became powerful enough to be a threat to the entire

system, as France did in 1688–1713 and again in 1792–1815, or when a single state of middle power sought to reverse a settlement that others had accepted, as Spain did in 1717–8, could something approaching a collective security system be said to have been put into operation.

Nor did any of the other institutions of the period do much more to maintain the peace. Third party settlement, though it was widely used, did not prevent wars from occurring – it only sometimes marginally increased the prospect of a settlement after they had happened: no country would ever agree from the start that an issue on which it felt deeply should be resolved by mediation, still less by arbitration, rather than by the traditional arbitrament of war. Guarantees had equally little influence on the traditional conduct of affairs, if only because they were almost never fulfilled. And the calling of conferences and "congresses" was never sufficiently institutionalised to act as a significant constraint on state actions: they too were used mainly to resolve the problems which occurred after war broke out, not to prevent them happening at all.

The institutional developments of the age should not be dismissed altogether. They did reflect a growing tendency to see events in continental, rather than local, terms. They did encourage a willingness to consider multilateral rather than bilateral or unilateral solutions. They did promote a greater understanding in all states about the interests and concerns of other states. What they did not do was to create an international environment that was significantly more peaceful or stable than had been known before.

BOOKS

Contemporary works

J. Bellers, *Some Reasons for an European State* (London, 1710).

Jeremy Bentham, *Plan for an Universal and Perpetual Peace*, 1786–9 (London, 1939).

I. Kant, *Perpetual Peace*, 1795, English trs. (London, 1927).

William Penn, *An Essay Towards the Present and Future Peace of Europe* (London, 1693–4).

Abbé Pierre, *A Project for Perpetual Peace* (Paris, 1712).

J.-J. Rousseau, *Essay on the Abbé Pierre's Project for Perpetual Peace*, 1782, English trs. (London, 1927).

Modern works

A. C. F. Beales, *The History of Peace* (London, 1931).
W. Evans Darby, *International Tribunals*, 4th edn (London, 1904).
Denys Hay, *Europe, the Emergence of an Idea* (London, 1957).
S. J. Hemleben, *Plans for World Peace through Six Centuries* (Chicago, 1943).
D. J. Hill, *A History of Diplomacy in the International Development of Europe* (London, 1921).
F. H. Hinsley, *Power and the Pursuit of Peace* (Cambridge, 1967).
G. Mattingly, *Renaissance Diplomacy* (London, 1955).
H. Nicolson, *The Evolution of Diplomatic Method* (London, 1954).
J. H. Ralston, *International Arbitration from Athens to Locarno* (Stanford, Conn., 1929).
Sir E. Satow, *A Guide to Diplomatic Practice* (London, 1917).
E. E. York, *Leagues of Nations* (London, 1919).

12 Rules

RULES OF INTERCOURSE

No society of states is totally anarchic. There are almost always some conventions and understandings among them about the way they should conduct themselves towards each other. During the period we are concerned with there was a general and growing recognition that some elementary rules of international behaviour were necessary, though there was frequent disagreement about the precise content of the norms required.

There were some areas in which the need for rules had been accepted from earlier times. One of these was the field of diplomatic practice. Communication between states could not be easily undertaken without diplomacy, and diplomacy itself could not be conducted without agreement concerning the way that diplomats should be treated. For this reason, for a century and a half before our period began some conventions had emerged about the privileges which governments should grant to the diplomats of other states. During this age those rules began to be more firmly established and more widely recognised.

It came to be more generally accepted, for example, both by legal writers and by governments, that an ambassador could not be arrested or prosecuted, even for serious offences:[1] in 1765 the British cabinet felt it necessary to intervene to halt proceedings brought against the French ambassador in London although a Grand Jury had indicted him for such an offence.[2] They were not even liable to civil suits by injured parties.[3] They could not be taxed. They were not liable to legal action for non-payment of debts (Queen Anne apologised profusely to Peter the Great after the Russian ambassador in London had been arrested for an unpaid debt and new legislation was introduced in 1709 to protect future ambassadors against such an insult). Nor could their goods be seized in settlement of such a debt.[4] These privileges were to be enjoyed not only by the ambassadors themselves, but by their staffs, their families and even their servants: the French ambassador in London was able to secure the imprisonment of constables who had ventured to arrest his servant to secure the payment of a debt in 1764. Ambassadors were also uniquely privileged in being able to conduct services of their own rite in their own private chapels even if that religion was not otherwise tolerated and there were many disputes about the admission to these services of co-religionaries of the state concerned (who had not that right) and the use of ministers who were nationals of those states.[5]

But there was still ample room for disagreement about the application of these rules. In the early part of the period, for example, some ambassadors continued to claim that not only their own servants but all those who lived in the vicinity of their residencies were immune from arrest (*"droit du quartier"*): in 1660 the Cardinal d'Este, France's representative in Rome, protested vigorously at the arrest of an Italian trader who lived near his quarters and there were other similar incidents (mainly involving France): it was not until 1693 that Louis XIV reluctantly agreed to abandon this claim.[6] Another disputed question concerned the right of ambassadors to give asylum to political refugees in their residences: the British government protested vigorously when the Spanish authorities violated the extra-territoriality of the British embassy in Madrid to arrest the former Spanish chief minister, Ripperda, in 1726. There was dispute about the degree to which ambassadors should be free from arrest even if they had engaged in political activities: the action of the British king George I in arresting Gyllemborg, the Swedish ambassador in London, who was believed to have been plotting with the Jacobin revolutionaries in 1717, was widely condemned in other countries.

It was generally agreed that there was a need for agreement on a more detailed code covering these and other questions, including the highly contentious problem of diplomatic precedence and ceremony which could ever be the cause of armed conflict. A special committee was set up to examine these questions at the Congress of Vienna in 1815 and reached agreement on a number of the more important points. This agreement, together with the protocol of Aix-la-Chapelle which supplemented it, established a body of rules concerning the treatment of diplomats which was generally accepted and became the recognised code on such questions for the next century and a half.

One of the rules that was generally accepted from before the period began was that the despatches sent by diplomats to their home governments were privileged and not to be opened. But once again there were many disputes on the question. The opening of diplomatic mail was widely practised and this led to many controversies. The Austrian government systematically intercepted and copied the official correspondence of other states, and maintained offices for that purpose at Liège, Brussels, Frankfurt and Ratisbon as well as Vienna.[7] Britain had a "secret office" engaged in similar activities which employed nine people in 1741.[8] Bribery was also often used to secure the betrayal of secrets: Frederick the Great secured valuable information about the alliance being formed against him in 1756 by bribing a Saxon official to betray diplomatic documents to him. There none the less remained a clear sense that actions of this kind violated the international code. It was for this reason that the interception of mail was always kept a close secret. And when Frederick, having invaded Saxony in 1756, proceeded to open diplomatic archives to discover further details of the coalition's plans against him, his action caused a widespread outcry all over Europe.

Rules also began to be formulated about the duty of governments to protect foreign diplomats. It was generally agreed that there was an obligation to respect the safe-conducts used by other governments to their own representatives travelling abroad: there was general horror when in 1739 the Swedish ambassador in Constantinople was murdered in Silesia by Russian agents while returning home. According to Vattel, a government that had granted a safe conduct, or had undertaken to respect that of another government, was bound not only to "forbear violating that security", but also to "protect and defend those to whom he has promised it".[9] Governments were also under a duty, when a war broke out, to provide safe conduct to the ambassadors at their own courts, to enable them to return home (quite contrary to the practice of the Turkish government, which normally arrested foreign ambassadors in those circumstances). Safe conducts were also given, as an act of courtesy, in other cases: for example, the British and French governments granted safe conducts to the vessels of the other which were engaged in voyages of exploration during the eighteenth century, so ensuring that their activities were not interfered with even if a war should break out.[10]

New rules also emerged about the negotiation of treaties. Those who undertook the negotiations had to be provided with "full powers" for that purpose by their sovereigns; and there were long debates before the conclusion of the Peace of Westphalia and on some subsequent occasions about the validity of the full powers provided for some of the negotiators (because, for example, they named their sovereigns as the rulers of territories which were in fact ruled by others). There was a growing acceptance of the doctrine of *uti possedetis*: that, unless a treaty specified otherwise, each party would continue to hold territory which it had conquered during the preceding war. In some cases, entire treaties were based on that principle, so that no withdrawals were made on the conclusion of a treaty: this was the case, for example, with the Peace of Carlowitz of 1699. On the other hand it was equally accepted that the restoration of territory implied the restoration of all the property that was on it: in other words it could not be looted or laid waste before the conquering troops departed. Finally, it came to be accepted that treaties should take effect from the time they were signed and that the signatories should ensure that their commanders undertook this, though they could not be held responsible for action which occurred after the signature if information had not been received in time.[11] (William III was generally excused on these grounds when his troops continued to fight against the French after the conclusion of the Peace of Nymegen.) Because the negotiators were supposed to hold full powers, their signature alone was sufficient to have this effect; and the need for ratification through the appropriate constitutional procedures, which would later have been regarded as essential, was not thought necessary in this age of absolutist governments.[12]

Another question about which there was much discussion was the limit of jurisdiction that a state could claim in the seas surrounding its coast. In earlier times a wide range of claims had been made, based on a variety of principles usually unrecognised by other states. Spain, for example, had claimed sovereignty over the seas on either side of her possessions in South America and reserved the right to deny passage to vessels of other powers. Portugal, having voyaged down the coast of Africa and established colonies there, claimed large areas of the South Atlantic. Venice laid claim to dominion over the Adriatic: a claim that was still maintained in a law book of 1669;[13] while Genoa maintained a comparable claim in the Ligurian Sea, also supported in a law book of 1641.[14] English writers claimed sovereignty in the seas off England's coast from the north coast of Spain to the coast of Germany and Norway: a claim propounded in Seldon's *Mare Clausum*, which was reissued in an English language version by the English Parliament in 1651, immediately before the first Dutch war which was fought partly about this issue.[15] Finally Denmark, in controlling passage through the Sound at the entrance of the Baltic, was in effect asserting her right to control navigation in that sea by non-Baltic powers. In all these cases entire seas, or substantial parts of them, were claimed to fall under the sovereignty of a particular state.

Grotius, just before our period began, had contested all claims of this sort. He supported the contention of his own country, the United Provinces, which as a trading nation had an interest in free navigation, that the open seas could not be subjected to appropriation by any state in any way. In his work, *Mare Librum*, written to support a claim brought by the Dutch against the Portuguese, he asked: "Can the vast, the boundless sea be the apanage of one country alone? . . . Can any one nation have the right to prevent other nations which so desire from selling to one another, bartering with one another, from communicating with one another?" On the contrary, every nation, he held, enjoyed an equal right to free access to the sea.

For long, most other nations upheld the earlier view. England continued to assert her sovereignty in the "British seas" and three wars were fought between England and the United Provinces between 1652 and 1674 partly about this question. At the end of the third of these, in 1674 the United Provinces fully recognised British sovereignty in the seas from Cape Finisterre to Staten, a claim reasserted in a treaty of 1784. With the rapid increase in her own foreign trade, however, Britain herself began to understand the benefits of the doctrine the Dutch had proclaimed. Eventually other nations too began to accept more limited conceptions of their sovereignty over the waters of their coasts.

But if such sweeping claims were no longer tenable, what were the areas they could reasonably claim? A number of proposals had been made in earlier times, both by lawyers and by statesmen. Gentile had proposed a limit of a hundred miles, while Grotius had suggested fifty miles or a sixty-mile maximum. Some suggested the distance which could be seen from the shore, others the mid-point of the oceans or straits.[16] Increasingly, however, it came to be accepted that the limits of jurisdiction must be related to the capacity of the coastal state to enforce it. Grotius had stated that a state could exercise authority off its coast "as far as they could be coerced to the same degree as if they had been upon the shore". Bynkershoek, in the early part of our age, was rather more specific, declaring that this meant an area that was in the range of canon fire (*une portée de canon*), though he did not specify what this was. Some writers who accepted that the area should be limited by the ability to exercise effective jurisdiction left the precise distance undefined. Vattel, for example, held that "in general the dominion of the state over the neighbouring sea, extends as far as her safety renders it necessary and her power is able to assert it". And on these grounds he recognised the claim of Venice in the

Adriatic "in the places of which she can keep possession and on which the possession is important for her own safety". For the rest, "the whole space of the sea within canon-shot of the coast is considered as making a part of the territory".[17] During the course of the period it came to be increasingly accepted, both in state practice and by legal writers, that the appropriate distance was a league or three miles. In 1758 the king of Sweden asserted the right do suppress privateering to a distance of three miles from the coast and at the beginning of the nineteenth century the British judge Lord Stowell, held that the gun-fire limit implied a distance of three miles.[18] Among legal writers, Martens, in his famous *Précis of International Law* (1789), Galiani, the Italian writer, and other authorities upheld this distance. And in general, though there was still no unanimity for another two centuries, by the end of our age this was the most commonly accepted limit of national jurisdiction in the "territorial sea".

One reason a limit was required was because it could affect the right of fishing off the coast of another state. A major cause of friction between England and the United Provinces at the beginning of our period was the resentment in England at widespread fishing by the Dutch off the coast in waters that most considered to be English; and similar disputes arose in some colonial areas, for example in the St Lawrence and Hudson Bay areas (see above). In earlier times, when most fishing was relatively close to the coast, there had been no rules on this question. Grotius had maintained that since the seas generally belonged to no state, there was no right to restrict or tax fishermen in these areas. "The right of fishing", he maintained, "ought everywhere to be exempt from tolls, lest a servitude be imposed upon the sea, which is not susceptible to a servitude."[19] In 1654 at the end of the first war between the two countries, the Dutch right to fish in British waters was recognised by England (provided they recognised these as British); and that agreement was maintained after the next two wars. But it gradually came to be accepted that a state did have the right to limit fishing in the waters off its coast. Thus Vattel, though he believed that the English had allowed their herring fishery to become "common . . . with other nations" by allowing them to fish there in the past, also believed that "if a nation had on their coast a particular fishery of a profitable nature . . . shall they not be permitted to appropriate to themselves that bounteous gift of nature . . . and to reserve to themselves the great advantages which their commerce may derive . . .?"[20] Even after a colonial conquest there was often a willingness to allow nations that had traditionally fished in a particular area to continue their activities there. Thus after Britain won a dominant position in the St Lawrence in 1713, she continued to recognise the right of French fishermen to fish and to dry their nets in British territory; and even after she won control of the whole of Canada, she still acknowledged a continuing French interest in fishing off the coasts, including sovereignty in St Pierre and Miquelon. There was even a willingness to recognise "fishing truces" permitting the fishermen of enemy states to continue fishing close to the coast during a war.[21]

There was also recognised to be a need for mutually acceptable rules governing trade. Commercial treaties had been reached among individual countries for centuries: providing, for example, for protection for the traders of one in the territory of the other; for their right to use harbours and other local facilities, to dwell in certain quarters, to buy and sell freely, to acquire warehouses and so on, in return for the obligation to respect local laws and conventions and to pay the specified customs and other taxes.[22] In the age that began in 1648, when commercial rivalry became more acute and the desire to win trade abroad began to displace the desire to secure an adequate supply of goods for home consumers, trading relationships altered. Policies became more protectionist, with subsidies, draw-backs, increased duties and other impediments to foreign traders. Though some international lawyers believed there was a duty in international law to afford freedom of commerce (Vattel held that a nation "ought not only to countenance trade, as far as it reasonably can, but even to protect and favour it" and should not "cramp it by unnecessary burdens"[23]), the new policies in many cases introduced an element of discrimination. The Methuen Treaty of 1703, between England and Portugal afforded each country favourable treatment in the markets of the other. Slowly the disadvantages of this discrimination began to be recognised. Dutch writers such as de la Court had long argued in favour of non-discrimination in trade, along the lines later pursued by Adam Smith. Whether or not as a result of these writings, states became increasingly willing in negotiating commercial treaties to undertake to afford each other conditions at least as favourable as those accorded to any other. This "most-favoured-nation" provision began to appear in an increasing number of treaties. And in consequence a convention of non-discrimination began slowly to be established.

During this age, therefore, the growing contacts which took place among states brought a desire for more general conventions governing their conduct. There continued to be many disagreements about details. The balance of advantage resulting from the new rules was not always equally shared: those that benefited small states were not always acceptable to large ones, while maritime countries favoured rules that were not always accepted by coastal states; and so on. But slowly and painfully, during the course of the age a framework of rules that was more or less widely accepted began to be developed.

NEUTRALITY

During the centuries before 1648 the concept of neutrality had been a nebulous one. During the Middle Ages there was no recognised status of "neutral" and those that were not "friends" were apt to be treated almost like enemies (see below). In the age of religious wars many held (like Dulles in a later ideological age) that neutralism was immoral: as Gustav Adolphus put it, denouncing the prudent in-action of Brandenburg in the Thirty Years War: "There can be no third way. . . . neutrality is nothing but rubbish, which the wind raises and carries away."[24] The rights of neutral states were thus in practice frequently violated. It was, for example, not uncommon for an army to march through, and even to occupy for long periods, the territory of a neutral state: for example imperial forces occupied Brandenburg territory for long periods during the Thirty Years War while its ruler remained neutral. Gradually during the period we are concerned with the concept of neutrality began to be more clearly defined and new rules about it emerged. These rules concerned both the conduct to be observed by the neutrals themselves and those to be adopted towards them by other states.

Grotius had asserted that the duties of a neutral depended on the justice of the cause of the states involved in the war. "It is the duty of those who stand apart from a war", he wrote "to do nothing which may strengthen the side whose cause is unjust, or which may hinder the movements of him who was carrying on a just war."[25] Some subsequent legal writers continued to maintain a distinction of this kind: for example Vattel held that the neutral should allow the passage of troops only to the side whose cause was more just (though he also asserted that the neutral should not discriminate between the combatants at all). But increasingly these subjective criteria were abandoned. Bynkershoek, the Dutch international lawyer, explicitly rejected it: "a neutral has nothing to do with the justice or injustice of the war: it is not for him to sit as judge between his friends".[26] And certainly in practice neutral countries themselves became more insistent on asserting their right to remain totally uninvolved in the wars of others.

This was increasingly accepted by international lawyers and by international opinion generally. "To themselves alone", Vattel declared, "it belongs to determine whether any reason exists to induce [neutrals] to join in the contest."[27] Neutrals claimed not only the right to trade with either belligerent power (see below) but even to provide ships or arms to one if they had undertaken to do so under a previous alliance: Denmark made that claim in securing assistance from Prussia in her war with Sweden in 1788 (and could claim the authority of Vattel in doing so).[28] Even belligerent states were increasingly willing to recognise neutrality chosen in this way. And there was outrage throughout Europe that Napoleon sent soldiers into neutral Baden to arrest the Duke d'Enghien whom he accused of plotting with foreign powers to overthrow him.

So far as the passage of troops was concerned, there were not at first any spectacular changes. Following Grotius,[29] the rulers of the period continued to march their armies across the territory of neutral countries. Louis XIV sent his armies across the territory of the Spanish Netherlands on their way to attack the United Provinces (with which he had no common border) in 1672 and Luxembourg in 1681. The emperor Leopold, when he wished to attack French positions in north Italy in 1701, sent his troops through neutral Venetian territory; and Austrian troops crossed the papal states in attacking Naples in 1743. Russian troops habitually crossed Polish territory when on their way to fight in the west; for example the Russian auxiliaries sent to help the United Provinces in the War of Austrian Succession, and again in the Seven Years War.[30] Even as late as the Napoleonic wars neutral status was blatantly disregarded: Swiss territory was violated by France, Austria and Russia in turn and a major campaign was fought in that country in 1799–1802. Sometimes neutral states voluntarily agreed to allow the passage of troops. Thus in 1701 the Duke of Savoy agreed with France to allow French troops through his territory, though he himself was to remain neutral; and at about the same time the duke of Mantua allowed the French to occupy a fortress on his territory without being involved in the war.[31] The most that can be said, therefore, is that, though the crossing of neutral territory remained common for much of the period, there was an increasing recognition that when it occurred the treatment of the local people should be humane and reasonable, and that no long-term occupation should be undertaken.

On the other hand it began to be recognised that belligerent powers themselves would sometimes benefit if particular countries or regions remained neutral. Thus the deliberate *neutralisation* of particular states or areas was increasingly proposed, and quite often agreed among a number of states. Sometimes this occurred when one or more states declared their own neutrality; and this was subsequently explicitly recognised by other nations. Switzerland had done this in 1515 (after suffering a major defeat by France) and for much of the period this permanent neutrality was recognised by other states. Leopold, the grand duke of Tuscany (1765–90), was insistent on the neutrality of that state, which he sought to establish as a permanent tradition of European diplomacy (though most other states felt some doubt about his impartiality given that his brother was the Austrian emperor). Increasingly two or more states became willing to group together to assert their neutrality. For example in 1691 Sweden and Denmark, normally bitter enemies, joined in a treaty of "armed neutrality", designed to prevent the Nine Years War affecting their territories or commerce. During the same war a group of German states, including those disaffected as a result of the emperor's creation of an eighth electorate without consultation (see above), created a "third party", a grouping which rejected his call to participate in the war on behalf of the empire. In 1756 Spain, the United Provinces and Denmark, with French encouragement, agreed on a treaty of "armed neutrality", committing them to defending their right to trade with belligerent powers free of interference. In 1780, during the War of American Independence, a more substantial grouping of active neutrals was established: under the leadership of Catherine II of Russia a League of Armed Neutrality was established, including Russia, Prussia, Sweden and Denmark, which was also committed to defend their right to trade without harassment by British warships. Finally, in 1800 yet another League of Armed Neutrality was established among a similar group of states and with similar objectives; this time they were willing to take stronger action to assert their rights, sequestering British property in Russian ports, for example, and closing German ports and rivers to British ships.

In all these cases neutrality was deliberately chosen by the countries involved. But there were other cases where neutralisation was imposed by *other* states. Sometimes this resulted from bilateral action. For example, in the 1660s France and the United Provinces discussed several times the neutralisation of the southern Netherlands, largely without reference to Spain, the sovereign power at the time; and the same two countries discussed the neutralisation of the same area in 1714, after the territory's transfer to Austria, again without reference to the sovereign power. In 1696, when Savoy changed sides to join Louis XIV in the Nine Years War, the two countries agreed that from that point the whole of north Italy should be neutralised: a decision that the other belligerent powers subsequently accepted. During the Great Northern War the neutralisation of the whole of Germany was agreed at the Hague Conference of 1710, and an army of 21,000 was promised to enforce it among powers, most of which were not German, nor had even participated in the war in question.[32] The Treaty of Baden at the end of the War of Spanish succession (1714), of which Savoy was the only Italian signatory, laid down (in Article XXI) that the whole of Italy was to be neutralised; and this was reaffirmed in the Quadruple Alliance Treaty of 1718 (Article I). In 1756 Prussia and Britain agreed in the Treaty of Westminster that Germany should be neutralised, without reference to the views of other German states.[33] Finally the Treaty of Vienna of 1815 created the "neutral" republic of Cracow (suppressed by Austria in 1846) and recognised the "permanent" neutrality of Switzerland: also examples of externally imposed or externally agreed neutralisation.

Multilateral neutralisation of this sort, and the greater recognition given everywhere to neutral status, served the common purposes of the European community. The neutralisation of Germany in the Great Northern War, of Italy after 1714 and of Switzerland in 1815, were intended to insulate those areas from European conflicts which might otherwise have engulfed them: not only in the interests of the inhabitants of those regions but of other countries, including the belligerents who would otherwise have found themselves drawn into the even more extensive conflicts that anyway occurred. The creation of "armed neutralities" served to protect the interests of a majority of the members of the system of deterring interference with their people's commercial activities from one or two more-powerful states, primarily Britain. The formulation of more-detailed rules about the rights and duties of neutral countries, which became part of the "Public Law of Europe", was intended to define and consolidate a status which had rested previously only on the basis of bilateral treaties or individual goodwill. Even for the belligerent powers a clarification of the rules provided some benefits. Those who were at peace were, even more obviously, protected from some of the ravages of war which might otherwise have afflicted them. As Lord Brougham put it towards the end of the period, the advantage of neutralisation was that "we thus narrow the evil operation of war . . . mitigate its suffering and . . . preserve our material chance of restoring peace when we retain as many neutrals as possible".[34]

MARITIME LAW

There was also a growing recognition of the need for a body of rules governing the uses of the seas. The extension of maritime trade to the furthest parts of the world meant that many more ships now used the seas and this alone made rules increasingly necessary. In addition, the growing dependence of many states on imports made them highly vulnerable in wartime to the activities of others determined to interfere with their commerce. And it was these activities which aroused most controversy and, it was felt, most required international regulation.

Neutral states were the most concerned that new rules should be established. From long before the beginning of this period there had been controversy over the right of a nation at war to capture at sea goods which were carried in neutral ships but were destined for its enemies. The most generally accepted guidelines on the question had been contained in the *Consulato del Mare*, a body of rules which became current in medieval times on maritime questions. This had accepted that in wartime a belligerent nation could take from neutral ships goods being traded to its enemies, provided that the ships were otherwise allowed to proceed peacefully.[35] Sometimes these rules had been explicitly accepted in bilateral treaties: for example in the series of treaties reached between England and Burgundy between 1406 and 1495. But the provisions of such treaties, even if they were respected, affected only the two states concerned. To others each state applied its own rules and some (including France at various times) went beyond the rules in holding that in wartime not only the neutral goods going to its enemies but the ship that was trading with it could be taken.[36]

During the first half of the seventeenth century the Dutch, as a people who lived on trade, had begun to challenge the traditional rules. They called for recognition of a new principle, that of "Free ship, free goods"; that is, if the ship itself was neutral, all the goods it carried should be allowed to go freely to its destination, even if that was in a state at war. But they were willing, like most other states, to accept the corresponding principle of "enemy ship, enemy goods"; that is, that a state at war could remove even neutral goods that were being carried on an enemy ship. In 1646, even before our period began they had persuaded France to abandon its former, more vigorous practice, and to recognise the freedom of a neutral ship, if not of the goods it carried. In the first two decades after 1648 they won recognition of the "free ship, free goods" principle from a number of other countries; from Spain in 1650, from England in 1654, 1668, 1674 and 1679; from Portugal in 1661 and even from France, during a period of cordial relations, in 1662.[37] The same principle was occasionally accepted in treaties between other powers: for example between England and Portugal (in 1654) and between France and Spain (in 1659). The fact that these undertakings were secured in the peace settlements reached at the end of major wars is an indication of the importance that was widely attached to the question.

Although the new principle suited the purposes of trading states and their merchants, it was not welcome to all countries. It was opposed in particular by the more powerful states (such as France) which did not like to see their freedom of action in war-time interfered with; and above all by strong naval states (such as Britain), which were reluctant to place limitations on an important capability – their capacity to weaken their opponents by cutting off their supplies of imports. These two countries, therefore, became increasingly hostile to the proposed rules. In 1681 Louis XIV passed an *ordonnance* which declared that all ships carrying enemy goods were lawful prize, so that the ships as well as the goods were subject to forfeiture; while Britain too signed a number of bilateral treaties which rejected the principle (for example with Sweden in 1661, 1666 and 1670, and with Denmark in 1670). The Dutch, for whom this was a major aim of foreign policy, were able, however, to secure at least temporary compliance from France at the end of her successful wars: at Nymegen (1678), Ryswick (1697) and Utrecht (1713) France was brought to accept the principle of "free ship, free goods". During the next 65 years she lapsed from time to time: for example in 1744 during the War of Austrian Succession she issued a new *règlement* restoring her former practice and applied it against the Dutch, then still neutral, in the following year. In 1778, however, she announced the adoption during the War of American Independence of the "free ships, free goods" principle, provided that Britain would do the same: a step which would have deprived Britain of one of her main capabilities. Britain declined to conform.

Britain had thus now become the main power to oppose the Dutch principle. In most of the wars of the period her navy continued to capture neutral vessels sailing to enemy ports and took them to prize ports, where the cargoes were condemned as "good prize". In doing so she finally aroused the anger of almost every country of the continent. Successive combinations were created to contest and resist her actions. The three "armed neutralities" of 1756, 1780 and 1800 were primarily directed against her. In establishing the League of 1780 Catherine the Great enunciated a set of principles of neutrality which included the doctrine of "free ships, free goods". The adherence to this League of so many significant states (Austria, France, Prussia, Spain, United Provinces, Sweden, Denmark, Portugal, Naples and the US, in addition to Russia) clearly demonstrated the isolation in which Britain now found herself. She was obliged to accept the contested principle in the settlement of the War of American Independence in 1783 and agreed to it again in the Eden Treaty with France in 1786. But she continued to negotiate bilateral treaties – with Russia in 1801 and Sweden in 1801 – in which she rejected it (as she continued to do till the middle of the nineteenth century). But her position was increasingly rejected, both in legal writings and in state policy. The doctrine of "free ships, free goods" was incorporated in three major international treaties: Utrecht, Aix-la-Chapelle and Paris. And by the end of the period it had won recognition by the great majority of the international community.

Closely connected with this was a parallel controversy concerning the definition of "contraband". Even states that accepted the Dutch doctrine on neutral trade accepted the right of a belligerent power to remove from neutral ships "contraband" (that is, war goods) destined for an enemy. But they did not agree on what represented "contraband". Grotius had distinguished three categories of goods: those that could be used only in war; those that could not be used for war at all; and those that could be used both in war and in peace, such as food, money, vessels and naval goods. The only difficulty concerned the third category. Grotius held that such goods could be taken by a belligerent in case of "necessity", but normally only on condition of restitution when that necessity no longer existed; and that they could also be prevented from reaching a beseiged city where they might make the difference between victory and defeat.[38] As in the other case there was some attempt to establish definitions in bilateral agreements: for example the Treaty of the Pyrenees between France and Spain (1659) included a detailed definition of what represented contraband, as did a number of other treaties of the period. But once again there was a difference of interest between the major naval powers – above all Britain – and the rest. Britain favoured a wider definition of contraband, permitting more sweeping seizures. In her treaties with the United Provinces in 1654 and with Sweden in 1661 she secured a definition which included food, money and ships as "contraband".

Other states, however, were increasingly resistant to such formulations and managed to secure in the various treaties of Utrecht the use of a more restricted list. There were bitter disputes about whether, for example, naval stores such as pitch, tar and hemp should be included (for example between Britain and the Scandinavian countries during the eighteenth century); or whether ship-building materials and food were covered (between Britain and the US during the Napoleonic wars).[39] Other conflicts concerned the right of a state to make its own decisions on such questions, sometimes in defiance of bilateral treaties: there was a bitter dispute between Britain and Prussia about Britain's action in seizing goods from Prussian ships which, Frederick the Great claimed, were not covered in the bilateral treaty between the two countries (causing him to refuse to make payments on the Silesian loan which he had taken over after his invasion of that province). Britain roundly rejected the idea that there was any general law of nations covering the question: an Admiralty prize court laid down that "sovereign princes at war may declare such and such things to be contraband and, after notice to their allies, their subjects may seize them".[40] On this basis the British Commissioner of Prizes determined in 1665 that contraband included wine, brandy, fish and all "things that tend . . . to the support of life".[41]

Most other states were therefore concerned to secure consensus on the point. Catherine the Great secured for herself a restrictive list in negotiating her commercial treaty with Britain in 1766; and in 1781 she declared that she believed this to be founded on "natural law" and would apply it in her dealings with other European states. Britain continued to resist such proposals and demanded the right to "pre-empt", that is, to confiscate goods in the marginal categories but to pay for them. But there was unmistakably a general movement towards limiting more closely the category of goods which could be seized as contraband (though the task of securing an accepted multilateral definition had to await the naval conference of 1908).[42]

A related subject of controversy concerned the right of blockade.

In earlier times, though from time to time rulers had sought to prevent trade with the ports of enemy states (for example Edward III of England gave orders in 1346 that every ship attempting to enter a French port should be taken and burnt), it had rarely been possible to institute effective naval blockades. During their war of independence the Dutch had regularly sought to impose blockades against Spanish shipping trying to reach the ports of Flanders. After 1648 something like a legal doctrine concerning blockades began to develop. A Dutch edict of 1630 relating to the southern Netherlands was used as the basis for the prize law adopted by England. Under this it was laid down that any ship trying to break a blockade even if neutral, was liable to be seized as prize, and could be captured at any moment before it reached the port in question (so that virtually any ship on any part of the seas might have to prove it was not bound for that port). The Dutch themselves declared blockades of English ports during her wars with that country, and of French ones in the war of 1672. Similarly the Dutch and English together, in their alliance treaty of 1689, declared their intentions to impose a blockade of trade with the French coast. Neutral shipping, therefore, became increasingly vulnerable and was liable to be stopped whether or not it was seeking to trade with a belligerent port. Here too the neutral powers rebelled – they became increasingly concerned to limit the right of belligerents to institute a "blockade". In particular they enunciated the doctrine that, to have any legal force a blockade must be "effective": that is, it must be effectively enforced (since otherwise the stopping of ships could be random and arbitrary). In some cases they instituted reprisals when their own ships were taken at sea, as Sweden and Denmark did in 1693 against England and the United Provinces. There were even attempts to define the number of ships needed to establish an "effective" blockade. The general resistance to the efforts of maritime powers to declare blockades mounted during the course of the period and by its end there was little disposition to countenance "paper" blockades based on decrees but without effective enforcement.

Another controversy, closely related to those concerning neutral trade, contraband and blockades, related to the right of search. A maritime power could only enforce the limitations it declared on trade with its enemies by stopping neutral ships on the high seas to see whether they were carrying goods of a certain type or were destined for a particular destination. The right to stop neutral ships for this purpose had been recognised in some earlier treaties and codes of maritime laws. But during our period actions of this kind became increasingly unacceptable to many states, and there were therefore attempts to lay down more precisely the circumstances in which it was justified and the formalities which were to be followed. The Treaty of the Pyrenees between France and Spain (1659) and the Treaty of Commerce between Britain and France of 1714, for example, both included provisions on this point. It was increasingly asserted by the neutral countries that merchant ships which were being convoyed by naval vessels should be free from search, or should be searched only if the naval commanders gave their assent. And they sought especially to place restraints on the brutal way in which searches of this kind were sometimes conducted (quite often by privateers as well as by naval vessels). Once again it was Britain, as the leading maritime power, and so the one most interested in controlling foreign shipping, which was most insistent in asserting this right (although Britain herself bitterly resented the actions of Spanish coastguards in the 1730s in stopping and searching English shipping in the Caribbean). British insistence on the right of search became a major cause of friction with other countries during the War of American Independence. It was one of the main causes of the formation of the League of Armed Neutrality of 1780 and of the outbreak of war between Britain and the United Provinces in that year. And it was a principal cause of the war of 1812 between her and the United States.

All these controversies reflected the deep differences of interest which existed between the states of the system. But they also clearly demonstrated the determination of the majority to establish principles of international behaviour which would protect them from arbitrary and high-handed action at the hands of one or two dominant naval powers, as well as a more general concern to establish order in place of anarchy on the high seas. Though differences of view continued to be expressed on many of these points throughout the period, increasingly the view of the majority prevailed. And the rules which that majority demanded eventually came to be accepted as representing the "public law" of the continent.

THE LEGITIMACY OF WAR

But the most important set of rules required within any international society are those that concern the making of war. Here too some new thinking developed during this period.

There were a few who maintained that war was always wrong. Just as Erasmus in an earlier day had inveighed against the propensity of the rulers of his time to make war against their rivals and to claim admirable reasons for doing so, so now such groups as the Quakers preached that the initiation of war could never be justified. However much it might be protested that a war was made for a "just" cause, in practice it resulted from the ambition and greed of men. William Penn, for example, in his work *An Essay Towards the Present and Future Peace of Europe* (1693–4) pointed out that "as war cannot in any sense be justified but upon wrong received and right . . . the generality of wars have their rise from some such pretention".[43] In fact, however, they rarely secured the ends intended: the aggressors seldom getting what they seek or performing, if they prevail, what they promised". The final result was only that "blood and poverty that usually attend the enterprise weigh more, on earth as well as in heaven, than what they lost or suffered".[44] Only the establishment of a system of justice, comparable to that which existed within states, would bring war to an end.

A larger and more influential group were the writers on international law. These did not suggest that war was always wrong. But they did seek to define more clearly than before the circumstances in which it was justified.

Writers on "just war" in the Middle Ages had held that a war was just if it intended to retake something unjustly taken, to secure reparation for a wrong, or to repel an injury or attack. On the other hand, war undertaken from envy, resentment or greed was not just. The writers of our age (many of whom quoted liberally from mediaeval writers, as well as from the Scriptures) elaborated these doctrines. Grotius, just before the period began, stated that a war was unjust if it resulted from a desire to secure "advantage" without necessity, to rule others against their will, from the desire for universal empire, the desire for richer land, the desire to take what others have discovered and lawfully acquired, and even the desire for freedom among subject peoples.[45] Pufendorf held that war was unjust if it resulted merely from the fear of a neighbour's designs, or the desire to intimidate him, or to extort a guarantee by force.[46] Wolff held that war was not just if it was brought "without preceding or threatened wrong", or for "quasi-justifying reasons", that is reason which "if properly reasoned out" could be recognised as "contrary to law".[47] Vattel held that a war was unjust if no injury had been suffered or intended by the attacker or if made from motives of advantage, or without any right, or if undertaken from a vicious motive even though there was just cause.[48]

Against this even these legal writers accepted that there were still many situations in which war was legitimate and justifiable. It could be undertaken, for example, not only to avenge or punish an injury but to anticipate it. Grotius held that a war undertaken to prevent "an injury not yet inflicted which menaces either persons or property"[49] was legally justified. Pufendorf held that a war was just if undertaken "to conserve and protect ourselves and our possessions against others who attempt to injure us or take from us or destroy what we have; to assert our claim to whatever others may owe us by perfect right"; to "obtain reparation for losses which we have suffered by injuries and to extort from him who did the injury guarantees that he will not so offend in future";[50] or if a state "refuses to fulfil some former pact legally entered into".[51] Wolff held that a just cause of war arose "when a wrong has been done or is likely to be done"; in "repairing the wrong if it can be repaired"; "satisfying the injured party if it cannot"; or "preventing the doing of wrong".[52] Vattel held that a war was just if undertaken in self-defence; for the maintenance of right; to prevent an intended or threatened injury; to recover what belongs or is due to us; to punish an offence or offender; to "anticipate the designs of another state" or to "prevent a recurrence of . . . attacks".[53]

Thus even if the rulers of the day wanted to claim that they acted in accordance with the law, there was no shortage of justifications drawn from impeccable authorities to use. Such writings were not entirely unknown. All the works quoted above were widely translated, and discussed throughout the continent. In a few cases international lawyers held influential positions at a ruler's court: both Grotius and Pufendorf held such positions at the Swedish court at different times (although there is little evidence that they influenced the conduct of the warlike Vasa kings they served). But in general it is doubtful whether most of the rulers of the day either knew or cared about the opinions of lawyers on the matter of making war.

Their own view of its legitimacy was clear enough from their conduct. Louis XIV in his own series of aggressive wars; the three rulers who together attacked Sweden in 1700; Frederick the Great in seizing Silesia, Austria in seeking to recover it; the partitioners of Poland; Napoleon in launching his attack on his ally Russia in 1812; these showed little concern about whether or not such actions conformed with the doctrines laid down by the lawyers. Although on his death-bed Louis XIV ruefully admitted that he had "loved war too much", in his youth he had said that he would rather acquire territory by war than by negotiation. Philip V of Spain, in declaring war against England in 1704, asserted that "war is the ultimate court of appeal for the sovereigns of this world and they may honestly and openly have recourse to it". Frederick the Great wrote that all wars

> whose sole design is to guard against usurpation, to maintain unquestionable rights, to guarantee public liberty and to ward off the oppression and violence of the ambitious, are agreeable to justice. When sovereigns engage in wars of this kind they have no reason to reproach themselves with bloodshed; frequently they are forced to it by necessity and in such circumstances war is a lesser evil than peace.[54]

Not only was there no general prohibition of war. New justifications of it were found. It was generally accepted, by most of the legal writers and almost all statesmen, that a nation had the right to use force to recover property that had been taken from it or to redress an injury if this could not be done through legal procedures.[55] It was commendable to assist an ally under a treaty obligation (though, according to most of the lawyers, only if their cause was just). Many (including Grotius) said it was justifiable to assist an uprising in another state among a people unjustly suppressed (as Louis XIV helped the rebels in Hungary and Ireland, and the Maritime Powers assisted Protestant dissidents in France). And it was almost universally accepted, both by lawyers and statesmen, that war to maintain the balance of power was justifiable.

Another reason believed to justify war, by statesmen at least though rarely by lawyers, was if it was undertaken to uphold the "honour" of the state. In declaring war against Spain in 1718, George I stated that he "could no longer stand idly by for our honour has been impeached, the territories of our friends and allies unjustly invaded": he was therefore compelled to make war "in a cause in which the honour of our crown, the faithful observance of solemn treaties and pledges, and the safeguarding of our subjects' rights and interests are at stake".[56] Charles XII of Sweden declined to make peace after fourteen years of war on the grounds that "better times would not come until we get more respect in Europe than we now have. Such respect would not come till we are stronger in the military sense and display our willingness to use the sword in our own defence".[57]

Frederick the Great wrote after his attack on Silesia that this had been done partly from "a desire for glory . . . the satisfaction of seeing my name in the papers, and later in the history books, seduced me";[58] and later wrote that if he could conquer West Prussia, Pomerania, Mecklenburg and other lands his country might "cut a fine figure among the great powers of the world".[59]

Thus the rules and conventions of the day scarcely discouraged the making of war. But they did begin to place some restraints on the way it was waged. In theory the launching of a war against another state should be preceded by a "declaration" of war. This was the clear view of Grotius,[60] although Bynkershoek stated that it was not essential: "though it is a thing which may properly be done" an undeclared war was perfectly lawful.[61] Sometimes it was also held that, after the declaration, subjects of the enemy state who had been resident in the state which declared war should be allowed time to settle their affairs and leave the country. In practice, however, many wars were never declared on either side.[62] Sometimes it was because an incident quickly led to wider hostilities, before either government had made a decision to make war: as the confrontation over naval salutes between English and Dutch naval commanders led to war in 1652. But even when war had been deliberately planned it was often not declared: the Dutch were on these grounds especially indignant when England failed to declare war when joining France in war against them in 1672. Neither the king of Denmark nor Augustus of Saxony/Poland declared war on Sweden at the beginning of the Great Northern War (though Peter the Great did). Sometimes a declaration of war followed long after hostilities had already begun. Prussia occupied the Swedish port of Stettin and the surrounding area in 1713 but did not declare war until two years later. Similarly Britain sent her fleet to help capture the Swedish ports of Rügen and Stralsund in 1715 but declared war only two years after that. Frederick the Great issued no declaration of war when attacking Saxony in 1756 (ignoring her offer of neutrality, and proceeding even to make use of her armed forces to assist his own). Occasionally a failure to declare war was made a major issue: Napoleon was so angry that Britain resumed war against him in 1803 without a declaration that he kept 10,000 Englishmen then resident in France as prisoners of war.[63] Nor was it always unequivocally clear whether two states were at war at all. Frequently unofficial wars took place in colonial territories without any declaration of war, and little participation by the mother countries. Thus Portugal and United Provinces were effectively at war for forty years, with their navies providing support for local colonists in many places, before war was finally declared in 1657. England and France were at war with each other in the West Indies a year before war broke out in January 1666, and in Canada and India for nearly three years before they were officially at war in 1756. Whatever the international lawyers might say, therefore, in practice governments frequently engaged in war against each other without going through the formal procedure of a declaration.

Some agreements were reached to mitigate the worst barbarities of war. There were, for example, attempts to secure some improvement in the treatment of prisoners of war, previously often barbarous. Arrangements were sometimes made for prisoners to be repatriated even while war continued: England and the United Provinces reached an agreement of this kind in 1666. Exchanges were often undertaken: usually an equal number of the same rank on either side, or sometimes one officer in exchange for several soldiers. Sometimes instead of an exchange, prisoners were ransomed. Louis XIV was willing to pay for the return of French officers and men in this way.[64] Gradually it became common for "commissioners" to be appointed by each side to arrange such exchanges: they would be allowed entry to the enemy's territory, would identify the prisoners, list them, supervise their accommodation and treatment, and prepare a rota for the exchange.[65] In some cases prisoners were released only on condition that they did not take part in hostilities for a specified period.[66] In addition there were genuine efforts to ensure that prisoners were reasonably treated. Catherine the Great issued a *règlement* in 1778 that Turkish prisoners "should be treated with great humanity, provided with provisions . . . and not be allowed to lack for anything". Prussia and the US reached an agreement in 1785 under which it was laid down that prisoners were to be housed in sanitary conditions, in cantonments large enough to permit of exercise, should be well fed and be regularly visited by a commissioner.[67]

Understandings also came to be reached about the care of the wounded in war. Improved arrangements for medical care within each army (especially well-developed in those of Louis XIV) were matched by agreements between commanders concerning the way they treated each other's wounded. In 1689, at the beginning of the Nine Years War, the commander of the French forces reached agreement with the elector of Brandenburg, commanding German contingents, in which both agreed to respect the hospital and the wounded of the other.[68] A similar agreement was reached during the

War of Austrian Succession: Marshal Noailles for France and Lord
Stair, commanding the British Pragmatic Army, undertook to treat
each other's wounded with consideration. In 1759 a more comprehensive agreement was reached between French and British commanders: they undertook that they would care for the wounded who
fell into their hands, that doctors and other hospital staff would not
be taken prisoner, that the wounded who were captured would be
allowed to stay in hospital under guard, and would be adequately fed
and cared for (the cost to be repaid in due course). In the French
revolutionary wars an agreement was made between the French and
Austrian commanders under which the roads leading to hospitals
would be marked by special signs; troops would avoid using such
roads wherever possible. Before the period ended there were proposals for multilateral agreements concerning the treatment of the
wounded[69] (proposals that were not to be implemented until 1856).

There was also a genuine concern to reduce the sufferings of
civilians in war and to prevent the type of barbarities which had so
widely occurred during the Thirty Years War. It was generally
accepted that an occupying army had the right to demand "contributions", that is payment in cash or kind, from the local population.[70]
But it was increasingly held that these should not be excessive. Vatell
declared that "if a general wishes to enjoy an unsullied reputation he
must be moderate in his demands for contributions and proportion
them to the abilities of those on whom they are imposed".[71] The
rights of civilians began to be protected in other ways. Cartels
between opposing commanders, setting out the scale of contributions
they would levy, were reached even while a war continued.[72] Such
agreements also laid down that arable fields, meadows and gardens
were not to be destroyed. Improved discipline in armies reduced
outrages against civilians. A number of states published codes of war
laying down the conduct they expected from their own forces: in 1665
a German publication, *Corpus Juris Militarii*, set out the rules then in
force in a number of European states. It is doubtful if such rules were
everywhere observed but at least there was a recognition of the need
for some kind of regulations in this field.

There was even an attempt to exclude the use of certain weapons
believed to be particularly inhumane. There were not yet any multilateral agreements on such matters (that effort had to await the
nineteenth century, but there were *ad hoc* agreements among local
commanders. Thus in one case a cartel banned the use, on pain of
death, of poisoned projectiles or missiles of tin and other metals.[73]

Others proposed the banning of bombs, red-hot balls and other destructive missiles, or even the bombardment of cities altogether, because of the losses of civilian lives they caused.[74] On the whole such agreements were of limited effect. According to one historian of the period, they had "no direct effect that we can trace".[75] Even international lawyers tended to accept that, at least in public and declared war, there was no limit to the damage a belligerent could inflict on an enemy,[76] and in general armies frequently continued to conduct themselves with great brutality towards the peoples of the areas they occupied. No concern for civilian property or life was shown, for example, during the two devastations of the Palatinate undertaken by Louis XIV in 1674 and 1688 or that of Savoy by his general, Catinat, in 1690, or that of Bavaria by the forces of the Grand Alliance in 1704, or of East Prussia by Russian forces during the Seven Years War, or in countless other cases. If any rules concerning such matters were acknowledged at all, they were totally disregarded under the pressure of war. The aim was to cause the maximum difficulty for the opposing army; and if it caused hardship to the local civilians this was not usually of great concern. In the way they conducted their operations the commanders of the day, and the soldiers who served them, themselves often subject to appalling hardships during their military service, showed little squeamishness, still less respect for international convention. Conduct of that kind however now aroused considerable public indignation elsewhere on the continent; and the consciousness of this reaction may have acted in some cases as a restraining influence.

It was above all this increased concern of public opinion, or at least of the most enlightened section of it, which, slowly and uncertainly, brought some slight improvement in the way in which war was conducted. It began to be recognised that a ruler could win honour not only in launching a successful campaign but in securing an honourable peace. As Pomponne, Louis XIV's dovish foreign minister argued at the end of the Nine Years War, "it is not enough to overawe the princes of the empire by a show of military might: we must persuade them of his majesty's desire to include a just and reasonable peace".[77] De Callières, another of Louis' servants, showed himself equally well aware of the necessity for a ruler to demonstrate to world opinion that he was reasonable and moderate in his actions.

Every Christian Prince [he declared] ought to lay it down as a principal maxim of his government not to have recourse to arms for the maintenance and defence of his rights until he has once tried what he can do by the force of reason and persuasion.

The international lawyers held that peaceful methods, including attempts to secure mediation or arbitration, should be tried before recourse to the final arbitrament of war. However tolerant they were of war for certain purposes, they all proclaimed the superior merits of peace, denouncing the use of false justification for warlike action or even the prosecution of a just war from dishonourable motives. As Vattel, who was so widely read, put it: "the law of nature every way obliges [nations] to seek and cultivate peace" and to "promote it as far as lies in their power".[78]

Most of the rules concerning war that developed during this age were inchoate, imprecise and disputed. Even where such rules were recognised they were scarcely demanding. War, even offensive war, was almost everywhere held to be justifiable in some circumstances. Yet there was an increasing number, both among rulers and their subjects, who became more conscious of the heavy human cost entailed (see, for example, the comments of Maria Theresa quoted above). For this reason there were attempts to devise some relatively mild restraints on its worst barbarities. There was even some recognition of the need for something more: for a more general acceptance among states that, as the price of their sovereignty, they owed certain duties and obligations. Appeal was increasingly often made to "the public law of Europe", by which the behaviour of states ought to be guided. The need for rules of some kind, at least in certain areas, began slowly to be accepted. What did not yet exist, however, was a set of rules sufficiently clearly defined or widely respected to create a peaceful order among the states of the system.

BOOKS

Contemporary works

J. Borough, *The Sovereignty of the British Seas* (London, 1651).
C. van Bynkershoek, *Questions of Public Law*, 1737, English trs. (Oxford, 1930).
Hugo Grotius, *De Jure Pacis ac Belli*, 1646, English trs. (Oxford, 1725).
——, *Mare librum*, 1608, English trs. (New York, 1916).
G. F. de Martens, *Summary of the Law of Nations*, 1801, English trs. (London, 1802).

S. Pufendorf, *De Jure Naturae et Gentium*, 1688, English trs. (Oxford, 1934).
John Selden, *Mare Clausum* (London, 1635).
E. Vattel, *The Law of Nations*, 1758, English trs. (Washington, 1916).
Robert Ward, *Enquiry into the Foundation and History of the Law of Nations* (London, 1795).
Christian Wolff, *The Law of Nations*, 1749, English trs. (Oxford, 1934).

Modern works

G. Butler and S. Maccoby, *The Development of International Law* (London, 1928).
D. W. Fulton, *The Sovereignty of the Seas* (Edinburgh, 1901).
P. Jessup and F. Peak, *Neutrality*, vol. I: *The Origins* (New York, 1935).
I. de Madariaga, *Britain, Russia and the Armed Neutrality of 1780* (London, 1962).
A. Nussbaum, *A Short History of International Law* (New York, 1947).
E. Nys, *Les Origines du droit international* (Brussels, 1894).
D. Owen, *Declaration of War: A Survey of the Position of Belligerents and Neutrals* (London, 1889).
R. Pares, *Colonial Blockade and Mutual Rights* (Oxford, 1935).
F. S. Ruddy, *International Law in the Enlightenment* (New York, 1975).
D. A. Walker, *History of the Law of Nations* (Cambridge, 1899).
H. Wheaton, *Elements of International Law* (including a "sketch of the history of the science") (Philadelphia, 1836).

Conclusions: The Nature of the System

We have now examined some of the more significant features of the system of international relations that operated in Europe during this period. What evidence does our survey provide about the character of that system?

International systems, like other systems, are characterised above all by the nature of the component units of which they are composed and the motive-forces that animate them. In analysing the character of this system, therefore, it is necessary first to consider the units of which it was made up and the motives that impelled them. Those units, as we saw in Chapter 2, were by no means uniform. But they did share in common a number of characteristics and attitudes which influenced their behaviour, and so the nature of the system as a whole.

They consisted typically of "states", national political structures, in which ultimate political authority was held by "sovereigns", rulers who held a substantial degree of personal power, sometimes declared to be "absolute", though in practice limited by a variety of restraints, constitutional or traditional, financial or political. Whatever the constitutional structure, whether they were monarchies or republics, the decisions within such units were taken by a relatively small group of people, usually dominated by a single figure. Public opinion in the wider sense, although never altogether impotent, exercised little influence. These ruling groups were usually engaged in a systematic process of state-building: that is, seeking to develop the military, financial, commercial and industrial strength of their country to enable it to compete more effectively with other such states of the system for territory, status and power.

Their behaviour within the wider international system reflected these objectives. A major characteristic was that they were highly *individualistic*. Each took its own decisions about its own actions independently of each other. They recognised no superior authority; neither that of the pope (even in the religious affairs of their own states), nor of the emperor (even in Germany); still less that of other states or groups of states. The demand for independence was expressed above all in the doctrine of "sovereignty", which upheld the right of the ruler (the "sovereign") in each state to determine all affairs according to his unfettered will (Chapter 4). It was seen in the general detestation of "universal monarchy", any attempt by an individual state or ruler to acquire domination over a substantial part of the continent, or indeed any excessive power. And it received its most extreme expression in the doctrine of sovereign *equality*, which rejected the notion of a graduated class-structure among states and maintained that small and weak nations had equal rights with the most powerful. Sometimes it was this belief which provided the main justification for the balance of power doctrine (as when von Gentz praised the benefits of a "federative system", based on the balance of power, which would "ensure the independence of the weaker states by erecting a formidable barrier against the ambitions of the more powerful"[1]). In practice, however, the capacity of each state to maintain its rights, or even its independence, varied widely. If they were small – like Lorraine, or Bremen, or Courland – or if the process of state-building had been unsuccessful (as in Poland), they sometimes proved incapable of ensuring their independence or even their survival. But this demonstrated a difference in capacity, not in ambition. The demand for maximum independence and self-sufficiency was one that was universally shared among the members of the system.

Secondly, the states were highly *competitive*. They were concerned not only to succeed, but to succeed better than others. This desire was demonstrated in its most extreme (and indeed ludicrous) form in the intense competition for status, title, precedence and honours (Chapter 5 above), in which each state struggled to demonstrate that it deserved a higher place than possible rivals. But this was only the outward and visible sign of attitudes and ambitions that underlay the conduct of foreign affairs generally. There was little sense that states might share *common* interests, and so benefit sometimes from co-operative activity. On the contrary there was continual emphasis on *conflicting* interests, and unending rivalry: on the "essential jealousy" and "permanent enmity" which Louis XIV declared to exist between France and Spain, for example, so that "it was impossible to raise one without humbling the other". The desire to win success for one's own state thus often brought a demand to cause the maximum damage to another; as when Colbert exulted to his master that France was "flourishing not only in itself but also by the want which it has inflicted upon all neighbouring states"[2] or when British merchants declared that there was not sufficient trade for England and the United Provinces to share so that "one must down". In the effort to outdo rivals trade was cut off, colonies were seized, alliances were formed, wars were waged. Mutual envy was one of the most powerful motive forces within the system.

Thirdly, the intensity of this national competition brought wide-spread *unscrupulousness* in the conduct of states. The doctrine of *raison d'état*, which was hailed by Louis XIV as the "first of all laws by common consent", was held to justify breaches of faith and violations of elementary moral principle which would never have been accepted in normal inter-personal contact. The belief that state interest overrode all other obligations and constraints created the belief that virtually any action could be justified if it promoted state interests: allies could be deserted, friends could be betrayed, enemies could be destroyed. One effect of this attitude was that policies towards other states were highly calculating. This mercenary attitude is shown in a crude form in the buying and selling of territory with their populations; in the purchase of support from other rulers and ministers by bribery; and in the effort to quantify the relative value of different territories by reference to their area, population and tax-bearing capacity. It is shown in the coolly calculating way in which alliances were sought and later discarded. Above all, the whole idea of the "balance" of power, often seen as the guiding principle of international politics, implied that power could be measured, weighed and calculated in the scales, according to the principles of mechanics then being so rapidly developed and discussed. This affected the conduct of foreign affairs in many ways. States gave their assent to the Pragmatic Sanction, not according to any objective appraisal of its constitutional appropriateness in Austria's situation, but according to the value of the political concessions that could be won in return. Territory was apportioned at the end of wars, not according to any objective principles relating to language, culture, race, still less the wishes of the people involved, but as a result of crude bargaining on the basis of a balance of state interests.

Fourthly, this in turn brought about the latent *opportunism* which characterised the behaviour of governments within the system. All relationships among the states were short-term in character. The country that had been an ally in one war would become an enemy in the next, and vice versa. As Frederick the Great declared, in politics a state "should have no preference for one state and aversion against another", but should "follow blindly the interests of the state" (see above). This reflected the fact that all relationships with foreign nations were seen in purely instrumental terms; they were not based on any deep sense of friendship or affinity, ideological sympathies or personal loyalty, but only on the immediate advantages that could be gained from them. Thus, though alliances might be negotiated for twenty years or more or even be declared "perpetual", they rarely lasted in practice for more than a few years, and in some periods they were changed almost from year to year. This opportunism sometimes took still more unattractive forms. A state would be attacked at the moment when it was in the greatest difficulty: as when Charles X of Sweden attacked Poland when she was already prostrate from other causes; or when Charles II of England joined Louis XIV against his recent ally, the United Provinces, in 1670; or when Frederick II seized Silesia from Austria in 1740 when the latter country, under a new and youthful ruler, appeared least able to resist this; or when Prussia and Austria both joined Napoleon in his attack on Russia in 1812. The idea that inter-state relationships could be founded on the basis of goodwill, good faith, still less on lasting principles of behaviour, was one that was nowhere recognised.

Another striking feature of the system was the indifference shown to the internal political character of states. In general another country would be chosen as an ally, or as an enemy, without regard to the system of government that operated there, or to any other domestic factor. Religion, previously so important, now counted for nothing. Lutheran Denmark fought Lutheran Sweden as regularly and as bitterly as Catholic France fought Catholic Austria; while, conversely, Catholic states would now willingly join with Protestant (and even Moslem) states if it served their national interests. Differences in political systems were equally without influence. Monarchies allied themselves with republics and vice versa. The way a government conducted itself towards its own population – its "human rights" record, as it would be termed today – was even less significant. Even states that were to all appearances of totally alien cultures could be made into allies if it appeared advantageous at the time: so France entered into alliances with the Barbary states as well as with Turkey from time to time; Russia signed treaties with the Cossacks and the Crimean Tartars. Conversely, states of similar system and attitudes could be frequently at war with each other. For this reason a change of government, or even of political system, did not bring the fundamental change of foreign policy that might have been expected. England fought the Dutch under Cromwell and under Charles II alike. Sweden fought Russia for territory under parliamentary and absolutist regimes alike. France pursued expansionist policies under Louis XIV, under a revolutionary government and under Napoleon. The fact was that the basic motivations in inter-state rivalry, the demand for status and territory, remained constant however the character of governments and political systems might change.

Our survey also provides some negative evidence: it shows what features this system does *not* display. It demonstrates, first, that the balance of power principle, although continually appealed to as the justification for policy, was in practice frequently ignored. Under a genuine balance of power policy, as we noted in Chapter 1, states should have been willing to ally themselves with a weaker state for the sake of preventing a strong one from becoming still more powerful. But in practice states often chose the easier, the *short-term* strategy (denounced by von Gentz) of allying with a powerful state to get the better of a weaker rival. So, to take only a few examples, Charles II allied himself with France in 1670 for short-term financial and political advantage, regardless of the long-term danger of French aggrandisement; Denmark and Saxony allied themselves with Russia in 1700, though the result was only to replace the immediate menace of Sweden with another that was ultimately far more dangerous, that of Russia; Austria allied herself with Russia against Turkey in 1735–9 and in 1787–91, though this ultimately helped Russia to become a far more dangerous rival than Turkey could ever be; France and other countries aided Prussia against Austria in 1740–5, though this assisted the emergence of the European power which was ultimately to be the major threat to France; almost every state of the continent allied itself with France at one time or another during the Napoleonic wars, and so made her ultimate defeat far more difficult. Such actions demonstrate that there was certainly no *automatic* process, as is sometimes suggested,[3] by which states followed enlightened balance-of-power policies. On the contrary, in calculating their interest at any one moment, they were often more influenced by the opportunity of *immediate* local gain than by any consideration of the long-term continental balance. The most that can be said is that when, eventually, the power of any single state came to be insupportable (like that of France in 1688 or in 1811–13) the majority could normally be relied on to join together to end that dominance.

Secondly, the history of the period scarcely supports the assertion, commonly made, that this was an age of limited objectives or general moderation, either in aims or methods. Because many of the governments of the period were of similar character, dominated by personal rulers and powerful aristocracies, served by ministers and diplomats of similar class background, it is sometimes suggested that they were willing to restrain their ambitions to decent proportions and to engage in gentlemanly combat which avoided excessive force or casualties.[4] It is true that wars in this age did not normally aim to secure the "unconditional surrender" of the enemy; but this has been a relatively infrequent demand in the whole history of warfare. Far from fighting restricted wars of "manoeuvre", the rival states fought strenuous campaigns, covering large geographical areas, in several different countries, over many years, to achieve highly ambitious objectives. The determination of Charles XII of Sweden, maintained over nearly twenty years, to conquer with a relatively small striking force most of the north of the continent; or of Peter the Great to fight, in two successive wars which lasted continuously for 35 years, to extend Russian borders vast distances to the west and south; of Frederick the Great challenging most of the other powers of the continent for six years almost single-handed; of Pitt the Elder seeking to wrest control of huge areas of Canada and India; or of Napoleon seeking to win domination of the entire continent, can scarcely be accused of being modest in ambition. Nor did the governments of the age show themselves willing to settle easily for compromise terms: on the contrary they sometimes (like the Grand Alliance in the War of Spanish Succession, to whom Louis XIV was willing to concede almost every demand in 1709) prevented a settlement being reached by maintaining unrealistic demands which went well beyond what the opposing side, even in extremity, was willing to concede. And far from being "moderate" in the conduct of warfare, the armies of this age often behaved with extreme brutality, destroying cities, burning crops and slaughtering large numbers of innocent civilians, over and above the bloodthirsty conduct of hand-to-hand warfare involving heavy casualties* and recognising few restraints.

Nor is it the case, as is often suggested** that there was a conven-

---

* Frederick the Great estimated that 1 in 9 of the population of Prussia perished during the Seven Years War: a higher proportion than has occurred even in the "total warfare" of modern times.

**Kaplan for example states in *System and Process* that it is one of the "essential rules" of this system that an actor should stop fighting rather than "eliminate an essential national actor" (pp. 23–4). E. W. Gulick in *Europe's Classical Balance of Power* (Ithaca, N.Y., 1955) suggests that the preservation of the system implied the "necessity of preserving the significant counterweights in the system of equilibrium" (pp. 33 and 76). Whether or not this is a rule that *ought* to have been observed in theory, it is not one that the members of the historical system appear to have known.

tion or "rule" of the system that no significant state should be eliminated. The historical record provides no basis for this contention. On the contrary, throughout the period not only were a large number of very small states continually disappearing from the map, but a significant number of middle-sized powers were also suppressed: Venice, Genoa, Tuscany, Lorraine, Courland, Holstein, Hamburg, Bremen and other German states, among others. Norway was absorbed by Denmark, Belgium by Austria, Lithuania by Poland, Estonia and Livonia (Latvia) by Russia, Hungary by Austria, and most of Italy by Spain and Austria. Nor were even the largest states spared from this fate. Poland, at the beginning of our period was the second largest and third most populous state of the system, controlling huge territories stretching from Cracow to Smolensk, from the Baltic to the Black Sea; yet, because of its political weakness, it was before the end of the period systematically eliminated by three of its neighbours, with little scruple or regret and without effective resistance from elsewhere. Nor was this an isolated case. In 1668 the rulers of Austria and France agreed between them the elimination of Spain, only recently the dominant power of the continent, from the face of Europe, by sharing out all its component parts among themselves. In 1725 Austria and Spain, in allying with each other, secretly agreed to partition France between them if there were a war. In 1732 France, Bavaria and Saxony discussed a partition of Austria if Maria Theresa were to inherit there; and in 1740–1 during the War of Austrian Succession the anti-Austrian alliance planned the virtual destruction of the Austrian state and the distribution of most of its component parts among each other. In 1756 Austria, Russia and France planned the virtual elimination of Prussia through a partition of her territories among themselves.[5] In 1778–84 Austria planned the elimination of Bavaria from the map of Europe. In 1795 Russia, Austria and Prussia planned the partition of Turkey. Napoleon had no hesitation in totally rewriting the atlas to suit his own purposes. And in 1814, on the eve of victory over France, Prussia seriously proposed the partitioning of French territory. If in practice, despite these ambitions, most of the major states survived, it was not because of some generally accepted convention or "rule" of the system, still less because of the "moderation" of governments, but because, as Frederick the Great noted, given the strength of the rival alliances, it was not usually in practice possible to achieve the overwhelming victory which alone would have secured those ends.[6] Most wars ended in a draw which frustrated attempts to destroy a rival utterly.

Nor, finally, can it be said, as is sometimes suggested, that the system was sustained by a general presumption that the previous status quo was to be restored,[7] still less that only minor territorial changes occurred. In fact huge territorial changes resulted from the wars of this period. Sweden was transformed from a large imperial power, controlling Finland and most of the south of the Baltic, to a small state confined to something like her present borders. Poland lost the Ukraine, Belorussia, Podolia and other substantial areas before being finally eliminated. Spain lost all her Italian territories, Franche Comté and the southern Netherlands. Turkey lost vast tracts of land in the north to Russia and Hungary and substantial parts of the Balkans to Austria. Prussia was changed from a group of scattered lands to a consolidated state with a population nearly three times bigger than before. Britain acquired important Mediterranean assets, as well as a huge collection of overseas colonies. Even a cursory glance at the maps on pp. 182–3 will give an idea of the extent of the territorial changes which occurred.

It is true that after one or two particular wars there was agreement to restore the status quo in most areas (for example, after the War of Austrian Succession in western Europe and after the Seven Years war in eastern Europe). But after many others (including the two large-scale Northern Wars, the Eastern War of 1683–99, the War of Spanish Succession and the Napoleonic wars, very great territorial changes took place. The theoretical concern for the status quo laid down in earlier treaties was often forgotten when the chance of useful acquisitions occurred. The only real constraint to territorial change was the power available to other states seeking to prevent it. And because the larger states were not in a position to destroy each other, the main territorial changes were, in practice, mainly at the expense of the smaller ones (often eliminated altogether), and of weaker ones, such as Sweden, Poland and Turkey (which lost large parts of their territory). The reality, therefore, is not of a general restoration of the status quo: it is the steady accretion in the power and territory of the larger states at the expense of the weaker ones.

THE EUROPEAN SOCIETY OF STATES

Whether or not they recognised the existence of a "system", the statesmen and writers of this period often accepted the existence of an international society of a kind: they recognised, that is, that there was a close interrelationship between the different states of the continent, and that this created – or at least ought to create – a sense of mutual obligation among them. Sometimes this even led to the idea that there existed a community of states which had interests of its own over and above those of the individual states.

No doubt this sentiment was not equally shared. Among the statesmen it was perhaps most clearly expressed by William III, the ruler of two European states and foremost advocate of balance-of-power policies, who habitually spoke and wrote of the "general interests of Europe" and of the need to defend the "liberty of all Europe".[8] Among writers there were many who held that "Europe" constituted a single, closely interrelated organism which might even be compared to a single state. Thus Fénelon described it as "a kind of society and general commonwealth";[9] Vattel wrote of it as a "sort of republic";[10] von Gentz as the "European commonwealth";[11] the Abbé de Pradt as a "single social body which one might rightly call a European Republic".[12] Vogt, a well-known writer on international relations and the balance of power, wrote a book entitled *About the European Republic*.[13] Voltaire used the same image in describing Europe as "a kind of great republic divided into several states".[14] John Bellers, the English Quaker, even wrote a work entitled *Some Reasons for a European State*,[15] proposing an annual European "Congress, senate, diet or parliament" to settle disputes about boundaries or rights; a "Supreme Court" to decide inter-state disputes "without bloodshed"; an agreement on the principles of a "standing European law"; and a universal guarantee among the states of the system[16] (that is, a continent-wide collective security system), not to speak of a General Council to settle disputes on doctrine among different Christian sects.[17]

Many went further. They accepted that recognition of this European entity implied the existence of a "system" of international relations within it. So, for example, Fénelon wrote of the "general system of Europe". Vattel held that "Europe forms a political system and integral body, closely connected by the relations and different interests of the nations inhabiting this part of the world".[18] Von Gentz wrote of "the political system of Europe" the balance of power ought to maintain.[19] Brougham wrote of the union of European states as "one connecting system, obeying certain laws and actuated for the most part by a common principle". De Callières believed that "all the states of Europe have the necessary ties with each other which makes them to be looked upon as members of the same Commonwealth".[20] The existence of this supposed system, it was generally accepted, placed certain restraints on the freedom of action of the individual states.

Some believed that the essential feature of the system was a recognition of common values and principles. So Voltaire, in the passage quoted before, asserted that, although some of the states of Europe were "monarchical, the others mixed, the former aristocratic, the latter popular", none the less all "have the same religious foundation, even if divided into several confessions. They all have the same principles of public law and politics, unknown to the other parts of the world.[21] Rousseau wrote that "all the powers of Europe form a kind of system among themselves, which unites them by the same religion, by the same law of nations, by morals, literature, and by a sort of an equilibrium which is a necessary result of them all, and which, though nobody studies to preserve it, is not so easily destroyed as many people imagine".[22] A similar idea was expressed by the international lawyer, Savigny who maintained that "international law as we see it existing among the Christian states of Europe" rested on a "community of ideas founded upon a common origin and religious base". And the better known international lawyer, Bynkershoek, believed that the European system depended, at root on a common recognition of the "law of nations", which he defined as "that which is observed . . . between nations, if not among all at least among the greater part, and those the most civilized".

This sense that the states of Europe all belonged to a common system, resting on common values and principles, was encouraged by the cosmopolitanism of the age. It was not only that most of the states (if Turkey is excluded) inherited a common (even if deeply divided) Christian faith. They shared the same European civilisation dating from classical times. Latin was still a widely used common language for all legal and philosophical works (even if increasingly replaced by French for diplomatic purposes). They enjoyed a similar level of material and technical development. They shared a common culture: well-educated Englishmen read Voltaire and Leibniz, just as the educated Frenchman (or Germans) knew Hobbes and Locke. This common culture was shared by many of the rulers and statesmen of the day: so Frederick II of Prussia and Catherine II of Russia welcomed to their courts writers and thinkers from all over Europe.

It was not only the culture that was transnational: so were the rulers themselves and their families. Many states were ruled by foreign dynasties, and the rest were deeply intermarried with them. Their senior ministers and advisers often came from foreign lands: such figures as von Fürstenburg, the German in the service of Louis XIV; Alberoni and Ripperda, Italian and Dutch ministers to Spanish rulers; Göetz, the German chief official of Charles XII of Sweden; Grotius and Pufendorf, the Dutch international lawyers who served his forebears; the Bernstorffs, the German ministers who controlled Danish policy for thirty years. Where a royal family ruled two separate states (as in Saxony/Poland and in Britain/Hanover) or retained close links with a foreign dynasty (like the Bourbon and Hapsburg rulers of Italian states) or ruled in two different countries (like William III), they inevitably acquired a vision that was more than purely national. These close inter-state links inevitably helped to inculcate the idea that all belonged to a common European system. It was for this reason that Burke could write in 1796 that "no European can be a complete exile in any part of Europe".[23]

It would be wrong to overstate the influence such ideas had on state behaviour. At most times statesmen were far more aware of the rights and interests of their own particular country than of its obligations to the system to which it belonged. The awareness of the wider society and the widespread deference paid to the European system or the European balance is thus at first sight something of a paradox. There has rarely been an age in which such emphasis was placed on the independence and sovereignty of the individual states, in which so little regard was paid to obligations to others or the rights of neighbours. Yet at the same time there has rarely been (at least until recent times) such frequent reference to the existence of a wider European "republic", "commonwealth" or "system" within which all shared a common existence.

This is perhaps ultimately not such a paradox as it appears. It was partly because the states of the period were so individualistic and self-seeking, because they were so frequently engaged in bitter and expensive conflicts with each other, that it became so necessary to insist on their obligations to the wider international society to which they belonged. Only this could reduce the risk of international anarchy, or the exploitation of superior power by the stronger states, above all the domination of the entire system by a single state. And perhaps the most striking expression of this demand for a recognition of the needs of the system as a whole was the continual reiteration of the need, in the interests of all, to maintain the "balance of power" among the members of the system.

WAS THERE A SYSTEM?

If this was the conception of the European community that existed
during this period, how far can there be said to have been a "system"
of international relations? When the statesmen and writers of the
period spoke of such a system, as they frequently did, did they
describe a reality of international life at the period or was it simply
empty rhetoric and wishful thinking?

It was suggested in Chapter 1 that for a set of social arrangements
to be described as a "system" four conditions need to be fulfilled. It
may be useful to recall these in seeking to answer this question.

The first condition was that there must be a clear *interconnection*
between the parts to make it a coherent and interrelated whole. How
far was this condition fulfilled in our society of states?

There was, it is true, a system of diplomatic relations which
represented the principal, formal link between the states. But most of
the states had diplomatic relations with only a few others; and smaller
states had them with none. In these circumstances the existence of
diplomatic links cannot be regarded as providing the kind of connections a system requires. If there was a system, membership was
clearly possible even where no diplomatic ties existed.

Which then were the states which can be regarded as members of
the system? Did it, for example, have clear international boundaries?
It would have been generally accepted that most of the states of Asia
and Africa, such as they were, did not belong to it. They were too
distant, too weak, too exotic, too "primitive", in the eyes of their
European contemporaries, to be accepted as viable members of the
system. Even states such as China, Persia and some Indian states,
having developed institutions and controlling large populations and
territories, were generally felt to be beyond its confines.

But there were some more difficult cases. There was a legitimate
difference of view whether, for example, Turkey belonged. According to some, only Christian states could be accepted as members of
the system, in which case Turkey clearly did not belong. She undoubtedly controlled substantial European territory, and exercised
dominant power in other parts (such as Wallachia and Moldavia)
which were not directly under her control. But she was, by culture
and religion and tradition, so different that in the eyes of most she
could not be regarded as a participant within the European concert.
Though even before this period began she had accepted diplomatic
representatives from elsewhere, she was not enthusiastic about the

custom[24] and did not send them to other courts until 1793, then only to four (Paris, Vienna, London and Berlin) and that only temporarily. She frequently violated the diplomatic codes that were generally accepted by other states (for example, by her habit of imprisoning the ambassadors of foreign countries as soon as war was declared against them). And even at the end of the period informed observers (such as Burke in debating the Ochakov issue in the British Parliament) denied that Turkey was generally accepted as belonging to the European system or the European balance of power.[25]

Even Russia was not generally considered to belong to the system at the beginning of the period. She had no diplomatic relations with any other state until the time of Peter the Great. She had no traditional links with western Europe. She had not participated in the wars of that part of the continent (not even the Thirty Years War), nor in the Westphalia peace-making. Even her participation in the war against Turkey of 1683–97 with other European powers and the (separate) treaty which she concluded at its end did not win for her full acceptance within the European system. The French *Almanach Royal* did not list the Romanovs among the reigning families of Europe until 1716.[26] Only when she signed the Treaty of Nystad in 1721 was Russia universally admitted as having joined the family of nations and the European "system".

But it was not only the geographical boundary of the system that was uncertain. There were comparable problems as a result of the huge disparities in size and power among the units. Could it really be said that the several hundred mini-states of Germany and Italy belonged in any meaningful sense to the same system of international relations as the fifteen or so largest countries of the continent? Apart from differences in size, there were considerable differences in their political status. Some were not fully independent, but were claimed to be under the ultimate authority of a "suzerain"; and these could scarcely be full members of the "system". Finally, there were also substantial cultural differences: were the Barbary states (which were sufficiently independent to sign treaties with West European countries), the Knights of Malta, the dukes of Courland and Holstein, or the Hanseatic cities of sufficiently similar political status and diplomatic tradition to be integrated within the same system of international relations as the governments of France, Austria, Britain and Sweden? In practice, because of such differences, there were *degrees* of participation. There was something like a two-tier system. Full membership was confined to a relatively small number of the larger and more politically organised states; while the great majority of smaller and weaker entities existed only on its fringes, deeply affected by the outcome of the rivalries and agreements among the more powerful, but able to do little to influence them.

Even among the independent states participation was not equal. The outermost states – Russia before 1700, Turkey and the Barbary states for most of the period, the principalities throughout – were only loosely and intermittently connected with the rest. There were also geographical divisions within the area. North and south were not always fully integrated with each other: the Scandinavian states took no part in the main wars of the western and southern states, while the latter took no part in the two Northern Wars and the subsequent conflicts between Sweden and Russia. On the other hand the abandonment of the system of separate secretaries of state for north and south Europe in both Britain and Prussia towards the end of the eighteenth century indicated that this division was thought to be diminishing. There was also an east–west division. For a time in the late eighteenth century (as we saw earlier) the two parts of the continent were largely disconnected, with the eastern powers preoccupied by Poland and other regional issues, while the western states were engaged in colonial and maritime conflicts outside Europe, and with little connection between the two halves. There were also non-geographical divisions. Some of the lesser states of the continent, having little power and few contacts, were only marginally connected with the main strand of European politics, and the larger states undertook their relations with each other with little or no regard for them. In considering the international "system" in this period, therefore, we are mainly considering the interactions of the twelve to fifteen principal powers of the continent. Only of these can it reasonably be said that they were sufficiently closely linked to represent a coherent system.

The second condition which we described for the establishment of a "system" was that there should be not only a connection but regular *communication* between its parts. This is because the operation of a social system must depend upon actions taken on the basis of knowledge obtained from other parts of the system. Such a network of information clearly existed within this society. It came partly from unofficial sources: from spies, travellers, newspapers, and other accounts, or from messengers sent for specific purposes. But it was mainly provided by the system of diplomacy. Among the major states this provided a reasonably regular and reliable source of information about events elsewhere. Even these states, it is worth remembering, had diplomatic representation only in a dozen or so capitals for most of the period, though for some the number had risen to twenty-odd by the time it ended (a far larger number of smaller states lacked even this source of information). Governments generally were thus far less well informed about events in other parts of the continent than they were to become in subsequent ages. But they were not so ignorant, and so cut off from each other, that a system of a kind could not be operated. On this count too, therefore, it must be accepted that, at least for the major states, the conditions for a system existed.

The third condition we suggested must be fulfilled in any social system was that there must be a tradition of intercourse sufficient to create common expectations among the members. For anything like a "system" to operate, it was necessary for one state to be able to rely on another responding to particular events and actions in a reasonably predictable fashion. Otherwise, even though information might have been transmitted, it could not have brought about the results which a functioning system requires. Among the principal states at least some such common pattern of expectations existed. If Turkey is excluded, all the states shared the traditions, ideas and objectives of "Christendom" (even if a sharply divided Christendom). They had developed rules and conventions concerning diplomatic procedures and inter-state intercourse which influenced and harmonised their actions towards each other. They possessed a common culture, a common literary and artistic tradition. They were linked by the inter-marriage of royal families and aristocracy, and the emerging cosmopolitan tradition in all the major capitals. As one of the major international lawyers of the day wrote:

> The resemblance in manners and religion, the intercourse of commerce, the frequency of treaties of all sorts, and the ties of blood between sovereigns have so multiplied the relations between each particular state and the rest, that one may consider Europe (particularly the Christian states of it) as a society of nations and states, each of which has its laws, its customs and its maxims, but which cannot be put in execution without observing a great deal of delicacy towards the rest of the society.[27]

In this respect too one of the basic conditions for the creation of a viable system existed.

The fourth and final condition we suggested for the establishment of a system was that there should be some *regularity* in the relationships undertaken. It is this above all which characterises anything that can properly be termed as a "system", and which we should need to find to be able to decide conclusively that there existed a system in this age. The regular responses which one might hope to find in this case are those needed to maintain the relationships characteristic of the system including a reasonable equilibrium among the parts. It would require, therefore, that, as soon as one state had acquired a power that was excessive, or "exhorbitant" (to use a term that was widely used at the time), others would combine together to hold it in check, to "reduce it to its due proportion of it". If this policy had been consistently pursued by every state, or even by the majority of states, it should at least have had the effect of preventing undue domination by a single nation; and, if the countervailing power had been mobilised early enough, it might even, by deterring the exercise of superior power by any state that had acquired it, have maintained peace within the system as well. These two objectives, to prevent domination and to maintain peace, are those that "balance of power" policies were most generally claimed to secure. Though frequently confused, they are distinct. And in assessing the effectiveness (if any) of the "system", it is necessary to consider each of them separately.

In considering the operation of the balancing system briefly in Chapter 3 we saw that, for much of the age, it worked reasonably well as a means of preventing any single state acquiring excessive power. In the first of the four periods we considered, alliances successfully countered the expansive policies of Sweden (1660) and France (1668 and, with somewhat less success, 1678). In the second period the policy was applied successfully against France (1697 and 1713–14), Turkey (1699 and 1718), Russia (1717–20) and Sweden (1721). In the third period there was a significant growth in the power of Prussia (1740–5) and of Britain (1748–63), but in each case this was checked or even reduced in subsequent wars fought largely for that purpose; though no significant steps were taken to prevent the considerable growth in Russian power during the same period. Finally, in the last quarter of the age, the dramatic growth that took place in France's power was eventually countered by the combined actions of other states, but only after prolonged hesitations and defections which placed major powers with, rather than against, the main threat to the balance. These had the effect that for a period of fifteen years, between 1797 and 1812, the balance of power failed to operate effectively, even among the major powers: a single state was allowed to succeed during that period in acquiring domination through the continent.

So far as the balance among the major powers is concerned, therefore, it could be held that the responses that they made to any threat that occurred were sufficiently regular to be regarded as "systematic"; and this did serve to prevent any prolonged dominance by a particular state. Though there were, inevitably, some changes in the relative position each state occupied, none was allowed to secure for long a position of unchallenged supremacy. This is not a particularly surprising or notable achievement: there is no reason why, given the distribution of population and resources among the principal states of the continent, any single one should ever have been in a position to dominate the rest; and even when on occasion one was able to do so temporarily (like France from 1797 to 1812), it is unlikely that it would have been able to maintain that domination for long. But if the *overall* balance within the continent is considered, then even on this count the system was scarcely a success. For if some kind of balance was maintained between the major states, this was often only at the expense of lesser powers. As we have seen, these were gradually weakened or even destroyed. Spain was progressively denuded of her possessions, both in the Netherlands and Italy. Sweden was stripped of a substantial part of its (admittedly inflated) territories; Poland was progressively pillaged and finally destroyed; Turkey, with a few intermissions, was consistently robbed of her possessions from 1699 onwards; Portugal and Saxony lost substantial territory; and the once-proud states of Italy were, with the exception of Savoy, reduced to puppets under foreign rulers, Spanish or Austrian. If the "balance of power" was taken to mean a stable equilibrium among the states of the continent as a whole, it was patently not achieved. On the contrary, the weak were made still weaker, quite often to the benefit of the strong. By the end of the period the affairs of the continent were to a large extent under the control of the five largest powers.

Still less was there any systematic attempt to preserve the peace. During the course of the period there were a dozen major wars, each involving a number of states, and many lesser ones. There was hardly a year in which a war was not taking place somewhere. The principal powers were at war for almost as long as they were at peace (in some cases longer): an incomparably larger proportion than in the century that followed, and scarcely less than in the years before 1648.[28] And many of these were long and expensive wars, often covering different regions of Europe, and sometimes extra-European areas as well.

The failure of the system to maintain the peace was to some extent inevitable. To a large extent war was the instrument by which the balance was maintained. There was little attempt to *anticipate* breaches of the peace and so prevent them. Only of the intentions of aggressive powers had been clearly known in advance and effective alliances established to deter warlike action, could the system have operated to maintain the peace. But in practice there was no inclination among the states of the period, however much they might proclaim their devotion to that end and to the balance of power as the means to it, to act in that way. When Louis XIV was preparing his war against the United Provinces in 1668–72, neighbouring states, far from allying to deter him, on the contrary flocked to his banner in order to share in the profit. When Austria was blatantly robbed of her territory by Prussia in 1740, other states of the continent, far from joining in an alliance to evict her, on the contrary joined her in seeking to despoil the victim of further territories. When, fifteen years later, Austria herself planned war against Prussia to recover the lost lands, her neighbours, far from allying with her enemy to protect it, joined her in a war of conquest. When France secured total domination of the continent from 1795 onwards, other major powers, far from joining together in resistance, from time to time joined her in further aggressions. In other words, there never existed a sufficient commitment to the goal of deterring and defeating aggression to induce the states of the system to act consistently against a potential threat to the peace. There never existed the willingness to renounce immediate national advantage to promote the common interest in resisting or preventing aggression on which a collective security system ultimately depends.

In other words, though there was a frequent *tendency* to combine against threats to the peace, it did not have the regularity and consistency which an effective system would have required. If there was a system at all, it did not result from a dedicated willingness among governments to place the general interest of the continent above that of their own state. It resulted only from an eventual and often unwilling decision to turn against a particular state (such as France under Louis XIV or Napoleon) when it had unquestionably become a menace to the independence of the others. In other words, the actions taken were reactive rather than planned: a response to a domination already secured, rather than a deliberate, "systematic" attempt to prevent domination being won in the first place. A willingness to react sooner or later (often later) after disaster had already occurred represented a fragile basis on which to erect a "system". It was not self-evident that governments would always be sufficiently far-sighted to put their long-term interest (in preventing domination by a single power) above their short-term interest (in profiting from his successes). If Napoleon's gamble in Russia had succeeded, if he had effectively brought that country under his control as he planned, would Austria and Prussia have so readily turned against him, as they did after his failure in 1812–13? It seems unlikely. In that case France's domination could have lasted for many years and even decades; and the balance of power mechanism would then, even more obviously, be seen to have failed.

On this final test, therefore, the system only narrowly qualifies. It is just possible to discern a tendency among the member-states to combine against a major threat. But this was spasmodic and unreliable, above all belated. It can therefore scarcely be reckoned as systematic. In so far as the required response occurred, it was not the result of commitment to the abstract principle that a balance be maintained. It was rather a recognition, by some states at least, that over the long term their own *particular* interests demanded that they should prevent any country from becoming all-powerful.

Even so, if we take our four tests together it would be hard to deny that a system of some sort existed in this age. The system was less clear-cut and consistent – in a word less systematic – than most of those who wrote about it so enthusiastically suggested. Individual states frequently acted in ways that were not consistent with the system. But there was sufficient regularity in behaviour among the majority of states in the majority of situations for it to be not altogether fanciful to maintain that they were operating within a system of a kind. However fragile, that tendency represented perhaps a foundation on which future generations might be able to build a more viable international system.

THE WEAKNESSES OF THE SYSTEM

But even if there did exist a system of a kind, it had manifest weaknesses.

First, the idea of the balance was fatally imprecise. A clear implication of the concept was that relative power could be accurately assessed so that it could be counteracted. But there was little serious effort to do this. There was, as we saw, at the end of the period an effort to compare the relative value of different *territories*, in terms of area, population, resources and financial strength, but there was no attempt to do the same for entire states. The surveys that were made of the states of the system – for example by Pufendorf,[29] Frederick the Great in his *Political Testaments*, Favier,[30] and others – compared them only in the most general outlines. Even the writers most concerned with the balance of power, such as David Hume, von Gentz and Brougham, did not suggest how the power of individual states was to be measured and compared. Very occasionally rulers did count up the armed forces of an opponent, to measure the likely outcome of a war: as Maria Theresa did, for example, in urging her son to abandon the War of Bavarian Succession in 1778–9.[31] But even when they were made, such comparisons often left out of account some of the factors that were in practice most important: administrative strength, financial system, leadership, the morale and effectiveness of armed forces, the loyalty of populations, for example. But it was these factors that had the decisive effect on the outcome of wars, and ultimately determined the balance. It was because of them that individual states were in practice able to defy apparently insuperable odds against them: as Louis XIV did in 1709–10, and Frederick the Great in 1760–1. Because of these imponderables the balance did not operate always as might have been expected. To operate a system which was said to be based on the balance of power it would have been necessary to undertake far more accurate measures of the balances that existed than were customarily made at this time and to mobilise them accordingly.

Secondly, there is little evidence that the balance of power, whether or not it was accurately known, had the effect on national conduct that the theory implied. According to the theory a state which had aggressive intentions would be deterred by the strength of the alliance formed against it: that "alliance of many princes and states" which, in the words of Frederick the Great, would create a balance "solely designed for maintaining the peace and security of mankind"; the "league well-concerted and strictly observed" by which, in the words of Walpole, "bounds would be set to the turbulence of ambition" and the "torrent of power restrained". But there was little evidence that in practice, even when confronted with overwhelmingly powerful coalitions, states were deterred. Louis XIV in 1688 had every reason to expect that any attack he made would be met with the combined force of most of the rest of Europe, yet he was not restrained from launching his assaults on Cologne and the Palatinate; Frederick the Great in 1756 was not deterred from invading Saxony by his knowledge that a far superior coalition was being built against him; revolutionary France was not deterred by the might of Austria and Prussia, and eventually most of the rest of Europe, in 1793–5. If even a *preponderance* of power had so little effect on the actions of states, it was unlikely that a *balance* could be expected to prevent warlike action by an ambitious ruler who saw the opportunity of aggrandisement. The theory, borrowing the language of mechanics, implied that the actions of states could be determined by mechanical forces. But it seriously underplayed the psychological factors influencing the behaviour of national leaders, which was often less rational and deterministic than the theory suggested. And the fact that the policy of states was so often determined by a single individual made these subjective factors even more important than they might otherwise have been.

Another weakness of the system was that it could operate effectively only if there existed a widespread commitment to the status quo: only, that is, if all agreed that whenever a state committed a breach of the peace, the majority would combine to bring about a restoration of the situation which existed before the war began. Unfortunately no such commitment existed. A large proportion of the states were continually seeking to change the status quo in their own favour. They were, therefore, only too willing to profit from a breach of the peace, and to seek further booty for themselves, rather than virtuously coming to the defence of the existing territorial settlement when any act of aggression took place. France was continually seeking the opportunity to expand towards her "natural" boundaries, Austria to win back Alsace or territory occupied by the Turks, Russia to secure access to the Baltic and Black Sea, Spain to win territory in Italy, Savoy to acquire a little more of the Milanese, Britain to win further colonies abroad, Prussia to acquire territory that would join her scattered lands, and so on. They were not therefore willing, when a breach of the peace occurred, to co-operate obediently in restoring the situation which had existed beforehand. Even if such a desire had existed, there was often disagreement about where the status quo lay: in whose hands, for example, would the status quo have placed Strasbourg after 1681, or Gibraltar after 1713, or Schleswig after 1720, or Silesia after 1740, to take only a few examples? Where the definitions of normality diverged so widely, a commitment to re-establish it could not provide a guide to effective common action.

Still less could the system operate, as some of the theorists held, to maintain the peace of the continent. This was in any case a highly ambitious objective. Warfare was so frequent, so institutionalised, that it was taken for granted that sooner or later – usually sooner – a new war would occur somewhere or other, and would quite likely engulf much of the continent. Many states were aligned within alliances that made it more likely that if any such conflict occurred they would become involved. War was widely extolled as a glorious endeavour. There was little attempt to distinguish between offensive and defensive actions. Preventive war was generally regarded as justifiable. The balance-of-power system did not significantly affect these attitudes, or, therefore, the likelihood of war. On the contrary, since the balance habitually failed to *deter* attacks by one state or another, it was only through war that the balance could be restored. Even if, therefore, the system operated somewhat uncertainly to prevent the domination of a single power, it can certainly not be said to have operated to maintain the peace of the continent.

This general toleration of warfare points to the final, and perhaps the most serious, weakness of the system. For the system did not rest on any generally accepted principles of international conduct that might have maintained stability, still less peace, among its members. There were no accepted rules about when, or whether, the use of force was justified. Though it was widely asserted that only "just" wars were permissible, there was no agreement about which wars were just and which were not. If there was any consideration of the matter at all (and probably few rulers cared deeply about the question) the most common presumption was that the wars that one's own nation engaged in were "just", and those of its enemies "unjust". The main duty of a ruler or a minister was to promote the interest of their own state; and there did not exist, even among the international lawyers, any higher morality, emphasising the iniquity of war in general, which might have restrained such action. Nor was the morality of warfare simple. Who was responsible, for example, for initiating the War of Spanish Succession: the emperor Leopold in sending his troops to take Milan in 1701, or Louis in accepting the will by which Charles II disposed of his own state? Who was responsible for causing the Seven Years War: Frederick II because he fired the first shot against Saxony, or Austria in preparing a war designed to recover lost territory, and perhaps to destroy Prussia permanently? Who was responsible for initiating the French revolutionary wars: Austria and Prussia in issuing successive threats and ultimata against the revolutionary government in France, or that government in finally declaring war against them? In a society where war was endemic, there were no generally accepted principles to provide clear answers to such questions.

Yet for all these weaknesses the system did represent an advance of a kind. For the true importance of the doctrine of the balance was that it asserted the principle that the states of the system had obligations beyond their own immediate interest. It recognised that they all had their being within a wider society, which had interests of its own, that transcended those of the individual states. Not many were as detached and disinterested as Fénelon who recommended that the other states of the system should take collective action against his own if it sought to profit unduly from the Spanish succession. But there was a general understanding that no state was an island (whatever its geographical situation); that it was one element within a wider whole; and that all had to take account of the effect of their actions on others who belonged to that society. Even a statesman as conservative as Metternich could, at the close of the period, write:

> what characterises the modern world and distinguishes it from the ancient is the tendency of states to draw near each other and to form a kind of social body based on the same principle as human society. . . . In the ancient world isolation and the practice of the utmost selfishness without other restraint than that of prudence was the sum of politics. . . . Modern society, on the other hand, exhibits the application of the principle of the balance of power between states. . . . The establishing of international relations, on the basis of reciprocity, under the guarantee of respect for acquired rights . . . constitutes in our time the essence of politics.[32]

However ineffective balance-of-power policies proved in preventing war, however imprecise the conception of the balance which they applied, at least they recognised an end of policy which went beyond the interests of the individual state: the interest of the wider community to which all the states of the continent belonged.

Notes

Notes to the Preface

1. Among the more prominent writers of the period who wrote of an international "system" were Fénelon, Vattel, von Gentz and Brougham.
2. For example, in "general systems theory" developed in the US in the 1940s and 1950s.
3. Notably by T. Parsons in *The Social System* (London, 1952) and other works, and by David Easton in *The Political System* (New York, 1953) and other works.
4. Among the best known of these were Charles McClelland, *Theory and the International System* (New York, 1966); Morton Kaplen, *System and Process in International Politics* (New York, 1957); Klaus Knorr and Sidney Verba (eds), *The International System: Theoretical Essays* (Princeton, 1961); Oran Young, *Systems of Political Science* (Englewood Cliffs, 1968).
5. For example in *Types of International Society* (London, 1976) and in *International Society* (London, 1969).
6. The author has set out the reasons for this belief at greater length in his *Types of International Society*.

Notes to Chapter 1: The Idea of the Balance

1. Polybius, Book I, Chapter 4. In recounting the story Polybius commented that "it is never right to help a power to acquire a predominance that will render it irresistible".
2. In "The Balance of Power", in *Essays, Moral, Political and Literary* (London, 1741) p. 339.
3. Philippe de Commynes, *Memoirs* (1498), trs. M. Jones (London, 1972) pp. 339–40.
4. Francesco Guicciardini, *The History of Italy*, trs. S. Alexander (New York, 1969) p. 4. Machiavelli, observing the same scene, had made a similar point: declaring that "a prince ought never to make common cause with one more powerful than himself with the object of injuring another, unless necessity forces him to it" (*The Prince*, Ch. XXI). But Machiavelli was inconsistent in the view he took on this question and more often held the position that the best thing was to be sure to be on the winning side. See Professor Butterfield's discussion of this point in his chapter on *The Balance of Power* in H. Butterfield and M. Wight, *Diplomatic Investigations* (London, 1966) p. 13.
5. Guicciardini, *History of Italy*.
6. Alberico Gentili, *De Jure Belli* (London, 1589), trs. J. C. Rolfe (London, 1953) p. 65.
7. Giovanni Botero, *Reason of State* (Venice, 1589), trs. P. D. and D. P. Waley (London, 1956) p. 125.

8. P. Paruta, *The Politick Discourses* (1599), trs. Henry Earl of Monmouth (London, 1657) p. 183. He commented: "To join in friendship and confidence with a more powerful prince . . . when the increase of power is intended by this conjuncture, is never to be done without constant danger."
9. A. F. Pollard, *Henry VIII* (London, 1902) p. 120.
10. A. F. Pollard, *Wolsey* (London, 1929) p. 119.
11. Thomas Rymer, *Foedera*, vol. III (dedication to Queen Anne) (London, 1712).
12. Richard Fiddes, *Life of Cardinal Wolsey* (London, 1724) (quoted in Pollard, *Wolsey*, p. 3).
13. Quoted in Butterfield, *The Balance of Power*, p. 164.
14. William Camden, *History of Elizabeth* (London, 1675) p. 223.
15. Abbé de Mably, *Collection complète d'oeuvres* (Paris, 1794–6) vol. V, p. 65. Francis Bacon, writing shortly after Elizabeth's death, had blessed the same policy, declaring that "there can be no general rule given . . . save one, which ever holdeth, which is that princes do keep due sentinal, that none of their neighbours do overgrow" (Francis Bacon, *Essays* (London, 1624) "On Empire").
16. See Butterfield and Wight, *Diplomatic Investigations*, p. 139.
17. P. de la Court, *The Interest of Holland* (Amsterdam, 1662) vol. II, p. 10.
18. F. P. de Lisola, *The Buckler of State and Justice*, English version (London, 1667) p. 300.
19. Ibid., p. 278.
20. S. Pufendorf, *Introduction to the History of the Principal States* (1684), trs. J. Crull (London, 1697) p. 75.
21. *Europe's Catechism* (London, 1741). This was one of a large number of pamphlets published during the first half of the eighteenth century in Britain which discussed the balance of power. For a discussion see M. S. Anderson, *Eighteenth Century Theories of Balance of Power*, in R. Hatton and M. S. Anderson (eds), *Studies in Diplomatic History* (London, 1970) pp. 187ff.
22. Daniel Defoe, *Review of the State of the Nation*, vol. III (1 June 1706) pp. 261–3.
23. Ibid. This last sentiment reflected the fear of many in England at this time that her own ally, Austria, which she was assisting to win control of Spain in place of France, might as a result become as dangerous a threat to the European balance as France had been: this is the theme of Defoe's later pamphlet, *The Ballance of Europe*, written in 1711 after Charles VI, whom Britain had hitherto supported in Spain, became emperor and so likely, as king of that country, to be at least as great a threat as the king of France.
24. This was intended not for Louis himself (with whom Fénelon had by then fallen out) but for the young Duke of Burgundy who was a possible successor.
25. François de Selignac Fénelon, *L'Examen de conscience sur les devoirs de la royauté* (c. 1700) Supplement, English trs. published as *Two Essays on the Ballance of Europe* (London, 1720) p. 1.
26. Ibid., p. 3.

27. David Hume, *Essays, Moral, Political and Literary* (London, 1741–2; Oxford, 1963) p. 345–6. Britain had in fact pursued precisely the balance of power principle Hume commended during those wars: she had been willing to negotiate a separate peace with her enemies at the expense of her allies in each of them (even if, apparently, not as rapidly as Hume saw as "prudent").

28. E. de Vattel, *The Law of Nations* (Neuchatel, 1758). English trs. (London, 1811) III.iii.47–9.

29. Ibid., III.iii.42.

30. Ibid., pp. 309–10. This view that preventative action could be taken against a threat to the balance of power was supported by later international lawyers, such as G. F. de Martens in his famous textbook *Précis du droit moderne de l'Europe* (Göttingen, 1801) p. 190.

31. J. H. G. von Justi, *Die Chimära des Gleichgewichts von Europa* (Altona, 1758).

32. Ibid., p. 65 (quoted in E. B. Hass, "The Balance of Power: Prescription, Concept or Propaganda", *World Politics*, vol. V, (July 1953) pp. 442–77).

33. Edmund Burke, *The Annual Register for 1760*, pp. 2–3. Burke later became far more favourable to the notion of the balance of power, justifying intervention in France partly on those grounds.

34. For example, in Britain "many politicians, especially if they were out of office tended to challenge the validity of the whole concept of a balance of power and to allege that it was being used by the government as a pretext to squander British money on foreign princes" (M. S. Anderson, *Europe in the Eighteenth Century, 1713–1783*, (London, 1961) p. 262).

35. Jean-Jacques Rousseau, *A Project for Perpetual Peace*, English trs. (Edinburgh, 1774) pp. 128–33.

    Kant too, though he had not always been so derisive of the idea (he referred quite favourably to the balance of power in his *Idée zu einer allgemeiner Geschichte* of 1784), later declared that "the maintenance of universal peace by means of the so-called balance of power in Europe . . . is a mere figment of the imagination" (*Verhältnis der Theorie zur Praxis im Völkerrecht* (1793) quoted in Wight, *The Balance of Power*, p. 170).

    The same sceptical attitude was shown later also by Fichte who asserted that "no state . . . strives to maintain the balance of power in the European Republic of Nations except upon account of its being unable to attain something more desirable, and because it cannot yet realise the purpose of its own individual aggrandisement".

36. It had been explicitly defended on these grounds by the Prussian statesman Hertzberg.

37. Vergennes, *Mémoire*, in *Politique des Cabinets de l'Europe* (Paris, 1774).

38. In Comte d'Hauterive, *L'État de la France a la fin de l'an VIII* (1800).

39. Friedrich von Gentz, *On the State of Europe before and after the French Revolution* (1802) (London, 1809) pp. 258–62.

40. Friedrich von Gentz, *Fragments Upon the Present State of the Political Balance of Europe*, English trs. (London, 1806) ch. 1.

41. Ibid., ch. 3.

42. Lord Brougham, *Balance of Power* (1803) (London, 1857) pp. 1–30, 49–50.

43. Hansard, *Parliamentary History*, vol. XII, pp. 168–9, quoted in E. V. Gulick, *Europe's Classical Balance of Power* (New York, 1955) p. 61.
44. Frederick the Great, *Anti-Machiavel*, English trs. (London, 1741) p. 107.
45. C. G. Koch, *Histoire abrégé des traites de paix, entre les puissances de l'Europe depuis la paix de Westphalie* (Paris, 1817–18) quoted in Gulick, *Europe's Classical Balance of Power*, p. 45.
46. Favier, S., *Politique de tous les cabinets* (Paris, 1773) quoted in ibid., p. 66.
47. Jonathan Swift, *A Tale of a Tub, and Other Early Works*, ed. Herbert Davis (Oxford, 1957) p. 197: Where there were "several states in a neighbourhood . . . it is not necessary that the Power should be equally divided between these three: the Balance may be held by the weakest who, by his Address and Conduct . . . may keep the scales duly poised".
48. G. F. von Martens, *Summary of the Law of Nations* (Philadelphia, 1795) pp. 126–7.
49. D'Hauterive, *L'État de la France* pp. 109–10.
50. For example, in the north of Europe (between Russia, Sweden and Denmark); in Italy; between the Bourbons and the Hapsburgs; in Germany; and between Papists and Protestants: see Duke de Ripperda, *Memoirs*, English trs. (London, 1740) p. 357.
51. William III was fully aware of this in building his coalition against France: "I have always been afraid of a war of religion, fearing that France and the emperor might come to a secret understanding" (see Andrew Lossky, *International Relations in Europe*, in *The New Cambridge Modern History*, vol. VI (Cambridge, 1970) p. 188.
52. Brougham, *The Balance of Power*, p. 8.

Notes to Chapter 2: The States

1. See *The Memoirs of Catherine the Great*, ed. D. Maroger (London, 1955) p. 361. Catherine also stated that "The glory of this country is my glory. This is my principle, a fine and happy one" (ibid., p. 379).
2. Frederick expressed this idea repeatedly in varying forms: "first servant and first magistrate of the state"; "first servant of the state"; "first minister (of the people)"; "first magistrate of the nation" (see F. Meinecke, *Machiavellism* (London, 1967) p. 308). But these differing formulations all had in common the idea of the ruler's primary responsibility to the purposes of the state he ruled.
3. Frederick the Great, *Testament politique* (1752) (Berlin, 1920) p. 48.
4. Louis XIV, *Memoires for the Instruction of the Dauphin*, ed. P. Sonnino (New York, 1970) p. 170. The text of this work (which is quoted extensively above) was originally drafted by a secretary, Perigny, making use of earlier texts prepared by Colbert. But it seems to have been heavily corrected by Louis himself and it can be taken as certain that the final text closely reflects his views.
5. Louis XIV, *Memoires*, pp. 23–8.
6. Ibid., p. 35.
7. R. R. Beltes, "The Hapsburg Lands", in *The New Cambridge Modern History*, vol. V (Cambridge, 1951) p. 475.
8. Frederick the Great, *Testament politique*, p. 70.

9. Louis XIV, *Memoires*, pp. 31–2.
10. See John Rule, "Colbert de Torcy and the Formulation of French Foreign Policy, 1698–1715", in R. M. Hatton (ed.), *Louis XIV and Europe* (London, 1976) p. 278.
11. Cf. R. M. Hatton, *Charles XII of Sweden* (London, 1968) p. 99: "Charles XI had established a system whereby the Council and high officials of the Chancellery debated and prepared foreign policy issues, while he read, listened and discussed, reserving the ultimate decision for himself after consultation with individuals whom he trusted".
12. Louis XIV, *Memoires*, p. 130.
13. J. R. Jones, *Britain and the World, 1649–1815* (Brighton, 1980) p. 23.
14. M. S. Anderson, *Europe in the Eighteenth Century, 1713–1783* (London, 1961) p. 137.
15. Ibid., p. 138.
16. See Geoffrey Symcox (ed.), *War, Diplomacy and Imperialism, 1618–1763* (New York, 1973) p. 23.
17. For a description of these systems, see ibid., pp. 22ff; and Anderson, *Europe in the Eighteenth Century*, p. 136.
18. For these and other figures of military expenditure, see W. L. Dorn, *Competition for Empire, 1740–1763* (New York, 1940) p. 50; Paul Kennedy, *The Rise and Fall of the Great Powers* (London, 1988) p. 99.
19. The close correlation between financial strength and military power was well-recognised at this time. For example, Josiah Child declared that "since the introduction of the new artillery of powder, shot and firearms in the world . . . success attends those that can most and longest spend money, rather than men; and consequently princes' armies in Europe are become more proportionate to their purses than the numbers of their people" (*A Discourse on Trade* (London, 1690) pp. 182–3).
20. See P. G. M. Dickson and John Sperling, "War Finance, 1689–1714", in *The New Cambridge Modern History*, vol. VI (Cambridge, 1970) pp. 284–315; P. G. M. Dickson, *The Financial Revolution in England* (London, 1967).
21. Symcox, *War, Diplomacy and Imperialism*, p. 30.
22. Louis XIV, *Memoires*, p. 36.
23. Ibid., p. 39.
24. "In effect William was his own foreign secretary, frequently negotiating with foreign ambassadors alone and penning his more important letters himself in the seclusion of his cabinet. . . . With few exceptions his envoys gathered and transmitted information rather than negotiated" (Andrew Lossky, "International Relations in Europe", in *The New Cambridge Modern History*, vol. VI (Cambridge, 1970) p. 176.
25. See D. B. Horn, *Great Britain and Europe in the Eighteenth Century* (Oxford, 1967) pp. 1–5. Horn concludes that at least to the closing months of William III's reign "England's foreign policy was both asserted and executed by the king, almost uninfluenced by his ministers and virtually unimpeded by parliament, if we accept its initial reluctance to vote supplies for a war".
26. Ibid., pp. 18–21, 90.
27. Frederick the Great, *Testament politique*, p. 20.

28. Ibid., p. 37.
29. See Lossky, "International Relations in Europe", p. 190.
30. Hatton, *Charles XII of Sweden*, p. 119.
31. Louis XIV, *Memoires*, p. 130.
32. Colbert, *Testament politique* (The Hague, 1694) p. 446.
33. François de Callières, *De la maniere de negocier avec les souverains*, trs. as *The Practice of Diplomacy* by A. M. Whyte (London, 1919) p. 46.
34. Louis XIV, *Memoires*, p. 130.
35. H. H. Rowen, *The Ambassador Prepares for War*, (The Hague, 1957) p. 60.
36. Ibid., p. 61.
37. Hatton, *Charles XII of Sweden*, p. 138.
38. Lossky, "International Relations in Europe", p. 189.
39. Louis XIV, *Memoires*, p. 16.
40. Ibid., p. 215.
41. For a description of its organisation see Rule, "Colbert de Torcy", pp. 265–78.
42. Ibid., pp. 278–9.
43. The Emperor Leopold is said to have "made it a rule to abide by the decisions of the majority of his Council even when he disagreed with them" (Lossky, "International Relations in Europe", p. 177).
44. See H. Kamen, *Spain in the Late Seventeenth Century* (London, 1980) p. 25.
45. For example, see Evan Luard, *War in International Society* (London, 1986) pp. 206–7.
46. Lossky, *International Relations in Europe*, p. 176.
47. See Rule, "Colbert de Torcy", pp. 280–1.
48. See G. Mattingley, "International Diplomacy and International Law", in *The New Cambridge Modern History*, vol. III (Cambridge, 1958) pp. 154–6.
49. See E. V. Gulick, *Europe's Classical Balance of Power* (Ithaca, 1955) p. 17. For a description of British representation abroad in this period, see D. B. Horn, *The British Diplomatic Service, 1689–1789* (Oxford, 1961) esp. pp. 12–41.
50. For a description of the growth of the French diplomatic service at this time see A. Picaved, *La Diplomatie française en temps de Louis XIV* (Paris, 1930).
51. De Callières, *De la manier de negocier*, pp. 11–12.
52. Ibid., pp. 41–2.
53. Ibid., pp. 39–40.
54. Ibid., p. 19.
55. Frederick the Great, *Testament politique*, p. 55.
56. See H. Snyder, "The British Diplomatic Service during the Godolphin Ministry", in R. Adams and M. S. Anderson (eds), *Studies in Diplomatic History* (London, 1970) p. 50 on the qualifications required by a British ambassador at the beginning of the eighteenth century. These were said to be "experience; the confidence of the ministry; wealth to sustain the considerable expenses to be borne, before reimbursement in domestic office; and social rank to satisfy the court by which they would be accredited".

57. De Callières, *De la manier de negocier*, p. 9.
58. See Rowen, *The Ambassador Prepares for War*, p. 33.
59. Ibid., p. 90.
60. Ibid., pp. 33 and 279.
61. Ibid., pp. 24–5.
62. Louis XIV, *Memoires*, p. 135.
63. Frederick the Great, *Testament politique*, p. 51.
64. Louis XIV, *Memoires*, p. 135.
65. Ibid.
66. For a general discussion see R. Hatton, "Gratifications and Foreign Policy", in R. Hatton and J. S. Bromley (eds) *William III And Louis XIV* (Liverpool, 1968).
67. Rowen, *The Ambassador Prepares for War*, pp. 101–3.
68. Ibid., p. 114.
69. See G. Livet, "Louis XIV and Germany", in R. Hatton (ed.), *Louis XIV and Europe* (London, 1976) p. 61.
70. F. Weiss, *Histoire des fonds secrets sous l'ancien régime*, quoted in Horn, *Great Britain and Europe*, pp. 37–8.
71. Frederick the Great, *Testament politique*, pp. 56–7.
72. Rowen, *The Ambassador Prepares for War*, p. 141.
73. Ibid., p. 151.
74. Anderson, *Europe in the Eighteenth Century*, p. 161.
75. Ibid., p. 162.

Notes to Chapter 4: Sovereignty

1. Justinian, *Institutiones*, I.ii.6.
2. Machiavelli, *The Prince*, trs. L. Ricci (London, 1952) pp. 44 and 46.
3. Ibid., pp. 74 and 73.
4. Jean Bodin, *Six Books of the Republic* (1576), English trs. N. J. Tooley (Oxford, 1955).
5. Thomas Hobbes, *Leviathan*, vol. II, ch. 17.
6. Ibid., ch. 20.
7. Although this particular phrase was not used in the Westphalia treaty, in asserting the full jurisdiction of the rulers it was taken to reaffirm their powers in this respect.
8. The king of Denmark made a similar declaration, equally asserting absolute power in 1660.
9. Quoted in A. Fanchier-Magnon, *The Smaller German Courts in the Eighteenth Century* (London, 1958) pp. 44–5.
10. Ibid., p. 45.
11. Jacques Benigne Bossuet, *Politics Drawn from the very words of the Scriptures*, Book II, Conclusions.
12. Ibid., Book III.
13. Ibid., Book IV.
14. Louis XIV, *Memoire for the Instruction of the Dauphin*, ed. Paul Sonnino (New York, 1970) pp. 244–5.
15. Ibid., p. 42.

16. By the terms of the Peace of Westphalia they were accorded only *jus territoriae et superioritatis.*
17. Emericu de Vattel, *The Law of Nations* (1756), English trs. (London, 1811) p. lxii.
18. Ibid., p. lxiii.
19. Ibid., p. lxiv.
20. Ibid., p. lxv.
21. Samuel Pufendorf, *Law of Nations* (1688) Book VIII, ch. 9, para. 5.
22. Vattel, *The Law of Nations*, p. lxvi.
23. J. J. Moser, *Essay on the Most Recent European Law of Nations Regarding Peace and War Based Principally on those Public Acts of the European Powers and on other Events which have Happened since the Death of Emperor Charles VI in 1740* (1777–80).
24. *Mare clausum* (1635) was the title of a book by John Selden, which he claimed was authorised by James I, declaring that the seas around the English coast were England's alone.
25. Louis XIV, *Memoire*, p. 44.
26. For accounts of their views see F. Meinecke, *Machiaevellism – The Doctrine of Raison d'état and its Place in Modern History*, English trs. (London, 1924) pp. 162–256.
27. Quoted in ibid., p. 301.
28. Frederick the Great, *First Political Testament* (Berlin, 1920) p. 75.
29. Ibid., p. 24.
30. Louis XIV, *Memoires*, p. 183.
31. Ibid., pp. 250–1.
32. Frederick the Great, *Testament politique* (1752) (Berlin, 1920) p. 76.
33. Meinecke, *Machiavellism*, p. 307.
34. Louis XIV, *Memoires*, p. 77.
35. Quoted in G. P. Gooch, *Frederick the Great* (London, 1947) pp. 3–4.
36. Quoted in G. Ritter, *Frederick the Great* (Heidelberg, 1954) p. 66.
37. Quoted in P. Sonnino, "Louis XIV and the Dutch War", in *Louis XIV and Europe*, ed. R. M. Hatton (London, 1976) p. 158.
38. Frederick the Great, *Anti Machiavel*, English trs. (London, 1741) p. 326.
39. Sir George Clark, *War and Society in the Seventeenth Century* (Cambridge, 1958) pp. 87 and 89.
40. This was not the end of the complications: parts of Sicily were claimed as fiefdoms by Spain too, even after it had been handed over to Savoy in 1713: see G. Symcox, *Victor Amadeus II* (London, 1983) p. 173.
41. Louis XIV had attempted to bribe the previous duke to hand over the duchy in return for financial inducements and appointment as a prince of the realm; but though the duke himself was willing, the plan came to nothing because of the objections of his heir (as well as those of the French royal family who objected to a devaluation of the princely title).
42. See R. M. Hatton, *Charles XII of Sweden* (London, 1958) pp. 102–7.
43. At one time the Dutch proposed that the barrier should be placed on French soil: in other words, on the territory of the very country against which it was directed.
44. The thinking behind this was expressed by Catherine too when she doubted whether "a despotic neighbour is more desirable for Russia than

the anarchy which reigns in Poland at the moment, and of which we can dispose at our wish" (quoted in D. Maroger (ed.), *The Memoirs of Catherine the Great* (London, 1955) pp. 383–4).

45. She claimed (like modern powers undertaking similar actions) to be intervening in response to a call from a group of rebels, but these themselves justified their cause on the basis of Russia's right to protect the earlier constitution.

46. Frederick the Great, *Political Testament* (1752), p. 73. France, Russia's enemy, favoured autocratic power in Sweden. In 1769 the French Ambassador offered six million livres to the Hat party to introduce a change in the constitution to strengthen royal powers, while Russia was at the same time offering almost as lavish a prize to prevent this.

47. It is worth noting that the writers on international law who had been most concerned with asserting the rights of sovereignty rejected interventions of this kind. So, for example, Vattel declared that "a nation has the right to draw up for itself its constitution, to uphold it, to perfect it, and to regulate at will all that relates to the government, without interference on the part of anyone. . . . All such matters are of purely national concern and no foreign power has any right to intervene otherwise than by its good offices, unless it be requested to do so or be let to do so by special reasons" (*Law of Nations*, vol. III, pp. 18 and 19).

48. On his own admission Louis XIV encouraged the Cromwell faction to "create some disturbances in London"; gave twenty thousand ecus to a professed revolutionary, Algernon Sidney, promising to send him all the aid he needed as soon as he could put it to good use; and planned to "land 400 men in Ireland as soon as the Catholic faction could receive them" (*Memoires*, pp. 177–8 and 214). Rulers of this age would indeed have had little to learn from the CIA about the conduct of covert operations to secure political change.

49. For example, six separate articles of the Treaty of Westminster of 1654 between England and the United Provinces were concerned with such prohibitions. There were similar provisions in the treaty between France and England of the following year, the treaty between France and Denmark of 1663 and many other treaties of the period.

50. Louis XIV, *Memoires*, p. 46.

51. J. R. Jones, *Britain and the World, 1649–1815* (Brighton, 1980) p. 108.

52. Ibid., p. 160.

53. Ibid., p. 126.

Notes to Chapter 5: Status

1. Louis XIV, *Memoires for the Instruction of the Dauphin*, ed. P. Sonnino (New York, 1970) p. 169.

2. G. Ritter, *Frederick the Great* (Heidelberg, 1954,) p. 37.

3. Cf. A. Fauchier-Magnon, *The Smaller German Courts in the Eighteenth Century*, English trs. (London, 1958) pp. 43–4 and 21–2; "The smallest princes of Germany, at all costs and by noisy ostentation . . . had to outshine the neighbouring court". Each "rivalled those who had been more favoured by fortune. . . . This resulted in constant agitation,

rivalry, hatred and conspiracy, in order to climb one step up the hierarchy ladder."

4. Louis XIV, *Memoire*, pp. 224–5.
5. Ibid.
6. Quoted in G. P. Gooch, *Frederick the Great* (London, 1947) pp. 24–5.
7. Louis XIV, *Memoire*, p. 37.
8. Ibid., p. 225.
9. Ibid., p. 46.
10. After the death of Clement X Louis pursued his vendetta by insisting, (successfully) that no Cardinal who had been friendly with that pope should be elected as his successor.
11. Louis believed that France had been largely responsible for securing the dependence of the United Provinces in 1648 and he was particularly resentful when that country joined the Triple Alliance which compelled him to make peace with Spain in 1668.
12. Quoted in Fauchier-Magnon, *The Smaller German Courts* pp. 44–5. Cf. F. L. Carsten, "The Empire after the Thirty Years War", in *The New Cambridge Modern History*, vol. v (Cambridge, 1951) pp. 450–1: "If they could not hope to rival the splendour of the French King, if their armies remained woefully inferior to his, they at least had to build a little Versailles on the banks of the Neckar or the Spree."
13. Louis XIV, *Memoires*, p. 96.
14. Fauchier-Magnon, *The Smaller German Courts*, p. 175.
15. M. S. Anderson, *Europe in the Eighteenth Century, 1713–1783* (London, 1961) p. 198.
16. Quoted in Robert Pick, *Empress Maria Thérèse*, (London, 1966) p. 203. See also the remark of the emperor Joseph II below.
17. Louis XIV, *Memoires*, p. 242.
18. Ibid., pp. 95–6.
19. Ibid., p. 77.
20. Quoted in H. H. Rowen, *The Ambassador Prepares for War* (The Hague, 1957) p. 12.
21. Gooch, *Frederick the Great*, p. 39.
22. Rowen, *The Ambassador Prepares for War* p. 12.
23. Pick, *Empress Maria Thérèse*, p. 262.
24. See G. P. Gooch, *Maria Theresa, and Other Studies* (London, 1985) p. 51.
25. Cf. D. B. Horn, *The British Diplomatic Service, 1678–1789* (Oxford, 1961) p. 205: "It was generally agreed that the Holy Roman Emperor, by virtue of his imperial title and ecumenical traditions, took precedence of all other general sovereigns."
26. Louis XIV, *Memoires*, pp. 49–51.
27. In the *Memoires* he wrote for his successor, Louis speaks of another battle of this sort with the emperor. After Leopold had been elected emperor in 1658 he awaited a message of congratulation from Louis, such as was customarily sent on those occasions; and would not make any communication with the French king until he had received it. Louis however refused to send such a message, and regarded this as a splendid victory (Louis XIV, *Memoires*, pp. 48–9).
28. Louis XIV, *Memoires*, pp. 72–5. Louis expressed the hope that his son

would show himself "just as sensitive as I have always been about the honour of the French crown" (p. 68). It was Louis personally who was so determined to win the victory on this occasion. Colbert recalls that the council called to consider the matter unanimously advised on a policy of moderation but the king had insisted on his view and had therefore won what Colbert himself accepted was a major diplomatic triumph (François Colbert, *Testament politique* (The Hague, 1694) p. 137).

29. Harold Nicolson, *The Evolution of Diplomatic Method* (London, 1954), p. 63.
30. Louis XIV, *Memoires*, p. 76.
31. Ibid., p. 70.
32. Cardinal Richelieu, *Testament politique*, ed. L. André (Paris, 1947) pp. 404–5.
33. Louis XIV, *Memoires*, pp. 202, 204 and 226.
34. For an account of some of these disputes see C. G. Zeller, "French Diplomacy and Foreign Policy in their European Setting", in *The New Cambridge Modern History*, vol. v (Cambridge, 1961) pp. 201–2.
35. See Horn *The British Diplomatic Service*, p. 213: "It was generally agreed that republics were lower in rank than monarchies and that amongst crowned heads hereditary monarchs rightly took precedence over such elected monarchs as the king of Poland."
36. See *The New Cambridge Modern History*, vol. VI (Cambridge, 1970) p. 170. The opening of many peace conferences was delayed because of disputes between the plenipotentiaries concerning the right of their masters to style themselves as rulers of particular territories, sometimes lost long ago. Rulers would make significant political concessions to secure recognition of their titles: for example, the king of Prussia was willing to allow Augustus of Saxony/Poland to send troops across his territory to attack Denmark in 1700 in return for recognition of his kingly title. They would also do deals with each other to secure mutual recognition: under the Treaty of Vienna of 1725 the rulers of Austria and Spain, though each renouncing the claim to be the sovereign of the other's state, agreed that they would both continue to use those titles, while ensuring that their successors would renounce them.
37. There was also considerable sensitivity about modes of address, which were supposed to follow from the titles held. Kings were supposed to address fellow-monarchs as "Frères", dukes as "Cousins", and lesser rulers as "Sieur" or "Monsieur". One way to acquire the title of course, was to be elected Holy Roman Emperor. It was by no means taken for granted in this age that the emperor must be a Hapsburg. Louis XIV was regarded as a serious candidate in 1658 and again in the 1670s and 1680s. In 1702 the Elector of Bavaria, governor of the Spanish Netherlands recognised the Bourbon succession there in return for a promise that the French would support him at the next election as emperor. Since it was still sometimes possible to buy the votes of the electors, or at least exercise substantial pressure on them, this was by no means an empty hope (the same Elector's son was able to secure every vote at the election following the death of Charles VI, when Austria's power was minimal: even the British king, as elector of Hanover, though an ally of Austria, gave him his vote).

38. A French writer of the period, the Comte de Ségur, commented on this ambition of the Electors: "The Electors . . . believed that they should have royal honours everywhere: they are unwilling to give precedence even to princes of the blood" (quoted in Fauchier-Magnon, *The Smaller German Courts*, p. 37). This was reflected in perennial disputes between the emperor and the Electors about the latter's demand to be styled "excellency".

39. Augustus showed his affection for the royal title when, having lost his crown in Poland after defeat by Charles XII in 1706, he soon declared himself a candidate for the thrones of Naples and Sicily, which he expected to be allocated at the conclusion of the War of Spanish Succession. His son, Augustus II, shared his taste. He hoped to be king of Saxony as well as Poland, but Maria Theresa (who, though not emperor, exercised much of his authority) would not agree. This was one reason why Augustus gave his support to France during the War of Austrian Succession, since France undertook to offer him a crown in the Hapsburg territories of Moravia and Lower Austria if they were acquired at the conclusion of the conflict (they were not).

40. Sir George Clark, "From the Nine Years War to the War of Spanish Succession", in *The New Cambridge Modern History*, vol. VI (Cambridge, 1970) p. 402.

41. Giorgio Spini, "Italy after the Thirty Years War", in *The New Cambridge Modern History*, vol. V (Cambridge, 1961) p. 463.

42. Geoffrey Symcox, *Victor Amadeus II* (London, 1983) pp. 117 and 135.

43. Somewhat similar problems arose over a claim to *regain* a royal title. While most of the rulers of Europe were quite willing to grant this to the rulers of Portugal after she regained her independence from Spain, Spain herself was most reluctant to concede it: the claim to a royal title was one of the last Portuguese demands they would accept when negotiating an end to the war of independence in 1667–8.

44. One of the reasons for the bitterness of the war for Cologne at that time was the fact that it would determine the religious balance among the electors.

45. See Horn, *The British Diplomatic Service* p. 207.

46. Ibid., p. 208.

47. Account was taken not only of the rank of the title but the prestige and age of the house: thus a count of Nassau was able to say to a minor prince at the coronation of Charles VI: "You must learn, sir, that a prince like you must walk behind counts like me" (quoted in Fauchier-Magnon, *The Smaller German Courts*, p. 65).

48. François de Callières, *De la manière de negocier avec les souverains*, trs. as *The Practice of Diplomacy* by A. M. Whyte (London, 1919), p. 23.

49. However it was possible for an ambassador to overreach himself in this endeavour. Thus when a newly appointed British ambassador to the French court prepared to make a "superb" public entry in the garden of the Tuileries in 1719, he was not permitted to make his entry with a six-horse carriage as he had planned, but was obliged to withdraw and return with only a two-horse carriage before he was admitted (see Horn, *The British Diplomatic Service*, p. 209).

50. Pick, *Empress Maria Thérèse*, p. 224.

51. Horn, *The British Diplomatic Service*, p. 208.
52. Ibid., p. 207. British envoys in Venice were particularly sensitive on such questions because of the honours done there to the son of the Young Pretender, which for a time in 1737–44, caused a total breach of relations.
53. Ibid., p. 209.
54. Ibid., pp. 209–10.
55. Ibid., p. 207.
56. Ibid., pp. 159 and 195.
57. See R. C. Anderson, *Naval Wars in the Levant, 1559–1853* (Liverpool, 1952) pp. 163–75.
58. Rowen, *The Ambassador Prepares for War*, p. 132.
59. Horn, *The British Diplomatic Service*, pp. 205–6.
60. Harold Nicolson, *The Evolution of Diplomacy* (2nd edition, New York, 1966) p. 64.

Notes to Chapter 6: Succession

1. The succession of Peter, who was only joint heir, occurred as a result of a counter-coup against his step-sister, Sophie, the regent, who he believed was attempting to eliminate him; that of his widow Catherine I, as a result of the support of the guards regiment after Peter had failed to make provision for a successor; that of Anna, Peter's niece (in preference to his daughter), resulted from the support of officers of the guard demanding a restoration of autocracy; that of Elizabeth, Peter's daughter, through the elimination of Anna's heir and successor Ivan VI, with the support of the army; and that of Catherine the Great, through the overthrow and subsequent murder of her husband, Peter II, by a group of army officers, with her own connivance.
2. It was on this ground, rather than because of the authority of Charles II's will, that Louis based the claims of his grandson in Spain after 1700: see Mark Thomson, "Origins of the War of Spanish Succession", in R. Hatton and J. S. Bromley (eds) *William II and Louis XIV* (Liverpool, 1968) pp. 142–3. Louis, however, was not consistent about the right of renunciation: he was only able to assert the claims of Philip in Spain by relying on the renunciations which had been made by the Dauphin and the Duc de Berry. But a denial of their right of renunciation implied that his aim was a union of the crowns, an objective which he (most of the time) denied.
3. Once again the argument that renunciations were illegal was not consistent, since it was generally believed that Philip planned to succeed to the French throne in place of the Spanish throne and not as well; and this implied that renunciation in the latter case was regarded as acceptable.
4. See Thomsom, "Origins of the War of Spanish Succession", p. 145. Once again Louis was not wholly consistent; he was willing to recognise William III's rights in the Treaty of Ryswick, so repudiating those of James II, yet proceeded to recognise James III as the rightful King of England after the death of James II, in 1701 apparently on the grounds that normal line of succession was restored on the death of the usurping king.

5. The power of the estates in this respect was, however, significantly weakened when it was agreed, at the instance of Russia at that time, that the new king should have the right to transmit the crown to a direct male heir.
6. Thomson, "Origins of the War of Spanish Succession", p. 241.
7. See J. O. Lindsay, "International Relations", in *The New Cambridge Modern History*, vol. VII (Cambridge, 1970) p. 191.
8. The third beneficiary of the 1698 treaty was also a son rather than a ruler: the heir to the Elector of Bavaria; and when he died suddenly in the following year it was not agreed that the Elector should inherit his son's expected portion.
9. During the negotiations for ending the Nine Years War Louis XIV had agreed to let the emperor's younger son inherit the *whole* Spanish inheritance, provided it was not united with Austria.
10. François de Selignac Fénelon, *L'Examen de conscience sur les devoirs de la royauré*, 1700 (London, 1720).
11. See D. McKay and H. M. Scott, *The Rise of the Great Powers 1648–1815* (London, 1983) p. 146.
12. Quoted in Robert Pick, *Empress Maria Theresa* (London, 1966) pp. 63–4.
13. *Histoire de la grande crise de l'Europe* (London, 1743) pp. 1–2; quoted in M. S. Anderson, "Eighteenth Century Notions of the Balance of Power", in Hatton and Anderson (eds), *Studies in Diplomatic History* (London, 1970) p. 191.
14. L. M. Kahle, *La Balance de Europe considerée comme la règle de la paix et la guerre* (Berlin, 1744) p. 147; quoted in ibid., p. 191.
15. In the Convention of Klein Schellendorf (1741), the Treaty of Breslau (1742) and the Treaty of Dresden (1745).
16. This method was not altogether obsolete however. Maria Theresa sought to acquire Modena by persuading the ruler to exclude his son from the inheritance (on the grounds of his dissolute behaviour) and instead to marry his 3-year old daughter to her own 6-year old grandson, thus ensuring that the territory finally became Austria's.
17. Writing to his ambassador in London in July 1698, Louis acknowledged that, though the Spaniards might accept, and even welcome, a Bourbon claim to an undivided kingdom, this would be likely to lead to a bitter war and that "no interest would seem to me to outweigh that of preserving the tranquility my people enjoy" (Thomson, "Origins of the War of Spanish Succession", p. 143). Over the course of the next three years Louis evidently changed his estimate to the relative desirability of maximising his claims and maintaining the European tranquillity.
18. The Swedish estates had invited Peter, Grand Duke of Holstein-Gottorp (later Peter III of Russia) to become the successor, a plan which was unacceptable to Elizabeth, the Russian empress.
19. This is usually known as the Quadrilateral Alliance treaty. More important than the alliance, however, was the settlement of succession questions.
20. In the same way, under the second treaty of Vienna of 1731 the emperor agreed in return for recognition of the Pragmatic Sanction, that an archduchess – that is a potential heiress to the throne – would not be

married to a Bourbon or to a member of the House of Brandenburg, thus giving assurance to other states that the balance of power would not be overturned.

21. H. H. Rowen, *The Ambassador Prepares for War* (The Hague, 1957) p. 67.
22. G. Symcox, *Victor Amadeus II: Absolutism in the Savoyard State, 1675–1730* (London, 1983) p. 136.
23. Ibid., p. 164.

Notes to Chapter 7: Territory

1. For a discussion of territorial motives in these ages, see Evan Luard, *War in International Society* (London, 1986) esp. ch. 4, pp. 153–61.
2. Frederick the Great, *Second Political Testament* (Berlin, 1920) p. 212.
3. Frederick the Great, *First Political Testament* (Berlin, 1920) p. 59.
4. Ibid., p. 49.
5. These were listed in ibid., pp. 62–5. Frederick repeated virtually the same list in his *Second Political Testament*, published in 1768, five years after the conclusion of the Seven Years War.
6. See L. R. Levitter, "Poland under the Saxon Kings", in *The New Cambridge Modern History*, vol. VII (Cambridge, 1957) pp. 389–90.
7. Frederick the Great, *First Political Testament*, p. 40.
8. Frederick the Great, *Les Principes du gouvernement prussien*, 1776 (Berlin, 1920) p. 239. Frederick wrote this after the failure of his attempt to annex Saxony twenty years earlier.
9. Louis XIV, *Memoires for the Instruction of the Dauphin*, ed. B. Sonnino (New York, 1970) p. 249.
10. Ibid., p. 87.
11. Ibid., p. 180.
12. Ibid., p. 213.
13. Frederick the Great, *First Political Testament*, p. 61.
14. Ibid., p. 63.
15. Ibid.
16. The provisions of the Treaty of Vienna of 1815 were designed to create similar barriers against France in the same three places.
17. Frederick the Great congratulated himself that, by acquiring the manufactures of Silesia, he had been enabled to turn a trade deficit into a surplus: see his *Reflexions sur l'administration des finances pour le gouvernement prussien*, 1784 (Berlin, 1920) p. 251.
18. Louis XIV, *Memoires*, p. 124.
19. Jerker, Rosen, "Scandinavia and the Baltic", in *The New Cambridge Modern History*, vol. V (Cambridge, 1961) p. 521.
20. See D. McKay and H. M. Scott, *The Rise of the Great Powers, 1648–1815* (London, 1983) pp. 287–8.
21. Louis XIV, *Memoires*, pp. 122–3.
22. Frederick the Great, *First Political Testament*, p. 63.
23. Not deterred by the failure of this strategy in the Seven Years War, Frederick described an almost exactly similar plan for acquiring Saxony in his *Second Political Testament*, written in 1768, five years after the

conclusion of that war: and after he had failed in that aim in the Seven Years War, he yet again, in his *Principes du gouvernement prussien* (1776), declared that the best way to secure it "would be to conquer Bohemia and Moravia and to exchange them for Saxony".

24. Maria Theresa, *Letters of an Empress*, trs. Eileen Taylor (London, 1939) letter of 25 January 1772, p. 9.
25. Ibid.
26. Letter of 2 January 1778, in Ibid., p. 43.
27. Frederick the Great, *First Political Testament*, p. 64.
28. Louis XIV, *Memoires*, p. 175.
29. Frederick the Great, *First Political Testament*, p. 64.
30. Ibid.
31. Ibid., p. 65.
32. Frederick the Great, *Second Political Testament*, p. 219.
33. Frederick the Great, *Les Principes du gouvernement prussien*, p. 242.
34. M. S. Anderson, "European Diplomatic Relations, 1763–1790", in *The New Cambridge Modern History*, vol. VIII (Cambridge, 1965) p. 270.
35. R. Hatton, "Charles XII and the Great Northern War", in *The New Cambridge Modern History*, vol. VI (Cambridge, 1970) p. 673.
36. Frederick the Great, *Second Political Testament*, p. 20.
37. The recovery of Alsace, and even of the three bishoprics of Metz, Toul and Verdun, were regarded by the emperors as their "German mission".
38. The agreement between Austria and Russia of 1783 providing for a division of Ottoman territories was similar in effect.
39. Frederick the Great recognised this motive in writing, two years before the first partition, that, because each of Poland's neighbours secretly desired to devour her but feared similar aspirations among its competitors, "it seems to be apparent that eventually these two powerful neighbours will reach an agreement to share the prey" (*Second Political Testament*, p. 199).
40. R. Pick, *The Emperor Maria Theresa* (London, 1966), p. 107.
41. The British proposed Milan, Naples or Sicily for this purpose but that idea was strongly resisted by the emperor.
42. See L. B. Lewitter, "The Partitions of Poland", in *The New Cambridge Modern History*, vol. VIII (Cambridge, 1965) esp. p. 359.
43. In particular, Austria wanted compensation for any gains made by Russia in Poland or by Prussia in Saxony. For a description of this bargaining, see E. V. Gulick, *Europe's Classical Balance of Power* (Ithaca, 1955) pp. 95–237.
44. Gulick, *Europe's Classical Balance of Power*, pp. 24–7.
45. Frederick the Great, *First Political Testament*, p. 68. As Frederick was pleased to note, this process would not only increase the power of the large states but reduce that of the emperor.
46. Frederick the Great, *Testament politique*, 1768 (Berlin, 1920) p. 228.

Notes to Chapter 8: Trade

1. C. W. Cole, *Colbert and a Century of French Merchantilism*, vol. I (New York, 1939) p. 342.

2. For a justification of traditional beliefs concerning the finite quantity of trade, see C. H. Wilson, "Trade, Society and the State", in *The Cambridge Economic History of Europe*, vol. IV (Cambridge, 1957) pp. 513–5.

3. J. B. Colbert, *Lettres, instructions et mémoires*, ed. P. Clément (Paris, 1859–82) pp. 264ff.

4. Ibid., vol. II, p. 62.

5. Quoted in Cole, *Colbert*, vol. I, p. 327.

6. Ibid.

7. J. Locke, *Some Considerations of the Consequences of the Lowering of Interest and Raising the Value of Money* (London, 1691, p. 13).

8. P. W. von Hörnigk, *Oestereich über Alles Wan es nur Ville* (1684), quoted in E. M. Heckscher, *Mercantilism*, vol. II (London, 1935) p. 22.

9. See Cole, *Colbert*, vol. II, p. 545: "Though Colbert went through the motions – and sometimes they were vigorous ones – of attempting to stop the export of coin and bullion, he placed his reliance on the indirect method connected with the fostering of industry, agriculture, colonies, shipping and so forth."

10. Thomas Mun, *England's Treasure Through Foreign Trade* (London, 1664) p. 33.

11. Matthew Decker, *Essay on the Causes of Decline of the Foreign Trade*, quoted in Wilson, "Trade, Society and the State", p. 503.

12. Mun, *England's Treasure*, p. 23.

13. Locke, *Some Considerations*, quoted in E. F. Hecksher, *Mercantilism*, vol. II, p. 197.

14. Mun, *England's Treasure*, p. 11.

15. Quoted in Heckscher, *Mercantilism*, p. 116.

16. C. Davenant, *An Essay on the East India Trade* (London, 1697) p. 30.

17. Lord Bolingbroke, *Letters on the Spirit of Patriotism* (London, 1749) pp. 184–5.

18. J. Child, *A Treatise Concerning the East India Trade* (London, 1681) p. 1.

19. Josiah Child, *A Discourse on Trade* (London, 1689) pp. 93–4.

20. Colbert, *Lettres*, vol. VI, pp. 260–70, quoted in Cole, *Colbert*, vol. I, p. 343.

21. Ibid., pp. 454 and 470.

22. Ibid., p. 438.

23. As Thomas Mun pointed out, if England carried more of its trade in its own ships it would "get not only the price of our wares . . . but also the merchants gains, the charger of insurance and freight to carry them beyond the seas" (*England's Treasure*, p. 20).

24. J. B. Colbert, *Memorandum to the King of France*, 1670; reproduced in A. Lossky (ed.), *The Seventeenth Century* (New York, 1987) pp. 292–3.

25. Ibid., pp. 246–7.

26. Ibid., p. 48.

27. This attitude was expressed by Colbert in 1669: "This state is flourishing not only in itself but also by the want which it has inflicted upon all the neighbouring states. Extreme poverty appears everywhere. There is only Holland which still resists, and its power in money decreases pitifully" (*Lettres*, vol. VII, quoted in Cole, *Colbert*, p. 344).

28. See C. Wilson, *Profit and Power* (London, 1957,) p. 31.
29. G. Symcox, *Victor Amadeus II* (London, 1983) p. 187.
30. See ibid., p. 160.
31. Colbert, *Lettres*, vol. VII, p. 230. On another occasion he commented that "it is always very advantageous for a state to make within the kingdom the goods that come from outside" and told Louis XIV that by establishing manufacturing industries he had "kept within his kingdom the money that used to go out of it to get all these goods from the Dutch and other foreigners" (see Cole, *Colbert*, p. 348).
32. Quoted in W. H. Bruford, "The Organisation and Rise of Prussia", in *The New Cambridge Modern History*, vol. VII (Cambridge, 1970) p. 313.
33. Mun, *England's Treasure*, p. 17.
34. Mun declared that the best policy was to "supply ourselves and prevent the importation of hemp, flax, cordage and tobacco and diverse other things which we now fetch from strangers to our great impoverishment" (*England's Treasure*, pp. 15–16).
35. J. Child, *A Discourse on Trade* (London, 1689) pp. 148–9.
36. See Cole, *Colbert*, vol. I, p. 360.
37. Ibid., p. 385.
38. Ibid., pp. 368ff.
39. Quoted in Wilson, "Trade, Society and State", p. 526.
40. Cole, *Colbert*, vol. I, p. 343.
41. Quoted in ibid., vol. I, p. 343.
42. Quoted in Wilson, "Trade, Society and State", p. 561.
43. Samuel Pepys, *Diary*, 2 February 1664.
44. For example, the English Navigation Act, the right of the English government to tax fishing, to search merchant vessels, and to demand a salute from Dutch vessels in the mid-Channel.
45. *Memorandum*, 1670, reproduced in A. Lossky (ed.), *The Seventeenth Century* (New York, 1967) pp. 292–3.
46. Cole, *Colbert*, vol. I, p. 446.
47. See C. H. Wilson, *Profit and Power* (London, 1957) p. 86.
48. J. R. Jones, *Britain and the World, 1649–1815* (Brighton, 1980) p. 101.
49. Sir G. Clark, "The Nine Years War, 1688–97", in *The New Cambridge Modern History*, vol. VI (Cambridge, 1970) p. 252.
50. Cf. J. B. Wolf, *The Emergence of the Great Powers, 1685–1715* (New York, 1951) p. 62: "Without doubt the new Spanish commercial policies convinced an important section of opinion in both England and the United Provinces that peace with France was impossible."
51. Quoted in E. F. Heckscher, *Mercantilism* (London, 1935) vol. II, p. 19.
52. Child, *Treatise Concerning the East India Trade*, pp. 6 and 4.
53. See Davenant, *Essay on the East India Trade*, p. 32.
54. Child, *Discourse on Trade*, pp. 144–5.
55. J. B. Colbert, *Letter to the Intendant at Rochefort* (Paris, 1666).
56. Child, *Discourse on Trade*, pp. 148–9.
57. Davenant, *Essay on the East India Trade*, p. 61.
58. J. Campbell, *The Present State of Europe*, 6th edn (London, 1761) p. 24.
59. J. V. Moreau, *Mémoires pour servir au l'histoire de notre temps* (Frankfurt, 1759–60) vol. I, p. 56.
60. He made a similar point in declaring of the English that "while pretend-

ing to protect the balance on land, which no one threatens . . . [they] are entirely destroying the balance at sea, which no one defends" (quoted in M. S. Anderson, *Europe in the Eighteenth Century 1713–1783* (London, 1961) p. 165).

61. Quoted in Wilson, "Trade, Society and the State", p. 537.
62. Quoted in ibid.
63. D. Defoe, *A Plan of the English Commerce* (London, 1737) p. 147.
64. Quoted in Anderson, *Europe in the Eighteenth Century*, p. 165.
65. See J. H. Plumb, *Chatham* (London, 1953) p. 90.
66. Quoted in W. Doyle, *The Old European Order, 1760–1800* (Oxford, 1978) p. 288.
67. P. C. de la Court, *The True Interest and Political Maxims of the Republic of Holland and West Friesland*, English trs. (London, 1702) pp. 243–4.
68. Rowen, *The Ambassador Prepares for War*, p. 186.
69. English Merchants were a strong influence in favour of peace in 1695–7, 1710–13, 1746–8, 1801–2 and 1809–12.
70. These points are made in de la Court, *The True Interest . . . of Holland*, pp. 69, 76–80, 88 and 363.
71. Wilson, "Trade, Society and the State", p. 542.

Notes to Chapter 9: Colonies

1. C. Montesquieu, *L'Esprit des lois* (Paris, 1748) vol. XXI, p. 21.
2. See J. H. Parry, *Trade and Dominion: The European Overseas Empires in the Eighteenth Century* (London, 1971) pp. 61–2.
3. For examples see K. Knorr, *British Colonial Theories, 1570–1850* (Toronto, 1944) esp. pp. 114–16.
4. C. Davenant, *Discourse on the Trade of England* (London, 1698) p. 208.
5. J. Child, *A Discourse on Trade* (London, 1690) p. 207.
6. A. Young, *Political Essays* (London, 1772) p. 329.
7. C. W. Cole, *Colbert and a Century of French Mercantilism* (New York, 1939) vol. I, p. 351.
8. P. de la Court, *The Interests of Holland* (1640) English trs. (London, 1712) vol. III, p. 1.
9. See Davenant, *Discourse on the Trade of England*, p. 208.
10. Quoted in Knorr, *British Colonial Theories*, pp. 126–7.
11. J. Tucker, *Brief Essays on the Advantages and Dis-advantages which Respectively Attend France and Great Britain in Regard to Trade* (London, 1750) p. 96.
12. See M. S. Anderson, *Europe in the Eighteenth Century, 1713–1783* (London, 1961) p. 267.
13. Montesquieu, *Esprit des lois*, vol. XXI, p. 21.
14. Cole, *Colbert*, vol. II, p. 27: "Of all Colbert's West Indian policies the most fundamental was the exclusion of foreigners, and especially the Dutch, from the Commerce with the Islands."
15. Ibid., p. 28.
16. Child, *Discourse on Trade*, p. 166.
17. See Davenant, *Discourse on the Trade of England*, p. 231. Davenant also

warned of the danger that the New England colonies might "carry the growth of our plantations to foreign countries and in exchange bring from thence such commodities and manufactures as they want": this would be to "the great hurt of the king's customs and to the damage of the general trade of England" (ibid., p. 206).

18. Robert Richardson, writing in the *London Chronicle*, 31 July 1764, quoted in Knorr, *British Colonial Theories*, p. 30.
19. Ibid., p. 130.
20. Cole, *Colbert*, vol. II, p. 34.
21. Quoted in Knorr, *British Colonial Theories*, p. 104.
22. See C. Davenant, *Discourses on the Public Revenues and the Trade of England* (London, 1698) vol. II, p. 204.
23. Parry, *Trade and Dominion*, p. 78.
24. For an account of some of these doubts, see Parry, *Trade and Dominion*, pp. 307–25; Knorr, *British Colonial Theories*, pp. 105–25; Anderson *Europe in the Eighteenth Century*, pp. 278–82.
25. See C. H. Wilson, "Trade, Society and the State", in *The Cambridge Economic History of Europe*, vol. IV (Cambridge, 1967) p. 501.
26. Cole, *Colbert*, vol. II, pp. 77–8. He told his Intendent that "it would be a great advantage and a great satisfaction to me if, on your return, you should bring to his Majesty the news of some good mines discovered", and urged in particular the desirability of opening up mines of copper, lead, iron and coal.
27. See Knorr, *British Colonial Theories*, pp. 34–5.
28. Sir Gilbert Heathecote, quoted in ibid., p. 84. For a number of similar statements by speakers and writers of the period, see pp. 83–6.
29. See Cole, *Colbert*, vol. II, pp. 77–80.
30. In fact the enterprise was largely a failure: the British Admiralty continued to favour Baltic over New England timber because of its superior quality (see Knorr, *British Colonial Theories*, p. 113).
31. Charles Davenant, for example, warned of the danger that "by such mistaken measures" England might "let them grow in naval strength and power" so that eventually "we cannot expect to hold them long in our subjection. If, as some have proposed, we should think to build ships of war there, we may teach them an art which will cost us some blows. . . . Some such cause may indeed put into their heads to erect themselves into independent commonwealths" (Davenant, *Discourses on the Public Revenues*, p. 205).
32. This view was put forward by Sir Francis Brewster in his *Essays on Trade and Navigation* (London, 1695) and by many other writers of the time.
33. See Cole, *Colbert*, vol. I, p. 475.
34. Young, *Political Essays*, p. 329.
35. House of Commons, 3 February 1738.
36. Erasmus Philips, *Miscellaneous Works* (London, 1751) p. 36.
37. For statements expressing this belief see Knorr, *British Colonial Theories*, pp. 86–8.
38. *Miscellaneous Works* (London, 1751) p. 32.
39. Quoted in Knorr, *British Colonial Theories*, p. 88.
40. See Davenant, *Discourse on the Trade of England*, p. 212. Josiah Child

made the same point: even if colonial goods were sometimes more expensive, "it would be no loss to the nation in general, because all freight would be paid to England, whereas the freight paid to the traders is all clear loss to the nation" (*A Discourse about Trade*, p. 100).

41. Daniel Defoe, *A Plan of the English Commerce* (London, 1728) p. xi.
42. Viscount Bolingbroke, *The Craftsman* (London, 1731-7) vol. IV, p. 53.
43. Letter from Sir John Wentworth to Pitt, 19 October 1760, quoted in Knorr, *British Colonial Theories*, p. 100.
44. For example one English pamphleteer wrote that the slave trade "may be justly esteemed an inexhaustible fund of wealth and naval power to this kingdom" (quoted in T. Williams, *The Expansion of Europe in the Eighteenth Century* (London, 1965) p. 41).
45. M. Decker, *Essay on the Cause of the Decline of Foreign Trade* (London, 1731) p. 178.
46. Davenant, *Discourse on the Trade of England*, p. 224.
47. Child, *Discourse on Trade*, p. 176.
48. See Knorr, *British Colonial Theories*, pp. 222-4.
49. Lord Henry Brougham, *Inquiry into the Colonial Policy of the European Powers* (London, 1803) vol. I, p. 214.
50. Frederick the Great, *Second Political Testament*, 1768 (Berlin, 1920) p. 227.
51. For examples of the arguments put on these points in Britain, see Knorr, *British Colonial Theories*, pp. 101-46.
52. J. Tucker, *Cui Bono?* (Gloucester, 1782) p. 129.
53. J. Bentham, *Principles of International Law* (London, 1789) p. 547.
54. Adam Smith, *The Wealth of Nations*, ed. E. Cannan (New York, 1937) p. 558.
55. Ibid., p. 559.
56. Ibid., p. 581.
57. J. Cary, *A Discourse on Trade* (London, 1745) p. 48.
58. Anderson, *Europe in the Eighteenth Century*, p. 267.
59. Quoted in D. Williams, *The Expansion of Europe in the Eighteenth Century* (London, 1956) p. 64.
60. For a discussion of Pitt's motives in organising this expedition see K. Hotblack, *Chatham's Colonial Policy* (London, 1917) p. 68: "the sole object of the expeditions which [Pitt] sent against Senegal and Goree was to make war upon trade".
61. Quoted in M. S. Anderson, "Eighteenth-Century Theories of the Balance of Power", in R. Hatton and M. S. Anderson (eds), *Studies in Diplomatic History* (London, 1970) p. 192.
62. M. Postlethwaite, *Great Britain's True System* (London, 1757) p. 234; quoted in Knorr, *British Colonial Theories*, p. 98.
63. Speech in the House of Commons, 8 March 1739, quoted in O. A. Sherrard, *Lord Chatham: A War Minister in the Making* (London, 1952) p. 66.
64. See Chapter 4 above.
65. Speech, 9 December 1762, quoted in Hotblack, *Chatham's Colonial Policy*, p. 68. Others stressed the financial, as well as the commercial, influence of colonies: George III in 1779 stressed the importance of

defending Britain's West Indies possessions, on the grounds that "if we lose our sugar islands it will be impossible to raise money to continue the war" (Anderson, "Eighteenth-Century Theories", p. 67.

66. Quoted in B. Kennedy, *The Rise and Fall of the Great Powers* (London, 1968) p. 113.
67. Brougham, *An Inquiry into the Colonial Policy*, p. 22.
68. G. Williams, *The Expansion of Europe in the Eighteenth Century* (London, 1956) p. 160.
69. Brougham, *An Inquiry into the Colonial Policy*, p. 51.
70. M. Postlethwaite, *The Universal Dictionary of Trade and Commerce* (London, 1774) quoted in Knorr, *British Colonial Theories*, p. 64.
71. Ibid., p. 65.
72. The negotiations failed because of disagreements about the right of search of neutral vessels but Britain did win recognition of her right to navigate in the Eastern Seas.
73. See Williams, *Expansion of Europe*, p. 162.
74. C. Talleyrand, *Essai sur les avantages à retirer de colonies nouvelles*, 1797.
75. After Napoleon withdrew, the British held Egypt for two years in 1801–3 before leaving it to fall into the hands of Mahamet Ali. The British reoccupied Alexandria in 1807 but were soon obliged to withdraw.

Notes to Chapter 10: Alliances

1. F. de Callières, *On the Manner of Negotiating with Princes*, trs. A. F. Whyte (London, 1919) p. 8.
2. J. B. Colbert in his *Political Testament* (The Hague, 1694) commented on the value of dynastic links for that purpose believing that the projected marriage of Louis XIV's brother into the family of German ruler "could serve as a pledge of the loyalty of some prince of the empire".
3. Religious factors were not entirely overlooked in the formation of alliances. Both Louis XIV and William III, when seeking alliances with Savoy in the Nine Years War, demanded religious concessions: so that the Duke was obliged to promise sterner persecution of his Protestants when allying with the former, and greater toleration of them when he switched alliance to the latter (see G. Symcox, *Victor Amadeus II* (London, 1983) pp. 99–102, 106–7).
4. Frederick the Great, *Testament Politique*, 1768 (Berlin, 1920) pp. 210–11. Most other states accepted that immediate self-interest was the only principle to apply in choosing allies. If an ally was needed badly enough, tempting inducements might be offered to win its support. When Britain was desperate for help during the War of American Independence, she not only considered acquiring auxiliaries from Russia, but offered her Minorca as a permanent base in the western Mediterranean, and even a colony in South America. Occasionally threats would be made for the same purpose. In the third Bourbon Family Compact of 1761 France and Spain demanded that Portugal should join in their war with Britain, declaring that she "cannot" remain neutral and adding

menacingly: "It is hoped that no threat will be necessary": in the following year Spain invaded Portugal. The two countries also sought the adhesion of other countries by inviting maritime powers "no less interested in bringing low the British colonies" to join them.

5. For example, Britain and Russia negotiated about an alliance for three years between 1753 and 1755, and France and Austria for two years from 1755 to 1757. In many other cases at least a year was required to secure agreement on the precise details of alliance treaties.

6. For a detailed account of these negotiations see H. H. Kaplan, *Russia and the Outbreak of the Seven Years War* (Berkeley, Cal., 1968) pp. 3–79.

7. For a discussion of these differing war aims see M. Thomson, "Louis XIV and the Grand Alliance, 1705–10", in R. M. Hatton and J. S. Bromley (eds), *William III and Louis XIV* (Liverpool, 1968) pp. 190–201.

8. Mainly on these grounds Britain deserted her allies in 1674, 1712, 1747–8 and 1761; Austria deserted hers in 1718, 1739 and 1790; Prussia deserted hers three times in five years during the course of the War of Austrian Succession.

9. Holstein-Gottorp and Portugal also switched sides at the same time (1702 and 1703).

10. This includes the convention of Kleinschellendorf of 1741 (under which Frederick committed himself not to oppose an Austrian attack on his French ally), the Peace of Breslau (1742) and that of Dresden (1745).

11. An alternative way of achieving the same end was to agree that the final peace terms would bring equal benefits to both parties. For example, in the third Bourbon Family Compact of 1761 France and Spain agreed in advance that "all losses and conquests in the war should be held to be mutual" and "should be shared among themselves as though they were one and the same power". How little such undertakings meant is indicated by the remark of Choiseul to Louis XVI in 1761 that (despite the provision described above) "if the event proved unfortunate, I had in mind that the losses of Spain would lessen those which France might suffer".

12. The wording of these undertakings is slightly different in each case, but in the compact of 1761 the two countries agreed "not to make peace . . . unless it be at one and the same time and by mutual consent", and "communicate to each other promptly and faithfully all direct and indirect propositions for peace that may be made to either one of them".

13. Frederick the Great, *Principes du gouvernement prussien*, 1776 (Berlin, 1920) p. 241.

14. J. B. Colbert, *Testament politique* (The Hague, 1699) pp. 261–2.

15. Quoted in E. V. Gulick, *Europe's Classical Balance of Power* (Ithaca, 1955) p. 11.

16. Frederick the Great, *Anti-Machiavel*, English trs. (London, 1741) p. 107.

17. The preliminaries to the Third Bourbon Family Contract (1761) explicitly justified it on the basis of the threat to the "balance of international seapower" resulting from British actions: the "English nation had demonstrated its design to make herself the absolute mistress of the

high seas and not to permit any other nation more than a modest trade under special licence from her". It was this, they claimed, which made it necessary for the two powers to join together in resisting her.

18. Quoted in D. P. Gooch, *Frederick the Great* (London, 1947) p. 218.
19. Frederick twice asked Maria Theresa to deny that she was planning to make war on him in 1756 or 1757, and it was her refusal to answer the query definitely that decided him to make the first move.

Notes to Chapter 11: Institutions

1. For an account of the procedures for peaceful settlement used in earlier international societies see J. H. Ralston, *International Arbitration from Athens to Locarno* (Stanford, Conn., 1959); E. Luard, *Types of International Society* (New York, 1976) ch. 13.
2. Gentili, the international lawyer, himself a Protestant, rejected the power of the pope to arbitrate (preferring arbitration by "experienced judges"), and Vattel, the Swiss, rejected the right of the pope to allocate territory by arbitration.
3. Louis XIV, *Memoires for the Instruction of the Dauphin*, ed. P. Sonnino (New York, 1970) p. 226.
4. See R. M. Hatton, *Charles XII of Sweden* (London, 1938) p. 156.
5. Ibid., pp. 61–2.
6. Ibid., p. 149.
7. Ibid., p. 383.
8. It is an interesting indication of the conviction that guarantees of this kind might be a useful way of promoting international stability that governments sometimes agreed to guarantee even treaties which they had not welcomed at the time. For example in their treaty of 1721 France and Spain undertook to guarantee both the Treaty of Utrecht, in which they had made the principal concessions, and the Quadruple Alliance treaty of 1718, which had been imposed on an unwilling Spain.
9. Hatton, *Charles XII of Sweden*, p. 104.
10. Britain acknowledged the legitimacy of the Westphalia treaties in the Treaties of Hanover (1725) and Aix-la-Chapelle (1748); Russia recognised them in the Treaty of Teschen (1779) of which she was a guarantor. See Sir E. Satow, *A Guide to Diplomatic Practice* (London, 1917) vol. II, p. 8.
11. William Penn, *An Essay Towards the Present and Future Peace of Europe* (London, 1693).
12. Abbé Pierre, *Project for Settling an Everlasting Peace on Europe* (Paris, 1714).
13. Emmanuel Kant, *Plan for a Universal & Perpetual Peace* (London, 1786–9).
14. In the treaty between Sweden and Brandenburg of 1686 the signatories undertook to maintain the settlements established at Westphalia and in the Truce of Ratisbon; the latter in fact represented a modification of earlier treaties since it recognised (for twenty years only) the gains made by France after 1679.

15. The only major peace treaty of the previous century not to be included in this and similar lists was the Treaty of the Pyrenees (1659) between France and Spain, which had been included in some earlier treaties. That treaty had involved humiliating concessions by Spain to France and its later omission probably reflected the French wish, after the Bourbon accession in Spain, not to cause offence in reaffirming the treaty.
16. Silesia had already been transferred under the treaties of Breslau and Dresden in 1742 and 1745.

Notes to Chapter 12: Rules

1. See for example Hugo Grotius, *De Jure Belli ac Pacis*, 1646, English trs. (Oxford, 1725) II. 18, 1–6.
2. Horn, D. B., *The British Diplomatic Service, 1689–1789* (Oxford, 1961) p. 214.
3. Emerich de Vattel, *Le Droit des gens*, vol. IV, p. 82.
4. Grotius, *De Jure*, II. 18, 9.
5. See Horn, *British Diplomatic Service*, pp. 215–16.
6. See E. Satow, *A Guide to the Diplomatic Practice* (London, 1917) pp. 304–16; and D. Butler and S. Maccoby, *The Development of International Law* (London, 1928) p. 90.
7. M. S. Anderson, *Europe in the Eighteenth Century* (London, 1961) p. 161.
8. Ibid., p. 162.
9. Vattel, *Le Droits des gens*, vol. III, p. 269.
10. Butler and Maccoby, *Development of International Law*, p. 281. Eventually, in 1907 the protection of ships undertaking scientific work was provided for in the Hague Convention, no. 11.
11. See Vattel, *Les Droits des gens*, vol. III, pp. 24–5.
12. See Butler and Maccoby, *Development of International Law*, pp. 94–5.
13. Ibid., p. 41.
14. Ibid.
15. Another work, Borough's *Sovereignty of the Seas* preaching the same doctrine, was published in the same year.
16. For a detailed description of the various claims which were made at this time, see E. W. Fulton, *The Sovereignty of the Sea* (London, 1928) *passim*.
17. Vattel, *Les Droits des gens*, vol. I, p. 289.
18. See Butler and Maccoby, *Development of International Law*, p. 57.
19. Hugo Grotius, *Mare Librum*, 1608, English trs. ed. J. B. Scott (New York, 1916).
20. Vattel, *Les Droits des gens*, vol. I, p. 284.
21. Butler and Maccoby, *Development of International Law*, p. 204.

22. A well-known example of a treaty of this kind, containing many detailed provisions for the conduct of trade between the two countries, was the *Intercursus Magnus* signed between England and Burgundy in 1496.
23. Vattel, *Les Droits des gens*, vol. II, pp. 21–3. Vattel recognised the right of states to "make such commercial treaties as it thinks proper to promote its own interests" such that only treaties which "paid to the general interest of mankind as great a degree of respect as possible and reasonable in a particular case" were "just and commendable" (ibid., p. 26).
24. See E. I. Beller, "The Thirty Years War", in *The New Cambridge Modern History*, vol. IV (Cambridge, 1970) p. 30.
25. See Grotius, *De Jure Belli ac Pacis*, vol. III, ch. 17. In a doubtful case the neutral should "act alike to both sides in permitting transit, in supplying provisions to the respective armies and in not assisting persons beseiged".
26. C. van Bynkershoek, *Questions of Public Law*, 1737, English trs. (Oxford, 1930) vol. I, ch. 9.
27. Vattel, *Les Droits des gens*, vol. III, p. 106.
28. Ibid.
29. Grotius, *Questions of Public Law*, vol. I, ch. 9.
30. At first sight this was uncontroversial since Prussia had already attacked the territory of Saxony/Poland, and it might have been supposed that this had already brought Poland into the war. In fact, though, only the Saxon part of the country became engaged in the war, while Poland remained neutral. Russia's ally, France, and her rival for influence in Poland, objected strongly to the idea that Russian troops should transit Poland, demanding that they pass only through the Baltic territories on their way to east Prussia. Turkey was also thought likely to object, and even possibly to enter the war on Prussia's side. France was eventually obliged to withdraw her objections and Russian troops entered Poland and spent much of the war there, despite the fact that Poland was supposed to be neutral. Frederick the Great then felt himself justified in invading Polish territory likewise and during the course of his occupation he debased the currency, causing substantial hardship to the Polish people despite their country's neutral status.
31. G. Symcox, *Victor Amadeus II: Absolutism, in the Savoyard State, 1675–1730* (London, 1983) pp. 138–9.
32. The Treaty was signed by Austria, the Maritime Powers, Prussia, Hanover, Russia, Denmark and Saxony, of which only the last three were involved in the war at the time.
33. Under the Treaty they undertook to maintain the "tranquillity" of Germany and to take armed action together against any power which infringed it.
34. Lord Henry Brougham, *Works* (London, 1855–61) vol. VIII, p. 88.
35. See Butler and Maccoby, *Development of International Law*, p. 268.
36. Ibid., p. 210.
37. For a more detailed account, see ibid., pp. 268–91.

38. Grotius, *De Jure Belli ac Pacis*, vol. III, p. 5.
39. Sometimes these controversies concerned the exact meaning to be attributed to the writings of leading international lawyers. There was thus much argument about the meaning of the word "necessity", as used by Grotius, and about the meaning of the definitions given by Vattel (*Les Droits des gens*, vol. III, p. 112) who said that contraband meant "commodities particularly useful in war", which he enumerated as "arms, ammunition, timber for shipbuilding, every kind of naval stores, horses, and even provisions, in certain junctures where we have hopes of reducing the enemy by famine" (the key point was what "juncture" justified the seizure of "provisions".
40. Quoted in Butler and Maccoby, *Development of International Law*, p. 287.
41. Ibid.
42. Even then, at British insistence belligerent powers were given the right to determine unilaterally if particular types of goods should be added to the two categories of "absolute" and "conditional" contraband.
43. William Penn, *An Essay Towards the Present and Future Peace of Europe* (London, 1693–4) p. 3.
44. Ibid., p. 4.
45. Grotius, *De Jure Belli ac Pacis*, vol. II, ch. 22.
46. J. Pufendorf, *On the Law of Nature and Nations*, 1673, English trs. (Oxford, 1934) VII, ch. 6.
47. Christian Wolff, *The Law of Nations*, 1749, English trs. (Oxford, 1934) vol. V, pp. 618 and 624.
48. Emericu Vattel, *The Law of Nations* (Neuchatel, 1758) English trs. (Washington) III, ch. 3, p. 3. 27, 32–33.
49. Grotius, *De Jure Belli ac Pacis*, vol. II, p. 2.
50. Pufendorf, *On the Law of Nature and Nations*, vol. VII, ch. 6.
51. Ibid., vol. III, ch. 7.
52. Wolff, *Law of Nations*, vol. V, pp. 617, 619.
53. Vattel, *Law of Nations*, vol. II, p. 4.
54. Frederick the Great, *Anti-Machiavel*, English trs. (London, 1741) p. 327.
55. Grotius, *De Jure Belli ac Pacis*, vol. II, ch. 1, p. 1; vol. III, ch. 2, p. 5; Pufendorf, *On the Law of Nature and Nations*, vol. VII, ch. 6; Wolff, *Law of Nations*, vol. V, pp. 589–606.
56. For the full text see W. H. Hargreaves-Mawdsley (ed.), *Spain under the Bourbons, 1700–1833* (London, 1973) p. 67.
57. Quoted in R. M. Hatton, *Charles XII*, (London, 1968) p. 375.
58. Quoted in G. B. Gooch, *Frederick the Great* (London, 1947) p. 39.
59. Quoted in G. Ritter, *Frederick the Great* (Heidelberg, 1964) p. 37.
60. Grotius, *De Jure Belli ac Pacis*, vol. III, ch. 3.
61. Bynkershoek, *Questions of Public Law*, vol. II, ch. 1, p.
62. C.f. M. S. Anderson, *Europe in the Eighteenth Century* (London, 1961) p. 60: "The openings of hostilities without any formal declaration of war, for example, remained a commonplace of international relations".
63. Butler and Maccoby, *Development of International Law*, p. 195.
64. Ibid., p. 205.
65. Ibid.

66. Ibid., p. 206.
67. Ibid., p. 207.
68. Ibid., p. 149.
69. Ibid., p. 151.
70. Vattel, *Droits des gens*, vol. III, ch. 9, p. 163.
71. Ibid.
72. See G. E. Zellor, "French Diplomacy and Foreign Policy", in *The New Cambridge Modern History*, vol. V (Cambridge, 1951) p. 204.
73. Sir George Clark, *War and Society in the Seventeenth Century* (Cambridge, 1958) pp. 86–7.
74. Ibid., p. 87.
75. Ibid.
76. A. A. Nussbaum, *A Concise History of the Law of Nations* (New York, 1947) p. 124.
77. Quoted in F. M. Tapié, "Louis XIV's Methods in Foreign Policy", in R. Hatton (ed.), *Louis XIV and Europe* (London, 1966) p. 10.
78. Vattel, *Droits des gens*, vol. IV, ch. 1, pp. 1, 2, 4.

Notes to Conclusions

1. F. von Gentz, *Select Despatches Relating to the Third Coalition against France*, 1804–5, quoted in E. P. Gulick, *Europe's Classical Balance of Power* (Westport, Conn., 1955) p. 32.
2. J. B. Colbert, *Lettres, instructions et mémoires*, ed. P. Clément (Paris, 1859–82), vol. VII, p. 230.
3. As by J.-J. Rousseau; by Hans Morgenthau in *Politics Among Nations* (New York, 1948, pp. 144–7); or by Morton Kaplan in *System and Process in International Politics*, 2nd edn (New York, 1964) (pp. 23–9), and other modern writers.
4. For example, by Kaplan, *System and Process*, pp. 30ff.
5. Russia would have acquired East Prussia; Austria Silesia and adjoining lands; France the Rhineland; Saxony parts of Brandenberg; and Sweden Prussia and Pomerania.
6. Frederick the Great made a similar point in his *First Political Testament* when he commented that the relatively equal division of forces in Europe would "prevent great conquests and make war unprofitable unless conducted from a position of great superiority and with invariable good fortune".
7. Even Gulick, generally a shrewd and well-informed observer of this system, states that "the second is indeed a remarkable one for the preservation of the status quo. Wars . . . repeatedly ended in a restoration of either the status quo or a close approximation of it" (*Europe's Classical Balance of Power*, p. 39). Still more astonishing is his statement that "in the period from 1648 to 1792 there were, generally speaking, no great territorial changes in Europe, except for the first partition of Poland". Neither statement has any basis in fact.
8. See A. Lossky, "International Relations in Europe", in *The New Cambridge Modern History*, vol. VI (Cambridge, 1970) p. 192.

9. See Chapter 8 above.
10. E. de Vattel, *The Law of Nations*, 1758, English trs. (London, 1811) vol. III, p. 251.
11. F. von Geirtz, *On the Balance of Power* (London, 1806) p. 69.
12. Abbé de Pradt, *La Prusse et sa neutralité* (London, 1800) pp. 86–7.
13. A. Vogt, *About the European Republic* (Frankfurt-am-Main, 1782–92).
14. Voltaire, *Siècle de Louis XIV*, quoted in Denys Hay, *Europe: The Emergence of an Idea* (Edinburgh, 1968) p. 123.
15. John Bellers, *Some Reasons for a European State* (London, 1710).
16. Bellers maintained, with some reason, that a general guarantee "through all Europe" would be more effective than one among the members of the Grand Alliance alone, and that "everybody, prince and state, having the benefit of it, they would all accord it in their interest to have it universally kept with such additional articles of agreement as may make it more lasting than guarantees usually are" (ibid., p. 2).
17. Bellers also proposed a limitation of armaments within the continent: "Considering Europe as one government, every kingdom . . . should be limited to what troops and ships of war they may keep up, that they may be disabled from invading their neighbours" (ibid., p. 2).
18. Vattel, *Law of Nations*, p. 311.
19. von Gentz, *On the Balance of Power*, pp. 12–13.
20. de Callières, op. cit., p. 33.
21. Voltaire, in Hay, *Europe*, p. 123.
22. J.-J. Rousseau, *Project for Perpetual Peace*, English trs. (Edinburgh, 1774) p. 119.
23. Edmund Burke, *Letters on a Regicide Peace* (London, 1796).
24. Under the Treaty of Constantinople of 1700 Turkey had to accept the right of Russia to send a diplomatic representative to that city. But after her victory over Russia in 1710–11, she won Russia's agreement to end the representation. Only after Austria had secured another military victory against her was Russia able in 1720 to get the decision reversed.
25. In that debate Burke declared that "he had never before heard it held forth that the Turkish Empire was ever considered as any part of the balance of power in Europe. They had nothing to do with European power; they considered themselves as only Asiatic . . . they despised and condemned all Christian princes as infidels, and only wished to subdue and exterminate them and their people" (Edmund Burke, speech in House of Commons, 29 February 1772.)
26. See M. S. Anderson, *Europe in the Eighteenth century, 1739–83* (London, 1961) p. 154. Russia, like Turkey, was not included among those states qualified to participate in European institutions in Sully's Grand Design at the beginning of the seventeenth century; but it was so included by Penn in his comparable plan put forward at the end of that century.
27. G. F. von Martens, *Summary of the Law of Nations* (Philadelphia, 1795) pp. 17–28.
28. For detailed statistics on this point see Evan Luard, *War in International Society* (London, 1986) pp. 24–68; Quincy Wright, *A Study of War*, 2nd edn (Chicago, 1965) pp. 220–3.

29. Pufendorf, *Introduction to the History of the Principal Kingdoms and States of Europe*, 1684, trs. J. Crull (London, 1697).
30. S. Favier, *Politique de tous les cabinets de l'Europe* (Paris, 1802).
31. See G. P. Gooch, *Maria Theresa, and Other Studies* (London, 1951) p. 85.
32. C. W. N. L. Metternich, *Mémoires, documents et ecrits divers* (Paris, 1880–4), quoted in H. du Coudray, *Metternich* (New Haven, Conn., 1936) pp. 167–8.

Index